Revolutions

Theoretical, Comparative, and Historical Studies

SECOND EDITION

Revolutions

Theoretical, Comparative, and Historical Studies

SECOND EDITION

Edited by

JACK A. GOLDSTONE

University of California, Davis

HARCOURT BRACE COLLEGE PUBLISHERS

Fort Worth   Philadelphia   San Diego   New York   Orlando   Austin   San Antonio
Toronto   Montreal   London   Sydney   Tokyo

TED BUCHHOLZ
Publisher

DAVID TATOM
Acquisitions Editor

NANCY LOMBARDI
Project Editor

NICK WELCH
Designer

JANE TYNDALL PONCETI
Production Manager

Address for Editorial Correspondence:
Harcourt Brace College Publishers, 301 Commerce Street, Suite 3700, Fort Worth, TX 76102.

Address for Orders:
Harcourt Brace & Company, 6277 Sea Harbor Drive, Orlando FL 32887.
1-800-782-4479, or 1-800-433-0001 (in Florida).

Copyrights and Acknowledgments appear on pages 327–328 and constitute a continuation of the copyright page.

Library of Congress Catalog Card Number: 92-75767

ISBN: 0-15-500385-2

Printed in the United States of America

4 5 6 7 8 9 0 1 2 016 9 8 7 6 5 4 3 2

PREFACE

When this book first appeared in 1986, revolutions were confounding U.S. and Soviet policy in Iran, Nicaragua, and Afghanistan. To understand these events, scholars still looked primarily to models of revolution based on the "great" revolutions of France in 1789, Russia in 1917, and China in 1949. These historical examples are still immensely valuable. However, they focused our thinking about revolutions on the weaknesses of traditional states, and on the problem of "peasant" uprisings.

It is now clear from examining the recent wave of contemporary revolutions—from Iran and Nicaragua in 1979, to the Philippines in 1986, to Eastern Europe and the Soviet Union in 1989—that traditional peasant revolutions provide an incomplete model for understanding modern revolutions. Modern revolutions have occurred in states that have begun industrialization and that have relatively modern bureaucracies and party apparatuses. They have been brought about primarily by urban, rather than rural, revolts. The Tiananmen Square uprising in China in 1989—a quintessentially urban revolt in a country that had been a model for peasant revolution —typifies this change in the character of revolutionary action.

As the world changes, so must our tools for teaching and understanding change with it. This revised edition retains its coverage of the great traditional revolutions. However, it also includes extensive new material on revolutions in modern dictatorships, on the revolutions of 1989 in the Soviet Union and Eastern Europe, and on the Tiananmen Square uprising. The introduction highlights new concerns about nationalism and emerging democracies. And a new section has been added examining the challenges faced by women and minority groups in revolutionary crises.

These revisions allow this book to be used in courses focusing either on the great traditional revolutions or on modern revolutions. Even more importantly, this book can now be used to examine changes in the revolutionary process through history, as well as how revolutionary events continue to shape our world.

This second edition was completed, and the new material for the Introduction and my essay in Chapter 3 composed, while I was a Fellow at the Center for Advanced Study in the Behavorial Sciences at Stanford University. I am grateful for financial support provided by National Science Foundation grant SES-9022192. Nancy Lombardi, my project editor at Harcourt Brace for the second edition, played a key role in improving the original. Her good cheer and careful attention to detail made the often laborious task of revision a pleasure. Leslie Leland Frank prepared the index for this edition.

Jack A. Goldstone
Stanford, CA

PREFACE TO THE FIRST EDITION

This book began as a course on "Revolution and Social Change." I wanted to include readings by major thinkers and writers that would encourage students to think about revolution in terms of social theory, major historical events, and contemporary politics. Colleagues with similar interests shared with me a number of their teaching needs. Those teaching general courses in introductory political science or political sociology wanted a collection of essays presenting the latest controversies and ideas on the theory of revolutions. Those teaching courses on comparative revolution—who usually examine events in France, Russia, China, and other great historical revolutions—wanted some up-to-date and theoretically informed material on Iran or Nicaragua. Those teaching courses in the history and politics of specific areas—Latin America, China, Russia, and Eastern Europe—wanted essays that would introduce theoretical issues about the sociology of revolution and political change that would be pertinent to their particular region.

This book evolved to meet these varied needs. I have designed it for use as the core book for courses on revolution or as a supplementary text for courses in comparative politics and political sociology.

Part I presents theories of revolution from Marx, de Tocqueville, Weber, Huntington, Tilly, and Skocpol and Trimberger. Parts II through IV analyze specific aspects of revolution—the origins, the role of peasants, the outcomes—through historical and comparative case studies. The case studies range from the English and French Revolutions to the Mexican, Russian, and Chinese Revolutions—from Iran and Nicaragua to Cuba and Eastern Europe.

These essays are addressed primarily to undergraduates who have some prior course work in social science. However, instructors can vary the scope of this volume by carefully selecting accompanying texts and lectures. My own students, from freshmen to beginning graduate students, have enjoyed this material and found it challenging.

The selections are analytical and thought-provoking, rather than merely descriptive: they assume that the reader has some knowledge of the outline of events in, for example, the French or Russian Revolutions. For readers who wish to learn more about specific events, suggestions for further reading at the back of the book list several of the more interesting works on individual revolutions.

All of the essays have appeared in books and academic journals; however, I have edited—and in some cases revised and updated—these texts for this book. I owe a great debt of thanks to the authors who worked with me. Of course, the responsibility for any errors in the way their work has been presented is mine alone.

In the interest of brevity, I have omitted footnotes and citations except for references to works likely to be found in most undergraduate libraries. Readers who want more detailed information on the sources of quotations and data should consult the original works listed in the Copyrights and Acknowledgments section at the back of the book.

The list of teachers, colleagues, and students who have stimulated my interest in revolutions is far too long to print. Daniel Chirot, Robert K. Merton, and Judith Stacey were instrumental in setting this volume in motion; I greatly appreciate their support and advice. Much of what I know about revolutions is due to the diligence of my teachers at Harvard—Theda Skocpol, George Homans, and S. N. Eisenstadt. In addition, Roderick Aya, Daniel Bell, Victoria Bonnell, Randall Collins, Arnold Feldman, Gary Hamilton, Michael Hechter, Nathan Keyfitz, Joel Mokyr, Charles Ragin, Arthur Stinchcombe, Charles Tilly, Mark Traugott, Harrison White, and Christopher Winship have all made valued contributions to my general education. Two superb graduate students, York Bradshaw and Larry Radbill, helped me discover how to make best use of this material in teaching undergraduates.

Northwestern University has generously supported my study of revolutions both with funds and with that most valuable commodity for scholars, free time for research. The swiftness and acumen of the secretarial staff of Northwestern's Department of Sociology—particularly Nancy Weiss Klein, who took on the difficult task of turning a mass of heavily edited photocopies and rough notes into a neatly typed manuscript—made work on the final manuscript a pleasure.

While writing the study of England in Chapter 6, I benefited from a fellowship from the American Council of Learned Societies and enjoyed the intellectual stimulation and facilities of the Graduate Group in Demography at the University of California, Berkeley.

Finally, it is unlikely that the idea of this volume would ever have been realized without the encouragement and expert support provided by Harcourt Brace College Publishers. I owe deep thanks to my acquisitions editor, Marcus Boggs, who helped to develop this volume; my manuscript editor, Gene Carter Lettau; my permissions editor, Eleanor Garner; and my production editor, Ruth Cornell. It is hard to imagine an editorial staff that could have been more helpful.

Jack A. Goldstone

CONTENTS

The Comparative and Historical Study of Revolutions

The laws are put out of doors. Men walk on them in the streets. . . . The king has been deposed by the rabble. . . . The people have reached the position of the highest divine court. . . . Every town saith: Let us drive out the powerful from our midst.

(*The Lament of Ipuwer*)

This excerpt from 2100 B.C. describes the fall of Pepi II, pharaoh of the Old Kingdom of Egypt. Written observations on revolution stretch back over 4000 years. Why have certain governments fallen at the hands of their own people? This question has fascinated students of politics for almost as long as governments have existed. Yet explaining why revolutions occur is not any easy task. Revolutions are complex events and originate in long and complicated causal processes. Ideas about how and why revolutions occur are widespread, but observers must constantly check those ideas against the evidence actual revolutions have left. Over the centuries, Plato, Aristotle, Machiavelli, de Tocqueville, Marx, and many others have added to the observations of Ipuwer. And the study of revolutions has been one of the most active areas of modern social science. Consequently, people have learned a great deal about revolutions. But the process of testing and refining our understanding through studying the history of revolutions is a long, and still continuing, process.

Theories of Revolution: The Basic Problems

The basic problems in building a theory of revolution become clear if we consider some common notions of why revolutions occur. One view widely held among laypeople is that "misery breeds revolt": When oppression becomes too much to bear, the masses will rise up against their oppressors. Although this view has an element of truth, it does not explain why revolutions have occurred in some countries but not in others. Revolt is only one of several paths the oppressed may take. The downtrodden may be so divided and powerless that they may be unable to organize an effective revolt or they may simply hope for a better life in the hereafter. Oppression and misery have been widespread throughout history, yet revolutions have been rare. Therefore, a theorist of revolution must ask, Does all oppression stir revolt? Or are there conditions under which people, no matter how oppressed, are unlikely to mount a revolution?

Another common view is that revolutions occur when a state faces unmanageable accumulation of difficulties. When a number of severe problems occur together—a royal bankruptcy, a famine, a conflict within the ruling family, a war—the state collapses, opening the floodgates of revolution. Again, this view has an element of truth, but it, too, fails to explain where and how revolutions have occurred. The great empires of Rome and Charlemagne faced such difficulties, yet they first crumbled at the edges and then fell into parts which minor lords ruled or external enemies conquered. These empires died with a whimper, not a bang. So the theorist of revolution must ask: When do pressures on a government lead to revolution, rather than to a break-up into lesser states or conquest by external enemies?

A third view is that revolutions arise when new, radical ideas shake people out of their accustomed lives. This idea also has merit, for people generally fight great revolutions under the banner of radical ideas. Yet what causes such ideas to take root and to lead men and women to revolt? Many ideals of a better, more just existence take the form of religious movements focused on a better life in the next world. And many radical ideas stimulate people to behave in different ways in different times and cultures. The ideas of democracy and citizenship were current among Greeks and Romans; why did they only become revolutionary ideas in Europe 2000 years later?

In sum, common observations about revolution, though not totally inaccurate, do not provide a full understanding of the historical pattern of revolution. Popular revolts, the process of the collapse of states, and the role of ideologies all need closer scrutiny.

In this century, studies of revolutions have moved through three generations of scholarship, each adding to our understanding: the *natural histories* of the 1920s and 1930s, the *general theories of political violence* of the 1960s and early 1970s, and the *structural theories* of the late 1970s and 1980s.

The Natural History of Revolutions

In the 1920s and 1930s, a number of historians and sociologists surveyed the most famous revolutions of the West: The English Revolution of 1640, the American Revolution of 1776, the French Revolution of 1789, and the Russian Revolution of 1917.[1] These writers wanted to identify common patterns of events in the process of revolution. They succeeded in finding a remarkable correspondence among the major events in each of these revolutions. Several of their observations on the "natural history" of revolutions have been valid so often that they appear to be lawlike empirical generalizations:

1. *Prior to a revolution, the bulk of the "intellectuals"—journalists, poets, playwrights, essayists, teachers, members of the clergy, lawyers, and trained members of the bureaucracy—cease to support the regime, write condemnations, and demand major reforms.* These attacks on the old regime even attract the attention of the regime's natural supporters. French aristocrats applauded the plays of Voltaire and Beaumarchais; English lords supported Puritan preachers; and Russian nobles demanded local parliaments and other democratic reforms.

Why is the mass desertion of the intellectuals so important? Primarily for what it portends. When hereditary nobles, high officials, and professionals countenance such public criticism, the regime must be failing to provide services important to its own supporters, such as security of property and rank, high-level positions for the children of prominent people, and victories and spoils in war. The desertion of the intellectuals on a vast scale thus implies an unusually widespread and pervasive dissatisfaction with regime performance. This dissatisfaction extends even to the highest ranks of government and society. Such uneasiness often presages a reluctance of elite leaders to suppress popular uprisings and even more often portends elite revolts against the regime.

2. *Just prior to the fall of the old regime, the state attempts to meet criticism by undertaking major reforms.* Examples from the past have included the reforms of Louis XVI in France, the Stolypin reforms in Russia, and the Boxer reforms in China. Such reforms often attempt to absorb additional groups into the regime without giving them any real influence by adding parliaments or councils with strictly advisory powers. However, such reforms generally serve further to undermine the regime. They act both as an admission that the regime is flawed and as an encouragement to others to pressure the government for further changes. This pattern bears out Machiavelli's warning to rulers: "If the necessity for [reforms] comes in troubled times, you are too late for harsh measures; and mild ones will not help you, for they will be considered as forced from you, and no one will be under any obligation to you for them."

3. *The actual fall of the regime begins with an acute political crisis brought on by the government's inability to deal with some economic, military, or political problem rather than by the action of a revolutionary opposition.* The crisis may take the form of a state bankruptcy or a weakening command of the armed forces. Revolutionary leaders, who may have been active but relatively powerless for a long time, suddenly find themselves with the upper hand because of the incapacity of the old regime. The sudden onset of revolution thus stems from a weakening or paralysis of the state rather than from a sudden gain in the strength of revolutionaries.

4. *Even where revolutionaries have united solidly against the old regime, following its collapse their internal conflicts eventually cause problems.* After enjoying a brief euphoria over the fall of the old regime, the revolutionary opposition becomes rapidly disunited. Usually the revolutionaries divide into three factions: conservatives who seek to minimize change (many of whom eventually return to support for the ousted regime), radicals who seek rapid and widespread change, and moderates who try to steer a middle course. The results of such disunity among revolutionaries range from coups to civil war.

5. *The first group to seize the reins of state are moderate reformers.* This axiom, observed in major revolutions a century and more ago, again proved accurate in Iran where Bazargan, the moderate critic, first took power after revolutionaries forced out the Shah.

6. *While the moderates seek to reconstruct rule on the basis of moderate reform and often employ organizational forms left over from the old regime, alternative, more radical centers of mass mobilization spring up with new forms of organization.* In France, the moderate Girondin assembly faced the radical Jacobin clubs; in America, the moderate Continental Congress had to deal with the more radical Patriots Societies; in modern Iran, the moderates of the executive branch (Bazargan, Bani-Sadr, Gotzbadeh) competed in their attempt to rule the country with the radical, mass-mobilizing Islamic theologians.

7. *The great changes in the organization and ruling ideology of a society that follow successful revolutions occur not when the old regime first falls, but when the radical, alternative, mass-mobilizing organizations succeed in supplanting the moderates.* This step generally occurs because the moderates, seeking continuity, do not rid the government of the liabilities that caused the old regime to fail. Hence they inherit the same inability to deal with urgent economic and military problems. The success of the radicals generally comes from their willingness to take extreme measures, both in dealing with pressing problems and in securing their rule.

However, as the American Revolution shows, the triumph of the radicals, though common, is not inevitable. Yet only to the extent that the moderates repudiate and dissociate themselves from the old regime—a task in which they are unlikely to equal the radicals—are they likely to succeed. Only in a war of colonial liberation—where the old regime enemy is clearly external—are moderates likely to have a chance for survival. For example, in Indonesia in 1945, in Algeria in 1962, and in Guinea in 1958, as in America in 1787, relatively moderate regimes were able to stay in power because in fighting colonial forces, the moderates could maintain unity with other factions. On the other hand, in Nicaragua and Iran, where the enemy of the revolutionaries was an internal regime, radical leaders supplanted the moderates.

8. *The disorder brought by the revolution and the implementation of radical control usually results in forced imposition of order by coercive rule.* This is the stage of "terror," familiar from the guillotine days of the French Revolution, and known to later generations through Stalin's *gulag* and Mao's Cultural Revolution.

9. *The struggles between radicals and moderates and between defenders of the revolution and external enemies frequently allow military leaders to move from obscurity to commanding, even absolute, leadership.* The long roster of national leaders who emerged in this fashion includes Washington, Cromwell, Napoleon, Attaturk, Mao, Tito, Boumedienne, and Mugabe.

10. *The radical phase of the revolution eventually gives way to a phase of pragmatism and moderate pursuit of progress within the new status quo.* In this phase, the radicals are defeated or have died, and moderates return to power. They condemn the "excesses" of the radicals and shift the emphasis from political change to economic progress within a framework of stable institutions. This phase began with the fall of Robespierre in France; Khrushchev's repudiation of Stalin in Russia; and the fall of Mao's allies, the "gang of four," in China.

These ten propositions, the legacy of the natural historians of revolution, provided a valuable guide to understanding the process of revolutions. However, using this approach alone left many basic questions unanswered. Chief among these was the question of causes: Why did revolutions arise? What were the sources of opposition to the old regime? These issues became the focus of a second generation of analysts who were adherents of the general-theory school.

General Theories of Political Violence

In the 1950s and 1960s, the emergence of new nations captured the attention of scholars. Political changes were clearly part of the process by which traditional societies, as they gained in education and economic growth, developed into modern states. Yet the wide-spread violence that accompanied these changes was striking: Revolutions, coups, riots, and civil wars suddenly seemed to arise everywhere. Some scholars developed general theories to explain all these kinds of political violence.

General theories of political violence took several forms. The psychological approach, as set forth by Davies and further refined by Gurr,[2] attempted to improve the view that "misery breeds revolt" by identifying precisely the kinds of misery likely to lead to political disorders. These authors argued that people generally accept high levels of oppression and misery if they expect such discomforts to be their natural lot in life. Only when people expect a better life, and have their expectations frustrated, are they likely to develop feelings of aggression and resentment. Therefore, any change in a society that raises people's expectations for a better life without providing the means of meeting those expectations can be politically destabilizing. Such expectations may include cultural contacts with more advanced societies or rapid but uneven economic growth. Davies argued that one combination of events in particular—a period of growing prosperity that raises people's expectations for a better life, followed by a sharp economic downturn that dashes those expectations (the "J-curve" of economic growth)—would yield exceptionally sharp feelings of deprivation and aggression.

A second general-theory approach, developed largely by Smelser and Johnson,[3] argued that instead of focusing mainly on popular discontent, scholars should examine social institutions. These authors stressed that when the various subsystems of a society—the economy, the political system, the training of young people for new positions—grow at roughly the same rate, the government will remain stable. However, if one subsystem starts to change independently, the resulting imbalance will leave people disoriented and open to considering new values. When such imbalance becomes severe, radical ideologies that challenge the legitimacy of the status quo will become widespread. During such periods, a war, a government bankruptcy, or a famine may bring the government down.

In an influential work, Huntington[4] synthesized these two approaches. He argued that modernization led to institutional imbalance because the resulting educational and economic growth would increase people's desire to participate in politics faster than political institutions could change to accommodate this desire. This gap between desire for change and accomplished change would create frustrated expectations about political life, which in turn could lead to riot, rebellion, and revolution.

The psychological and the system-disequilibrium theories of revolution tried to explain why popular discontent and opposition to the regime arose. Tilly[5] developed a third general-theory approach focusing on resource mobilization. He pointed out that discontent alone is unlikely to lead to revolution if the discontented remain unorganized and lack resources. Arguing that discontent and conflict are a normal part of politics, he stressed that political violence is likely to occur only when aggrieved parties have the means to make such violence count—namely, when they have the resources and the organization to take significant actions. In this view, although modernization may bring discontent, it does not necessarily lead to revolution. Instead revolution will probably occur only when opponents are able to mobilize the massive resources needed to take command of a geographical area and effectively challenge the old regime.

General theories thus moved from (1) approaches stressing relative deprivation and frustration to (2) approaches stressing institutional imbalance to (3) Tilly's approach stressing resource mobilization by challengers. This work led scholars to study not merely individual discontent, but changes in institutions and resource mobilization by organized groups. Still, *all* the general theory approaches had certain problems in explaining where and how revolutions occurred.

First, the general theories viewed revolutions as purposive movements of an opposition that sought to wrest control of the state. They explained revolutions mainly by explaining the origins of the opposition and its recourse to violence. Yet often revolutions began not from the acts of a powerful opposition but from the internal breakdown and paralysis of state administrations which rendered states incapable of managing normally routine problems. The general theories of revolution and collective violence provided no help in understanding the conditions behind the internal breakdown of states.

Second, during the period when theorists of revolution debated whether modernization engendered revolutions by raising expectations, by disequilibrating the sectors of society, or by shifting resources from authorities to regime opponents, our view of modernization greatly changed. Scholars recognized that the notion that all societies would face the same general process of modernization was too simple. Moore[6] argued that different kinds of societies experienced different kinds of social change. For example, Moore demonstrated that whether or not modernization led to revolution and what *kind* of revolution occurred depended on the relationship between peasants and landlords, a relationship that was very different in England from that in France or Germany, and different again in Russia and China. Scholars recognized that in order to explain why revolutions occurred in some countries but not in others and to understand their outcomes, they needed to study in detail *differences* among political structures and agrarian relationships. The general theories of revolution overlooked these differences.

So scholars in their search for the bases for revolutions turned from general theories of political violence to historical and comparative studies of the structure of different kinds of states and agrarian relationships. These studies have led to structural theories of revolution.

Structural Theories of Revolution

Structural theories posit that states vary in structure, and thus are vulnerable to different kinds of revolution. They further contend that revolutions begin from some combination of state weakness, conflicts between states and elites, and popular uprisings.

STATES AND ELITES

Structural theories of revolution start from a few straightforward observations about states: (1) All states are organizations that gather resources from their society. (2) States are in competition with other states for territory, for military strength, and for trade. (3) Some kinds of state organizations are likely to fare badly in such competition and experience severe political crises. Therefore structural theorists ask, What kinds of state organizations are apt to experience fiscal or military crises in competition with other states? Scholars have found several answers.

States with relatively backward and unproductive economies, compared to the states with which they are competing, may face overwhelming outside pressures. The extreme case of this is Russia in World War I. The Russian state collapsed under defeats by more advanced Germany; these defeats ushered in the Russian Revolution. Other countries have faced similar, if less severe pressures; France, fighting more economically advanced England in the eighteenth century; and Japan, China, and Turkey, fighting the more advanced Western powers, in the nineteenth and twentieth centuries.

Yet states sometimes do collapse without defeat in war. The probability of an internal collapse generally depends on the relationship of the state to members of the elite, whether they are hereditary nobles, local landlords, or clergy. Skocpol[7] has pointed out that attempts of the state to meet international competitive pressures by increasing government income or authority often run counter to elite interests, for state goals may require suspension of traditional elite privileges and may threaten the resources of elites. The vulnerability of the state to a political crisis then depends on the extent to which elites can influence the state and can use resources against it.

For example, the eighteenth century French monarchy required the cooperation of noble-controlled *parlements,* independent judicial bodies that could block and challenge the directives the Crown issued. More recently the Iranian clergy, because of their financial supporters in the bazaar economy, their role in the traditional courts, and their network of influence in the mosques and schools, retained control of resources with which to mount a challenge to the Shah. Thus when conflicts between the monarchy and elites arose—in France over the state bankruptcies arising from the Anglo-French wars of the eighteenth century and in Iran over the Shah's rapid modernization plans—the elite's opposition was able to cripple and paralyze the central government.

The loyalty of the army is also crucial. Where the government openly recruits officers from all classes, provides long training for the rank and file, and keeps troops isolated from civilians, the army is usually a reliable tool for suppressing domestic disorders. Yet where army officers come primarily from a landed elite, they may sympathize with their own class in a conflict between the central government and elites. Where troops are recently recruited and fraternize with the populace, their sympathy for their civilian fellows may override their allegiance to their officers. In either of the latter two cases, the unreliability of the army increases the vulnerability of the state to revolution.[8]

In sum, where a powerful elite outside the state bureaucracy has the resources to paralyze the state in times of conflict, and outside allegiances weaken the army, severe political crises are liable to occur when states attempt to increase their authority or resources. This kind of conflict became crucial during the French, English, Chinese, and Iranian Revolutions.

However, two other kinds of societal structure are also prone to state breakdown. And again, the relationship between states and elites is the key factor. First, even if there is no strong independent elite outside the state bureaucracy, conflicts between states and elites may still occur. Trimberger[9] has argued that this is likely when officials who lack great personal landholdings or ties to landlord classes, but who share a tradition of state service and elite training, hold positions *within* the bureaucracy or armed forces. This may occur when a state provides certain civil or military officials with special status or elite training. If exceptional military or economic pressures from abroad threaten the state, and this elite decides the state is failing to meet those pressures, the elite is likely to initiate what Trimberger calls an "elite revolution." Powerful civil or military officials may seize control of the central administrative apparatus and reshape the pattern of resource distribution and extraction in an effort to solve the military and economic difficulties that threaten the nation. Lacking a vested interest in the current economic structure, such officials are free to respond to international pressures by implementing radical reforms— including land reform, abolition or attenuation of traditional status distinctions, and rapid industrialization. Examples include the Meiji restoration in 1868 in Japan, Attaturk's takeover of Turkey in 1923, and Nasser's revolutionary coup in 1952.

Second, certain states (labeled "neo-patrimonial" by Eisenstadt[10]) have a structure characterized by a high degree of patronage. In such states, the government is extremely personal. The chief executive maintains his or her position not with a strong bureaucracy that enforces the law, but with the support of the elites and bureaucrats secured through an extensive and informal system of personal rewards. In such a state, the leader may keep the bureaucracy and armed forces weak and divided, while he or she may encourage corruption to keep military and civil officials dependent on the patronage of the chief executive.

This kind of state is particularly vulnerable to economic downturns or military pressures. A period of economic stability and growth provides the executive with the resources to build an extended patronage network; however, a sharp economic downturn or military setback may then deprive the executive of the means to continue to reward followers. In this event, the patronage network may begin to crumble, and the competition once encouraged within the bureaucracy may reduce the loyalty of the followers. If at this juncture even a limited popular uprising occurs, the internal divisions and corruption of the bureaucracy and armed forces may limit the state's ability to suppress it quickly, and this failure may lead to the fall of the state.

This type of revolution is distinct from other revolutions in that its leaders' first aim is overthrowing the personal rule of the discredited chief executive, not changing the system of government. Indeed, the chief executive is often attacked for betraying an already-existing democratic constitution, which the regime's opponents promise to restore. Nonetheless, because the government is bound up with the person of the chief executive, the crumbling of the patronage network combined with a limited popular uprising can bring the collapse of the entire regime. The reconstruction of the state may then bring far-reaching changes in government and social organization. Such a revolution at first generally lacks a strong ideological component, and considerable time may pass before the revolutionaries decide what form of government should replace the old personal state. Examples include the Mexican Revolution, the Cuban Revolution, and the recent Nicaraguan Revolution.

Certain state structures lack the vulnerability of the preceding types. These are relatively resistant to revolution even in times of crisis. One such type is the open, public state typical of modern democracies. Another is the elite or aristocratic government where the state is effectively a committee of a united ruling elite. Historical examples include the ancient Roman republic and the English landlord state of the seventeenth and eighteenth centuries. In the contemporary world, rule by a unified elite more often takes the form of rule by a united military regime, or by a particular ethnic group. The Republic of South Africa has been a clear example of the latter. States ruled by unified military or ethnic elites can be quite repressive and unjust; nonetheless, the unity among their elite rulers provides them with considerable stability. As long as the elites remain united in support of the regime, and have the financial and military resources to support their rule, they can withstand significant challenges and retain power.

In all these cases, revolution depends on elites with independent resources who have substantial grievances against the state over taxation, corruption, attacks on the elite, or the state's failure to stand up to foreign pressures. Over 2000 years ago, Plato observed, "All political changes originate in divisions of the actual governing power; a government which is united . . . cannot be moved" (*Republic,* Book VII). This observation is no less true today: Precisely those states that are structurally prone to internal conflicts between states and their elites are most vulnerable to revolution.

Yet the paralysis of the state is only one component of revolution. Elite opposition may disable a state and open it to coups or elite revolution, but a full-scale revolution only occurs through the conjunction of such opposition with widespread popular uprisings.

POPULAR UPRISINGS

Popular uprisings range from traditional food riots to modern industrial strikes. For convenience, we may divide them into two kinds of uprisings that have been critical in actual revolutions: peasant revolts and urban workers' uprisings.

Peasant Revolts Peasants the world over have a long history of oppression. Their control over the land they farm is often weak, and they frequently must pay one-third to one-half of their crop to landlords and to the state as rents and taxes. In agrarian societies, outbreaks of peasant protest over the terms of these payments and over control of land have been as common as factory strikes in industrial societies. However, most peasant revolts are small-scale, local, and easily suppressed. A successful peasant revolt is likely only where several key relationships exist simultaneously: peasant solidarity, peasant capacity, and landlord vulnerability.[11]

Peasant revolts generally stem from obvious grievances such as landlords taking over peasant lands, major increases in state taxation or in rents, or famines and military disasters. As Scott has remarked, "The great majority of peasant movements historically, far from being affairs of rising expectations, have rather been defensive efforts to preserve customary rights or to restore them once they have been lost.[12]

Yet what appears to be important is not merely the level of grievances, but whether such grievances are widely shared and widely directed at the same target. When the state sharply increases taxes, or landlords raise the dues of whole villages or seek to take over village lands, entire villages share common grievances toward obvious targets. But where villages have few or no communal lands, or where each family holds land under different obligations to landlords, some families may suffer great hardships and yet whole villages will not rise in revolt.

Peasants also must have the organizational capacity to plan and act in common before revolts can be successful. This is readily possible where self-governing village councils traditionally exist. Such councils played an important role in the peasant villages of Old Regime France and Tsarist Russia and in the Indian communal villages of rural Mexico. Where peasants have no traditional self-government but are under the close supervision of local landlords or their agents as in England after 1500, in Eastern Germany after 1600, and in Latin America haciendas, major revolts are extremely rare.

The vulnerability of landlords is also a factor. Landlords having their own means of coercion and strong local governing bodies able to deal with food shortages and local disturbances can generally stand firm against the early stages of peasant uprisings without relying on aid from the state. Such landlords can maintain their authority even if the central government is temporarily disabled. Such landlords may even tolerate or promote peasant protests against higher taxes or other intrusions of the central government. But landlords who must rely almost entirely on central government troops to maintain local order are extremely vulnerable when war or economic distress incapacitates the state. Russian landlords during World War I and French landlords during the Crown's bankruptcy in 1788–1789 had to face peasant uprisings without state protection, and they had no other means to defend themselves. So peasant revolts spread rapidly through the countryside.

Still, the transformation of peasant revolts into peasant revolutions requires the action of groups outside the peasantry. Peasants tend to be very local in their outlook and goals. Without national leadership or actions by other groups, peasant revolts tend to dissolve into numerous unconnected local uprisings. But if other efforts join with peasant protest, the rural groups can contribute to a national revolution in two ways.

In the first pattern, an urban elite leaves the cities to work with the peasantry and forge links between peasant groups. Building peasant guerilla armies and peasant organizations, these elites can provide both organizational capacity and national goals. This is particularly important where peasants lack their own self-government free of landlord control. This pattern occurred in the Chinese and Vietnamese Revolutions and, in varying degrees, in Cuba, Nicaragua, and El Salvador.

A second pattern, found in the French and Russian Revolutions, is for peasant revolts to coincide with urban revolts. Urban revolts have often provided the first "shock troops" of revolution by combining with elite protests to paralyze the state. Where appropriate conditions prevailed in the countryside, such as peasant solidarity and landlord vulnerability, the paralysis of the state then allowed peasant revolts to spread and to undermine rural landlords.

Peasant grievances do play a role in peasant movements. But usually the peasants who have suffered the most are *not* those who undertake major revolts. Instead, the peasants with moderate grievances but greater solidarity and organizational capacity who face more vulnerable landlords have been the major actors in social revolutions.

Urban Uprisings In the countryside, major uprisings have depended on key relationships among peasants, landlords, and the state. In urban settings such relational factors are less important. The concentration of large masses of workers and the presence of obvious targets for violence such as state buildings and palaces in capital cities provide revolutionary crowds with ready access to potential supporters and targets. The chief factors in urban uprisings are the level of workers' grievances and such physical factors as the scale and layout of cities and the size and effectiveness of urban police forces.

In seeking the roots of urban uprisings, we must first discard some old myths. Whether we look at the residents of growing cities in eighteenth-century France or twentieth-century Mexico, we find they are *not* isolated, ignorant, disoriented masses. Instead, urban migrants tend to be better educated and more highly skilled than the compatriots they leave behind in the countryside, generally have family contacts already in the city, and maintain frequent contacts, through circular migration, with rural kin. Moreover, when we examine the backgrounds of the participants in riots and revolutionary tumults, whether in eighteenth-century towns or in twentieth-century American ghettos, we find that the rioters tend to be among the better educated residents of their communities and are more likely to be long-term residents than recent arrivals.[13] These urban rioters are generally laborers or artisans for whom swings in prices and employment have a powerful impact, rather than the poorest, hard-core unemployed. In short, they are people who are responding to current grievances and not criminals or rabble.

Two grievances stand out as the chief causes of revolutionary urban tumults: the cost of food and the availability of employment. Food riots have occurred in sixteenth-century England and twentieth-century Poland, whereas urban rioting has accompanied unusually high levels of unemployment from the French Revolution to twentieth-century Britain and the United States. In the great revolutions of France, England, Russia, and China, and throughout Europe in 1848, high unemployment and sharp jumps in food prices combined to drive the laboring poor into large-scale antigovernment protests.

In the absence of such grievances, the mere rapid growth of cities or increases in rural-to-urban migration are not necessarily politically destabilizing. Indeed, if the urban economy is expanding and providing jobs and better conditions for underemployed rural residents, urban expansion may increase political stability. Only when urban growth is combined with food shortages and outpaces the availability of jobs do grievances grow that may stimulate political violence.

Of course, riots are not always successful. The outcome of urban revolts depends on how much crises and elite opposition have weakened the state. The size and discipline of police forces and the layout of cities (narrow streets and strongly cohesive neighborhoods make good bases for revolts) also affect the likelihood of success.

We must add a final word about the interaction of urban and rural revolt. Urban riots alone do not make a revolution. Though urban disorders have often been at the leading edge of revolution—in Paris in 1789, in Petersburg in 1917, in Tehran in 1980—no revolution has succeeded solely on the basis of rioting and seizure of the political capital by the populace. The state can isolate and defeat revolutionaries in the capital city if the revolutionaries lack support in the provinces and the countryside, as members of the Paris Commune of 1871 and the Chinese Communists of the 1920s discovered. Still, the enormous growth of urban populations in Third World countries since World War II has created a situation in which urban discontent and opposition may play the primary role in giving rise to social revolutions; rural uprisings may play a lesser role.[14]

In summary, popular uprisings grow from specific grievances that threaten the livelihood of peasants and workers. In the countryside these are grievances that peasants share widely and direct at landlords or the state; in the city, grievances center on high food prices and unemployment. When such grievances combine with conducive structural conditions—peasant autonomy and landlord vulnerability in the countryside, and weakly policed and isolated enclaves in the cities—the conditions for popular uprisings exist. When such popular uprisings also coincide with conflicts between states and powerful independent elites, all the ingredients for a full-scale revolution are at hand.

Frontiers of Research

We now better understand that revolutions arise from a complex blending of state weakness, elite conflicts, and urban and rural revolts. However, beyond the causes of revolution, further issues excite lively discussion. First, what are the outcomes of revolutions? Second, what part have nationalism and ethnic conflict played in revolutionary unrest? Third, what have various ideologies contributed to revolutions? Fourth, if a concurrence of severe state/elite conflicts and popular uprisings is necessary for revolutions, why do such occurrences arise at some times and not others? What large scale patterns in world history account for these rare conjunctures?

OUTCOMES

Many experts agree that full-scale revolutions, whether liberal or socialist, from the American colonies to the Chinese republic, have led to more centralized, more powerful governments than had existed under the old regimes. What observers still debate hotly, however, is whether most victorious revolutions have been successful in implementing the goals expressed during the revolution. Scholars are now beginning to develop quantitative evidence to test these questions; the result is some of the most controversial work in historical sociology. Eckstein[15] has argued that in Latin America, among states with similar levels of economic development and forms of economic organization, those states that have experienced revolutions have generally given rise to a more equitable allocation of land. Also, Cuba, in particular, has made greater strides in health care and education than states that did not undergo revolutions. However, countries that have experienced revolutions do not appear to be better off in terms of income equality or economic growth than countries that have not. Also at issue is whether revolutions have succeeded in reducing differences in opportunity among citizens, or if they have yielded to what Kelley and Klein[16] provocatively label "the rebirth of inequality."

In addition, the ability of nations to acquire democratic governments through revolution is questionable. A major set of natural "experiments" is now underway among the former communist states of Eastern Europe and Central Asia. In general, the level of violence that accompanies revolution has led military or authoritarian governments to step in to restore order. The names of Napoleon, Stalin, and Mao Zedong are synonymous with revolution, but these leaders did not implement democratic regimes. It appears that only where revolutions are relatively nonviolent, and leave no major counterrevolutionary threats or ethnic conflicts in their wake, is there hope for a democratic outcome to the revolutionary struggle. Thus, today in Nicaragua after the end of the Contra threat, and in the Philippines, we may see democracy develop, although such an outcome is by no means certain.

NATIONALISM AND REVOLUTION

The break-up of the Soviet Union and Yugoslavia has brought renewed attention to the role of nationalism in revolutions. Interestingly, Marx believed that once capitalist class relations had been overcome by revolution, nationalism would also cease to motivate workers, who would instead perceive their common needs. In this, as in much else, Marx was mistaken. Nationalism appears to provide a sense of purpose and belonging that people value, especially in times of crisis.

Nationalism has played a variety of different roles in the process of revolution. In early modern revolutions against European monarchs, the "nation" became an alternative focus for loyalty, replacing the person of the king. Nationalism thus became the basis for antimonarchical coalitions in the English and French Revolutions. In the nineteenth and twentieth centuries, the desire to liberate "the nation" from foreign domination was a key factor in anticolonial revolutions from Algeria and Vietnam to Angola and Mozambique. In recent years, the belief that certain rulers—the Shah of Iran, Marcos in the Philippines, Somoza in Nicaragua—were too dependent on U.S. aid, and hence were following foreign interests rather than their *own* nations' interests, played a major role in building support for movements to topple those leaders. Finally, in the last decade, belief that communist systems had become corrupt, and that the people's interest would be better served by "national" governments rather than Soviet rule, was crucial to the collapse of central authority in the Soviet Union and Yugoslavia.

While the passions aroused by nationalism are obvious, the actual definition and construction of nationalism is often problematic. Who belongs to the "nation"? How is membership defined—by territory, ancestry, or claims of allegiance? Often in times of revolutionary crisis, the struggle to dominate the nationalist issue pits different groups against each other, and brings persecution to minorities, as Gurr's essay in this volume makes painfully clear.

The question of how nations are constructed, the meaning they have for their members, and how that construction and meaning change in times of crisis are still very much issues of argument and study. The emergence of dozens of "new nationalisms" in the former Soviet Union, as well as the reemergence of centuries-old nationalisms in former Yugoslavia, continue to present puzzles to social scientists regarding how nationalism is born, survives, and grows.

THE ROLE OF IDEOLOGY

Communist ideology, though often the focus of attention in political rhetoric, has played a limited role in inducing revolutions. In neopatrimonal revolutions in Mexico, Cuba, and Bolivia, communist ideology was either nonexistent or relatively unimportant until after the old regime had already succumbed. In Russia, communism became a major force only after the fall of the old regime. In examining more recent Third World revolutions, Migdal[17] has pointed out that Communists gained adherents among peasantries not because of the inherent attractiveness of communist thought, but because communist parties were the most effective groups in undertaking the tasks of organizing peasants for land reform and protecting traditional village communities from state or landlord depredations. Communism's major effect has not been to induce revolutions but to provide an ideology for reconstruction after the old regime has fallen. Whether, given the examples of the Soviet Union and Cuba, this ideal of reconstruction will continue to be influential remains unresolved, but seems unlikely.

Eisenstadt[18] has noted that the key to revolution lies in the combination of diverse movements—peasant uprisings, elite political revolts, religious heterodoxies—in time of crises into widespread attacks on the institutions of the old regime. Therefore, the main role of ideologies in revolutions is to bring together diverse grievances and interests under a simple and appealing set of symbols of opposition. For this purpose, any ideology that features a strong tension between good and evil, emphasizes the importance of combatting evil in this world through active remaking of the world, and sees politics as simply one more battlefield between good and evil, may serve as the foundation for a revolutionary ideology. Thus puritanism, liberalism, communism, and more recently, Islam, all provided appealing ideologies for revolutions. Recent studies of peasant and worker revolts have stressed that traditional ideologies—the norms of the peasant village or the corporatism of the craft guild—can play a similar role.[19] Though none of these ideologies themselves have brought down governments, they have been crucial in providing a basis for uniting diverse existing grievances under one banner and encouraging their active resolution.

Yet ideologies are not merely *sources* of revolutions; ideologies are the *products* of revolution as well. Modern communism was not merely drawn from the ideas of Karl Marx: In Russia it was the product of Leninism; in China, the product of Maoism; and in Yugoslavia, something slightly different again. In each case, the ideology under which the revolution consolidated developed out of a collision between the initial ideas and the actual experience of particular revolutionaries who struggled for power and built postrevolutionary regimes.[20] Indeed, the particular problems revolutionaries face in seizing and holding power and the manner in which they choose to solve them contribute more to the final shape of postrevolutionary society than does the ideological banner under which they proclaimed the revolution. Understanding the actual role of ideologies and how varied ideologies—including traditional beliefs—affect revolutionary struggles will remain a problem of practical politics as well as of continued research.

Finally, ideology shapes revolutions, as well as being shaped by them. Revolutionary rhetoric rarely provides a blueprint for the development of a revolution, since struggles for power and unforeseen difficulties can powerfully shape events. Still, the development of revolutions is affected by whether revolutionary leaders have a deep commitment to democratic principles, or to a particular kind of party-led politics, or whether their experience has been shaped by power struggles that have produced a cynical pragmatism. For the most part, revolutionary leaders with deep commitments to democracy have been rare. However, where such leaders have gained power—such as Cory Aquino in the Philippines—their commitment has helped sustain early movement toward democratic rule. Unfortunately, most of the leaders of the new post-Soviet and East European regimes appear to be of the pragmatic type; their prospects for democracy will dim if economic or political struggles require severe government actions. On the other hand, much remains to be discovered about the ways in which ideology can change, and shape, the long-term outcomes of states born in revolutionary crises.

THE PROBLEM OF CONJUNCTURE

If the availability of an appropriate ideology helps to explain the coalescence of extant grievances, it does little to explain why at certain times the grounds for state crises, increased state/elite conflict, and popular uprisings should arise simultaneously. Experts have often suggested that the pressures of defeat in war are what bring diverse social problems to a head and that these pressures precipitate both state/elite conflicts and widespread revolt. However, although in some instances war has led to revolution, empirical studies have shown that the relationship between wars and internal political instability in general is weak. To give only the most striking example, in Europe the period from 1670 to 1763 was one of almost constant warfare, from the wars of Louis XIV to the Seven Years' War. States used the largest armies seen on the continent up to that time. Yet not a single revolution occurred anywhere in Europe. When revolution did come to France in 1789, France had not suffered a military defeat in more than twenty-five years, and had been at peace for six years following its victory over Britain in the American Revolution. Moreover, twenty of the twenty-six years preceding 1789 were years of peace. Similarly, Germany, Austria, and Russia were free from revolution during their defeats in the Napoleonic wars; revolutionary crises came to Germany and Austria only in 1848 after thirty years of peace. For these two centuries, the broad relationship between defeat in war and revolution is virtually nil.

What then might be the source of revolutionary conjuncture? I have suggested that the roots of revolutionary crises might lie in the pattern of long waves of population growth and rising prices.[21] In the sixteenth and seventeenth centuries, when Europe's population was growing, prices rose steadily. As population increased, high food prices and growing unemployment afflicted the cities. Governments, in order to keep themselves abreast of rising prices, raised taxes and sought to increase control of the countryside. At the same time, rising prices divided the landed elites. Some landlords, dependent on fixed rents, saw their real incomes decline with rising prices and therefore sought to raise rents and dues; others, who directly controlled the marketing of products, reaped bonanzas. In short, the steady rise of population and prices produced increasing divisions among the landed elite; attempts by the state to raise taxes and gain greater control of the land; and increased problems of dues and taxes, unemployment, and rising food costs for the populace.

These forces may well have been the major causes behind the conjuncture of state/elite conflicts and popular uprisings that swept across Europe during 1560–1660, with revolution in England and revolts in France, Russia, Austria, and Italy comprising a "crisis of the Seventeenth Century." When Europe's population ceased growing between 1660 and 1730, so did prices, and the cycle of political discontent receded. But when population and prices continued their upward march from 1750 to 1850, political instability returned to much of Europe until cheap American and Russian wheat broke the link between population increase and rising prices. If this hypothesis is correct in linking revolutionary conjunctures with problems of population growth, state financial distress, food shortages, and increasing prices, much of the Third World, particularly Africa, may well experience an extended period of revolution, similar to that of Europe in 1789–1848, in the next few decades.

In the contemporary world, the problems of coping with population growth continue to impose strains on governments. However, population growth by itself is not sufficient to topple a regime. Rather, what appears to matter is whether the economy and political system respond constructively to changes in the size, age, and distribution of the population. The stability of government may be threatened where urban populations grow rapidly without a supporting growth of jobs; where feeding a growing population requires growing state indebtedness; where the government's revenue sources fail to keep pace with the spending required to meet goals for development, welfare, and security; where aspiring elites and middle classes find no opportunities or outlets for their ambitions; or where natural disasters, such as earthquakes or floods, reveal the incapacity of a corrupt government to assist a struggling population. Whenever such imbalances become widespread, so too does the risk of revolutions.

Finally, a key element in revolutionary conjunctures in the modern world is the willingness of international superpowers to support, or resist, revolutionary movements. As Goldfrank points out in his essay in this volume, a permissive or supportive world context increases the chance that an unstable situation will blossom into open revolution. Thus when the United States in 1979, or the Soviet Union in 1989, became less willing to expend effort to enforce the status quo (as in Nicaragua, Iran, the Philippines, Afghanistan, and Eastern Europe), a wave of revolutions spread as regimes that were shaky, and relied heavily on foreign support, were forced to depend on their own frail resources. With the end of the cold war, the inclination of Europe and the United States to shore up shaky regimes in Africa and other developing regions is likely to decline; if past patterns hold, this may lead to yet another wave of revolutions in the decades ahead.

Conclusion

In this century, scholars have contributed greatly to our knowledge of the course of revolutions, and of the structural conditions conducive to them. In addition, they are giving closer scrutiny to the outcomes of revolutions, to nationalism, to the role of ideologies, and to the links between macro-social and international changes and the conjunctures that comprise revolutionary crises.

Yet the study of revolutions remains much like the study of earthquakes. When one occurs, scholars try to make sense of the data they have collected and to build theories to account for the next one. Gradually, we gain a fuller understanding of revolutions and of the conditions behind them. And yet the next one still surprises us. Our knowledge of revolutions, like that of earthquakes, remains limited. We can detail the patterns in those that have occurred, and we can list some of the conditions conducive to them, but a better and more exact understanding of precisely when they are likely to occur still lies in the future.

REFERENCES

1. Edwards (1927); Pettee (1938); Brinton (1938)
2. Davies (1962); Gurr (1970).
3. Smelser (1963); Johnson (1966).
4. Huntington (1968).
5. Tilly (1978).
6. Moore, Jr. (1966).
7. Skocpol (1979).
8. Chorley (1943); Russell (1974).
9. Trimberger (1978).
10. Eisenstadt (1978).
11. Paige (1975).
12. Scott (1977), p. 237.
13. Rudé (1964).
14. Gugler (1982); Dix (1983); Farhi (1990).
15. Eckstein (1982).
16. Kelley and Klein (1977).
17. Migdal (1974).
18. Eisenstadt (1978).
19. Scott (1976); Sewell, Jr. (1980); Calhoun (1983).
20. Dunn (1972).
21. Goldstone (1991).

PART ONE

Theories of
Revolutions

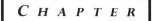

Classic Approaches

During the nineteenth and early twentieth centuries, scholars concentrated their efforts to understand revolution on the French Revolution of 1789. Attempts to develop general theories of revolution began with the French Revolution as a model, for it was the most dramatic and best known revolution in European history.

The following selections embody the most influential thinking about revolution to emerge from this period. These classic statements by Marx and Engels, de Tocqueville, and Weber form the starting point for modern studies of revolution.

MANIFESTO OF THE COMMUNIST PARTY

Karl Marx and Frederick Engels

In the nineteenth century Karl Marx and Frederick Engels first formulated many of the key issues in the study of revolution. Their "Manifesto of the Communist Party," published in 1848, has undoubtedly been the most influential essay on revolution ever written. Marx and Engels viewed European history since the Middle Ages as a progression through various modes of production—feudal, capitalist, and in the future, socialist—each more fruitful than the last. They postulated that the transition between these modes had not been—and would not be—peaceful, however, since in each of these modes a particular social class dominated society. This dominant class would have to be dislodged by a revolution before the transition to the next mode of production could be completed. The French Revolution of 1789 was an example of a revolution waged to dislodge the privileged feudal aristocracy and clear the way for capitalism. However, Marx and Engels argued that the new political freedoms and material benefits following the overthrow of the aristocracy went only to the class of professionals and businessmen—the bourgeoisie— who dominated the capitalist society. The French Revolution was thus essentially a "bourgeois" revolution. A further revolution— in the name of workers—was necessary to extend the benefits of modern industrial technology to all. The major tenets of this view are that revolutions are related to great historical transitions, that revolution is a necessary agent of change, and that revolutions are progressive and beneficial. Also, capitalism, even though it is progressive, benefits only a minority so that socialist revolutions are needed to benefit all society.

These tenets have become articles of faith for many modern revolutionaries. Asking to what extent these conclusions of Marx and Engels are valid poses one of the chief research problems for modern scholars.

In the following excerpt from the *Manifesto*, Marx and Engels outline their theory of history, applaud the accomplishments of capitalism, and predict its future demise.

The history of all hitherto existing society is the history of class struggles.

Freeman and slave, patrician and plebeian, lord and serf, guild-master and journeyman, in a word, oppressor and oppressed, stood in constant opposition to one another, carried on an uninterrupted, now hidden, now open fight, a fight that each time ended, either in a revolutionary re-constitution of society at large, or in the common ruin of the contending classes.

In the earlier epochs of history, we find almost everywhere a complicated arrangement of society into various orders, a manifold gradation of social rank. In ancient Rome we have patricians, knights, plebeians, slaves; in the Middle Ages, feudal lords, vassals, guild-masters, journeymen, apprentices, serfs; in almost all of these classes, again, subordinate gradations.

The modern bourgeois society that has sprouted from the ruins of feudal society has not done away with class antagonisms. It has but established new classes, new conditions of oppression, new forms of struggle in place of the old ones.

Our epoch, the epoch of the bourgeoisie, possesses, however, this distinctive feature: it has simplified the class antagonisms: Society as a whole is more and more splitting up into two great hostile camps, into two great classes directly facing each other: Bourgeoisie and Proletariat.

From the serfs of the Middle Ages sprang the chartered burghers of the earliest towns. From these burgesses the first elements of the bourgeoisie were developed.

The discovery of America, the rounding of the Cape, opened up fresh ground for the rising bourgeoisie. The East-Indian and Chinese markets, the colonization of America, trade with the colonies, the increase in the means of exchange and in commodities generally, gave to commerce, to navigation, to industry, an impulse never before known, and thereby, to the revolutionary element in the tottering feudal society, a rapid development.

The feudal system of industry, under which industrial production was monopolized by closed guilds, now no longer sufficed for the growing wants of the new markets. The manufacturing system took its place. The guild-masters were pushed on one side by the manufacturing middle class; division of labor between the different corporate guilds vanished in the face of division of labor in each single workshop.

Meantime the markets kept ever growing, the demand ever rising. Even manufacture no longer sufficed. Thereupon, steam and machinery revolutionized industrial production. The place of manufacture was taken by the giant, Modern Industry, the place of the industrial middle class, by industrial millionaires, the leaders of whole industrial armies, the modern bourgeois.

Modern industry has established the world-market, for which the discovery of America paved the way. This market has given an immense development to commerce, to navigation, to communication by land. This development has, in its turn, reacted on the extension of industry; and in proportion as industry, commerce, navigation, railways extended, in the same proportion the bourgeoisie developed, increased its capital, and pushed into the background every class handed down from the Middle Ages.

We see, therefore, how the modern bourgeoisie is itself the product of a long course of development, of a series of revolutions in the modes of production and of exchange.

Each step in the development of the bourgeoisie was accompanied by a corresponding political advance of that class. An oppressed class under the sway of the feudal nobility, an armed and self-governing association in the medieval commune; here independent urban republic (as in Italy and Germany), there taxable "third estate" of the monarchy (as in France), afterwards, in the period of manufacture proper, serving either the semi-feudal or the absolute monarchy as a counterpoise against the nobility, and, in fact, corner-stone of the great monarchies in general, the bourgeoisie has at last since the establishment of Modern Industry and of the world-market, conquered for itself, in the modern represen-tative State, exclusive political sway. The executive of the modern State is but a committee for managing the common affairs of the whole bourgeoisie.

The bourgeoisie, historically, has played a most revolutionary part.

The bourgeoisie, whenever it has got the upper hand, has put an end to all feudal, patriarchal, idyllic relations. It has pitilessly torn asunder the motley feudal ties that bound man to his "natural superiors," and has left remaining no other nexus between man and man than naked self-interest, than callous "cash payment." It has drowned the most heavenly ecstasies of religious fervor, of chivalrous enthusiasm, of philistine sentimentalism, in the icy water of egotistical calculation. It has resolved personal worth into exchange value, and in place of the numberless indefeasible chartered freedoms, has set up that single, unconscionable freedom—Free Trade. In one word, for exploitation, veiled by religious and political illusions, it has substituted naked, shameless, direct, brutal exploi-tation.

The bourgeoisie has stripped of its halo every occupation hitherto honored and looked up to with reverent awe. It has converted the physician, the lawyer, the priest, the poet, the man of science, into its paid wage-laborers.

The bourgeoisie has torn away from the family its sentimental veil, and has reduced the family relation to a mere money relation.

The bourgeoisie has disclosed how it came to pass that the brutal display of vigor in the Middle Ages, which Reactionists so much admire, found its fitting complement in the most slothful indolence. It has been the first to show what man's activity can bring about. It has accomplished wonders far surpassing Egyptian pyramids, Roman aqueducts, and Gothic cathedrals; it has conducted expeditions that put in the shade all former Exoduses of nations and crusades.

The bourgeoisie cannot exist without constantly revolutionizing the instruments of production, and thereby the relations of production, and with them the whole reactions of society. Conservation of the old modes of production in unaltered form, was, on the contrary, the first condition of existence for all earlier industrial classes. Constant revolutionizing of production, uninterrupted disturbance of all social conditions, everlasting uncertainty and agitation distinguish the bourgeois epoch from all earlier ones. All fixed, fast-frozen relations, with their train of ancient and venerable prejudices and opinions, are swept away, all new-formed ones become antiquated before they can ossify. All that is solid melts into air, all that is holy is profaned, and man is at last compelled to face with sober senses his real conditions of life, and his relations with his kind.

The need of a constantly expanding market for its products chases the bourgeoisie over the whole surface of the globe. It must nestle everywhere, settle everywhere, establish connections everywhere.

The bourgeoisie has through its exploitation of the world-market given a cosmopolitan character to production and consumption in every country. To the great chagrin of Reactionists, it has drawn from under the feet of industry the national ground on which it stood. All old-established national industries have been destroyed or are daily being destroyed. They are dislodged by new industries, whose introduction becomes a life and death question for all civilized nations, by industries that no longer work up indigenous raw material, but raw material drawn from the remotest zones; industries whose products are consumed, not only at home, but in every quarter of the globe. In place of the old wants, satisfied by the productions of the country, we find new wants, requiring for the satisfaction the products of distant lands and climes. In place of the old local and national seclusion and self-sufficiency, we have intercourse in every direction, universal interdependence of nations. And as in material, so also in intellectual production. The intellectual creations of individual nations become common property. National one-sidedness and narrow-mindedness become more and more impossible, and from the numerous national and local literatures, there arises a world literature.

The bourgeoisie, by the rapid improvement of all instruments of production, by the immensely facilitated means of communication, draws all, even the most barbarian nations into civilization. The cheap prices of its commodities are the heavy artillery with which it batters down all Chinese walls, with which it forces the barbarians' intensely obstinate hatred of foreigners to capitulate. It compels all nations, on pain of extinction, to adopt the bourgeois mode of production; it compels them to introduce what it calls civilization into their midst, i.e., to become bourgeois themselves. In one word, it creates a world after its own image.

The bourgeoisie has subjected the country to the rule of the towns. It has created enormous cities, has greatly increased the urban population as compared with the rural, and has thus rescued a considerable part of the population from the idiocy of rural life. Just as it has made the country dependent on the towns, so it has made barbarian and semi-barbarian countries dependent on the civilized ones, nations and peasants on nations of bourgeois, the East on the West.

The bourgeoisie keeps more and more doing away with the scattered state of the population, of the means of production, and of property. It has agglomerated population, centralized means of production, and has concentrated property in a few hands. The necessary consequence of this was political centralization. Independent, or but loosely connected provinces, with separate interests, laws, governments and systems of taxation, became lumped together into one nation, with one government, one code of laws, one national class-interest, one frontier and one customs-tariff.

The bourgeoisie, during its rule of scarce one hundred years, has created more massive and more colossal productive forces than have all proceeding generations together. Subjection of Nature's forces to man, machinery, application of chemistry to industry and agriculture, steam-navigation, railways, electric telegraphs, clearing of whole continents for cultivation, canalization of rivers, whole populations conjured out of the ground—what earlier century had even a presentiment hat such productive forces slumbered in the lap of social labor?

We see then: the means of production and of exchange, on whose foundation the bourgeoisie built itself up, were generated in feudal society. At a certain stage in the development of these means of production and of exchange, the conditions under which feudal society produced and exchanged, the feudal organization of agriculture and manufacturing industry, in one word, the feudal relations of property became no longer compatible with the already developed productive forces; they became so many fetters. They had to be burst asunder; they were burst asunder.

Into their place stepped free competition, accompanied by a social and political constitution adapted to it, and by the economical and political sway of the bourgeois class.

A similar movement is going on before our own eyes. Modern bourgeois society with its relations of production, of exchange and of property, a society that has conjured up such gigantic means of production and of exchange, is like the sorcerer, who is no longer able to control the powers of the nether world whom he has called up by his spells. For many a decade past the history of industry and commerce is but the history of the revolt of modern productive forces against modern conditions of production, against the property relations that are the conditions for the existence of the bourgeoisie and of its rule. It is enough to mention the commercial crises that by their periodical return put on its trial, each time more threateningly, the existence of the entire bourgeois society. In these crises a great part not only of the existing products, but also of the previously created productive forces, are periodically destroyed. In these crises there breaks out an epidemic that, in all earlier epochs, would have seemed an absurdity—the epidemic of over-production. Society suddenly finds itself put back into a state of momentary barbarism; it appears as if a famine, a universal war of devastation had cut off the supply of every means of subsistence; industry and commerce seem to be destroyed; and why? Because there is too much civilization, too much means of subsistence, too much industry, too much commerce. The productive forces at the disposal of society no longer tend to further the development of the conditions of bourgeois property; on the contrary, they have become too powerful for these conditions, by which they are fettered, and so soon as they overcome these fetters, they bring disorder into the whole of bourgeois society, endanger the existence of bourgeois property. The conditions of bourgeois society are too narrow to comprise the wealth created by them. And how does the bourgeoisie get over these crises? On the one hand by enforced destruction of a mass of productive forces; on the other, by the conquest of new markets, and by more thorough exploitation of the old ones. That is to say, by paving the way for more extensive and more destructive crises, and by diminishing the means whereby crises are prevented.

The weapons with which the bourgeoisie felled feudalism to the ground are now turned against the bourgeoisie itself.

But not only has the bourgeoisie forged the weapons that bring death to itself; it has also called into existence the men who are to wield those weapons—the modern working class—the proletarians.

In proportion as the bourgeoisie, i.e., capital, is developed, in the same proportion is the proletariat, the modern working class, developed—a class of laborers, who live only so long as they find work, and who find work only so long as their labor increases capital. These laborers, who must sell themselves piece-meal, are a commodity, like every other article of commerce, and are consequently exposed to all the vicissitudes of competition, to all the fluctuations of the market.

Owing to the extensive use of machinery and to division of labor, the work of the proletarians has lost all individual character, and consequently, all charm for the workman. He becomes an appendage of the machine, and it is only the most simple, most monotonous, and most easily acquired knack, that is required of him. Hence, the cost of production of a workman is restricted, almost entirely, to the means of subsistence that he requires for his maintenance, and for the propagation of his race. But the price of a commodity, and therefore also of labor, is equal to its cost of production. In proportion, therefore, as the repulsiveness of the work increases, the wage decreases. Nay more, in proportion as the use of machinery and division of labor increases, in the same proportion the burden of toil also increases, whether by prolongation of the working hours, by increase of the work exacted in a given time or by increased speed of the machinery, etc.

Modern industry has converted the little workshop of the patriarchal master into the great factory of the industrial capitalist. Masses of laborers, crowded into the factory, are organized like soldiers. As privates of the industrial army they are placed under the command of a perfect hierarchy of officers and sergeants. Not only are they slaves of the bourgeois class, and of the bourgeois State; they are daily and hourly enslaved by the machine, by the over-looker, and above all, by the individual bourgeois manufacturer himself. The more openly this despotism proclaims gain to be its end and aim, the more petty, the more hateful and the more embittering it is.

The less the skill and exertion of strength implied in manual labor, in other words, the more modern industry becomes developed, the more is the labor of men superseded by that of women. Differences of age and sex have no longer any distinctive social validity for the working class. All are instruments of labor, more or less expensive to use, according to their age and sex.

No sooner is the exploitation of the laborer by the manufacturer, so far, at an end, that he receives his wages in cash, than he is set upon by the other portions of the bourgeoisie, the landlord, the shopkeeper, the pawnbroker, etc.

The lower strata of the middle class—the small tradespeople, shopkeepers, and retired tradesmen generally, the handicraftsmen and peasants—all these sink gradually into the proletariat, partly because their diminutive capital does not suffice for the scale on which modern industry is carried on, and is swamped in the competition with the large capitalists, partly because their specialized skill is rendered worthless by new methods of production. Thus the proletariat is recruited from all classes of the population.

The proletariat goes through various stages of development. With its birth begins its struggle with the bourgeoisie. At first the contest is carried on by individual laborers, then by the workpeople of a factory, then by the operatives of one trade, in one locality, against the individual bourgeois who directly exploits them, They direct their attacks not against the bourgeois conditions of production, but against the instruments of production themselves; they destroy imported wares that compete with their labor, they smash to pieces machinery, they set factories ablaze, they seek to restore by force the vanished status of the workman of the Middle Ages.

At this stage the laborers still form an incoherent mass scattered over the whole country, and broken up by the mutual competition. If anywhere they unite to form more compact bodies, this is not yet the consequence of their own active union, but of the union of the bourgeoisie, which class, in order to attain its own political end, is compelled to set the whole proletariat in motion, and is moreover yet, for a time, able to do so, At this stage, therefore, the proletarians do not fight their enemies, but the enemies of their enemies, the remnants of absolute monarchy, the landowners, the non-industrial bourgeois, the petty bourgeoisie. Thus the whole historical movement is concentrated in the hands of the bourgeoisie; every victory so obtained is a victory for the bourgeoisie.

But with the development of industry the proletariat not only increases in number; it becomes concentrated in greater masses, its strength grows, and it feels that strength more. The various interests and conditions of life within the ranks of the proletariat are more and more equalized, in proportion as machinery obliterates all distinctions of labor, and nearly everywhere reduces wages to the same low level. The growing competition among the bourgeois, and the resulting commercial crises, make the wages of the workers ever more fluctuating. The unceasing improvement of machinery, ever more rapidly developing, makes their livelihood more and more precarious; the collisions between individual workmen and individual bourgeois take more and more the character of collisions between two classes. Thereupon the workers begin to form combinations (Trade Unions) against the bourgeois; they club together in order to keep up the rate of wages; they found permanent associations in order to make provision beforehand for these occasional revolts. Here and there the contest breaks out into riots.

Now and then the workers are victorious, but only for a time. The real fruit of their battles lies, not in the immediate result, but in the ever-expanding union of the workers. This union is helped on by the improved means of communication that are created by modern industry and that place the workers of different localities in contact with one another. It was just this contact that was needed to centralize their numerous local struggles, all of the same character, into one national struggle between the classes. But every class struggle is a political struggle. And that union, to attain which the burghers of the Middle Ages, with their miserable highways, required centuries, the modern proletarians, thanks to railways, achieve in a few years.

This organization of the proletarians into a class, and consequently into a political party, is continually being upset again by the competition between the workers themselves. But it ever rises up again, stronger, firmer, mightier. It compels legislative recognition of particular interests of the workers, by taking advantage of the divisions among the bourgeoisie itself. Thus the ten-hours' bill in England was carried.

Altogether collisions between the classes of the old society further, in many ways, the course of development of the proletariat. The bourgeoisie finds itself involved in a constant battle. At first with the aristocracy; later on, with those portions of the bourgeoisie itself, whose interests have become antagonistic to the progress of industry; at all times, with the bourgeoisie of foreign countries. In all these battles it sees itself compelled to appeal to the proletariat, to ask for its help, and thus, to drag it into the political arena. The bourgeoisie itself, therefore, supplies the proletariat with its own elements of political and general education, in other words, it furnishes the proletariat with weapons for fighting the bourgeoisie.

Further, as we have already seen, entire sections of the ruling classes are, by the advance of industry, precipitated into the proletariat, or are at least threatened in their conditions of existence. These also supply the proletariat with fresh elements of enlightenment and progress.

Finally, in times when the class struggle nears the decisive hour, the process of dissolution going on within the ruling class, in fact within the whole range of society, assumes such a violent, glaring character, that a small section of the ruling class cuts itself adrift, and joins the revolutionary class, the class that holds the future in its hands. Just as, therefore, at an earlier period, a section of the nobility went over to the bourgeoisie, so now a portion of the bourgeoisie goes over to the proletariat, and in particular, a portion of the bourgeois ideologists, who have raised themselves to the level of comprehending theoretically the historical movement as a whole.

Of all the classes that stand face to face with the bourgeoisie today, the proletariat alone is a really revolutionary class. The other classes decay and finally disappear in the face of modern industry; the proletariat is its special and essential product.

The lower middle class, the small manufacturer, the shopkeeper, the artisan, the peasant, all these fight against the bourgeoisie, to save from extinction their existence as fractions of the middle class. They are therefore not revolutionary, but conservative. Nay more, they are reactionary, for they try to roll back the wheel of history. If by chance they are revolutionary, they are so only in view of their impending transfer into the proletariat; they thus defend not their present, but their future interests, they desert their own standpoint to place themselves at that of the proletariat.

The "dangerous class," the social scum, that passively rotting mass thrown off by the lowest layers of old society, may, here and there, be swept into the movement by a proletarian revolution; its conditions of life, however, prepare it far more for the part of a bribed tool of reactionary intrigue.

In the conditions of the proletariat, those of old society at large are already virtually swamped. The proletarian is without property; his relation to his wife and children has no longer anything in common with the bourgeois family-relations; modern industrial labor, modern subjection to capital, the same in England as in France, in America as in

Germany, has stripped him of every trace of national character. Law, morality, religion, are to him so many bourgeois prejudices, behind which lurk in ambush just as many bourgeois interests.

All the preceding classes that got the upper hand sought to fortify their already acquired status by subjecting society at large to their conditions of appropriation. The proletarians cannot become masters of the productive forces of society, except by abolishing their own previous mode of appropriation, and thereby also every other previous mode of appropriation. They have nothing of their own to secure and to fortify; their mission is to destroy all previous securities for, and insurances of, individual property.

All previous historical movements were movements of minorities, or in the interests of minorities. The proletarian movement is the self-conscious, independent movement of the immense majority, in the interests of the immense majority. The proletariat, the lowest stratum of our present society, cannot stir, cannot raise itself up, without the whole superincumbent strata of official society being sprung into the air.

Though not in substance, yet in form, the struggle of the proletariat with the bourgeoisie is at first a national struggle. The proletariat of each country must, of course, first of all settle matters with its own bourgeoisie.

In depicting the most general phases of the development of the proletariat, we traced the more or less veiled civil war, raging within existing society, up to the point, where that war breaks out into open revolution, and where the violent overthrow of the bourgeoisie lays the foundation for the sway of the proletariat.

Hitherto, every form of society has been based, as we have already seen, on the antagonism of oppressing and oppressed classes. But in order to oppress a class, certain conditions must be assured to it under which it can, at least, continue its slavish existence. The serf, in the period of serfdom, raised himself to membership in the commune, just as the petty bourgeois, under the yoke of feudal absolutism, managed to develop into a bourgeois. The modern laborer, on the contrary, instead of rising with the progress of industry, sinks deeper and deeper below the conditions of existence of his own class. He becomes a pauper, and pauperism develops more rapidly than population and wealth. And here it becomes evident, that the bourgeoisie is unfit any longer to be the ruling class in society, and to impose its conditions of existence upon society as an over-riding law. It is unfit to rule because it is incompetent to assure an existence to its slave within his slavery, because it cannot help letting him sink into such a state, that it has to feed him, instead of being fed by him. Society can no longer live under this bourgeoisie, in other words, its existence is no longer compatible with society.

The essential condition for the existence, and for the sway of the bourgeois class, is the formation and augmentation of capital; the condition for capital is wage-labor. Wage-labor rests exclusively on competition between the laborers. The advance of industry, whose involuntary promoter is the bourgeoisie, replaces the isolation of the laborers, due to competition, by the revolutionary combination, due to association. The development of modern industry, therefore, cuts from under its feet the very foundation on which the bourgeoisie produces and appropriates products. What the bourgeoisie, therefore, produces, above all, is its own grave-diggers. Its fall and the victory of the proletariat are equally inevitable.

The French Revolution and the Growth of the State

Alexis de Tocqueville

Alexis de Tocqueville wrote at the same time as Marx and Engels; his book on The Old Regime and the French Revolution appeared in 1848, the same year as the Manifesto of the Communist Party. Yet de Tocqueville saw the French Revolution very differently. De Tocqueville agreed that the Revolution destroyed the power of the old aristocracy and those laws and practices associated with feudal society. But where Marx and Engels saw the defeat of feudalism as a triumph for a new class—the bourgeoisie—that a later socialist revolution would in turn dislodge, de Tocqueville saw the triumph of the centralized state. To de Tocqueville, when the French Revolution destroyed class privileges and set all men equal before the law it also removed all the obstacles to the authority of the state. Before the Revolution, privileged and powerful groups had existed alongside the state; after the Revolution the state stood alone, gathering all power to itself. If Marx has inspired a tradition that sees revolution as progressive and beneficial, de Tocqueville inspires caution, noting that revolution often strengthens the power of the state rather than weakening it.

No great historical event is better calculated than the French Revolution to teach political writers and statesmen to be cautious in their speculations. What was its true significance, its real nature, and what were the permanent effects of this strange and terrifying revolution? What exactly did it destroy, and what did it create?

One of the earliest enterprises of the revolutionary movement was a concerted attack on the Church, and among the many passions inflamed by it the first to be kindled and last to be extinguished was of an anti-religious nature. Nevertheless, it is easy enough to see today that the campaign against all forms of religion was merely incidental to the French Revolution, a spectacular but transient phenomenon, a brief reaction to the ideologies, emotions, and events which led up to it—but in no sense basic to its program. The Church was hated not because its priests claimed to regulate the affairs of the other world but because they were landed proprietors, lords of manors, tithe owners, and played a leading part in secular affairs; not because there was no room for the Church in the new world that was in the making, but because it occupied the most powerful, most privileged position in the old order that was now to be swept away.

What I have said about Church authority applies even more strongly to the authority of the central power. Those who saw the Revolution overthrowing all the institutions and customs which had hitherto shored up the social hierarchy and prevented men from running wild were naturally inclined to think that the Revolution spelled the end of all things; not merely of the old order, but of any order in the State, not merely that of any given form of government, but of any government at all—that in fact the nation was heading towards sheer anarchy. Yet, in my opinion, those who held this view were misled by appearances.

Since the object of the Revolution was not merely to change an old form of government but to abolish the entire social structure of pre-revolutionary France, it was obliged to declare war simultaneously on all established powers, to destroy all recognized prerogatives, to make short work of all traditions, and to institute new ways of living, new conventions. Thus one of its first acts was to rid men's minds of all those notions which had ensured their obedience to authority under the old regime. Hence its so markedly anarchic tendencies.

But beneath the seemingly chaotic surface there was developing a vast, highly centralized power which attracted to itself and welded into an organic whole all the elements of authority and influence that hitherto had been dispersed among a crowd of lesser, uncoordinated powers: the three Orders of the State, professional bodies, families, and individuals. Never since the fall of the Roman Empire had the world seen a government so highly centralized. This new power was created by the Revolution, or, rather, grew up almost automatically out of the havoc wrought by it.

Despite its magnitude it was as yet invisible to the eyes of the multitude, but gradually time has made amends and contemporary monarchs, in particular, are fully alive to its significance. They contemplate it with envy and admiration; not only those who owe their present eminence to the Revolution but also those who are least in sympathy with, or frankly hostile to, its achievement. Thus we see all these rulers doing what they can to abolish privileges and remove immunities within their territories. Everywhere they are breaking down class distinctions, leveling out inequalities, replacing members of the aristocracy with trained civil servants, local charters with uniform regulations, and a diversity of powers with a strong, centralized government. They are putting through these revolutionary measures with unflagging energy and sometimes even have recourse to the methods and maxims of the Great Revolution when obstacles arise. Thus we often find them championing the poor man's cause against the rich man's, the commoner's against the nobleman's, the peasant's against his lord's. In short, the lesson of the Revolution has not been lost even on those who have most reason to detest it.

BUREAUCRACY AND REVOLUTION

Max Weber

Max Weber amplified de Tocqueville's ideas on the strengthening of state power. Weber, a German sociologist who wrote in the early twentieth century, argued that bureaucracy—a system in which authority derives from legally defined offices rather than from hereditary position or privileges—thrives when governments abolish such privileges. Weber thus suggested that the revolutionary leveling that de Tocqueville described would lead to increasing bureaucratization. Moreover, the superior efficiency of bureaucracy would lead to its growing entrenchment. Revolution, therefore, had permanent bureaucracy as a likely outcome.

The Leveling of Social Differences

Bureaucratic organization has usually come into power on the basis of a leveling of economic and social differences. This leveling has been at least relative, and has concerned the significance of social and economic difference for the assumption of administrative functions.

Bureaucracy inevitably accompanies modern *mass democracy** in contrast to the democratic self-government of small homogeneous units. This results from the characteristic principle of bureaucracy: the abstract regularity of the execution of authority, which is a result of the demand for 'equality before the law' in the personal and functional sense— hence, the horror of 'privilege.' Such regularity also follows from the social preconditions of the origin of bureaucracies. The nonbureaucratic administration of any large social structure rests in some way upon the fact that existing social, material, or honorific preferences and ranks are connected with administrative functions and duties;. This usually means that a direct or indirect economic exploitation or a 'social' exploitation of position, which every sort of administrative activity gives to its bearers, is equivalent to the assumption of administrative functions.

Bureaucratization and democratization within the administration of the state therefore signify and increase the cash expenditures of the public treasury. And this is the case in spite of the fact that bureaucratic administration is usually more 'economical' in character than other forms of administration. Until recent times—at least from the point of view of the treasury—the cheapest way of satisfying the need for administration was to leave almost the entire local administration and lower judicature to the landlords of Eastern Prussia. The same fact applies to the administration of sheriffs in England. Mass democracy makes a clean sweep of the feudal, patrimonial, and—at least in intent—the plutocratic privileges in administration. Unavoidably it puts paid professional labor in place of the historically inherited avocational administration by notables.

This not only applies to structures of the state. For it is no accident that in their own organizations, the democratic mass parties have completely broken with traditional notable rule based upon personal relationships and personal esteem. Yet such personal structures frequently continue among the old conservative as well as the old liberal parties. Democratic mass parties are bureaucratically organized under the leadership of party officials, professional party and trade union secretaries, et cetera. In Germany, for instance, this has happened in the Social Democratic party and in the agrarian mass-movement;

*By *mass democracy*, Weber means *equality* of all before the law, whether or not all participate in governing society.

and in England, for the first time, in the caucus democracy of Gladstone-Chamberlain, which was originally organized in Birmingham and since the 1870's has spread. In the United States, both parties since Jackson's administration have developed bureaucratically. In France, however, attempts to organize disciplined political parties on the basis of an election system that would compel bureaucratic organization have repeatedly failed. The resistance of local circles of notables against the ultimately unavoidable bureaucratization of the parties, which would encompass the entire country and break their influence, could not be overcome. Every advance of the simple election techniques, for instance the system of proportional elections, which calculates with figures, means a strict and inter-local bureaucratic organization of the parties and therewith an increasing domination of party bureaucracy and discipline, as well as the elimination of the local circles of notables—at least this holds for great states.

The progress of bureaucratization in the state administration itself is a parallel phenomenon of democracy, as is quite obvious in France, North America, and now in England. Of course one must always remember that the term 'democratization' can be misleading. The *demos* itself, in the sense of an inarticulate mass, never 'governs' larger associations; rather, it is governed, and its existence only changes the way in which the executive leaders are selected and the measure of influence which the *demos*, or better, which social circles from its midst are able to exert upon the content and the direction of administrative activities by supplementing what is called 'public opinion.' 'Democratization,' in the sense here intended, does not necessarily mean an increasingly active share of the governed in the authority of the social structure. This may be a result of democratization, but it is not necessarily the case.

We must expressly recall at this point that the political concept of democracy, deduced from the 'equal rights' of the governed, includes these postulates: (1) prevention of the development of a closed status group of officials in the interest of a universal accessibility of office , and (2) minimization of the authority of officialdom in the interest of expanding the sphere of influence of 'public opinion' as far as practicable. Hence, wherever possible, political democracy strives to shorten the term of office by election and recall and by not binding the candidate to special expertness. Thereby democracy inevitable comes into conflict with the bureaucratic tendencies which, by its fight against notable rule, democracy has produced. The generally loose term 'democratization' cannot be used here, in so far as it is understood to mean the minimization of the civil servants' ruling power in favor of the greatest possible 'direct' rule of the *demos*, which in practice means the respective party leaders of the *demos*. The most decisive thing here—indeed it is rather exclusively so—is the *leveling of the governed* in opposition to the ruling and bureaucratically articulated group,which in its turn may occupy a quite autocratic position, both in fact and in form.

In Russia, the destruction of the position of the old landed nobility through the regulation of the Mjeshtshitelstvo (rank order) and the permeation of the old nobility by an office nobility were characteristic transitional phenomena in the development of bureaucracy. In China, the estimation of rank and the qualification for office according to the number of examinations passed mean something similar, but they have had consequences which, in theory at least, are still sharper. In France, the Revolution and still more Bonapartism have made the bureaucracy all-powerful. In the Catholic Church, first the feudal and then all independent local intermediary powers were eliminated. This was begun by Gregory VII and continued through the Council of Trent, the Vatican Council, and it was completed by the edicts of Pius X. The transformation of these local powers into pure functionaries of the central authority was connected with the constant increase in the factual significance of the formally quite dependent chaplains, a process which above all was based on the political party organization of Catholicism. Hence this process meant an advance of bureaucracy and at the same time of 'passive democratization,' as it were, that is, the leveling of the governed. The substitution of the bureaucratic army for the self-equipped army of notables is everywhere a process of 'passive' democratization, in the sense in which every establishment of an absolute military monarchy in the place of a feudal state or of a republic of notables is. This has held, in principle, even for the development of the state in Egypt in spite of all the peculiarities involved. Under the Roman principate the bureaucratization of the provincial administration in the field of tax collection, for instance, went hand in hand with the elimination of the plutocracy of a capitalist class, which, under the Republic, had been all-powerful. Ancient capitalism itself was finally eliminated with this stroke.

It is obvious that almost always economic conditions of some sort play their part in such 'democratizing' developments. Very frequently we meet with the influence of an economically determined origin of new classes, whether plutocratic, petty bourgeois, or proletarian in character. Such classes may call on the aid of, or they may only call to life or recall to life, a political power, no matter whether it is of legitimate or of Caesarist stamp. They may do so in order to attain economic or social advantages by political assistance. On the other hand, there are equally possible and historically documented cases in which initiative came 'from on high' and was of a purely political nature and drew advantages from political constellations, especially in foreign affairs. Such leadership exploited economic and social antagonisms as well as class interests merely as a means for their own purpose of gaining purely political power. For this reason, political authority has thrown the antagonistic classes out of their almost always unstable equilibrium and called their latent interest conflicts into battle. It seems hardly possible to give a general statement of this.

The extent and direction of the course along which economic influences have moved, as well as the nature in which political power relations exert influence, vary widely. In Hellenic Antiquity, the transition to disciplined combat by Hoplites, and in Athens, the increasing importance of the navy laid the foundation for the conquest of political power by the strata on whose shoulders the military burden rested. In Rome, however, the same development shook the rule of the office nobility only temporarily and seemingly. Although the modern mass army has everywhere been a means of breaking the power of notables, by itself it has in no way served as a leverage for active, but rather for merely passive, democratization. One contributing factor, however, has been the fact that the ancient citizen army rested economically upon self-equipment, whereas the modern army rests upon the bureaucratic procurement of requirements.

The advance of the bureaucratic structure rests upon 'technical' superiority. This fact leads here, as in the whole field of technique, to the following: the advance has been realized most slowly where older structural forms have been technically well developed and functionally adjusted to the requirements at hand. This was the case, for instance, in the administration of notables in England and hence England was the slowest of all countries to succumb to bureaucratization or, indeed, is still only partly in the process of doing so. The same general phenomenon exists when highly developed systems of gaslight or of steam railroads with large and fixed capital offer stronger obstacles to electrification than in completely new areas which are opened up for electrification.

The Permanent Character of the Bureaucratic Machine

Once it is fully established, bureaucracy is among those social structures which are the hardest to destroy. Bureaucracy is *the* means of carrying 'community action' over into rationally ordered 'societal action.' Therefore, as an instrument for 'societalizing' relations of power, bureaucracy has been and is a power instrument of the first order—for the one who controls the bureaucratic apparatus.

Under otherwise equal conditions, a 'societal action,' which is methodically ordered and led, is superior to every resistance of 'mass' or even of 'communal action.' And where the bureaucratization of administration has been completely carried through, a form of power relation is established that is practically unshatterable.

The individual bureaucrat cannot squirm out of the apparatus in which he is harnessed. In contrast to the honorific or avocational 'notable,' the professional bureaucrat is chained to his activity by his entire material and ideal existence. In the great majority of cases, he is only a single cog in an ever-moving mechanism which prescribes to him an essentially fixed route of march. The official is entrusted with specialized tasks and normally the mechanism cannot be put into motion or arrested by him, but only from the very top. The individual bureaucrat is thus forged to the community of all the functionaries who are integrated into the mechanism. They have a common interest in seeing that the mechanism continues its functions and that the societally exercised authority carries on.

The ruled, for their part, cannot dispense with or replace the bureaucratic apparatus of authority once it exists. For this bureaucracy rests upon expert training, a functional specialization of work, and an attitude set for habitual and virtuoso-like mastery of single yet methodically integrated functions. If the official stops working, or if his work is forcefully interrupted, chaos results, and it is difficult to improvise replacements from among the governed who are fit to master such chaos. This holds for public administration as well as for private economic management. More and more the material fate of the masses depends upon the steady and correct functioning of the increasingly bureaucratic organizations of private capitalism. The idea of eliminating these organizations becomes more and more utopian.

The discipline of officialdom refers to the attitude-set of the official for precise obedience within his *habitual* activity, in public as well as in private organizations. This discipline increasingly becomes the basis of all order, however great the practical importance of administration on the basis of the filed documents may be. The naive idea of Bakuninism of destroying the basis of 'acquired rights' and 'domination' by destroying public documents overlooks the settled orientation of *man* for keeping to the habitual rules and regulations that continue to exist independently of the documents. Every reorganization of beaten or dissolved troops, as well as the restoration of administrative orders destroyed by revolt, panic, or other catastrophes, is realized by appealing to the trained orientation of obedient compliance to such orders. Such compliance has been conditioned into the officials, on the one hand, and, on the other hand, into the governed. If such an appeal is successful it brings, as it were, the disturbed mechanism into gear again.

The objective indispensability of the once-existing apparatus, with its peculiar, 'impersonal' character, means that the mechanism—in contrast to feudal orders based upon personal piety—is easily made to work for anybody who knows how to gain control over it. A rationally ordered system of officials continues to function smoothly after the enemy has occupied the area; he merely needs to change the top officials. This body of officials continues to operate because it is to the vital interest of everyone concerned, including above all the enemy.

During the course of his long years in power, Bismarck brought his ministerial colleagues into unconditional bureaucratic dependence by eliminating all independent statesmen. Upon his retirement, he saw to his surprise that they continued to manage their offices unconcerned and undismayed, as if he had not been the master mind and creator of these creatures, but rather as if some single figure had been exchanged for some other figure in the bureaucratic machine. With all the changes of masters in France since the time of the First Empire, the power machine has remained essentially the same. Such a machine makes 'revolution,' in the sense of the forceful creation of entirely new formations of authority, technically more and more impossible, especially when the apparatus controls the modern means of communication (telegraph, et cetera) and also by virtue of its internal rationalized structure. In classic fashion, France has demonstrated how this process has substituted *coups d'etat* for 'revolutions': all successful transformations in France* have amounted to *coups d'etat.*

---

*Weber here refers to changes in French regimes after the Revolution of 1789.

The Debate on Modernization

In the twentieth century, the French Revolution no longer dominates discussions of revolution. Scholars must also confront the many revolutions in this century: in Mexico in 1910; in Russia in 1917; in China from 1911 to 1949; in Persia in 1905; in the Ottoman Empire (Turkey) in 1919; and in a host of Third World countries, including Vietnam, Bolivia, and Cuba, in the 1950s and 1960s. As de Tocqueville and Weber suggested, such revolutions usually led to stronger, more centralized, and more bureaucratic states. But the origins of these revolutions rarely fit the pattern that Marx and Engels had set forth. Instead of occurring after bourgeois, capitalist revolutions, socialist revolutions have occurred in relatively poor countries, just beginning the modernization of their economies. Moreover, instead of industrial laborers carrying out socialist revolutions, peasants have often played the major role. Although theorists of revolution continue to value Marx's insight that revolutions arise from the struggle of different groups competing for dominance, revolutions clearly can arise in ways Marx did not foresee. These revolutions have therefore prompted scholars to reinvestigate the causes of revolution and to seek connections between modernization and revolution.

In the following selections two prominent scholars discuss the different ways in which revolutions can arise. Their debate suggests that modernization per se need not lead to revolution; the key issue is whether modernization leads to a change in the balance of power among those groups in a society who are contending for political power.

REVOLUTION AND POLITICAL ORDER

Samuel P. Huntington

Huntington argues that a key aspect of modernization is the demand for increased participation in politics. Where certain groups do not have access to political power, their demands to change and broaden government may lead to revolution.

In discussing a wide range of revolutions, including those in France, Russia, China, Mexico, Turkey, Vietnam, and Persia (Iran was called Persia at the time of the fall of the Qajar dynasty in 1925), Huntington identifies different patterns of revolution and examines the roles of moderates, counterrevolutionaries, and radicals.

A revolution is a rapid, fundamental, and violent domestic change in the dominant values and myths of a society, in its political institutions, social structure, leadership, and government activity and policies. Revolutions are thus to be distinguished from insurrections, rebellions, revolts, coups, and wars of independence. A coup d'etat in itself changes only leadership and perhaps policies; a rebellion or insurrection may change policies, leadership, and political institutions, but not social structure and values; a war of independence is a struggle of one community against rule by an alien community and does not necessarily involve changes in the social structure of either community. What is here called simply "revolution" is what others have called great revolutions, grand revolutions, or social revolutions. Notable examples are the French, Chinese, Mexican, Russian, and Cuban revolutions.

Revolutions are rare. Most societies have never experienced revolutions, and most ages until modern times did not know revolutions. More precisely, revolution is characteristic of modernization. Revolution is the ultimate expression of the modernizing outlook, the belief that it is within the power of man to control and to change his environment and that he has not only the ability but the right to do so. For this reason, as Hannah Arendt observes, "violence is no more adequate to describe the phenomenon of revolution than change; only where change occurs in the sense of a new beginning, where violence is used to constitute an altogether different form of government, to bring about the formation of a new body politic . . . can we speak of revolution."[1]

Revolution is thus an aspect of modernization. It is not something which can occur in any type of society at any period in its history. It is not a universal category but rather an historically limited phenomenon. It will not occur in highly traditional societies with very low levels of social and economic complexity. Nor will it occur in highly modern societies. Like other forms of violence and instability, it is most likely to occur in societies which have experienced some social and economic development and where the processes of political modernization and political development have lagged behind the processes of social and economic change.

Political modernization involves the extension of political consciousness to new social groups and the mobilization of these groups into politics. Political development involves the creation of political institutions sufficiently adaptable, complex, autonomous, and coherent to absorb and to order the participation of these new groups and to promote social and economic change in the society. The political essence of revolution is the rapid expansion of political consciousness and the rapid mobilization of new groups into politics at a speed which makes it impossible for existing political institutions to assimilate them. Revolution is the extreme case of the explosion of political participation. Without this explosion there is no revolution. A complete revolution, however, also involves a second phase: the creation and institutionalization of a new political order. The successful revolution combines rapid political mobilization and rapid political institutionalization. Not all revolutions produce a new political order. The measure of how revolutionary a revolution is is the rapidity and the scope of the expansion of political participation. The measure of how successful a revolution is is the authority and stability of the institutions to which it gives birth.

A full-scale revolution thus involves the rapid and violent destruction of existing political institutions, the mobilization of new groups into politics, and the creation of new political institutions. The sequence and the relations among these three aspects may vary from one revolution to another. Two general patterns can be identified. In the "Western" pattern, the political institutions of the old regime collapse; this is followed by the mobilization of new groups into politics and then by the creation of new political institutions. The "Eastern" revolution, in contrast, begins with the mobilization of new groups into politics and the creation of new political institutions and ends with the violent overthrow of the political institutions of the old order. The French, Russian, Mexican, and, in its first phases, Chinese Revolutions approximate the Western model; the latter phases of the Chinese Revolution, the Vietnamese Revolution, and other colonial struggles against imperialist powers approximate the Eastern model.

The first step in a Western revolution is the collapse of the old regime. Consequently, scholarly analysis of the causes of revolution usually focuses on the political, social, and economic conditions which existed under the old regime. Implicitly, such analyses assume that once the authority of the old regime has disintegrated, the revolutionary process is irreversibly underway. In fact, however, the collapse of many old regimes is not followed by full-scale revolution. The events of 1789 in France led to a major social upheaval; those of 1830 and 1848 did not. The fall of the [Chinese] Manchu and [Russian] Romanov dynasties was followed by great revolutions; the fall of the [Austrian] Hapsburg, [German] Hohenzollern, [Turkish] Ottoman, and [Persian] Qajar dynasties was not. The overthrow of traditional dictatorships in Bolivia in 1952 and in Cuba in 1958 set loose major revolutionary forces; the overthrow of traditional monarchies in Egypt in 1952 and in Iraq in 1958 brought new elites to power but did not completely destroy the structure of society. In virtually all these instances, the same social, economic, and political conditions existed under the old regimes whose demise was not followed by revolution as existed under the old regimes whose demise was followed by revolution. Old regimes—traditional monarchies and traditional dictatorships with concentrated but little power—are continually collapsing but only rarely is this collapse followed by a major revolution. The factors giving rise to revolution, consequently, are as likely to be found in the conditions which exist after the collapse of the old regime as in those which exist before its downfall.

In the "Western" revolution very little overt action by rebellious groups is needed to overthrow the old regime. "The revolution," as Pettee says, "does not begin with the attack of a powerful new force upon the state. It begins simply with a sudden recognition by almost all the passive and the active membership that the state no longer exists." The collapse is followed by an absence of authority. "Revolutionists enter the limelight, not like men on horseback, as victorious conspirators appearing in the forum, but like fearful children, exploring an empty house, not sure that it is empty."[2] Whether or not a revolution develops depends upon the number and the character of the groups entering the house. If there is a marked discrepancy in power among the remaining social forces after the old regime disappears, the strongest social force or combination of forces may be able to fill the vacuum and to reestablish authority, with relatively little expansion of political participation. The collapse of every old regime is followed by some rioting, demonstrations, and the projection into the political sphere of previously quiescent or suppressed groups. If a new social force (as in Egypt in 1952) or combination of social forces (as in Germany in 1918–19) can quickly secure control of the state machinery and particularly the instruments of coercion left behind by the old regime, it may well be able to suppress the more revolutionary elements intent on mobilizing new forces into politics (the Moslem Brotherhood, the Spartacists) and thus forestall the emergence of a truly revolutionary situation. The crucial factor is the concentration or dispersion of power which follows the collapse of the old regime. The less traditional the society in which the old regime has collapsed and the more groups which are available and able and inclined to participate in politics, the more likely is revolution to take place.

If no group is ready and able to establish effective rule following the collapse of the old regime, many cliques and social forces struggle for power. This struggle gives rise to the competitive mobilization of new groups into politics and makes the revolution revolutionary. Each group of political leaders attempts to establish its authority and in the process either develops a broader base of popular support than its competitors or falls victim to them.

Following the collapse of the old regime, three social types play major roles in the process of political mobilization. Initially, as Brinton and others have pointed out, the moderates (Kerensky in Russia, Madero in Mexico, Sun Yat-sen in China) tend to assume authority. Typically, they attempt to establish some sort of liberal, democratic, constitutional state. Typically, also, they describe this state as the restoration of an earlier constitutional order: Madero wanted to restore the constitution of 1856; the liberal Young Turks the constitution of 1876; and even Castro in his initial moderate phase held that his goal was the restoration of the constitution of 1940. In rare cases, these leaders may adapt to the subsequent intensification of the revolutionary process: Castro was the Kerensky and the Lenin of the Cuban Revolution. More frequently, however, the moderates remain moderate and are swept from power. Their failure stems precisely from their inability to deal with the problem of political mobilization. On the one hand, they lack the drive and the ruthlessness to stop the mobilization of new groups into politics; on the other, they lack the radicalism to lead it. The first alternative requires the concentration of power, the second its expansion. Unable and unwilling to perform either function, the liberals are brushed away either by counterrevolutionaries who perform the first or by more extreme revolutionaries who perform the second.

In virtually all revolutionary situations, counterrevolutionaries, often with foreign assistance, attempt to stop the expansion of political participation and to reestablish a political order in which there is little but concentrated power. Kornilov in Russia, Yuan Shih-kai in China, Huerta in Mexico, and, in sense, Reza Shah in Persia and Mustafa Kemal in Turkey all played these roles in the aftermath of the downfall of the Porfirian regime and of the Romanov, Ch'ing, Qajar, and Ottoman dynasties. As these examples suggest, the counterrevolutionaries are almost invariably military men. Force is a source of power, but it can have longer range effectiveness only when it is linked to a principle of legitimacy. Huerta and Kornilov had nothing but force and failed in the face of the radicalization of the revolution and the mobilization of more social groups into politics. Yuan Shih-kai and Reza Shah both attempted to establish new, more vigorous traditional systems of rule on the ruins of the previous dynasty.

That Yuan Shih-kai failed to establish a new dynasty while Reza Shah Pahlevi succeeded is due primarily to the fact that political mobilization had gone much further in China than it had in Persia. The middle-class in the Chinese cities was sufficiently well developed to have supported a nationalist movement since the 1890s. Students and intellectuals played a crucial role in Chinese politics while they were almost absent from the Persian scene. The lower level of social mobilization in Persia made it possible to give new vigor to traditional forms of rule.

The radical revolutionaries are the third major political group in a revolutionary situation. For ideological and tactical reasons, their goal is to expand political participation, to bring new masses into politics, and thereby to increase their own power. With the breakdown of the established institutions and procedures for co-opting groups into power and socializing them into the political order, the extremists have a natural advantage over their rivals. They are more willing to mobilize more groups into politics. Hence the revolution becomes more radical as larger and larger masses of the population are brought into the political scales. Since in most modernizing countries the peasants are the largest social force, the most revolutionary leaders are those who mobilize and organize the peasants for political action. In some instance, the appeals to the peasants and other lower class groups may be social and economic; in most instances, however, these will be supplemented by nationalist appeals. This process leads to the redefinition of the political community and creates the foundations for a new political order.

In Western revolutions the symbolic or actual fall of the old regime can be given a fairly precise date: July 14, 1789; October 10, 1911; May 25, 1911; March 15, 1917. These dates mark the beginning of the revolutionary process and the mobilization of new groups into politics as the competition among the new elites struggling for power leads them to appeal to broader and broader masses of the people. Out of the competition one group eventually establishes its dominance and reestablishes order either through force or the development of new political institutions. In Eastern revolutions, in contrast, the old regime is modern, it has more power and legitimacy, and hence it does not simply collapse and leave a vacuum of authority. Instead it must be overthrown. The distinguishing characteristic of the western revolution is the period of anarchy or statelessness after the fall of the old regime while moderates, counterrevolutionaries, and radicals are struggling for power. The distinguishing characteristic of the Eastern revolution is a prolonged period of "dual power" in which the revolutionaries are expanding political participation and the scope and authority of their institutions of rule at the same time that the government is, in other geographical areas and at other times, continuing to exercise its rule. In the Western revolution the principal struggles are between revolutionary groups; in the Eastern revolution they are between one revolutionary group and the established order.

In the Western revolution the revolutionaries come to power in the capital first and then gradually expand their control over the countryside. In the Eastern revolution they withdraw from central, urban areas of the country, establish a base area of control in a remote section, struggle to win the support of the peasants through terror and propaganda, slowly expand the scope of their authority, and gradually escalate the level of their military operations from individual terroristic attacks to guerrilla warfare to mobile warfare and regular warfare. Eventually they are able to defeat the government troops in battle. The last phase of the revolutionary struggle is the occupation of the capital.

In a Western revolution the capture of the central institutions and symbols of power is usually very rapid. In January 1917 the Bolsheviks were a small, illegal, conspiratorial group, most of whose leaders were either in Siberia or in exile. Less than a year later they were the principal, although far from undisputed, political rulers of Russia. "You know," Lenin observed to Trotsky, "from persecution and a life underground, to come so suddenly into power. . . . *Es schwindelt!*"[3] The Chinese Communist leaders, in contrast, experienced no such exhilarating and dramatic change in circumstances. Instead they had to fight their way gradually and slowly to power over a 22-year period from their retreat into the countryside in 1927, through the fearsome battles of Kiangsi, the exhaustion of the Long March, the struggles against the Japanese, the civil war with the Kuomintang, until finally they made their triumphal entry into Peking. There was nothing "dizzying" about this process. During most of these years the Communist Party exercised effective political authority over substantial amounts of territory and numbers of people. It was a government attempting to expand its authority at the expense of another government rather than a band of conspirators attempting to overthrow a government. The acquisition of national power for the Bolsheviks was a dramatic change; for the Chinese Communists it was simply the culmination of a long, drawn-out process.

One major factor responsible for the differing patterns of the Western and Eastern revolutions is the nature of the prerevolutionary regime. The Western revolution is usually directed against a highly traditional regime headed by an absolute monarch or dominated by a land-owning aristocracy. The revolution typically occurs when this regime comes into severe financial straits, when it fails to assimilate the intelligentsia and other urban elite elements, and when the ruling class from which its leaders are drawn has lost its moral self-confidence and will to rule. The Western revolution, in a sense, telescopes the initial "urban breakthrough" of the middle class and the "green uprising" of the peasantry into a single convulsive, revolutionary process. Eastern revolutions, in contrast, are directed against at least partially modernized regimes. These may be indigeneous governments that have absorbed some modern and vigorous middle-class elements and that are led by new men with the ruthlessness, if not the political skill, to hang on to power, or they may be colonial regimes in which the wealth and power of a metropolitan country gives the local government a seemingly overwhelming superiority in all the conventional manifestations of political authority and military force. In such circumstances no quick victory is possible and the urban revolutionaries have to fight their way to power through a prolonged rural insurrectionary process. Western revolutions are thus precipitated by weak traditional regimes; Eastern revolutions by narrow modernizing ones.

In the Western revolution the principal struggle is usually between the moderates and the radicals; in the Eastern revolution it is between the revolutionaries and the government. In the Western revolution the moderates hold power briefly and insecurely between the fall of the old regime and the expansion of participation and conquest of power by the radicals. In the Eastern pattern, the moderates are much weaker; they do not occupy positions of authority; and as the revolution gets under way, they are crushed by the government or the revolutionaries or they are forced by the polarization process to join one side or the other. In the Western revolution, terror occurs in the latter phases of the revolution and is employed by the radicals after they come to power primarily against the moderates and other revolutionary groups with whom they have struggled. In the Eastern revolution, in contrast, terror marks the first phase of the revolutionary struggle. It is used by the revolutionaries when they are weak and far removed from power to persuade or to coerce support from peasants and to intimidate the lower reaches of officialdom. In the Eastern pattern, the stronger the revolutionary movement becomes the less it tends to rely on terrorism. In the Western pattern the loss of the will and the ability to rule by the old elite is the first phase in the revolution; in the Eastern model it is the last phase and is a product of the revolutionary war waged by the counterelite against the regime. Emigration, consequently, reaches its peak at the beginning of the revolutionary struggle in the Western model but at the end of the struggle in the Eastern pattern.

Institutional and Social Circumstances of Revolution

Revolution, as we have said, is the broad, rapid, and violent expansion of political partic- ipation outside the existing structure of political institutions. Its causes thus lie in the interaction between political institutions and social forces. Presumably revolutions occur when there is the coincidence of certain conditions in political institutions and certain circumstances among social forces. In these terms, the two prerequisites for revolution are, first, political institutions incapable of providing channels for the participation of new social forces in politics and of new elites in government, and, secondly, the desire of social forces, currently excluded from politics, to participate therein, this desire normally arising from the group's feeling that it needs certain symbolic or material gains which it can achieve only by pressing its demands in the political sphere. Ascending or aspiring groups and rigid or inflexible institutions are the stuff of which revolutions are made.

The many recent efforts to identify the causes of revolution have given primary emphasis to its social and psychological roots. They have thus tended to overlook the political and institutional factors which affect the probability of revolution. Revolutions are unlikely in political systems which have the capacity to expand their power and to broaden participation within the system. It is precisely this fact that makes revolutions unlikely in highly institutionalized modern political systems—constitutional or commu- nist—which are what they are simply because they have developed the procedures for assimilating new social groups and elites desiring to participate in politics. The great revolutions of history have taken place either in highly centralized traditional monarchies (France, China, Russia), or in narrowly based military dictatorships (Mexico, Bolivia,

Guatemala, Cuba), or in colonial regimes (Vietnam, Algeria). All these political systems demonstrated little if any capacity to expand their power and to provide channels for the participation of new groups in politics.

Perhaps the most important and obvious but also most neglected fact about successful great revolutions is that they do not occur in democratic political systems. This is not to argue that formally democratic governments are immune to revolution. This is surely not the case, and a narrowly based, oligarchical democracy may be as incapable of providing for expanded political participation as narrowly based oligarchical dictatorship. Nonetheless, the absence of successful revolutions in democratic countries remains a striking fact, and suggests that, on the average, democracies have more capacity for absorbing new groups into their political systems than do political systems where power is equally small but more concentrated. The absence of successful revolutions against communist dictatorships suggests that the crucial distinction between them and the more traditional autocracies may be precisely this capacity to absorb new social groups.

Revolution requires not only political institutions which resist the expansion of participation but also social groups which demand that expansion. In theory, every social class which has not been incorporated into the political system is potentially revolutionary. Virtually every group does go through a phase, brief or prolonged, when its revolutionary propensity is high. At some point, the group begins to develop aspirations which lead it to make symbolic or material demands on the political system. To achieve its goals, the group's leaders soon realize that they must find avenues of access to the political leaders and means of participation in the political system. If these do not exist and are not forthcoming, the group and its leaders become frustrated and alienated. Conceivably this condition can exist for an indefinite period of time; or the original needs which led the group to seek access to the system may disappear; or the group may attempt to enforce its demands on the system through violence, force, or other means illegitimate to the system. In the latter instance, either the system adapts itself to accord some legitimacy to these means and thus to accept the necessity of meeting the demands which they were used to support, or the political elite attempts to suppress the group and to end the use of these methods. No inherent reason exists why such action should not be successful, provided the groups within the political system are sufficiently strong and united in their opposition to admitting the aspiring group to political participation.

Frustration of its demands and denial of the opportunity to participate in the political system may make a group revolutionary. But it takes more than one revolutionary group to make a revolution. A revolution necessarily involves the alienation of many groups from the existing order. It is the product of "multiple dysfunction" in society. One social group can be responsible for a coup, a riot, or a revolt, but only a combination of groups can produce a revolution. Conceivably, this combination might take the form of any number of possible group coalitions. In actuality, however, the revolutionary alliance must include some urban and some rural groups. The opposition of urban groups to the government can produce the continued instability characteristic of a praetorian state. But only the combination of urban opposition with rural opposition can produce a revolution. In 1789, Palmer observes, "Peasant and bourgeois were at war with the same enemy, and this is what made possible the French Revolution."[4] In a broader sense, this is what makes possible every revolution. To be more precise, the probability of revolution in a modernizing country depends upon: (a) the extent to which the urban middle class—intellectuals, professionals, bourgeoisie—are alienated from the existing order; (b) the extent to which the peasants are alienated from the existing order; and (c) the extent to which urban middle class and peasants join together not only in fighting against "the same enemy" but also in fighting for the same cause. This cause is usually nationalism.

Revolutions are thus unlikely to occur if the period of the frustration of the urban middle class does not coincide with that of the peasantry. Conceivably, one group might be highly alienated from the political system at one time and the other group at another time; in such circumstances revolution is improbable. Hence a slower general process of social change in a society is likely to reduce the possibility that these two groups will be simultaneously alienated from the existing system. To the extent that social-economic modernization has become more rapid over time, consequently, the probability of revolution has increased. For a major revolution to occur, however, not only must the urban middle class and the peasantry be alienated from the existing order, but they must also have the capacity and the incentive to act along parallel, if not cooperative, lines. If the proper stimulus to joint action is missing, then again revolution may be avoided.

REFERENCES

1. Arendt (1963), p. 28.
2. Pettee (1938), pp. 100–101.
3. Trotsky (1930), p.337, quoted in Fainsod (1953), p. 84.
4. Palmer (1959–1964), vol. I, p. 484.

DOES MODERNIZATION BREED REVOLUTION?

Charles Tilly

In this essay Tilly offers a critical appraisal of Huntington's views. Tilly argues that Huntington's theory of revolution is "needlessly weak" because of ambiguities and contradictions. Tilly notes that the terms "modernization" and "instability" require more precise definition than Huntington offers. How would we know modernization when we see it? How would we go about estimating the probabilities of revolution within the next few years if we had been in France in 1788 (or for that matter in Iran in 1978)? Focusing on modernization, Tilly claims, is more an orientation than a predictive theory.

Tilly suggests that when we study a society, we ask the following questions: What groups are contending for power? What claims are they making on the central government? What ability do contending groups and the government have to mobilize resources—money, human resources, weapons, information, and leadership—in order to enforce their claims? Revolution is only likely when powerful groups press competing claims on the government, and the government lacks the resources either to satisfy the claims of contending groups or to defeat them.

Tilly's theory is, therefore, one of "collective mobilization." It emphasizes the mobilization of resources by contending groups and the conflict of such groups with the state.

I want to ask whether modernization breeds revolution. That first formulation of the question is compact, but ambiguous. We shall, unfortunately, have to put a large part of our effort into the preliminary task of reducing the ambiguities. "Modernization" is a vague, tendentious concept. "Revolution" is a controversial one as well.

Instead of trying to pace off modernization precisely, I shall ordinarily substitute for it somewhat better defined processes, such as industrialization or demographic expansion. Instead of trying to grasp the essential genius of revolution, I shall offer a rather arbitrary set of definitions which appear to me to have considerable theoretical utility. I shall compensate for my arbitrariness by discussing violence, instability, and political conflict more extensively than a strict concentration on revolution would justify.

Huntington's Synthesis

One of the most sophisticated recent syntheses of the standard views concerning all these matters comes from Samuel Huntington. In his *Political Order in Changing Societies*, Huntington argues that the widespread domestic violence and instability of the 1950s and 1960s in many parts of the world "was in large part the product of rapid social change and the rapid mobilization of new groups into politics, coupled with the slow development of political institutions."[1]

Huntington applies this lead-lag model to Western revolutions, treating them as extreme cases of the conflicts which emerge when political institutionalization proceeds too slowly for the pace of large-scale social change (which Huntington treats as more or less identical with "modernization") and of mobilization. Moreover, John Gillis has recently argued that the model applies specifically to the European modernizing revolutions of the eighteenth and nineteenth centuries.[2] It is therefore legitimate to ask how strong a grip on the Western experience with revolutions and violent conflict Huntington's analysis gives us. My answer is that the grip is needlessly weak—weak, because the scheme founders in tautologies, contradictions, omissions and failures to examine the evidence seriously. Needlessly, because several of the main arguments concerning mobilization, political participation, and conflict improve vastly on the usual social-psychological tracing of "violence" or "protest" back to "strain" or "discontent."

Although it would be worth trying, this article will not attempt to wrench Huntington's theory into shape. I shall dwell on it in other ways, for other reasons, because in one manner or another it sums up most of the conventional wisdom connecting revolution to large-scale structural change; because Huntington places an exceptional range of contemporary and historical material within its framework; because the variables within it appear to be of the right kind; and because it is sturdy enough to exempt me from the accusation of having erected, and then burned, a straw man as I build up an alternative line of argument.

Huntington offers several criteria for the institutionalization of the existing political organization: adaptability, complexity, autonomy, coherence (with the latter essentially meaning consensus among the active participants in the political system). This sort of definition-making increases the risk that Huntington's arguments will become tautological. To the extent that one judges adaptability, complexity, autonomy, and coherence on the basis of the absence of containment of domestic violence and instability, the circle of truth by definition will close.

Nevertheless, Huntington's balanced-development theory is appealing in its combination of three factors—rapid social change, mobilization, and political institutionalization—which other authors have employed separately in one-factor explantions of stability and instability. It does, furthermore, provide a plausible explanation of the twentieth-century concentration of revolution, governmental instability, and collective violence in the poorer (but not the poorest) countries of the world; the more plausible because it appears to dispose of the anomaly that by many standards the relatively peaceful richer countries are also the faster changing. Huntington's stress on the importance of group claims on the political system by mobilizing segments of the population is a distinct improvement over the more usual model of accumulating individual grievances. Indeed, the most attractive general feature of Huntington's scheme is its deliberate flight from psychologism, from the assumption that the central things to be explained by a theory of revolution are why, when, and how large numbers of individual men and women become discontented.

Huntington on Revolution

Huntington restricts the term *revolution* to the deep and rapid transformations of whole societies, which others have called Great Revolutions; the French, Chinese, Mexican, Russian, and Cuban revolutions epitomize what he has in mind. Nevertheless, Huntington asserts a fundamental continuity between revolution and lesser forms of conflict:

> Revolution is thus an aspect of modernization. It is not something which can occur in any type of society at any period in its history. It is not a universal category but rather an historically limited phenomenon. It will not occur in highly traditional societies with very low levels of social and econmic complexity. Nor will it occur in highly modern societies. Like other forms of violence and instability, it is most likely to occur in societies which have experienced some social and economic development and where the processes of political modernization and political development have lagged behind the processes of social and economic change.[3]

Thus the imbalances which account for other forms of "disorder" also account for revolution: "The political essence of revolution is the rapid expansion of political consciousness and the rapid mobilization of new groups into politcs at a speed which makes it impossible for existing political institutions to assimilate them. Revolution is the extreme case of the explosion of political participation."[4]

Huntington then distinguishes between an Eastern and a Western pattern of revolution. In the *Eastern*, new groups mobilize into politics, they fashion new political institutions, and they overthrow the old order; anticolonial revolutions are the type case. In the *Western*, the old political insitutions disintegrate and only then do new groups mobilize into politics, create new political institutions, and come to power. The Russian Revolution is typical. The "decay" of established institutions plays a large part in the Western pattern, according to Huntington, and a small part in the Eastern, As a result, the sequences are rather different. Nevertheless, in both cases the immediate cause of revolution is supposed to be the discrepancy between the performance of the regime and the demands being made upon it. In both cases that discrepancy is supposed to increase as a consequence of the mobilization of new groups into politics, which in turn occurs as a more or less direct effect of rapid social and economic change.

The danger of circular argument is just as apparent here as before. In his detailed argumentation, Huntington does not really escape the fateful circularity of judging the extent of the discrepancy from the character of the revolution which presumably resulted from the discrepancy. He tells us, for example, that:

> The great revolutions of history have taken place either in highly centralized traditional monarchies (France, China, Russia), or in narrowly based military dictatorships (Mexico, Bolivia, Guatemala, Cuba), or in colonial regimes (Vietnam, Algeria). All these political systems demonstrated little if any capacity to expand their power and to provide channels for the participation of new groups in politics.[5]

Suppose we suppress the urge to blurt out questions about England in the 1640s or the United States in the 1860s and stifle suspicions that the implicit standard for great revolutions at work in this passage simply restricts them logically to centralized, authoritarian regimes. We still must wonder how we could have known before the fact of revolution that the expansive capacity of these governments was inferior to that of the many other monarchies, military dictatorships, and colonial regimes which did not experience revolutions.

Huntington does not answer. In its present form his scheme does not, it appears, give us any solid guidance in the anticipation or production of revolutions. Not even in the weak sense of projecting ourselves back into the France of 1788 and saying how we would have gone about estimating the probabilities of revolution within the next few years. That is true of the whole argument, and not just of the treatment of revolution. Even in principle, the scheme is not really a predictive one. It is an orientation, a proposal to weight several clusters of variables differently from the way they have been estimated in the past, and a presentation of an exceptionally wide range of observations in the light of the orientation and the weighting.

Alternatives

How else could we proceed? We should hold onto several of Huntington's perceptions: (a) that revolutions and collective violence tend to flow directly out of a population's central political processes, instead of expressing diffuse strains and discontents within the population; (b) that the specific claims and counterclaims being made on the existing government by various mobilized groups are more important that the general satisfaction or discontent of those groups, and that claims for established places within the structure of power are crucial; (c) that large-scale structural change transforms the identities and structures of the potential aspirants for power within the population, affects their opportunities for mobilization, governs the resources available to the government, and through it to the principal holders of power. Accepting those insights will encourage us to concentrate our analysis on processes of mobilization, on structures of power, and on the changing demands linking one to the other.

We have to go further. By contrast with Huntington's global strategy, we must clearly distinguish among different forms of conflict before seeking to identify their connections; we must disaggregate revolution into its components instead of treating it as a unitary phenomenon; we must investigate the precise ways in which urbanization or political centralization affect the mobilization and demobilization of different segments of the population; and we must specify and trace the relations of each major segment to the changing structure of power.

A Model of Political Conflict

First, a simple model of political action. Let us distinguish three kinds of social units within any specified population. A *government* is an organization which controls the principal concentrated means of coercion within the population; a *contender for power* is a group within the population which at least once during some standard period applies resources to influence that government; and a *polity* is the set of contenders which routinely and successfully lays claims on that government. (We may call these individual contenders *members* of the polity, while *challenger* is a good name for a contender laying claims in an irregular or unsuccessful fashion.) Almost any population beyond a very small scale will include more than one contender. Almost any large population will include more than one government, hence more than one polity. But many theoretically possible contenders will not contend during any particular period; some will never contend. A group gains the capacity to contend by mobilizing; by acquiring collective control over resources—land, labor, information, arms, money, and so on—which can be applied to influence the government; it loses that capacity by demobilizing—losing collective control over resources.

Every polity, then, collectively develops tests of membership. The tests always include the capacity to bring considerable numbers of men into action; they may also include the possession of wealth, certified birth, religious stigmata, and many other characteristics. Challengers acquire membership in the polity by meeting the tests, despite the fact that existing members characteristically resist new admissions and employ the government's resources to make admissions more difficult. The members also test each other more or less continuously; a member failing the tests tends to lose membership in the polity. Each change in membership moves the tests in a direction harmonious with the characteristics and capacities of the set of members emerging from the change. The members of the polity come to treat the prevailing criteria of membership as having a special moral virtue. Challengers denied admission tend to define themselves as being deprived rights due them on general grounds. Members losing position tend, in contrast, to accent tradition, usage, and particular agreements in support of their claims to threatened privileges and resources. Thus contenders both entering and leaving the polity have a special propensity to articulate strongly moral definitions of their situations.

The scheme permits us to specify the close relationship between collective violence and the central political process: (a) political life consists largely of making collective claims for resources and privileges controlled by governments; (b) collective violence is largely a by-product of situations in which one contender openly lays such claims and other contenders (or, especially, the government) resist these claims; (c) such situations occur with particular frequency when groups are acquiring or losing membership—that is, partly because testing tends to take that form, partly because the moral orientations of the groups whose memberships are disputed encourage the individuals within them to take exceptional risks of damage or injury, partly because the activation of the coercive forces of the government increase the likelihood of damage or injury to other participants; (d) hence collective violence tends to cluster around major or multiple entries and exits; (e) governments themselves act to maintain priority over substantial concentrations of coercive resources, so that a contender accumulating such resources outside the control of the government is likely to find itself in acute conflict with the agents of the government.

Revolutions

We now have the means of moving on to revolution. The multiplication of polities is the key. A revolution begins when a government previously under the control of a single, sovereign polity becomes the object of effective, competing, mutually exclusive claims from two or more separate polities. A revolution ends when a single polity—by no means necessarily the same one—regains control over the government. This multiple sovereignty can result from the attempt of one polity to subordinate another heretofore independent polity; from the assertion of sovereignty by a previously subordinate polity; from the formation of a bloc of challengers which seizes control of some portion of the government apparatus; from the fragmentation of an existing polity into blocs, each of which controls some part of the government. Many observers would prefer to restrict the label "revolution" to the action by challengers; many others would prefer to call each of these a different major type of revolution: civil war, national revolution, and so on. I begin with an exceptionally broad definition to call attention to the common properties of the various paths through multiple sovereignty.

What observable political conditions, then, ought to prevail before a revolution begins? Three conditions appear to be necessary, and a fourth strongly facilitating. The three apparently necessary conditions are:

1. The appearance of contenders or coalitions of contenders, advancing exclusively alternative claims to the control over the government currently exerted by the members of the polity;
2. commitment to those claims by a significant segment of the subject population;
3. unwillingness or incapacity of the agents of the government to suppress the alternative coalition or the commitment to its claims.

The strongly facilitating condition is:

4. formation of coalitions between members of the polity and the contenders making the alternative claims.

Let me confess at once that the list contains little news not already borne by the definition of revolution as a state of multiple sovereignty. The purpose of the list is simply to focus the explanation of revolution on the structure of power, and away from the general level of strain, discontent, disequilibrium, or mobilization. At first approach, the argument therefore resembles Huntington's; both of them attach great importance to encounters between existing political arrangements and specific mobilized groups making new and powerful demands on the government. This analysis veers away from Huntington's, especially in denying the significance of a discrepancy between the overall rates of mobilization and institutionalization, in attaching great importance to conflicts over claims, duties, privileges, and conceptions of justice embedded in particular contenders for power, and in drawing attention to the important possibility that the crucial contenders will be disaffected members of a polity rather than newcomers to power.

The explanation of revolution, within this formulation, becomes the identification of the probable causes for the three necessary conditions and the fourth facilitating condition: the appearance of a bloc advancing exclusive alternative claims, commitment to those claims, failure of repression and formation of coalitions between the alternative bloc and members of the polity. An alternative bloc can come into being via three different routes: (a) the mobilization of a new contender outside the polity; (b) the turning away of an existing challenger from acceptance of the polity's current operating rules; (c) the turning away of an existing member from its established place in the polity. In order to gauge the probabilities of employment of any of the routes, we would have to know a good deal about the operating rules of the polities involved. But several general conditions very likely increase those probabilities: contraction of the resources available to the government for the meeting of its commitments, a shift in the direction of structural change within the base population such that not just new groups but new *kinds* of groups are coming into being, disappearance of the resources which make possible the membership in the polity, and the continuing collective life of some contender.

The expansion of commitment to the claims of the alternative bloc occurs both through their acceptance by groups and individuals not belonging to the bloc and through the further mobilization of the bloc itself. The two undoubtedly reinforce each other. Acceptance of the alternative claims is likely to generalize when: the government fails to meet its established obligations; it greatly increases its demands on the subject population; the alternative claims are cast within the moral framework already employed by many members of the population; there is a strong alliance between the existing government and a well-defined enemy of an important segment of the population; and the coercive resources of the alternative bloc increase.

The Marxist account of the conditions for radicalization of the proletariat and the peasantry remains the most powerful general analysis of the process, expanding commitment to a revolutionary bloc. Where it falls down is in not providing for contenders (communities, ethnic minorities, religious groups, and so on) which are not class-based, and in obscuring the revolutionary importance of defensive reactions by segments of the population whose established positions are threatened. Eric Wolf's superb study of twentieth-century peasant wars makes apparent the revolutionary potential of such defensive responses to land enclosure, expansion of the market, and the encroachment of capitalism. [See the essay by Wolf in this volume.—Ed.]

The agents of the government are likely to become unwilling or unable to suppress the alternative bloc and the commitment to its claims when their coercive resources contract, their inefficiency increases, and inhibitions to their use arise. Defeat in war is a quintessential case, for casualties, defections, and military demobilization all tend to decrease the government's coercive capacity; the destruction of property, disruption of routines, and displacement of population in defeat are likely to decrease the efficiency of the established coercive means; and the presence of a conqueror places constraints on the government's use of coercion. (The routine of modern military occupation, however, tends to substitute the coercive capacity of the victors for that of the vanquished.) The end of any war, won or lost, tends to restore men with newly acquired military skill to most of the contenders in the political system. Where military demobilization proceeds rapidly, it is likely to shift the balance of coercive resources away from the government, and may shift it toward an alternative bloc. Even without war, the increase in the coercive resources of the alternative bloc (which can occur through theft, purchase, training, the imposition of military discipline, and the lending of support by outsiders) is equivalent to the contraction of the government's own coercive resources. The efficiency of governmental coercion is likely to decline, at least in the short run, when the character, organization, and daily routines of the population to be controlled change rapidly; this appears to be one of the most direct effects of large-scale structural change on the likelihood of revolution. Inhibitions to the use of coercion are likely to increase when the coercive forces themselves are drawn from (or otherwise attached to) the populations to be controlled, when new members of the polity act against the coercive means that were employed to block their acquisition of membership, and effective coalitions between members of the polity and revolutionary challengers exist.

The final condition for revolution—this one strongly facilitating rather than necessary—is the formation of just such coalitions between polity members and revolutionary challengers. Modern European history, for example, provides many examples of temporary coalitions between professionals, intellectuals, or other fragments of the bourgeoisie well established within the polity and segments of the working class excluded from power. The revolutions of 1830 and 1848 display this pattern with particular clarity. The payoff to the challengers consists of a hedge against repression, some protection against the devaluation of their resources, and perhaps the transfer of information and expertise from the member. The payoff to the member consists of an expansion of the resources available for application to the government and to other members of the polity—not least the ability to mount a credible threat of mass action. This sort of coalition-formation is likely to occur, on the one hand, when a challenger rapidly increases the store of resources under its control and, on the other, when a member loses its coalition partners within the polity, or the polity is more or less evenly divided among two or more coalitions, or an established member is risking loss of membership in the polity through failure to meet the tests of other members.

The History of Revolution in the West

In the West of the past five centuries, perhaps the largest single factor in the promotion of revolutions and collective violence has been the great concentration of power in national states. (I concede that the rise of the national state depended to such a large degree on the growth of production, the expansion of large-scale marketing, the strengthening of the bourgeoisie, and the proliferation of bureaucracy that such a statement commits a dramatic oversimplification.) This factor shows up most clearly in the frequency of tax rebellions in Western countries over those centuries, and in the prominence of grievances concerning taxation in revolutions, such as those of the 1640s or the 1840s. The frequency of violent resistance to military conscription points in the same direction.

States are warmakers, and wars are state-makers. At least in modern Europe, the major increases in the scope and strength of national states (as indicated by national budgets, national debts, powers of intervention, and sizes of staffs,) have, on the whole, occurred as a direct result of war-making or preparation for war. What is more, the armed forces have historically played a large part in subordinating other authorities and the general population to the national state. They backed up the collection of taxes, put down tax rebellions, seized and disposed of the enemies of the crown, literally enforced national policy. The relationship was neatly reciprocal: war provided the incentive, the occasion, and the rationalization for strengthening the state, while war-makers assured the docility of the general population and the yielding of the resources necessary to carry out the task. The fairly recent division of labor between specialized police forces for domestic control and military forces for the remaining tasks has not fundamentally changed the relationship.

The connection matters here because a series of important relationships between war and revolution also exists. It is not just that they overlap to some extent. In some circumstances, war promotes revolution. That assertion is true in several different ways: the extraction of resources for the prosecution of war has repeatedly aroused revolutionary resistance; the defeat of states in war has often made them vulnerable to attacks from their domestic enemies; the complicity of some portion of the armed forces with the revolutionary bloc has been absolutely essential to the success of the modern revolution, and the most frequent variety of revolution—the coup—has depended mainly on the alignments of armed forces; the waning phases of major movements of conquest (the weakening of the Napoleonic regimes outside of France, the Nazi regimes outside of Germany, and the Japanese regimes outside of Japan being prime examples) are strikingly propitious for revolution; and the periods of readjustment immediately following large international conflicts also seem favorable to revolution, often with the collusion of major parties to the conflict. All of this suggest a strong connection between realignments in the international system and conflicts within individual countries, a connection mediated by the repressive policies and capacities of the governments involved.

Those who find at least some of the preceding analysis useful and plausible will do well to reflect on the sorts of variables that have been in play. Despite the many recent attempts to psychologize the study of revolution by introducing ideas of anxiety, alienation, rising expectations, and the like, and to sociologize it by employing notions of disequilibrium, role conflict, structural strain, and so on, the factors which hold up under close scrutiny are, on the whole, political ones. The structure of power, alternative conceptions of justice, the organization of coercion, the conduct of war, the formation of coalitions, the legitimacy of the state—these traditional concerns of political thought provide the main guides to the explanation of revolution. Population growth, industrialization, urbanization, and other large-scale structural changes do, to be sure, affect the probabilities of revolution. But they do so indirectly, by shaping the potential contenders for power, transforming the techniques of government control, and shifting the resources available to contenders and governments. There is no reliable and regular sense in which modernization breeds revolutions.

REFERENCES

1. Huntington (1968), p. 4.
2. Gillis (1970), pp. 344–70.
3. Huntington (1968), p. 265.
4. Huntington (1968), p.266.
5. Huntington (1968), p.275.

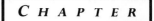

C H A P T E R

3

Multicausal Analyses of Revolutions

The classical and modernization debates on revolutions made it clear that revolutions are too complex to be captured by a simple, one-cause formula, such as "class struggle" or "modernization." Current theories of revolution therefore examine *multiple* causes behind the occurrence development of revolutions. In discussing these causes, Eric R. Wolf shows that a number of different social processes contribute to the mobilization of peasants into revolutionary movements. Theda Skocpol and Ellen Kay Trimberger examine several different relationships among the state, elites, and popular groups, and find that all were important in the development of great revolutions. Jack A. Goldstone demonstrates that multiple vulnerabilities lie behind the revolutionary overthrow of modern dictatorships. In each essay, although the precise causes differ for different revolutions, the authors agree on a fundamental principle: Explaining revolutions depends on understanding how multiple causes combine to create a situation in which states are weakened, and in which elites and popular groups have both the capacity and the motivation to revolt.

PEASANTS AND REVOLUTIONS

Eric R. Wolf

In this essay, Wolf notes that peasant rebellions are generally defensive. The participants wish to protect traditional lifestyles against mounting strains. Wolf identifies three sources of such strains: (1) population growth, (2) commercialization and the growth of markets, and (3) dislocation among the local elites that traditionally mediate peasants' interactions with government authorities and the outside world.

However, mobilizing the peasantry for revolution is no easy task. Wolf argues that peasants are only able to translate their resistance to such pressures into active rebellion if they have "tactical freedom" to act. Such freedom may be available to peasants who own their own resources—that is, a landowning middle peasantry; to peasants who live in areas far from the strongholds of central authority, especially in defensible mountainous regions; and to peasants who live in self-administering communal villages not under the direct supervision of landlords. Each kind of peasantry forms a potential enclave of rebellion in times of mounting pressures on peasants' traditional ways of life.

Still, peasant rebellions have only become revolutions when combined with the actions of dissident elites. Wolf describes the problematic nature of this connection and its role in building revolutions.

Six major social and political upheavals, fought with peasant support, have shaken the world of the twentieth century: the Mexican Revolution of 1910; the Russian Revolutions of 1905 and 1917; the Chinese Revolution, which metamorphosed through various phases from 1921 on; the Vietnamese Revolution, which had its roots in World War II; the Algerian Revolution of 1954; and the Cuban Revolution of 1958–59. All of these were to some extent based on the participation of rural populations. It is to the analysis of this participation that the present paper directs its attention.

Romantics to the contrary, it is not easy for a peasantry to engage in sustained rebellion. Peasants are especially handicapped in passing from passive recognition of wrongs to political participation as a means for setting them right. First, a peasant's work is most often done alone, on his own land, rather than in conjunction with his fellows. Moreover, all peasants are to some extent competitors for available resources within the community, as well as for sources of credit from without. Second, the tyranny of work weighs heavily upon peasants—their life is geared to an annual routine and to planning for the year to come. Momentary alterations of routine threaten their ability to take up the routine again later. Third, control of land enables him, more often than not, to retreat into subsistence production, should adverse conditions affect his market crop. Fourth, ties of extended kinship and mutual aid within the community may cushion the shocks of dislocation. Fifth, peasants' interests—especially among poor peasants—often crosscut class alignments. Rich and poor peasants may be kinfolk, or a peasant may be at one and the same time owner, renter, sharecropper, laborer for his neighbors, and seasonal hand on a nearby plantation. Each different involvement aligns him differently with his fellows and with the outside world. Finally, past exclusion of the peasant from participation in decision-making beyond the bamboo hedge of his village deprives him all too often of the knowledge needed to articulate his interests with appropriate forms of action. Hence peasants are often merely passive spectators of political struggles, or they long for the sudden advent of a millenium, without specifying, for themselves and their neighbors, the many rungs on the staircase to heaven.

If it is true that peasants are slow to rise, then peasant participation in the great rebellions of the twentieth century must obey some special factors that exacerbate the peasant condition. We will not understand that condition unless we keep constantly in mind that it has suffered greatly under the impact of three great crises: the demographic crisis, the ecological crisis, and the crisis in power and authority. The demographic crisis is most easily depicted in bare figures, though its root causes remain ill understood. Yet the bare numbers suffice to indicate the seriousness of the demographic problem. Mexico had a population of 5.8 million at the beginning of the nineteenth century; in 1910—at the outbreak of the revolution—it had 16.5 million. European Russia had a population of 20 million in 1725; at the turn of the twentieth century it had 87 million. China numbered 265 million in 1775, 430 million in 1850, and close to 600 million at the time of the revolution. Vietnam is estimated to have sustained a population of between 6 and 14 million in 1820; it had 30.5 million inhabitants in 1962. The indigenous population of Algeria numbered 10.5 million in 1963, representing a fourfold increase since the beginnings of French occupation in the first part of the nineteenth century. Cuba had 550,000 inhabitants in 1800; by 1953 it had 5.8 million. Population increases alone and by themselves would have placed a serious strain on inherited cultural arrangements.

The ecological crisis is in part related to the sheer increase in numbers; yet it is also an important measure independent of it. Population increases of the magnitude just mentioned coincided with a period of history in which land and other resources were increasingly converted into commodities to be bought and sold. As commodities, they were subjected to the demands of a market that bore only a very indirect relation to the needs of the rural populations subject to it. Where in the past market behavior had been largely subsidiary to the problems of subsistence, now existence and its problems became subsidiary to the market. The alienation of peasant resources proceeded directly through outright seizure or through coercive purchase, as in Mexico, Algeria, and Cuba, or it took the form—especially in China and Vietnam—of stepped-up rents, which resulted in the transfer of resources from those unable to keep up to those able to pay. In addition, the peasant economy was burdened by the pressure of taxation, by demands for redemption payments, and by increased need for industrially produced commodities on the part of the peasantry itself. All together, these various pressures disrupted the precarious ecological balance of peasant society. Where the peasant had required a certain combination of resources to effect an adequate living, the pressures on these resources broke that ecological nexus. This is perhaps best seen in Russia, where successive land reforms threatened continued peasant access to pasture, forest, and plowland. Yet it is equally evident in cases where commercialization threatened peasant access to communal lands (Mexico, Algeria, Vietnam), to unclaimed land (Mexico, Cuba), to public granaries (Algeria, China), or threatened the balance between pastoral and settled populations (Algeria). At the same time that commercialization disrupted rural life, it also created new and unsettled ecological niches in industry. Disruptive change in the rural area went hand in hand with the opening up of incipient but uncertain opportunities for numerous peasants. Many of these retained formal ties with their home villages (Russia, China, Algeria); others migrated between country and industry in continuous turnover (especially Vietnam). Increased instability in the rural areas was thus accompanied by a still unstable commitment to industrial work.

Finally, both the demographic and the ecological crisis converged in the crisis of authority. The development of the market produced a rapid circulation of the elite. The manipulators of the new "freefloating resources"—labor bosses, merchants, industrial entrepreneurs—challenged the inherited power of the controllers of fixed social re- sources—the tribal chief, the mandarin, the landed nobleman. Undisputed and stable claims thus yielded to unstable and disputed claims. This rivalry between primarily economic powerholders contained its own rules: the economic entrepreneur did not concern himself with the social cost of his activities; the traditional powerholder was often too limited in his power to offer assistance or was subject to cooptation by his successful rivals. The advent of the market thus produced not merely a crisis in peasant ecology; it deranged the numerous middle-level ties between center and hinterland, urban and rural sectors. Commercialization disrupted the hinterland; at the very same time it also lessened the ability of powerholders to perceive and predict changes in the rural area. The result was an ever widening gap between the rules and the ruled. That such a course is not inevitable is perhaps demonstrated by Barrington Moore,[1] who shows how traditional feudal forms were utilized in both Germany and Japan to prevent the formation of such a gap in power and communication during the crucial period of transition to a commercial and industrial order. Where this was not accomplished—precisely where an administrative, militarized feudalism was absent—the continued widening of the power gap invited the formation of a counterelite that could challenge both a disruptive leadership based on the operation of the market and the impotent heirs of traditional power, while forging a new consensus through communication with the peasantry. Such a counterelite is most frequently made up of members of provincial elites, relegated to the margins of commercial mobilization and political office; of officials or professionals who stand midway between the rural area and the center, and are caught in the contradictions between the two; and of intellectuals who have access to a system of symbols which can guide the interaction between leadership and rural area.

Sustained mobilization of the peasantry is, however, no easy task. Such an effort will not find its allies in a rural mass that is completely subject to the imperious demands of necessity. Peasants cannot rebel successfully in a situation of complete impotence; the powerless are easy victims. Therefore only a peasantry in possession of some tactical control over its own resources can provide a secure basis for ongoing political leverage. Power, as Richard Adams has said, refers ultimately

> to an actual physical control that one party may have with respect to another. The reason that most relationships are not reduced to physical struggles is that parties to them can make rational decisions based on their estimates of tactical power and other factors. Power is usually exercised, therefore, through the common recognition by two parties of the tactical control each has, and through rational decision by one to do what the other wants. Each estimates his own tactical control, compares it to the other, and decides he may or may not be superior.[2]

The poor peasant or the landless laborer who depends on a landlord for the largest part of his livelihood (or the totality of it) has no tactical power; he is completely within the power domain of his employer, without sufficient resources of his own to serve him as resources in the power struggle. Poor peasants and landless laborers, therefore, are unlikely to pursue the course of rebellion, *unless* they are able to rely on some external power to challenge the power that constrains them. Such external power is represented in the Mexican case by the action of the Constitutionalist Army in Yucatán, which liberated the peons from debt bondage "from above"; by the collapse of the Russian Army in 1917 and the reflux of the peasant soldiery, arms in hand, into the villages; by the creation of the Chinese Red Army as an instrument designed to break up landlord power in the villages.

Where such external power is present, the poor peasant and landless laborer have latitude of movement; where it is absent, they are under almost complete constraint. The rich peasant, in turn, is unlikely to embark on the course of rebellion. As employer of the labor of others, as moneylender, as notable coopted by the state machine, he exercises local power in alliance with external power holders. His power domain within the village is derivative; it depends on the maintenance of the domains of power holders outside the village. Only when an external force, such as the Chinese Red Army, proves capable of destroying these other superior power domains, will the rich peasant lend his support to an uprising.

There are only two components of the peasantry that possess sufficient internal leverage to enter sustained rebellion. These are (1) a landowning "middle peasantry" or (2) a peasantry located in a peripheral area outside the domains of landlord control. Middle peasantry refers to a peasant population that has secure access to land of its own and cultivates it with family labor. Where these middle peasant holdings lie within the power domain of a superior, possession of their own resources provides middle peasants with the minimal tactical freedom required to challenge their overlords. The same, however, holds for a peasantry, poor or middle, whose settlements are only under marginal control from the outside. Here land holdings may be insufficient for the support of the peasant household; but subsidiary activities such as casual labor, smuggling, livestock raising—not under the direct constraint of an external power domain—supplement land in sufficient quantity to grant the peasantry some latitude of movement. We mark the existence of such a tactically mobile peasantry in the villages of Morelos in Mexico, in the communes of the Central Agricultural Region of Russia, in the northern bastion established by the Chinese Communists after the Long March, as a basis for rebellion in Vietnam, among the fellahin in Algeria, and among the squatters of Oriente Province in Cuba.

Yet this recruitment of a "tactically mobile peasantry" among the middle peasants and the "free" peasants of peripheral areas poses a curious paradox. This is also the peasantry in whom anthropologists and rural sociologists have tended to see the main bearers of peasant tradition. If our account is correct, then (strange to say) it is precisely this culturally conservative stratum that is the most instrumental in dynamiting the peasant social order. This paradox dissolves, however, when we consider that it is also the middle peasant who is relatively the most vulnerable to economic changes wrought by commercialism, while his social relations remain encased within the traditional design. He is in a balancing act in which his balance is continuously threatened by population growth, the encroachment of rival landlords, the loss of rights to grazing, forest, and water, falling prices and unfavorable conditions of the market, and interest payments and foreclosures. Moreover, it is precisely this stratum that depends most on traditional social relations of kin and mutual aid between neighbors; middle peasants suffer most when these relations are abrogated, just as they are least able to withstand the depredations of tax collectors or landlords.

Finally—and this is again paradoxical—middle peasants are also the most exposed to influences from the developing proletariat. The poor peasant or landless laborer, in going to the city or the factory, also usually cuts his tie with the land. The middle peasant, however, stays on the land and sends his children to work in town; he is caught in a situation in which one part of the family retains a footing in agriculture, while the other undergoes "the training of the cities." This also makes the middle peasant a transmitter of urban unrest and political ideas. The point bears elaboration: it is probably not so much the growth of an industrial proletariat as such that produces revolutionary activity, as it is the development of an industrial work force still closely geared to life in the villages.

Thus, it is the very attempt of the middle and free peasant to remain traditional that makes him revolutionary.

If we now follow out the hypothesis that it is middle peasants and poor but "free" peasants—not constrained by any power domain—that constitute the pivotal groupings for peasant uprisings, then it follows that any factor that serves to increase the latitude granted by that tactical mobility reinforces their revolutionary potential. One of these factors is peripheral location of the peasantry with regard to the center of state control. In fact, frontier areas quite often show a tendency to rebel against the central authorities, regardless of whether they are inhabited by peasants or not. South China has constituted a hearth of rebellion within the Chinese state, partly because it was first a frontier area in the southward march of the Han people, and later because it provided the main zone of contact between Western and Chinese civilization. The Mexican North has similarly been a zone of dissidence from the center in Mexico City, partly because its economy was based on mining and cattle raising rather than maize agriculture, and partly because it was open to influences from the United States to the north. In South China it was the dissident gentry with a peasant following that frequently made trouble for the center; in the Mexican North it was the provincial businessmen, ranchers, and cowboys. Yet when a poor peasantry is located in such a peripheral area beyond the normal control of the central power, the tactical mobility of such a peasantry is "doubled" by its location. This has been the case with Morelos in Mexico, Nghe An Province in Vietnam, Kabylia in Algeria, and Oriente in Cuba. The tactical effectiveness of such areas is "tripled" if they also contain defensible mountainous redoubts—this has been true of Morelos, Kabylia, and Oriente. The effect is "quadrupled" where the population of these redoubts differs ethnically or linguistically from the surrounding population. Thus we find that the villagers of Morelos were Nahuatl speakers; the inhabitants of Kabylia, Berber speakers. Oriente Province showed no linguistic differences from the Spanish spoken in Cuba, but it did contain a significant Afro-Cuban element. Ethnic distinctions enhance the solidarity of the rebels; possession of a special linguistic code provides an autonomous system of communication.

It is important, however, to recognize that separation from the state or the surrounding populace need not be only physical or cultural. The Russian and the Mexican cases both demonstrate that it is possible to develop a solid enclave population of peasantry through state reliance on a combination of communal autonomy with the provision of community services to the state. The organization of the peasantry into self-administering communes with stipulated responsibilities to state and landlords created, in both cases, veritable fortresses of peasant tradition within the body of the country itself. Held fast by the surrounding structure, they acted as sizzling pressure cookers of unrest which, at the moment of explosion, vented their force outward to secure more living space for their customary corporate way of life. Thus we can add a further multiplier effect to the others just cited. The presence of any one of these will raise the peasant potential for rebellion.

But what of the transition from peasant rebellion to revolution, from a movement aimed at the redress of wrongs to the attempted overthrow of society itself? Marxists in general have long argued that peasants without outside leadership cannot make a revolution; our case material would bear them out. Where the peasantry has successfully rebelled against the established order—under its own banner and with its own leaders— it was sometimes able to reshape the social structure of the countryside closer to its heart's desires; however, it did not lay hold of the state, of the cities that house the centers of control, of the strategic nonagricultural resources of the society. Zapata stayed in his Morelos; the "fold migration" of Pancho Villa simply receded after the defeat at Torreon; the Ukrainian rebel Nestor Makhno stopped short of the cities; the Russian peasants of the Central Agricultural Region simply burrowed more deeply into their local communes. Thus a peasant rebellion that takes place in a complex society already caught up in commercialization and industrialization tends to be self-limiting and hence anachronistic.

The peasant utopia is the free village, untrammelled by tax collectors, labor recruiters, large landowners, or officials. Ruled over, but never ruling, peasants also lack any acquaintance with the operation of the state as a complex machinery; rather, they experience it only as a "cold monster." Willing to defend the peasants if it proved to be in their own interest, the traditional local power holders provided a weak, unreliable shield against the hostile force of the state. Thus, for the present, the state is a negative quality, an evil, to be replaced in short shrift by their own "homemade" social order. That order, they believe, can run without the state; hence peasants in rebellion are natural anarchists.

Often this political perspective is reinforced still further by a wider ideological vision. The peasant experience tends to be dualistic, in that he is caught between his understanding of how the world ought to be properly ordered and the realities of a mundane existence, beset by disorder. Against this disorder, the peasant has always set his dreams of deliverance—the vision of a *mahdi* who would deliver the world from tyranny, of a Son of Heaven who would truly embody the mandate of Heaven, of a "white tsar" as against the "black tsar" of the disordered present. Under conditions of modern dislocation, the disordered present is all too frequently experienced as world order reversed, and hence evil. The dualism of the past easily fuses with the dualism of the present. The true order is yet to come, either through miraculous intervention, rebellion, or both. Peasant anarchism and an apocalyptic vision of the world together provide the ideological fuel that drives the rebellious peasantry.

Thus, the processes of rebellion and of revolution involve not merely organizational changes, but also changes in the perception and understanding of the world one inhabits. The Mexican Revolution was preceded by the wide spread of anarchist ideals. The Algerian Revolution was preceded by the Badissa, a reformist Islamic movement. The Chinese Revolution of 1911 was preceded by the Taiping, Nien, and Boxer rebellions, and the mushroomings of heterodox secret societies. The Russian Revolution was prepared by the secession of the Old Believers and the spread of a millenarian ideology among the peasantry. The Vietnamese Revolution followed after the growth of novel sects like the Cao Dai and the Hoa Hao. Such ideological movements provide the opportunity to imagine alternatives to present conditions, to experiment mentally with alternative forms of organization, and to ready the population for the acceptance of changes to come. They are the mental rehearsals of revolutionary transformations.

Given these volatile cultural and ideological characteristics of peasant societies and the triple crisis impacting the peasant order in the modern age, what other social groupings and processes intercede to give certain twentieth-century peasant rebellions their revolutionary character? The pressures that affect the peasantry affect in other ways the middlemen who stand guard over the relays of communication and power between the developed sector and the hinterland. These middlemen are not homogeneous; they are not in any way like a European middle class. They include economic brokers, members of the lower orders of bureaucracy, and teachers. They also include the middlemen of the past social order, now shattered by the interrelated crises of overpopulation, ecological imbalance, and eroded authority. These are the landlords clinging to a decaying grandeur; the notables whose words were once decisive in the deliberations of the village assemblies; the literati learned in the canons of an outworn wisdom. But rarely do such men make good revolutionaries themselves. Their sons, however, characteristically caught between the decadent style of their fathers and the new and raucous style of their competitors in the business of social brokerage, can envision a future purged of the contradictions of the present. Such middlemen—old and new—are the social agents of articulation; but they are also society's victims. They occupy the social positions of greatest strain. Middlemen and middle peasants together constitute the population from which the revolution recruits its army. The middle peasants furnish the first infantry battalions; the middlemen, the first officers of line and staff. But not all peasants or all brokers participate in the revolutionary process. Rather, the political process leading to revolution is a process of social selection—different political groups compete with each other in articulating their interests into viable coalitions. Recent revolutions exhibit a patterned sequence of such attempts. First, the middle layers produce a set of political leaders who agitate for ameliorative reforms. Next follows a phase of coalition-building in which various political groups compete in making contacts with urban artisans and wage workers. The urban artisans produce "petty bourgeois anarchist" demands; the workers initiate trade-union demands. Then follows the third and most problematic phase, the social selection of some group or groups of cadre capable of linking up with the potential peasant rebels. I know of no twentieth-century revolution in which such a coalition was achieved without revolutionary warfare.

Revolutionary warfare is the strongest catalyst in effecting the link between cadre and rebels. In peaceful times, revolutionary leaders may scour the countryside in attempts to "go to the people," in the words of the pre-1905 Russian Narodniki. Yet, all too frequently they do so as outsiders, as people city-bred and city-trained, drawing their behavior patterns and cultural idioms from the dominant sector and the enclave society. They must first unlearn these patterns, if they are to enter into successful contact with the peasant rebels. Any anthropologist who has worked with peasants will appreciate the unreality suggested by the picture of the dedicated commissar, newly descended upon the peasant village, busily molding the minds of five hundred, a thousand, or two thousand peasants. This is not to say that the revolutionary leaders do not build and extend mechanisms of control wherever and whenever they can—but this building and extension of control must involve a complex dialogue with the villagers in which the outsider learns as much, if not more, about local organization and criteria of relevance than the local inhabitants. Guerrilla warfare both speeds and deepens this learning as cadre and peasant activists synchronize their behavior and translate from one cultural idiom to the other.

This phase is clearly the most problematical. First, mutual learning and consequent synchronization may fail. Second, the cadre may not be able to effect the transition from urban-based political activity to revolutionary warfare in the hinterland. Third, even if successful, the rebels among the peasantry rarely exceed ten percent of the peasant population. Hence the movement must gain tacit as well as overt support of the peasantry. To this end, the revolutionaries must construct, in the backward sector, a network of institutions (an "infrastructure" or "parallel hierarchy"), or at least inhibit the capacity of the government to exercise or extend its own power in the hinterland.

Such a new infrastructure cannot be built from whole cloth; it can only be the outcome of a complex interaction between leaders and followers. More often than not, the resultant form of organization is based on already existing peasant patterns and experience. Behind the new revolutionary organization of Mexican villages lies an age-old experience with communal land tenures; behind the sudden rise of the Russian soviets lies the experience of the traditional Russian village community of the *mir*. Behind the new organization of the population of Chinese villages, we discern quite traditional patterns of village associations, as well as the organizational experience gained by peasant rebels in such uprisings as the Taiping and the Nien. Even behind the organization of the Chinese Communist Party lie such traditional patterns of secret society as the Ko Lao Hui. This is not to say that no new patterns are introduced into the villages. Frequently, it is warfare itself—and the break it represents with the past—that allows the rural population to accept innovations under their *own* auspices, innovations they would have resisted if imposed by the agents of the dominant sector.

Such a self-made social structure speeds learning. By removing the constraints of the inherited order, it releases the manifold contradictions hitherto held in check—the opposition of old and young, men and women, rich and poor—and directs the energies thus freed into new organizational channels. It is this, above all, that makes revolution irreversible. It also speeds the rise of leaders from the peasantry itself, providing new channels of mobility not contained in the old system, and intensifying the fusion between peasantry and leadership which sparked the revolutionary effort.

REFERENCES

1. Moore, Jr. (1966).
2. Adams (1966), pp. 3–4.

REVOLUTIONS: A STRUCTURAL ANALYSIS

Theda Skocpol and Ellen Kay Trimberger

Building on the work of Karl Marx, Skocpol and Trimberger argue for a "structural" approach to revolutions that examines multiple relationships among important political actors. Beginning with a concern for the power of the state, they focus on several key relationships that may reinforce or undermine state power—relationships between states and elite groups, between peasants and landlords, and between states competing in the international arena. Skocpol and Trimberger thus find the causes of revolutions in the very structure of certain states and societies.

Marx on Revolution: A Critique

Karl Marx's theory of revolution was elegant, powerful, and politically relevant because it linked the causes and consequences of revolutions directly to the historical emergence and transcendence of capitalism. Nevertheless, events and scholarship since Marx's time show that there is a need for revised ways of understanding revolutions in relation to the world-historical development of capitalism.

Before we launch into critical discussion, let us briefly underline some aspects of Marx's approach to revolutions that are still compelling and which we want to recapitulate in our own approach. First, unlike many contemporary academic and social scientists, Marx did not try to create a general theory of revolution relevant to all kinds of societies at all times. Instead, he regarded revolutions as specific to certain historical circumstances and to certain types of societies.

Second, Marx developed a social-structural theory of revolutions which argued that organized and conscious movements for revolutionary change succeed only where and when there is an objectively revolutionary situation, due to contradictions in the larger societal structure and historical situation: thus Marx's oft-quoted saying that men make their own history, but not in circumstances of their own choosing and not just as they please.

Third, Marx made class domination central to his conception of social order, and class conflict a defining feature of revolution, and we retain such concerns.

Taking off from these continuities with Marx's approach to revolutions, we can now identify various points at which Marx's original theory of revolutions stands in need of revision when juxtaposed to historical revolutions as we understand them. We shall discuss in turn issues about causes, processes, and outcomes or revolutions.

CAUSES

Marx held that a revolutionary situation occurs when an existing mode of production reaches the limits of its contradictions. The decisive contradictions are *economic* contradictions that develop between the social forces and the social relations of production. In turn, intensifying class conflict is generated between the existing dominant class and the rising, revolutionary class. Thus Marx theorized that revolutionary contradictions are internally generated within a society. What is more, his perspective strongly suggested that revolutions should occur first in the most economically advanced social formations of a given mode of production.

Actual historical revolutions, though, have not conformed to Marx's theoretical expectations. From the French Revolution on, they have occurred in predominantly agrarian countries where capitalist relations of production were only barely or moderately developed. In every instance, political-military pressures from more economically advanced countries abroad have been crucial in contributing to the outbreak of revolution. Marx began an analysis of uneven world capitalist development, but he did not link this directly to the cause of revolutions. Nor do we agree that the objective conditions within the old regimes that explain the emergence of revolutionary situations have been primarily economic. Rather, they have been *political* contradictions centered in the structure and situation of states caught in cross-pressures between, on the one hand, military competitors on the international scene and, on the other hand, the constraints of the existing domestic economy and (in some cases) resistance by internal politically powerful class forces to efforts by the state to mobilize resources to meet international competition. To mention some examples: the Japanese Meiji Restoration (a bureaucratic revolution from above) occurred because the Tokugawa state (which was already highly bureaucratic) came under severe and novel pressures from imperialist capitalist Western powers; the French and Chinese Revolutions broke out because the Bourbon and Manchu regimes were caught in contradictions between pressures from economically more developed foreign states and resistance from dominant class forces at home; and the Russian Revolution broke out because the Tsarist bureaucracy and military dissolved under the impact of World War I upon economically backward Russia. Thus, it is conflict between nation-states in the context of uneven development of world capitalism that is central to the genesis of revolutions.

PROCESSES

Marx theorized that, given a revolutionary situation, revolutions are fundamentally accomplished through class struggles led by that class which emerges within the womb of the old mode of production and becomes central to the new, post-revolutionary mode of production. Historically, only two classes play this leading revolutionary role. In bourgeois revolutions, a capitalist class that has grown up within feudalism plays the leading role. In socialist revolutions in advanced capitalist societies, the proletariat plays the leading role.

On the basis of the historical record, a reservation must be made on which classes actually are central to revolutions. In our view, revolutionary leadership has never come from those who controlled the means of production. Hence, we find no instance of a class-conscious capitalist bourgeoisie playing the leading political role in a revolution (though of course some revolutions have contributed in their outcomes to the further or future growth of capitalism and bourgeois class dominance). Moreover, because social revolutions from below have occurred in agrarian states situated in more or less disadvantaged positions within developing world capitalism, their successful occurrence has not been determined by the struggle of proletarians against capitalists, but rather by the class struggles of *peasants* against dominant landed classes and/or colonial or neo-colonial regimes.

OUTCOMES

Finally, we arrive at the issue of what revolutions immediately accomplish, once they have successfully occurred. Marx held that revolutions mark the transition from one mode of production to another, that they so transform class relations as to create conditions newly appropriate for further economic development. Transformations of ideology and the state also occur, but these were seen by Marx as parallel to and reinforcing the fundamental changes in class relations.

Yet, historically, revolutions have changed *state structures* as much as, or more than, they have changed class relations of production and surplus appropriation. In all of the cases of revolution from above and below that we studied, state structures became much more centralized and bureaucratic. Moreover, Third World revolutions since World War II have broken or weakened the bonds of colonial and neocolonial dependency above all by creating truly sovereign and, in some cases, mass-mobilizing national governments.[1] Equally important, the effects that revolutions have had upon the subsequent economic development of the nations they have transformed have been traceable not only to the changes in class structures but also to the *changes in state structures and functions* that the revolutions accomplished. As Immanuel Wallerstein has very aptly argued, "development [i.e., national economic development] does require a 'breakthrough.' But it is a political breakthrough that in turn makes possible the far more gradual economic process"[2]

Social Structure and Revolution

If Marx's original, elegant theory is no longer entirely adequate, then how can we make sense in new ways of revolutions in relation to the development of capitalism? Obviously, we are not going to be able to provide complete answers here. But we can propose three analytic principles that we have found especially useful in our own efforts to explain revolutions from above and below in agrarian states situated within developing world capitalism. These are: (1) a non-reductionist conception of states; (2) social-structural analyses of the situation of the peasantry within the old and new regimes; and (3) a focus on international military competition among states within the historically developing world capitalist economy. Let us elaborate each point in turn.

THE STATE AND POLITICAL CRISES

We believe that states should be viewed theoretically as conditioned by, but not entirely reducible to, economic and/or class interests. States are not mere instruments of dominant class forces. Rather, states are fundamentally administrative and military organizations that extract resources from society and deploy them to maintain order at home and to compete against other states abroad. Consequently, while it is always true that states are greatly constrained by economic conditions and partly shaped and influenced by class forces, nevertheless, state structures and activities also have an underlying integrity and a logic of their own. These are keyed to the dynamics of international military rivalries and to the geo-political as well as world-economic circumstances in which given states find themselves.

This conception of states helps to make sense of certain facts about the causes of revolutions that seemed so jarring when placed in juxtaposition with Marx's original notions. For if states are coercive organizations not reducible to class structures, then it makes sense that processes that serve to undermine state strength should be crucial in bringing about revolutions.

In all of the five countries that we have studied most intensively—France, Russia, China, Japan and Turkey—there were, prior to the revolutions, relatively centralized and partially bureaucratic monarchical states, none of which had been incorporated into a colonial empire. As they came under pressure in a capitalist world, these states tried to mobilize national resources to stave off foreign domination—something that occurred through revolution from above in Japan and Turkey, whereas the old regimes broke down completely in France, Russia, and China, clearing the way for revolutions from below. Thus, Trimberger has demonstrated how in Japan military bureaucrats undertook a revolution from above without mass participation, which destroyed the traditional aristocracy, and established a modern state that fostered capitalist development. With more difficulty and less success, a similar process took place in Turkey. But in Bourbon France and Imperial China, as Skocpol has shown, politically powerful landed classes were able to resist state bureaucrats, undermining their attempts at modernizing reforms and causing the disintegration of centralized repressive controls over the lower classes. In Russia, the landed nobility was much less politically powerful vis-à-vis reforming state authorities, but the agrarian class structure nevertheless limited Russia's ability to prepare for the exigencies of modern warfare, so that the Tsarist state was overwhelmed and destroyed in World War I. The theoretically relevant point that applies to all of these cases regardless of the various patterns is that if one treats states theoretically as potentially autonomous vis-à-vis the existing dominant class, then one can explore the dynamic *interactions* between the state organizations and dominant class interests. In situations of intense foreign political and military pressure, these interactions can lead either to military bureaucrats' action against dominant class interests or to dominant classes acting in ways that undermine the state. Thus, our theoretical approach to the state helps make sense of the specifically political crises that launch revolutions.

This conception of the state also helps to render understandable those aspects of the processes and outcomes of revolutions that Marx's class conflict theory of revolutions seems to downplay or ignore. Revolutions are not consolidated until new or transformed state administrative and coercive organizations are securely established in the place of the old regime. Consequently, it makes sense that political leaderships—parties or bureaucratic/military cliques—that act to consolidate revolutionized state organizations should play a central role in revolutionary processes. And if states are extractive organizations that can deploy resources to some extent independently of existing class interests, then it makes sense that revolutions create the *potentials* for breakthroughs in national economic development in large part by giving rise to more powerful, centralized, and autonomous state organizations. This was true for all of the revolutions from above and below that we studied, although the potential for state-guided or initiated national economic development was more thoroughly realized in Japan, Russia, and China than it was in France and Turkey. Thus, the actual realization of the revolution-created potential depends upon the international and world-historical economic constraints and opportunities that are specific to each case after the revolution.

THE SITUATION OF THE PEASANTRY

In addition to looking at states as relatively autonomous and in dynamic interrelation with dominant classes, one should pay careful attention to the situation of the peasantry in relation to the state and dominant class. Historically, mass-based social revolutions from below have successfully occurred only if the breakdown of old-regime state organizations has happened where peasants, as the majority, producing class, possess (or obtain) sufficient local economic and political autonomy to revolt against landlords. Such revolts occurred successfully in the French, Russian, and Chinese Revolutions alike. By contrast, the German Revolution of 1848–50 failed largely because conditions conducive to peasant rebellion were absent East of the Elbe. And it was certainly an important condition for revolutions *from above* in Japan and Turkey that peasants in those countries remained immured within traditional structures not conducive to widespread revolts against landlords.

THE INTERNATIONAL STATE SYSTEM

Finally we arrive at an analytic emphasis that can help make sense of the entire context within which the causes and outcomes of revolutions have been shaped and their consequences determined. This point has two parts: (a) capitalism should be conceived not only as a mode of production based upon a relationship between wage labor and accumulating capital, but also as a world economy with various zones that are interdependent and unequal; and (b) capitalism from its inception has developed within, around, and through a framework of "multiple political sovereignties"—that is, the system of states that originally emerged from European feudalism and then expanded to cover the entire globe as a system of nations.

The analysis of capitalism as a competitive world system helps us to understand why there has been continual disillusionment when revolutionary outcomes have failed to mesh with ideological claims. Although there have been important variations in the state structures that have emerged from revolutions, all revolutions during the evolution of world capitalism have given rise to more bureaucratized and centralized states. We do not completely reject analyses that trace post-revolutionary bureaucratization to influences of the old regime or revolutionary parties. But our analysis does shift the emphasis to the necessity faced by the revolutionized regimes of coping with international pressures comparable to those that helped create the revolutionary crises in the first place. It is not just revolutions from above, but all revolutions that have become "bureaucratic revolutions"— in the specific sense of creating larger, more centralized, and more autonomous state organizations than existed under the old regimes. Revolutionary leaders have sought to enhance national standing and have seen the state apparatus as the most important tool to achieve this, especially where the state could be used to guide or undertake national industrialization. International pressures have been more effective in determining the outcomes of revolutions than internal pressures for equality, participation and decentralization. Even in China, where organized interests have fought for more equality and participation, China's vulnerable international situation has always encouraged centralization and bureaucracy.

How are we, finally, to reason about the consequences of revolutions for the development of capitalism and its eventual transformation into socialism? For Marx, this problem could be straightforwardly handled: some revolutions (i.e., bourgeois revolutions) established capitalism, while others (i.e., socialist revolutions) abolished capitalism and created the conditions for the rapid emergence of communism.

But actual revolutions have not readily conformed to the types and sequences originally projected by Marx or his successors. Certainly no country has had two successive revolutions, one bourgeois and the other socialist, and even revolutions that bear certain superficial resemblances to the "bourgeois" and "socialist" types do not really fit. Revolutions from above and below that have furthered bourgeois-capitalist development have not been "made by" class conscious bourgeoisie. As for "socialist revolutions," there have been revolutions made in part through class revolts from below that have culminated in the abolition of private property and the bourgeois class; yet these have occurred in "backward" agrarian countries, and not solely or primarily through proletarian class action. The outcomes of these revolutions can be described as "state socialist" in the sense that party-states have taken direct control of national economies. Yet these regimes act, so to speak, in the place of the bourgeoisie to promote national industrialization and do not conform to (or converge upon) Marx's original vision of socialism or communism.

From the perspective that capitalism is transnational in scope, we see why Marx's original typology of revolutions cannot hold. Since revolutions have occurred only in specific countries within the capitalist world economy and the international state system, and at particular times in their world-historical development, it follows that no single revolution could possibly either fully establish capitalism or entirely overcome capitalism and establish socialism.

Still, some revolutions have done better than others, and different international circumstances provide only part of the reasons. The specific societal configurations of state, economic, and class forces make a great difference in structuring the type of revolutionary outbreak and its consequences for both national and world-capitalist development.

REFERENCES

1. Dunn (1972).
2. Wallerstein (1971), p. 364.

REVOLUTIONS IN MODERN DICTATORSHIPS

Jack A. Goldstone

Great revolutions have transformed the distant past, but they have also shaken this century. Not just kings and emperors, but modern dictators such as Porfirio Díaz in Mexico, Fulgencio Batista in Cuba, Anastasio Somoza in Nicaragua, the Shah of Iran, and Ferdinand Marcos in the Philippines were overthrown by revolutionary movements. Theories of revolution must try to explain how these events arose, and how they differed from revolutions in traditional monarchies and empires.

The classic revolutions of France in 1789, Russia in 1917, and China in 1911–1949 were revolutions against traditional monarchies or imperial states. These were premodern states dominated by traditional elites, and their revolutions drew heavily on revolts by rural peasants. However, the twentieth century has seen a different kind of revolution—revolutions against modern dictatorships. In Mexico in 1911, in Cuba in 1959, in Nicaragua and Iran in 1979, and in the Philippines in 1986, dictators who ruled semimodern states, led by modernized bureaucracies and armies instead of traditional landed elites, were overthrown. Although peasants played a significant role in several of these revolutions, a greater role was played by urban groups—both workers and modern professionals.[1] Indeed, in Iran and the Philippines, urban groups were solely responsible for the revolutions. These new kinds of revolutions call for new explanations: What were the vulnerabilities of these states that led to the overthrow of seemingly all-powerful dictators?

Revolutions occurred in traditional monarchies and imperial states, such as France, Russia, and China, when those states faced either overwhelming foreign pressures, as Russia did in World War I, or moderate foreign pressures combined with paralyzing opposition to needed economic and administrative change from traditional elites. Failure to cope with war or paralysis due to the opposition of traditional elites opened the way for popular revolts that undermined the old regime. Modernizing elites drawn from urban professional and middle-class groups completed the dismantling of old regime institutions and sought to restructure state and society on a more modern basis.

Foreign pressures, conflict with elites, and popular revolts have all combined in bringing about recent revolutions, and we shall return to many of these themes. However, one key lesson of comparative studies is that the vulnerability of states to revolutions differs among states with different institutions. Thus we need to consider how contemporary states differ from traditional monarchies and imperial states, and why modern dictatorships have been vulnerable to revolution.

Contemporary states generally have governments in which the chief executive's and other officials' rule are based on some form of constitutional and parliamentary political arrangements rather than simply hereditary authority, and in which traditional landed elites have no institutionalized roles in administration. Instead, the chief executive's role is organized through political party mechanisms and sanctioned through a combination of electoral, bureaucratic, and military rule.

Some contemporary states seem to show such modern party-based governments, but in fact these governments are so strongly manipulated by a single, powerful individual that they are, in practice, dictatorships. Among such states, the United States has often sought regional allies based on personal relationships with strong leaders, such as the Somozas in Nicaragua or the Shah in Iran. However, these states have characteristics that make them vulnerable to revolution. To understand the processes that can lead such states to revolution, we need to examine the structure and the weaknesses of these states.

The Neopatrimonial State and Its Vulnerabilities

S. N. Eisenstadt (1978) has described as "neopatrimonial" those partially modernized states in which there appears to be modern bureaucratic and party-based government, but in fact a single powerful person rules society through an extensive system of personal patronage, rather than obedience to impersonal laws. Such states may have democratic trappings, including parliaments and political parties, constitutions and elections. However, it is recognized by all that the decisions of the chief of state are quite secure, as the patronage system, plus coercion where necessary, secures the compliance of the legislature and the political parties, the favorable interpretation of the constitution, and electoral victories. Examples include Mexico under Porfirio Díaz, Nicaragua under the Somozas, the Philippines under Ferdinand Marcos, and Iran under the Shah.

In such states, the masses are generally depoliticized. They may participate in periodic elections under the eye of local state servants; however, their interest in the economy and the polity is largely defensive. Their goal is merely to preserve their livelihood, with as little contact with the state authorities as possible. Whether in urban or rural settings, a secure if modest income and traditional habitations and culture are their requisites.

The elites in such states, by contrast, are highly politicized. The chief executive therefore is in a situation where he or she must broker among highly active elite segments. These commonly include traditional oligarchs, new professionals, and military/bureaucratic elites. Traditional oligarchs are generally strong supporters of the state; they usually depend on ownership of land, and while they have traditionally enjoyed the support of the state, they have also controlled their own networks of patronage and coercion. New professionals are the product of the introduction of modern systems of education, law, medicine, and communication. Engineers, journalists, lawyers, doctors, teachers, and business people, they are characteristically rooted in urban settings, and have strong contacts with international business and culture. If one adds skilled workers to these groups, they constitute the bulk of the urban middle classes.

The military/bureaucratic elites comprise the arms of the state. However, they are a force unto themselves with their own interests. They may support the old oligarchs, the new professionals, or the chief executive in the event of policy or financial conflicts. Or they may be rendered impotent by internal splits and corruption. Their loyalty to the chief executive varies, for that loyalty too depends on the workings of the patronage system. In short, neopatrimonial states rely on the support of a diverse assemblage of elites, themselves often divided, to maintain authority over a largely depoliticized population.

This kind of state has varied vulnerabilities. First, since it relies chiefly on elite support, rather than on mass support, alienation of too many segments of the elite can be fatal. Second, since the elites themselves are divided, the chief executive must perform a complex balancing act to preserve the alliance of diverse elites while fending off their intra-elite conflicts. Third, since the population is depoliticized, the state can be threatened by mass-mobilizing movements that place new forces in the political arena. Thus, the defection of elites, plus the willingness of elites to mobilize masses against the state, can leave the chief executive with few defenses other than sheer armed force, whose loyalty itself is never assured.

How does the chief executive maintain authority, indeed an authority that seems near-absolute, in such precarious conditions? The typical strategy is a mix of divide and conquer, carrot and stick, and indispensability approaches.

In neopatrimonial states, the chief executive generally faces elites with divided goals. Rather than attempt to unify them, the executive generally chooses to reinforce their divisions. The armed forces, political parties, urban professionals, landed oligarchs, and state bureaucrats are each encouraged to form direct, competing links to the chief executive's patronage network. The armed forces, political party leaders, and state officials may be encouraged to share in corruption or in secret deals and partnerships in order to isolate them from other groups. As a result, different elite segments find themselves in competition for the ear of, and the official power and financial advantages conferred by, the chief executive. The chief executive then becomes the crucial broker of power in the society, its sole political "center." The divisions among the elites make reliance on the chief executive essential for political coordination and conflict management.

Of course, the ability of the executive to manage such conflict and provide central coordination depends on the ability to dispense resources valued by the elite, chiefly money and political power. Thus chief executives seek to implement policies for rapid economic growth, or for massive infusions of foreign aid. Such growth enriches the executive, of course, but it also provides the essential fuel to power political machinery.

Contemporary neopatrimonial states usually seek to turn economic growth to modernization of the armed forces, growth of enterprises requiring professional and skilled workers, and growth of the state bureaucracy. This gives the executive the ability to dispense the carrots of military and bureaucratic posts, and economic contracts that will profit the elite. In addition, securing the loyalty of the landed elite generally requires that land reforms be kept moderate. Depoliticization of the masses is also served by economic growth sufficient to allow growing populations to sustain themselves at traditionally accustomed levels of food, clothing, and shelter.

Policies for promotion of economic growth are coupled with the stick—the threat of loss of wealth, position, liberty, or life for opposing the chief executive. Potential opposition leaders are often jailed or exiled, political freedoms (including freedom of speech) are limited, and even loyal aides whose accomplishments or influence threaten to make them alternative leaders may be promptly disposed of.

In addition to these strategies, the chief executive seeks to increase his or her "indispensability" by monopolizing key contact points in the society. The chief executive may be the only contact between the military and the civilian elites. The executive (and his or her close associates) may monopolize contact with foreign nations, seeking to become the indispensable conduit for foreign aid and investment. The chief executive generally seeks to avoid appointing, or even favoring, possible successors. Thus, the executive seeks to reinforce the fear that, if he or she is lost, political coordination, conflict management, and the flow of foreign resources will fail, leading to chaos.

These are potent strategies. Provided that economic growth provides resources, a politically adept chief executive, by skillful manipulation of elite aspirations and rewards, forging of strong ties to foreign resources, and limited coercion, can achieve and maintain a substantial concentration of power. The Shah of Iran, the Somozas in Nicaragua, the Diem regime in South Vietnam, Marcos in the Philippines, Fulgencio Batista in Cuba, Chiang Kai-shek in China, and Díaz in Mexico are examples of chief executives who typify this pattern.

Pressures and Problems in Neopatrimonial States

Despite the success of neopatrimonial executives, their vulnerabilities do not disappear; indeed, they may increase over time.

First, as economic growth continues, the ability of the executive to broker the conflicting demands of the elites becomes more difficult. As foreign investment grows, domestic urban and professional elites may seek greater domestic control of the economy. Nationalism then becomes a potent ideology among a segment of the elites. The executive must thus balance increased reliance on foreign aid and foreign investment, which increases the resources that the executive controls but requires satisfaction of foreign investors and states, against satisfying the demands of domestic professional and economic elites for national self-determination.

Second, as urbanization and industry grow, the urban and professional elite and skilled workers may seek a domestic economy more geared to satisfaction of domestic consumption than to export growth and luxury imports. Yet establishing light industry and a domestic consumer market requires improving the education and economic status of the populace, including the peasantry. This goal can come into conflict with the desires of the landed oligarchy to maintain their control of land and the rural labor force.

Third, as the state bureaucracy expands, it eventually comes into conflict with traditional organizations, including guilds, local village councils, and religious organizations. Where the state is successful in absorbing or circumventing the influence of these bodies, state power may increase. Yet this is difficult where the autonomy of these organizations is well established, and the traditional organizations control considerable resources and cultural authority. Conflicts between state and church may arise over secularization of economic life, over control of popular education and local justice, over disposal of church resources, and over cultural and ideological hegemony. Any of these conflicts can spur religious elites to seek alliances with other elite segments against the state, or to support popular mobilization against the state, as happened in Iran.

Fourth, the temptation to monopolize resources may become a self-defeating one. If the chief executive concentrates power and the proceeds of corruption too closely in the hands of family and cronies, the flow of carrots to diverse elite segments diminishes. Where elites find themselves excluded from their traditional, albeit limited, share in government and wealth, dependency on the chief executive quickly turns to animosity. Overuse of the stick and restriction of carrots is one of the most common errors of neopatrimonial executives over the course of their rule.

Fifth, a temptation to rely too heavily on foreign support may become fatal. Foreign support, whether in terms of financial aid through grants and foreign investment, or military aid, is highly attractive to neopatrimonial executives. It is a source of economic and political resources and, most importantly, a source over which the chief executive can establish exclusive control. As it becomes more difficult to satisfy conflicting demands and aspirations, and since there is no mass popular base to counterbalance the elites, there is a temptation to rely increasingly on foreign support. Yet this can further alienate the elites by frustrating their nationalist ambitions, and leaves the executive in a highly extended and vulnerable position if foreign support should fall.

Finally, the economic growth that fuels the patronage machine may falter. Growth may also fail to trickle down to the masses, or population increase may outrun economic growth, resulting in growing inequality and failure to meet traditional popular aspirations for diet, habitation, and family life.

If several of these problems develop at the same time, this combination of pressures can cause a patrimonial regime to unravel with astonishing rapidity. Economic setbacks and overuse of coercion may begin a trend of elite defection and attempts at mobilizing the masses against the state. Overdependence on foreign support may leave the chief executive isolated and vulnerable to nationalist movements. Finally, if elites overcome their divisions to unite against the executive, and if the loyalty of the army should falter or be pressed by widespread popular mobilization against the regime in urban or rural revolts, revolution becomes nearly inevitable. This course of events unfolded in the Mexican, Cuban, Nicaraguan, Philippine, and Iranian revolutions.

The very indispensability of the chief executive works against a smooth transfer of power to another leader, and against maintenance of existing institutions. These are too deeply identified with the chief executive's system of personal rule to survive his or her fall from power. For example, the solution of "Somozism without Somoza" in Nicaragua, or of a new minister (Bahktiar) at the head of the Shah's state in Iran, had little appeal to elites seeking to establish their autonomy, reverse their exclusion from control of the state, and satisfy the aspirations of their now-mobilized popular supporters. Once the chief executive has lost elite support, and the masses are mobilized against him or her, the result is almost certain to be transformation of state institutions and unpredictable turns in policy and economic organization as elite segments vie for state control, court popular support, and seek to reconstruct state institutions.

The Role of International Superpowers in Modern Revolutions

International pressures have always been an important factor in the development of revolutionary crises. Such pressures have become even more important in the contemporary world, as international superpowers—the United States and the Soviet Union—have sought to support or undermine regimes in developing states in pursuit of geopolitical strategy. Yet U.S. efforts to support regional allies in Vietnam, Nicaragua, Iran, and the Philippines have been overturned by revolutions. In light of U.S. support for these fallen regimes, we need to ask: How did U.S. policy exacerbate the vulnerability of neopatrimonial states? And what effect did U.S. actions have once a revolution had begun?

U.S. policy eventually weakened neopatrimonial regimes in three ways. First, over-dependence on the United States was encouraged. A massive flow of foreign and military aid often precluded the need for a foreign executive to build a domestic base. Instead, the resource flow encouraged the executive to continue to play the game of selectively dispensing or withholding patronage resources.

Second, overidentification of the chief executive with U.S. aid irritated elites and provoked nationalist opposition to the regime. In the eyes of many elites and popular groups, opposition to the chief executive became synonymous with opposition to the United States and with asserting national self-determination.

Third, while the United States sought to increase the dependence of the chief executive on U.S. aid, it also sought to impose domestic policies that weakened the executive— limits on coercion, greater political expression for professional elites and skilled workers, meaningful elections, and restrictions on corruption. All of these are desirable steps in the democratization of regimes; however, these steps also undermine the power of dictatorship. U.S. policy thus sought inherently contradictory objectives; choosing neopatrimonial rulers as allies and seeking to support their regimes meant that the overriding goal of U.S. foreign policy—encouraging democratization—was incompatible with keeping these geopolitical allies, for democratization would undermine the rulers that the United States claimed to support.

U.S. policy thus swung back and forth between its contradictory goals. Initially, the United States would support the neopatrimonial rulers with arms and money, while giving only lip service to the goals of greater human rights, political freedom, and democratization in these states. Later, when the ruler's abuses of power became too visible, the United States would demand that neopatrimonial rulers take action to pursue democratization. These policy swings precipitated disasters by putting neopatrimonial rulers in an impossible position—if they enacted liberalizing reforms, they undermined the basis of their rule; if they did not enact such reforms, they lost the U.S. aid essential to maintaining the patronage that supported their rule.

Moreover, such policy swings not only guaranteed that the neopatrimonial rulers would falter, but they also reduced the credibility and influence of the United States with opponents and likely successors of the regime. In times when the United States seemed satisfied with lip service regarding protection of human rights and democratization, the United States came to be viewed by domestic elites and popular groups as an insincere and untrustworthy advocate of popular rights and national self-determination. Thus, in the event that the executive faltered, successor elites were unlikely to view the United States favorably, either as a mediator for succession or as a continuing ally.

Exactly this course was followed in Iran and Nicaragua in the late 1970s. After decades of almost unconditional support of the Shah and the Somoza family, during which time the privileges of domestic elites were gradually curtailed and the chief executive was aggrandized through manipulation of growing foreign investment and aid, the United States began to insist on a human rights policy that undermined the neopatrimonial patterns of rule. The result was greater room to maneuver for the domestic opposition to the Shah in Iran, and to Somoza in Nicaragua. Yet the Shah and Somoza sought to enact only limited reforms, to change as little as possible while still satisfying the United States. Continued support for the Shah and for Somoza thus brought policy debacles: The domestic elites perceived the United States as hypocritically supporting reforms that changed little, and maintaining support for a repressive regime; yet the atmosphere of reform and U.S. pressure hindered the chief executives while emboldening the oppositions in their quest for change. The increased vigor of the oppositions, and the ambiguous, shifting support for the rulers, initiated an escalation of opposition that culminated in 1979 in revolutions in both Iran and Nicaragua. Both revolutions brought to power elites who were hostile to the United States and who sought to realign the foreign policy of what had been a steadfast ally. Even in the Philippines, where a similar pattern of support for Marcos' neopatrimonial regime had been changed more dramatically (although at the last moment), to support for the democratic opposition, the credibility of the United States had been so damaged by its former support for Marcos that nationalist and anti–United States feelings remained strong. As a result, the United States lost the use of major military installations in the Philippines, and is still viewed with suspicion by the shifting set of elites who have replaced the Marcos regime.

Conclusion

Modern personalist dictatorships, which are structured as neopatrimonial regimes, can appear very strong in the short term. When they can keep elites divided, use patronage to keep key elites and the military loyal, and keep the population depoliticized, neopatrimonial rulers can maintain their regimes for decades. But they are vulnerable on several points. First, the regime has a precarious dominance over diverse elites; elite loyalty can quickly be withdrawn if the regime fails to provide the rewards the elites have come to expect. Second, lacking its own mass base, the regime is highly vulnerable to mass mobilization by domestic elites in opposition to the regime. Moreover, many trends in early economic development—growing inequality; failure of popular income to provide traditional levels of food, habitation, and family lifestyles; the growth of urban professional and skilled workers; dependence on exports subject to cycles of boom and bust; international debt; and inflation—are precisely those that encourage mass mobilization. Third, superpower influence can be beneficial in limited amounts, but also can be pernicious and threatening to national self-determination in large amounts. Indeed, superpower influence can be fatal to neopatrimonial regimes when superpower policy swings between contradictory goals, undermining the basis for such regimes.

All of these vulnerabilities can rapidly appear once a neopatrimonial regime starts to lose its control of economic resources or foreign support. Thus, the same dictatorships that appeared so strong can quickly become the site of modern revolutions.

REFERENCE

1.   The special characteristics of revolutions in modern dictatorships have been pointed out by Dix (1983), Farhi (1990), Gugler (1982), Liu (1988), and Shugart (1989).

PART TWO

Comparative and Historical Studies of Revolutions

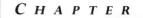

The Origins of Revolutions

The following readings examine the origins of revolutions from early modern Europe (in England and France) to Latin America (Mexico and Nicaragua) and the Middle East (Iran). The revolutionary struggles begun in 1989 in Eastern Europe and China are also discussed.

All these authors have a common message: Understanding revolutions requires going beyond a study of the general problems of poverty, injustice, or modernization. Rather, we must pay close attention to the social structure in various countries; examine the roles that the state, elites, and popular groups play; and analyze the relationships among them.

FRANCE, RUSSIA, CHINA: A STRUCTURAL ANALYSIS OF SOCIAL REVOLUTIONS

Theda Skocpol

Skocpol uses a structural analysis to probe the origins of three major social revolutions. She notes that modernization is not only a process that occurs within nations; it is also a process of increasing contact and competition among nations. The modernization of the leading western powers—first England, then Europe as a whole—put great military and economic pressures on states around the world. States restricted in their ability to raise resources for improving their economic and technological position were poorly equipped to meet that challenge. Restrictions might include the presence of powerful elites whose tax exemptions and other privileges kept resources beyond the reach of the state (such as the French nobility before 1789 and the Chinese gentry before 1911) or a technically backward and unproductive agricultural system (as in Russia before 1917). State weaknesses could then lead to fiscal crises or military defeats. Such political crises, not mere popular discontent or the actions of a revolutionary opposition, triggered revolutionary situations.

Such weakened states with large numbers of peasants who could readily organize to revolt against landlords contained the seeds for social revolutions that destroyed the power of the traditional landowning aristocracy. Peasant organization could arise from traditional peasant communities if they were relatively free from direct supervision by landlords, as in France or Russia, or from the efforts of revolutionary parties, as in China. In either case, the weakness of the state, combined with the organization of peasant groups, rendered society vulnerable to upheavals from below.

Still, peasants by themselves did not make revolutions; "marginal elites" also played a crucial role. These individuals had the training of social leaders. They were university students, teachers, journalists, lawyers, and civil servants—but lack of proper family background or connections or state policies that excluded certain groups from government kept them from leading social positions or important roles in government. These marginal elites capitalized on the opportunity a weakened state and peasant revolts provided to seize political power. The replacement of former ruling elites by previously marginal elites constituted the climactic phase of the revolution.

"A revolution," writes Samuel P. Huntington in *Political Order in Changing Societies*, "is a rapid, fundamental, and violent domestic change in the dominant values and myths of a society, in its political institutions, social structure, leadership, and government activities and policies." In *The Two Tactics of Social Democracy in the Democratic Revolution*, Lenin provides a different, but complementary perspective: "Revolutions," he says, "are the festivals of the oppressed and the exploited. At no other time are the masses of the people in a position to come forward so actively as creators of a new social order."

Together these two quotes delineate the distinctive features of *social revolutions*. As Huntington points out, social revolutions are rapid, basic transformations of socio-economic and political institutions, and—as Lenin so vividly reminds us—social revolutions are accompanied and in part effectuated through class upheavals from below. It is this combination of thoroughgoing structural transformation and massive class upheavals that sets social revolutions apart from coups, rebellions, and even political revolutions and national independence movements.

If one adopts such a specific definition, then clearly only a handful of successful social revolutions have ever occurred. France, 1789, Russia, 1917, and China, 1911–49, are the most dramatic and clear-cut instances. Yet these momentous upheavals have helped shape the fate of the majority of mankind, and their causes, consequences, and potentials have preoccupied many thoughtful people since the late eighteenth century.

Explaining the Historical Cases: Revolution in Modernizing Agrarian Bureaucracies

Social revolutions in France, Russia and China occurred during the earlier world-historical phases of modernization in agrarian bureaucratic societies situated within, or newly incorporated into, international fields dominated by more economically modern nations abroad. In each case, social revolution was a conjuncture of three developments: (1) the collapse or incapacitation of central administrative and military machineries; (2) widespread peasant rebellions; and (3) marginal elite political movements. What each social revolution minimally "accomplished" was the extreme rationalization and centralization of state institutions, the removal of a traditional landed upper class from intermediate (regional and local) quasi-political supervision of the peasantry, and the elimination or diminution of the economic power of a landed upper class.

In the pages that follow, I shall attempt to explain the three great historical social revolutions, first, by discussing the institutional characteristics of agrarian states, and their special vulnerabilities and potentialities during the earlier world-historical phases of modernization, and second, by pointing to the peculiar characteristics of old regimes in France, Russia, and China, which made them uniquely vulnerable among the earlier modernizing agrarian states to social-revolutionary transformations.

An agrarian bureaucracy is an agricultural society in which social control rests on a division of labor and a coordination of effort between a semi-bureaucratic state and a landed upper class. Clear-cut instances were China, Russia, France, Prussia, Austria, Spain, Japan, and Turkey. The landed upper class typically retains, as an adjunct to its landed property, considerable (though varying in different cases) local and regional authority over the peasant majority of the population. The partially bureaucratic central state extracts taxes and labor from peasants either indirectly through landlord intermediaries or else directly, but with at least minimal reliance upon cooperation from individuals of the landed upper class. In turn, the landed upper class relies upon the backing of a coercive state to extract rents and/or dues from the peasantry. At the political center, autocrat, bureaucracy, and army monopolize decisions, yet (in varying degrees and modes) they accommodate the regional and local power of the landed upper class and (again, to varying degrees) recruit individual members of this class into leading positions in the state system.

Agrarian bureaucracies are inherently vulnerable to peasant rebellions. Subject to claims on their surpluses, and perhaps their labor, by landlords and state agents, peasants chronically resent both. To the extent that the agrarian economy is commercialized, merchants are also targets of peasant hostility. In all agrarian bureaucracies at all times, and in France, Russia and China in non-revolutionary times, peasants have had grievances enough to warrant, and recurrently spur, rebellions. Economic crises (which are endemic in semi-commercial agrarian economies anyway) and/or increased demands from above for rents or taxes might substantially enhance the likelihood of rebellions at particular times. But such events ought to be treated as short-term precipitants of peasant unrest, not fundamental underlying causes.

Agrarian bureaucracies faced new challenges from the rapid modernization of the world economy that began in the eighteenth century. Modernization is best conceived not only as an *intra*social process of economic development, but also as a world-historic *inter*-societal phenomenon. Thus,

> a necessary condition of a society's modernization is its incorporation into the historically
> unique network of societies that arose first in Western Europe in early modern times and

today encompasses enough of the globe's population for the world to be viewed for some purposes as if it consisted of a single network of societies.[1]

In the first phase of world modernization, England's thoroughgoing commercialization, capture of world markets, and expansion of manufactures (both before and after the technological Industrial Revolution which began in the 1780s), put immediate pressure for reforms, if only to facilitate the financing of competitive armies and navies, upon the other European states and especially upon the ones with less efficient fiscal machineries. In the second phase, as Europe modernized and further expanded its influence around the globe, similar militarily compelling pressures were brought to bear on those non-European societies which escaped immediate colonization, usually the ones with pre-existing centralized state institutions.

But agrarian bureaucracies faced enormous difficulties in meeting the challenge of modernization. Governmental leaders' realm of autonomous action tended to be severely limited, because few fiscal or economic reforms could be undertaken which did not encroach upon the advantages of the traditional landed upper classes which constituted the major social base of support for the authority and functions of the state in agrarian bureaucracies. Only so much revenue could be squeezed out of the peasantry, and yet landed upper classes could often raise formidable obstacles to rationalization of tax systems. Economic development might mean more tax revenues and enhanced military prowess, yet it channelled wealth and manpower away from the agrarian sector. Finally, the mobilization of mass popular support for war tended to undermine the traditional local authority of landlords or landed bureaucrats upon which agrarian bureaucratic societies partly relied for the social control of the peasantry.

Agrarian bureaucracies could not indefinitely "ignore" the fiscal and military crises that grew out of involvement with a modernizing world, yet they could not adapt without undergoing fundamental structural changes. Social revolution helped accomplish "necessary" changes in some but was averted by reform or "revolution from above" in others. Relative stagnation, accompanied by sub-incorporation into international power spheres, was still another possibility (e.g., Portugal, Spain?). Social revolution was never deliberately "chosen." Societies only "backed into" social revolutions.

All modernizing agrarian bureaucracies have peasants with grievances and face the unavoidable challenges posed by modernization abroad. So, in some sense, potential for social revolution has been built into all modernizing agrarian bureaucracies. Yet, only a handful have succumbed. Why? A major part of the answer, I believe, lies in the insight that "not oppression, but weakness, breeds revolution."[2] It is the breakdown of social control which allows and prompts social revolution to unfold. In the historical cases of France, Russia and China, the unfolding of social revolution depended upon the emergence of revolutionary crises occasioned by the incapacitation of administrative and military organizations. That incapacitation, in turn, is best explained not as a function of mass discontent and mobilization, but as a function of a combination of pressures on state institutions from more modernized countries abroad, and (in two cases out of three) built-in structural incapacities to mobilize increased resources in response to those pressures.

France, Russia and China were also special among all agrarian bureaucracies in that their agrarian institutions afforded peasants not only the usual grievances against landlords and state agents but also "structural space" for autonomous collective insurrection. Finally, once administrative/military breakdown occurred in agrarian bureaucracies with such especially insurrection-prone peasantries, then, and only then, could organized revolutionary leaderships have great impact upon their societies' development—though not necessarily in the ways they originally envisaged.

Breakdown of Societal Controls: Foreign Pressures and Administrative/Military Collapse

If a fundamental cause and the crucial trigger for the historical social revolutions was the incapacitation of administrative and military machineries in modernizing agrarian bureaucracies, then how and why did this occur in France, Russia and China? What differentiated these agrarian bureaucracies which succumbed to social revolution from others which managed to respond to modernizing pressures with reforms from above? Many writers attribute differences in response to qualities of will or ability in governmental leaders. From a sociological point of view, a more satisfying approach might focus on the interaction between (a) the magnitude of foreign pressures brought to bear on a modernizing agrarian bureaucracy, and (b) the particular strutural characteristics of such societies that underlay contrasting performances by leaders responding to foreign pressures and internal unrest.

Overwhelming foreign pressures on an agrarian bureaucracy could cut short even a generally successful government program of reforms and industrialization "from above." Russia is the obvious case in point. Had she been able to sit out World War I, Russia might have recapitulated the German experience of industrialization facilitated by bureaucratic guidance. But participation in World War I forced Russia to fully mobilize her population, including her restive peasantry. Army officers and men were subjected to years of costly fighting, and civilians to mounting economic privations—all for nought. For, given Russia's "industrial backwardness . . .", plus the "inferiority of the Russian military machine to the German in everything but sheer numbers . . . , military defeat, with all of its inevitable consquences for the internal conditions of the country, was very nearly a foregone conclusion."[3] The result was adminstrative demoralization and paralysis, and the disintegration of the army. Urban insurrections which brought first middle-strata moderates and then the Bolsheviks to power could not be suppressed, owing to the newly-recruited character and war weariness of the urban garrisons. Peasant grievances were enhanced, young peasant men were politicized through military experiences, and, in consequence, spreading peasant insurrections from the spring of 1917 on could not be controlled.

The Russian Revolution occurred in 1917 because Russia was too inextricably entangled with foreign powers, friend and foe, economically and militarily more powerful than she. Foreign entanglement must be considered not only to explain the administrative and military incapacitation of 1917, but also entry into World War I. That involvement cannot be considered "accidental." Whatever leadership "blunders" were involved, the fact remains that in 1914 both the Russian state and the Russian economy depended heavily on West European loans and capital. Moreover, Russia was an established part of the European state system and could not remain neutral in a conflict that engulfed the whole of that system.

Foreign pressures and involvements so inescapable and overwhelming as those that faced Russia in 1917 constitue an extreme case for the earlier modernizing agrarian bureaucracies we are considering here. For France and China the pressures were surely no more compelling than those faced by agrarian bureaucracies such as Japan, Germany and Russia (1858–1914), which successfully adapted through reforms from above that facilitated the extraordinary mobilization of resources for economic and military development. Why were the Bourbon and Manchu regimes unable to adapt? Were there structural blocks to effective response? First, let me discuss some general characteristics of all agrarian states, and then point to a peculiar structural characteristic shared by Bourbon France and Manchu China which I believe explains these regimes' inability to meet snow-balling crises of modernization until at last their feeble attempts triggered administrative and military disintegration, hence revolutionary crises.

Inherent in all agrarian bureaucratic regimes were tensions between, on the one hand, state elites interested in preserving, using, and extending the powers of armies and administrative organizations and, on the other hand, landed upper classes interested in defending locally and regionally based social networks, influence over peasants, and powers and privileges associated with the control of land and agrarian surpluses. Such tensions were likely to be exacerbated once the agrarian bureaucracy was forced to adapt to modernization abroad because foreign military pressures gave cause, while foreign economic development offered incentives and models, for state elites to attempt reforms which went counter to the class interests of traditional, landed upper strata. Yet there were important variations in the ability of semi-bureaucratic agrarian states to respond to modernizing pressures with reforms which sharply and quickly increased resources at the disposal of central authorities. What can account for the differences in response?

Leaving aside value-orientations and individual characteristics, we must look at the class interests and connections of state officials. *The adaptiveness of the earlier modernizing agrarian bureaucracies was significantly determined by the degree to which the upper and middle ranks of the state administrative bureaucracies were staffed by large landholders.* Only state machineries significantly differentiated from traditional landed upper classes could undertake modernizing reforms which almost invariably had to encroach upon the property or privileges of the landed upper class.

Thus, in an analysis of what she calls "elite revolutions" in Japan (1863) and Turkey (1919), Ellen Kay Trimberger argues that segments of the traditional leaderships of those agrarian bureaucracies were able to respond so effectively to intrusions by more modern powers only because "the Japanese and Turkish ruling elites were political bureaucrats without vested economic interests. . . ."[4] But where—as in Bourbon France and late Manchu China—regionally-based cliques of landed magnates were ensconced within nominally centralized administrative systems, the ability of the state elites to control the flow of tax resources and implement reform policies was decisively undermined. By their *resistance* to the mobilization of increased resources for military or economic purposes in modernization crises, such landed cliques of officials could engender situations of acute administrative/military disorganization—potentially revolutionary crises of governmental authority.

The French monarchy struggled on three fronts throughout the eighteenth century. Within the European state system, France's "amphibious geography" forced her to compete simultaneously with the great continental land powers, Austria and (after mid-century) Prussia, and with the maritime powers, above all, Britain. Britain's accelerating commercial and industrial development put France at an ever increasing disadvantage in trade and naval strength. And the French monarchy had to fight on a "third front" at home—against the resistance of its own privileged strata to rationalization of the tax system.

The French administrative system in the eighteenth century afforded landlords (and wealth-holders generally) strategic points of institutional leverage for obstructing royal policies.

> A substantial number of the [nobility] was obviously still trying to live in terms of the old feudal structure that had lost its functional justification at least two centuries before . . . [T]he residue is not hard to identify or describe. Characteristically it was composed of the larger landowners, but not the princes of the realm nor even the constant residents at Versailles. The latter had obviously, if not necessarily willingly, cast their lot with the King. Similarly, many of the lesser nobles had, whether from ambition or necessity, taken service in the army or, occasionally, in the administration. The remaining survivors of the old feudal classes, however, tended to live on their properties in the provinces, serve and subvert the local bureaucracy, seek preferment in the Church, and find expression and defense of their interests through the provincial estates and *parlements*.[5]

The *parlements*, or sovereign courts, nominally a part of the administrative system, were the most avid and strategically located of the institutional defenders of property and privilege. For the French monarchy had sold its key judicial offices to raise cash. Thus, "the monarch was almost completely powerless in the face of his judges, whom he could not dismiss, transfer, or promote."[6]

Magistrates of the *parlements* varied markedly in the length of their noble pedigrees, but virtually all were men of considerable wealth, ". . . for their fortunes included not only their offices, in themselves representing large investments, but also a formidable accumulation of securities, urban property, and rural seigneuries."[7] Not surprisingly, given their property interests and extensive connections with non-magisterial propertied families, the *parlementaires* were avid defenders of the rights and privileges of the upper classes in general. By their dogged defense of tax and property systems increasingly inadequate to the needs of the French state in a modernizing world, the *parlements* throughout the eighteenth century repeatedly blocked attempts at reform.

France fought at sea and on land in each of the general European wars of the eighteenth century: the War of the Austrian Succession; the Seven Years War; the war over American Independence. In each conflict, her resources were strained to the utmost and her vital colonial trade disrupted, yet no gains, indeed losses in America and India, resulted. The

War for American Independence proved to be the last straw. "[T]he price to be paid for American Independence was a French Revolution:"[8] royal treasurers finally exhausted their capacity to raise loans from financiers and were forced (again) to propose reforms of the tax system. The usual resistance from the *parlements* ensured, and an expedient adopted in an attempt to circumvent it—the summoning of an Assembly of Notables in 1787— only provided privileged interests yet another platform for voicing resistance. A last-ditch effort to override the *parlements* crumbled in the face of concerted upper-class defiance, popular demonstrations, and the unwillingness of army officers to direct forcible suppression of the popular resistance.

The army's hesitance was especially crucial in translating fiscal crises and political unrest into general administrative and military breakdown. Recruited from various priv- ileged social backgrounds—rich noble, rich non-noble, and poor country noble—the officers had a variety of longstanding grievances against other officers and, significantly, against the Crown, which could never satisfy them all. But it is likely that the decisive explanation for their behavior lies in the fact that they were virtually all privileged, socially and/or economically, and hence identified during 1787–88 with the *parlements*. In her *Armies and the Art of Revolution*, Katharine Chorley concludes from comparative historical studies that, in preindustrial societies, army officers generally identify with and act to protect the interests of the privileged strata from which they are recruited.[9] During its opening phases, until after the King had capitulated and agreed to convene the Estates General, the French Revolution pitted all strata, led by the privileged, against the Crown. The army officers' understandable reluctance to repress popular unrest during that period created a general crisis of governmental authority and effectiveness which in turn unleashed social divisions, between noble and non-noble, rich and poor, that made a subsequent resort to simple repression by the Old Regime impossible.

The officers' insubordination early in the Revolution was all the more easily translated into rank-and-file insubordination in 1789 and after, because of the fact that French soldiers were not normally insulated from the civilian population. Soldiers were billeted with civilians, and those from rural areas were released during the summers to help with the harvest at home. Thus, during 1789, the *Gardes Francaises* (many of whom were married to Parisian working-class women) were won over to the Paris revolution in July, and peasant soldiers spread urban news in the countryside during the summer and returned to their units in the autumn with vivid tales of peasant revolt.

Like the Bourbon Monarchy, the Manchu Dynasty proved unable to mobilize resources sufficient to meet credibly the challenges posed by involvement in the modernizing world. Part of the explanation for this inability lay in a characteristic which the Chinese state shared with other agrarian states: lower and middle level officials were recruited from the landed gentry, paid insufficient salaries, and allowed to engage in a certain amount of "normal" corruption, witholding revenues collected as taxes from higher authorities. Yet, if the Manchu Dynasty had encountered the forces of modernization at the height of its powers (say in the early eighteenth century) rather than during its declining phase, it might have controlled or been able to mobilize sufficient resources to finance modern industries and equip a centrally controlled modern army. But, as it happened, the Manchu Dynasty was forced to try to cope with wave after wave of imperialist intrusions, engineered by foreign industrial or industrializing nations anxious to tap Chinese markets and finances, immediately after a series of massive mid-nineteenth-century peasant rebellions. The Dynasty had been unable to put down the Taiping Rebellion on its own, and the task had fallen instead to local, gentry-led, self-defense associations and to regional armies led by complexly interrelated gentry who had access to village resources and recruits. In consequence of the gentry's role in putting down rebellion, governmental powers formerly accruing to central authorities or their bureaucratic agents, including, crucially, rights to collect and allocate various taxes, devolved upon local, gentry-dominated, sub-district governing associations and upon provincial armies and officials increasingly aligned with the provincial gentry against the center.

Unable to force resources from local and regional authorities, it was all Peking could do simply to meet foreign indebtedness, and after 1895 even that proved impossible.

> Throughout the period from 1874 to 1894, the ministry [of Revenue in Peking] was engaged in a series of largely unsuccessful efforts to raise funds in order to meet a continuing series of crises—the dispute over Ili with Russia, the Sino-French war [1885], floods and famines, the Sino-Japanese War [1895]. . . . After 1895 the triple pressure of indemnity payments, servicing foreign loans, and military expenditures totally wrecked the rough balance between income and outlay which Peking had maintained [with the aid of foreign loans] until that time.[10]

The Boxer Rebellion of 1900, and subsequent foreign military intervention, only further exacerbated an already desperate situation.

Attempts by dynastic authorities to remedy matters through a series of "reforms" implemented after 1900—abolishing the Confucian educational system and encouraging modern schools; organizing the so-called "New Armies" (which actually formed around the nuclei of the old provincial armies); transferring local governmental functions to provincial bureaus; and creating a series of local and provincial gentry-dominated representative assemblies—only exacerbated the sorry situation, right up to the 1911 breaking point. "Reform destroyed the reforming government."[11] The last series of reforms, those that created representative assemblies, ironically provided cliques of gentry with legitimate representative organs from which to launch the liberal, decentralizing "Constitutionalist movement" against the Manchus.

What ultimately precipitated the "revolution of 1911" was a final attempt at reform by the central government, one that directly threatened the financial interests of the gentry power groups for the purpose of strengthening central government finances and control over national economic development:

> The specific incident that precipitated the Revolution of 1911 was the central government's decision to buy up a [railroad] line in Sichuan in which the local gentry had invested heavily. . . . The Sichuan uprising, led by the moderate constitutionalists of the Railway Protection

League, sparked widespread disturbances that often had no connection with the railway issue. . . .[12]

Conspiratorial groups mainly composed of Western-educated students and middle-rank New Army Officers joined the fray to produce a series of military uprisings. Finally,

> . . . the lead in declaring the independence of one province after another was taken by two principal elements: the military governors who commanded the New Army forces and the gentry-official-merchant leaders of the provincial assemblies.[13]

The Chinese "Revolution of 1911" irremediably destroyed the civilian-elite ties—traditionally maintained by the operation of Confucian educational institutions and the central bureaucracy's policies for recruiting and deploying educated officials so as to strengthen "cosmopolitan" orientations at the expense of local loyalties—which had until that time provided at least the semblance of unified governance for China. "Warlord" rivalries ensued as gentry interests attached themselves to regional military machines, and this condition of intra-elite disunity and rivalry (only imperfectly and temporarily overcome by Chiang Kai-Shek's regime between 1927 and 1937) condemned China to incessant turmoils and provided openings (as well as causes) for lower-class, especially peasant, rebellions and for Communist attempts to organize and channel popular unrest.

Peasant Insurrections

If administrative and military breakdown in a modernizing agrarian bureaucracy were to inaugurate social revolutionary transformations, rather than merely an interregnum of intra-elite squabbling, then widespread popular revolts had to coincide with and take advantage of the hiatus of governmental supervision and sanctions. Urban insurrections provided indispensable support during revolutionary interregnums to radical political elites vying against other elites for state power: witness the Parisian *sans culottes'* support for the Jacobins; the Chinese workers' support for the Communists (between 1920 and 1927); and the Russian industrial workers' support for the Bolsheviks. But fundamentally more important in determining final outcomes were the peasant insurrections which in France, Russia and China constituted irreversible attacks on the powers and privileges of the traditional landed upper classes.

Agrarian bureaucracy has been the only historical variety of complex society with differentiated, centralized government that has, in certain instances, incubated a lower-class stratum that was *simultaneously strategic* in the society's economy and polity (as payer of rents and taxes, and as provider of corvee and military manpower), and yet *organizationally autonomous* enough to allow the "will" and "tactical space" for collective insurrection against basic structural arrangements.

As Eric Wolf has pointed out, "ultimately, the decisive factor in making a peasant rebellion possible lies in the relation of the peasantry to the field of power which surrounds it. A rebellion cannot start from a situation of complete impotence. . . ."[14] If they are to act upon, rather than silently suffer, their omnipresent grievances, peasants must have "internal leverage" or "tactical mobility." They have this to varying degrees according to their position in the total agrarian social structure. Institutional patterns which relate peasants to landlords and peasants to each other seem to be the co-determinants of degrees of peasant "tactical mobility." Sheer amounts of property held by peasants gain significance only within institutional contexts. If peasants are to be capable of self-initiated rebellion against landlords and state officials, they must have (a) some institutionally based collective solidarity, and (b) autonomy from direct, day-to-day supervision and control by landlords in their work and leisure activities. Agricultural regimes featuring large estates worked by serfs or laborers tend to be inimical to peasant rebellion—witness the East Elbian Junker regime—but the reason is not that serfs and landless laborers are economically poor, rather that they are subject to close and constant supervision and discipline by landlords or their agents. If large-estate agriculture is lacking, an agrarian bureaucracy may still be relatively immune to widespread peasant rebellion if landlords control sanctioning machineries, such as militias and poor relief agencies, at local levels. On the other hand, landlords as a class, and the "system" as a whole, will be relatively vulnerable to peasant rebellion if: (a) sanctioning machineries are centralized; (b) agricultural work and peasant social life are controlled by peasant families and communities themselves. These conditions prevailed in France and Russia and meant that, with the incapacitation of central administrative and military bureaucracies, these societies became susceptible to the spread and intensification of peasant revolts which in more normal circumstances could have been contained and repressed.

It is worth emphasizing that peasant actions in revolutions are not intrinsically different from peasant actions in "mere" rebellions or riots. When peasants "rose" during historical social revolutionary crises, they did so in highly traditional rebellious patterns: bread riots, "defense" of communal lands or customary rights, riots against "hoarding" merchants or landlords, "social banditry." Peasants initially drew upon traditional cultural themes to justify rebellion. Far from becoming revolutionaries through adoption of a radical vision of a desired new society, "revolutionary" peasants have typically been "backward-looking" rebels incorporated by circumstances beyond their control into political processes occurring independently of them, at the societal "center." [See the essay by Eric Wolf in this volume.—Ed.]

In the highly abnormal circumstances of social revolution, administrative breakdown, political rebellions of marginal elites, and peasant insurrections *interacted* to produce transformations that none alone could have occasioned or accomplished. Because peasants could rebel on their own in France and Russia, they did not have to be *directly mobilized* by urban radicals. In China, such mobilization was ultimately necessary, but it was for the most part a military mobilization which conformed with important modifications to an age-old pattern of elite/peasant coordination of effort to accomplish "dynastic replacement." As we shall see, China is the exception that proves the rule about peasant insurrectionary autonomy and social revolution.

At the end of the Old Regime, "France was unique in Europe in that seigneurial privilege co-existed with a free peasantry owning a good deal of land"[15] and largely controlling the process of agrarian production. Averaging across regions, peasants owned about one-third of the land, subject to tithes, taxes, and seigneurial dues, and peasants probably cultivated most of the remainder as renters or sharecroppers (metayers), for large landowners rarely directly exploited their own holdings. The development of regional and national markets for grain and other agricultural products, a process directly and indirectly encouraged by government activities, spurred class differentiation within the ranks of the peasantry and fueled intra-village tensions. Laboureurs (rich peasants) with sufficient land and equipment could profit from rising prices for grain and land, but swelling masses of smallholders with insufficient land to support families were hard-pressed by rising rents and by bread prices that outstripped wage rates for agricultural or industrial labor. Nevertheless, virtually all peasants shared resentment of taxes, tithes, and seigneurial dues, and community institutions reinforced propensities and capacities to act together against common enemies.

> One important effect of the traditional agricultural system was to foster a strong community-feeling in the village. The management of the open fields required uniformity of cultivation and the commons were administered by the village as a whole . . . and the allocation of taxes was a matter of common concern. The village shared rights which it might have to defend in the courts. . . . In a system both traditional and partly communal there was little scope for individualism, and peasants, whole recognizing the private ownership of land, were inclined to regard the harvest as the property of the community.[16]

In general peasant communities looked after their own affairs. Seigneurs or their agents still exercised prerogatives of "feudal" justice on their estates, but military forces to back up judicial decisions to enforce order were controlled by the central government.

Peasant participation in the Revolutionary drama began in the spring of 1789 with bread riots, a long-established form of popular response to conditions of grain scarcity and high bread prices. The winter of 1788 had been unusually severe, and an industrial depression had been underway since 1786. "Irrespective of political events, there would have been widespread rioting and disorder in France during the summer of 1789."[17] But then, ". . . under the impact of economic crisis and political events, the peasant movement developed from early protests against prices, through attacks on enclosure, gaming [sic] rights, and royal forests, to a frontal attack on the feudal land system itself."[18]

The political events leading up to the calling and convening of the Estates General, and then to the fall of the Bastille and the assertion of national sovereignty by the Assembly, accelerated and focused the peasant rebellion in indirect ways. The spread of anti-aristocratic rhetoric by [revolutionary] spokesmen encouraged peasants to symbolize their own difficulties in terms of an "aristocratic plot." And divisions within the elite, pitting Crown and central administration against the privileged, and nobles against non-nobles, served to disorganize the army. Thus the peasantry, during the spring and summer of 1789 (and, in fact, thereafter for several years) was left largely free to push rebellion in rural areas beyond the largely ritualized form of the bread riot and was encouraged by what it perceived of urban upheavals to focus its attack upon *one* of its traditional enemies in particular: the seigneur.

> The real enemy of the majority of the peasants was the large landowner, noble, bourgeois or *laboureur* (yeoman farmer), whose acquisitiveness was threatening them with expropriation. But the main landowner in the village was often the seigneur, who was also responsible for the . . . burden of seigneurial dues. It was not difficult to lay most economic grievances at the seigneur's door. Royal taxation would have been lighter if the nobility had paid its full share. . . . The tithe, in very many cases, went not to the local *cure*, but to maintain the aristocratic abbot of an almost empty monastery in luxury at Versailles, while the impoverished contributors had to make supplementary grants to maintain the village church. The countryman thus found himself locked in a circle of frustration of which privilege seemed to hold the key to every door. Consequently, the village was able, for a time, to submerge its internal divisions in a common assault on the privileges of the nobility. . . . [T]he insurgent peasants made not for their seigneur's valuables but for their feudal title-deeds.[19]

The "choice" of enemy was encouraged by the fact that urban forces had also singled him out, but mainly as it was inherent in the agrarian structure of the Old Regime. That structure ". . . tended to maintain the cohesion of the rural community in opposition to the landed nobility"[20] yet rendered the landed noble (and other owners of seigneurial rights) dependent upon sanctioning machineries controlled from the center. When those machineries ceased to function effectively, the fate of seigneurial property was sealed.

Historians agree that the Russian Emancipation of the serfs in 1861, intended by the Czar as a measure to stabilize the agrarian situation, actually enhanced the rebellious potential of the ex-serfs. Heavy redemption payments and inadequate land allotments fuelled peasant discontent. More important, legal reinforcement of the *obshchina*'s (peasant commune's) authority over families and individuals left communes largely free to run their own affairs subject only to the collective fulfillment of financial obligations to the state. Estate owners were deprived of most direct authority over peasant communities.

Not surprisingly, given this agrarian situation, widespread peasant rebellions erupted in Russia in 1905, when the Czarist regime simultaneously confronted defeat abroad and anti-autocratic movement of the middle classes, the liberal gentry, and the working classes at home. "Economic hardship created a need for change; peasant tradition, as well as revolutionary propaganda, suggested the remedy [i.e., attacks on landlords and land seizures]."[21]

Although the disorders of 1905 were suppressed, "any shrewd observer of Russian conditions who weighed the lessons of the agrarian disorders of 1905 could have foreseen that a breakdown of central authority was almost certain to bring an even greater upheaval." And, indeed, between the spring and the autumn of 1917, when military defeats had incapacitated the Tsarist state, "side by side with the mutiny of the Russian army marched a second great social revolutionary movement: the seizure of the landed estates by the peasantry."[22] Their revolt, together with the Bolshevik's victory, "sealed forever the doom of the old landed aristocracy."[23]

The Chinese case presents decisive contrasts with France and Russia but nevertheless confirms our general insight about the importance of structurally conditioned "tactical space" for peasant insurrections as a crucial factor in the translation of administrative/military break-down into social revolution.

Except in infertile and marginal highland areas, Chinese peasants did not live in their own village communities clearly apart from landlords.

> The Chinese peasant . . . was a member of two communities: his village and the marketing system to which his village belonged ["typically including fifteen to twenty-five villages . . ." dependent on one of 45,000 market towns]. An important feature of the larger marketing community was its elaborate system of stratification. . . . Those who provided *de facto* leadership within the marketing community *qua* political system and those who gave it collective rep-resentation at its interface with larger polities were gentrymen—landed, leisured, and liter-ate. . . . It was artisans, merchants, and other full-time economic specialists, not peasants, who sustained the heartbeat of periodic marketing that kept the community alive. It was priests backed by gentry temple managers . . . who gave religious meaning to peasants' local world.[24]

Thus kinship, associational and clientage ties cut across class distinctions between peasants and landlords in traditional China. Gentry controlled at local levels a variety of sanctioning machineries, including militias and other organizations which functioned *de facto* as channels of poor relief.

Not surprisingly, therefore, settled Chinese peasant agriculturalists did not initiate class-based revolts against landlords, either in pre-modern or in revolutionary (1911–49) times. Instead, peasant rebellion manifested itself in the form of accelerating rural violence and social banditry, spreading outward from the mountainous "border areas" at the edges of the empire or at the intersections of provincial boundaries. Social banditry invariably blossomed during periods of central administrative weakness or collapse and economic deflation and catastrophe. Precisely because normal traditional Chinese agrarian-class re-lations were significantly commercialized, local prosperity depended upon overall admin-istrative stability, and peasants were not cushioned against economic dislocations by kin or village communal ties. During periods of dynastic decline, local (marketing) communities "closed in" upon themselves normatively, economically, and coercively, and poorer peasants, especially in communities without well-to-do landed elites, lost property and livelihood, and were forced to migrate. Such impoverished migrants often congregated as bandits or smugglers operating out of "border area" bases and raiding settled communities. Ultimately they might provide (individual or group) recruits for rebel armies led by marginal elites vying for imperial power.

The nineteenth and first half of the twentieth centuries constituted a period of dynastic decline and interregnum in China, complicated in quite novel ways by Western and Japanese economic and military intrusions. Peasant impoverishment, local community closure, spreading social banditry and military conflicts among local militias, bandit groups, and warlord and/or "ideological" armies, characterized the entire time span, and peaked during the mid-nineteenth and mid-twentieth centuries.

The Communist movement originated as a political tendency among a tiny fraction of China's nationalist and pro-modern intellectual stratum and created its first mass base among Chinese industrial workers concentrated in the treaty ports and to a lesser degree among students and southeast Chinese peasants. But after 1927, the Chinese Communists were forced out of China's cities and wealthier agrarian regions by Kuomintang military and police repression. The would-be imitators of the Bolsheviks were thus forced to come to terms with the Chinese agrarian situation. This they did initially (between 1927 and 1942) by recapitulating the experiences and tactics of traditional rebel elite contenders for imperial power in China. Scattered, disorganized and disoriented Communist leaders, along with military units of varying degrees of loyalty, retreated to mountainous border areas, there often to ally with already existing bandit groups. Gradually the fruits of raiding expeditions, plus the division and weakness of opposing armies, allowed the "Communist" base areas to expand into administrative regions.

Only after a secure and stable administrative region had finally been established in Northwest China (after 1937) could the Communists finally turn to the intra-market-area and intra-village political organizing that ultimately bypassed and then eliminated the gentry, and so made their drive for power unique in China's history. Before roughly 1940, ideological appeals, whether "Communist" or "Nationalist," played little role in mediating Communist elites' relations to peasants; and spontaneous class struggle, fuelled from below, played virtually no role in achieving whatever (minimal) changes in agrarian class *relations* were accomplished in Communist base areas. To be sure, ideology was important in integrating the Party, an elite organization, and in mediating its relationship with the Red Army. But until Party and Army established relatively secure and stable military and administrative control over a region, Communist cadres were not in a position to penetrate local communities in order to provide organization, leadership, and encouragement for peasants themselves to expropriate land. This finally occurred in North China in the 1940s. Once provided with military and organizational protection from landlord sanctions and influence, peasants often reacted against landlords with a fury that exceeded even what Party policy desired. Perhaps Communist ideology appeals were partially responsible for peasant insurrection. More likely, even at this state, the Communist organizations' important input to local situations was not a sense of grievances, or their ideological articulation, but rather simply *protection* from traditional social controls.

Even to gain the military strength they needed to defeat the Kuomintang, the Chinese Communists had to shove aside—or encourage and allow peasants to shove aside—the traditional landed upper class and establish a more direct link to the Chinese peasantry than had ever before been established between an extra-local Chinese rebel movement and local communities. The Chinese Communists also established more direct links to peasants than did radical elites in Russia or France. The Chinese Revolution, at least in its closing stages, thus has more of the aspect of an elite/mass movement than the other great historical social revolutions. Yet the reasons for this peasant mass-mobilization aspect have little to do with revolutionary ideology (except in retrospect) and everything to do with the "peculiarities" (from a European perspective) of the Chinese agrarian social structure. That structure did not afford settled Chinese peasants institutional autonomy and solidarity against landlords, yet it did, in periods of political-economic crisis, generate marginal poor-peasant outcasts whose activities exacerbated the crises and whose existence provided potential bases of support for oppositional elite-led rebellions or, in the twentieth-century world context, a revolutionary movement. Thus Chinese Communist activities after 1927 and ultimate triumph in 1949 depended directly upon *both* the insurrectionary potentials and the blocks to peasant insurrection built into the traditional Chinese social structure.

Radical Political Movements and Centralizing Outcomes

Although peasant insurrections played a decisive role in each of the great historical social revolutions, nevertheless an exclusive focus on peasants—or on the peasant situation in agrarian bureaucracies—cannot provide a complete explanation for the occurrence of social revolutions. Russia and China were recurrently rocked by massive peasant rebellions, yet peasant uprisings did not fuel structural transformations until the late eighteenth century and after. Obviously agrarian bureaucracies were exposed to additional and unique strains and possibilities once English and then European commercialization-industrialization became a factor in world history and development. The stage was set for the entry of marginal elites animated by radical nationalist goals.

Who were these marginal elites? What sectors of society provided the social bases for nationalist radicalisms? *Not* the bourgeoisie proper: merchants, financiers and industrialists. These groups have had surprisingly little *direct* effect upon the politics of modernization in any developing nation, from England to the countries of the Third World today. Instead, their activities, commerce and manufacturing, have created and continuously transformed, indeed revolutionized, the national and international *contexts* within which bureaucrats, professionals, politicians, landlords, peasants, and proletarians have engaged in the decisive political struggles. To be sure, in certain times and places, the "bourgeois" commercial or industrial context has been pervasive enough virtually to determine political outcomes, even without the overt political participation of bourgeois actors. But such was not the case in the earlier modernizing agrarian bureaucracies, including France, Russia and China.

Instead, nationalist radicals tended to "precipitate out" of the ranks of those who possessed specialized skills and were oriented to state activities or employments, but either lacked traditionally prestigious attributes such as nobility, landed wealth, or general humanist education, or else found themselves in situations where such attributes were no longer personally or nationally functional. Their situations in political and social life were such as to make them, especially in times of political crises, willing to call for such radical reforms as equalization of mobility opportunities, political democracy, and (anyway, before the revolution) extension of civil liberties. Yet the primary orientation of these marginal elites was toward a broad goal that they shared with all those, including traditionally prestigious bureaucrats, whose career, livelihoods, and identities were intertwined with state activities: the goal of extension and rationalization of state powers in the name of national welfare and prestige.

In Bourbon France, radicals (of whom the Jacobins were the most extreme) came primarily from the ranks of the non-noble, non-wealthy lawyers, professionals, or state functionaries, and disproportionately from the provinces.

> The royal bureaucracy, with its host of minor juridico-administrative officers, the professional civil servants of the great ministeries, the crowds of lawyers, the doctors, surgeons, chemists, engineers, lower army officers . . . all of these formed a social nexus which provided the men who did most of the work of government as well as of the professions, but who were kept out of the higher offices by lack of *noblesse* or of sufficient wealth to purchase it, and humiliated socially by the thought that they belonged to a lower caste.[25]

In Russia, by 1917, the revolutionary sects, such as the Bolsheviks and the Left Social Revolutionaries, constituted the surviving politically organized representatives of what had earlier been an outlook much more widespread among university-educated Russians: extreme alienation, disgust at Russia's backwardness, preoccupation with public events and yet refusal to become involved in the round of civil life. As Russia underwent rapid industrialization after 1890, opportunities for university education were extended beyond the nobility—a circumstance which helped to ensure that universities would be hotbeds of political radicalism—yet, before long, opportunities for professional and other highly skilled employments also expanded. Especially in the wake of the abortive 1905 Revolution, Russia's university-educated moved toward professional employments and liberal politics. Yet when events overtook Russia in 1917, organized radical leadership was still to be found among the alienated intelligentsia.

In China, as in Russia, radical nationalist modernizers came from the early student generations of university-educated Chinese. Yet with the abolition of the Confucian educational system in 1904, and the collapse of the imperial government in 1911, even traditionally prestigious attributes and connections lost their meaning and usefulness. At the same time, neither warlord regimes, nor the Nationalist government after 1927 offered much scope for modern skills or credentials; advancement in these regimes went only to those with independent wealth or personal ties to military commanders. Gradually, the bulk of China's modern-educated, and especially the young, came to support the Communist movement, some through active commitment in Yena, others through passive political support in the cities.

Two considerations help to account for the fact that radical leadership in social revolutions came specifically from the ranks of skilled and/or university-educated marginal elites oriented to state employments and activities. First, agrarian bureaucracies are "statist" societies. Even before the era of modernization official employments in these societies constituted both an important route for social mobility and a means for validating traditional status and supplementing landed fortunes. Second, with the advent of economic modernization in the world, state activities acquired greater-than-ever objective import in the agrarian bureaucratic societies which were forced to adapt to modernization aboard. For the concrete effects of modernization abroad first impinged upon the state's sphere, in the form of sharply and suddenly stepped up military competition or threats from more developed nations abroad. Understandably, as agrarian bureaucracies confronted modernization abroad, the state was viewed by virtually everyone, from conservative reformers to radicals and revolutionaries, as the likely tool for implementation of reforms at home and enhancement of national standing in the international context. This was true for eighteenth-century France, as well as for pre-revolutionary Russia and China.

The earlier modernizing agrarian bureaucracies that (to varying degrees) successfully adapted to challenges from abroad did so either through revolution, or basic reforms "from above" or social revolution "from below." Either traditional bureaucrats successfully promoted requisite reforms or else their attempts precipitated splits within the upper class which could, if the peasantry were structurally insurrection-prone, open the door to social revolution. In the context of administrative/military disorganization and spreading peasant rebellions, tiny, organized radical elites that never could have created revolutionary crises on their own gained their moments in history. As peasant insurrections undermined the traditional landed upper classes, and the old regime officials and structures tied to them, radical elites occupied center stage, competing among themselves to see who would seize and build upon the foundations of central state power.

"A complete revolution," writes Samuel Huntington, ". . . involves . . . the creation and institutionalization of a new political order."[26] A social revolution was consummated when one political elite succeeded in creating or capturing political organizations—a revolutionary army, or a revolutionary party controlling an army—capable of restoring minimal order and incorporating the revolutionary masses, especially the peasantry, into national life. No political elite not able or willing to accept the peasants' revolutionary economic gains could hope to emerge victorious from the intra-elite or inter-party conflicts that marked revolutionary interregnums. Elites with close social or politico-military ties to traditional forms of landed upper-class institutional power (i.e., the privileged rentier bourgeoise of France, the Kerensky regime in Russia, the [post-1927] Kuomintang in China) invariably lost out.

The historical social revolutions did not culminate in more liberal political arrangements. At opening stages of the French, Russian (1905) and Chinese Revolutions, landed upper-class/middle-strata political coalitions espoused "parliamentary liberal" programs. But events pushed these groups and programs aside, for the organized elites who provided the ultimately successful leadership in all social revolutions ended up responding to popular turmoil—counterrevolutionary threats at home and abroad, peasant anarchist tendencies, and the international crises faced by their societies—by creating *more* highly centralized, bureaucratized and rationalized state institutions than those that existed prior to the revolutions. The strengthening and rationalizing of central state powers was the result of the French Revolution as surely as of the Russian and Chinese.

Thus, what changed most thoroughly in *all* of the historical social revolutions was the mode of societal control of the lower strata. Landed upper classes lost (at least) their special socio-political authority and their roles in controlling the peasantry (however feebly) through local and regional quasi-political institutional arrangements—the *parlements* and seigneurial courts in France; *zemstovs* and landed estates in Russia; clans, associations, subdistrict, district and provincial governments in China. The peasantry and the urban lower strata were directly incorporated into now truly *national* politics and economies, institutionally and symbolically.

Let me sum up what this essay has attempted to do. To explain the great historical social revolutions, I have, first, conceptualized a certain type of society, the agrarian bureaucracy, in which social control of the lower strata (mainly peasants) rests with institutions locally and regionally controlled by landed upper classes, together with administrative and military machineries centrally controlled; and second, I have discussed differences between agrarian bureaucracies which did and those which did not experience social revolutions in terms of (a) institutional structures which mediate landed upper-class relations to state apparatuses and peasant relations to landed upper classes and (b) types and amounts of international political and economic pressures (especially originating with more developed nations) impinging upon agrarian bureaucracies newly incorporated into the modernizing world. According to my analysis, social revolutions occurred in those modernizing agrarian bureaucracies—France, Russia and China—which *both* incubated peasantries structurally prone to autonomous insurrection *and* experienced severe administrative and military disorganization due to the direct or indirect effects of military competition or threats from more modern nations abroad.

References

1. Hopkins and Wallerstein (1967), p. 39.
2. Lasch (1967), p. 141.
3. Chamberlin (1965), pp. 64–65.
4. Trimberger (1972), p. 192.
5. Fox (1971), p. 69.
6. Dorn (1963), p. 26.
7. Ford (1965), p. 248.
8. Cobban (1957), p. 122.
9. Chorley (1943).
10. Feuerwerker (1970), pp. 40–41.
11. Fincher (1968), p. 202.
12. Chang (1968), p. 50.
13. Fairbank (1983), p. 132.
14. Walter (1980), p. 73.
15. Hampson (1963), p. 23.
16. Hampson (1963), p. 24.
17. Hampson (1963), p. 69.
18. Rudé (1964), p. 103.
19. Hampson (1963), p. 78.
20. Lefebvre (1963).
21. Robinson (1969).
22. Chamberlin (1965), pp. 257, 242.
23. Chamberlin (1965), p. 256.
24. Skinner (1971). pp. 272–273.
25. Cobban (1957), p. 134.
26. Huntington (1968), p. 266.

THE ENGLISH REVOLUTION: A STRUCTURAL–DEMOGRAPHIC APPROACH

Jack A. Goldstone

Marx and Engels often suggested that the English Revolution of 1640 was a "bourgeois" revolution, in which the growth of capitalism in trade and agriculture overturned a feudal, backward-looking monarchy. The following essay examines the causes of the English Revolution and finds that the evidence does not support the Marxist model. Instead, the essay offers an alternative structural analysis, stressing the impact of population changes on the key social relationships of early modern England—between Crown and landlords, between landlords and peasants, and between members of the landed elite.

In 1640 Scottish troops crossed into England. The King of England and Scotland, Charles I, had angered the Scots by attacking their religious organization and the privileges of their nobility. The King had also claimed title to Scottish noblemen's lands and asked them to pay new taxes. Charles asked the English Parliament for money for a settlement with the Scots. Yet instead of money the King received attacks on his ministers and a long list of complaints about royal misgovernment. While King and Parliament locked in debates over the King's authority, riots broke out in London and in the English countryside, and a full-scale revolt began in Ireland. The King left London to raise an army to reassert his authority; his opponents in Parliament raised an army to defend themselves. Drawing on the wealth of London and the support of a broad range of landowners, farmers, small merchants, and artisans, the Parliamentary army led by Oliver Cromwell defeated the King and installed a revolutionary government.

Marx and Engels called these events a "bourgeois" revolution: The emergence of capitalism brought the rise of bourgeois classes—capitalist farmers among the landlord "gentry" and merchant capitalists among the growing overseas trading companies—who chafed at the restrictions on their activity which a still largely feudal aristocracy allied with the Crown imposed. Conflict between the rising capitalist classes and the older feudal classes thus lay behind the revolution. Identifying the Parliamentary forces as capitalist and bourgeois and the royalist forces as feudal, Marx and Engels saw the victory of Parliament as the victory of capitalist forces over feudalism.

However, historians have challenged this view by demonstrating that political divisions ran through every social and geographic category: Members of the House of Lords and the House of Commons, merchants and urban oligarchs, the gentry of nearly every county in England, and even members of many single families suffered internal division: All these groups included supporters of Parliament *and* supporters of the Crown. Explanations of the Revolution in terms of class conflict have thus largely receded.

Many English historians, particularly the youngest generation of scholars, have simply abandoned the search for long-term social changes as causes of the English Revolution.

Instead they have rallied around G. R. Elton's cry that "the failure of Charles's government was not rendered 'inevitable' by deep divisions in society or inherited stresses . . . but was conditioned by the inability of the King and his ministers to operate any political system."[1] Therefore, Charles's choice of policies and advisors precipitated the political crisis of the 1640s. In the words of one younger historian, it was a "crisis of counsel" that formed "the central crisis of early Stuart government."[2]

Yet this interpretation is unsatisfactory for at least two reasons. First, by blaming the Revolution on Charles's missteps, the historians render the enormous scale of the conflict—two civil wars in a decade and the overthrow of all royal courts, the Anglican Church, the House of Lords, and the monarchy itself—a mystery. Indeed, Englishmen had deposed and even murdered unpopular Kings before and after—William Rufus, Edward II, Richard II, and James II—without England's political institutions or the monarchy itself coming under assault. How was it that by 1640, the bumbling policies of a King—in and of themselves—led to popular uprisings, an urban revolution in London, the fracturing of the entire nation, and twenty years of civil war and interregnum?

Second, the research of recent scholars has made it clear that a key reason for the increasingly sharp conflict in 1642, both between King and Parliament and within Parliament, was the spread of popular uprisings throughout England, including both rural tumults and riots in London. Hill is certainly partly correct in stating that "what mattered in the English Revolution was that the ruling class was deeply divided at a time when there was much combustible material among the lower classes."[3] The exclusive focus on Charles's bumbling precludes an understanding of why so much "combustible material" existed in England in the 1640s. Without having some plausible answer to this issue, the course of the mid-century upheaval is hard to explain.

Neo-Marxist sociologists have taken another road. Barrington Moore, Jr., Perry Anderson, and Immanuel Wallerstein, have—to varying degrees—revised the Marxist view of the capitalist origins of the English Revolution by putting aside the notion of a distinctive bourgeois "class" as the necessary spearhead of revolution. Instead, these scholars have argued that the diffusion of capitalist economic and legal relations throughout society—shown by the agricultural improvements associated with extensive enclosures, and a vast increase in overseas trade—gradually undermined traditional English life and sharpened conflicts throughout the nation. In particular, the emergence of capitalist economic practices intensified conflicts between landlords and tenants, multiplied the misery and poverty of the peasantry, and motivated the popular protests that marked the sixteenth and early seventeenth centuries. At the same time, the greater dependence of England's economy on capitalist international trade left the nation highly vulnerable to cyclical downswings that significantly increased tensions both within the ruling gentry class and between the gentry and the Crown.

Unfortunately, both the neo-Marxist view and the view of the new generation of political historians with its narrow focus on elite politics and the failings of Charles I run into difficulties when confronted with the evidence. As an alternative I suggest a structural analysis of the origins of the English Revolution, one that stresses political conflicts but highlights long-term causes for such conflicts. In particular, I draw upon recent research in demographic history to suggest that the long-term causes of England's political crisis were mainly *demographic* changes, and that many of the effects mistakenly attributed to the growth of capitalism in early modern England were in fact changes in the scale, or the distribution, of traditional occupations, practices, and incomes, due to the rapid population growth of the years 1500–1640.

The Neo-Marxist View of the Capitalist Origins of the English Revolution: A Critique

According to the Neo-Marxist view, in the sixteenth and early seventeenth centuries landlords deprived small farmers of their land. Landlords denied villagers their traditional rights to use village common lands, assembled their property into large commercial farms or sheep pastures, enclosed them with fences or hedges, and turned their former tenants and farmers away. Enclosing landlords thus created a landless proletariat whose members spread unrest through the countryside; enclosers also brought to agriculture a new capitalist spirit that was at odds with the conservative spirit of the monarchy. Struggles between enclosing lords and tenants thus contributed to the conflict between landlords and the Crown. At the same time, England's expanding overseas trade, exploiting the growing capitalist world-system, supported new interest opposed to the Crown's control of commerce. These commercial forces added their weight to that of the landlords in the conflict with the monarchy. Instead of a distinct "bourgeoisie" facing feudal landlords, the neo-Marxist view ascribes the Revolution to commercial elements *within* the ruling landlord class, who created a landless proletariat and in so doing came into conflict with the "traditionalist" Crown. The Revolution was then fought between the commercial elements of the gentry, with help from the merchant and manufacturing interests in London, and the King and his aristocratic loyalists.

This story is told, in varying forms, by Moore, Wallerstein, and Anderson. Thus Moore:

> During the sixteenth century the most significant [enclosures] were encroachments made by lords of manors or their farmers upon the land over which the manorial population had common rights. . . . The peasants were driven off the land; ploughed strips and common alike were turned into pastures. . . . Those who promoted the wave of agrarian capitalism, the chief victors in the struggle against the old order, came from the yeomanry and even more from the landed upper classes. . . . [C]ommercially minded elements among the landed upper classes, and to a lesser extent among the yeomen, were among the main forces opposing the King and royal attempts to preserve the old order, and therefore an important cause . . . that produced the Civil War.[4]

Wallerstein and Anderson are even more forceful. Thus Wallerstein: "Encroachment led to the abandonment of villages and migration," as yeomen "usurped (by enclosure) the lands" of their laborers. The spread of the new practices and market orientation within the gentry led to a conflict of interests within the ruling landlord class "between the new capitalists and the old aristocrats."[5] And Anderson: "The English monarchy was felled at the center by a commercialized gentry [and] a capitalist city" which faced in Charles I's absolutism the attempted "political refortification of a feudal state."[6]

Undoubtedly the English economy underwent a profound change between the fifteenth and the eighteenth centuries. In the fifteenth century, though local commerce and marketing were well established, England was primarily a nation of small farmers producing for local consumption, towns with more than a few thousand inhabitants were rare, and overseas trade was modest. By the late eighteenth century, though a substantial number of family farms remained, large parts of England's agricultural output came from the efforts of wage laborers on farms producing for regional or national markets, the urban sector had expanded massively and provided a substantial share of production and consumption, and large segments of the economy depended on overseas trade. The issue is not whether these changes occurred—that is indisputable—but whether these changes adequately account for the conflicts that led to the English Revolution. In the neo-Marxist view, precisely these changes led to increasing conflict and set the stage for the revolutionary crisis. To evaluate this view, we need to look closely at the course of agricultural change in the sixteenth and seventeenth centuries and then examine the hypothesized links between such change, and also changes in manufacturing and overseas trade, and the Revolution.

Enclosures, Agrarian Capitalism, and Rural Unrest

In parts of England the medieval pattern of landholding was for copyholders and other tenants to hold scattered strips of land in open fields with large areas set aside for common use for grazing. In the fifteenth century areas of the open fields and commons began to be enclosed with hedges or fences.

Yet the type of enclosure that was held to have important social and political consequences—the enclosure by a landlord of common fields in order to turn out tenants and create sheep pasture—in fact constituted only a small portion of enclosures and occurred over a limited time span, primarily from 1450 to 1550 and from 1650 to 1750. The largest amount of such enclosure seems to have occurred before 1510; by the 1530s enclosures were generally used for intensive grain farming or mixed sheep and corn husbandry.

Also significant is the fact that in this period enclosures were rarely the work of the manorial lord who possessed all or virtually all of the enclosed lands. Instead, the tenants usually agreed on enclosures to increase the intensity of cultivation. The Chancery rolls of the sixteenth and seventeenth centuries reveal that tenants initiated scores of enclosures by agreement that benefitted all concerned. By 1580 the enclosure movement was as much a movement of small farmers and copyholders as of large landlords.

Sharp's recent study of the enclosure of the Western Forests nicely traces this pattern. The traditional view was that these enclosures and the riots that accompanied them constituted an arbitrary extinction of the common rights of small farmers and tenants (in

England called yeomen, copyholders, husbandmen, or freeholders), who rose to defend their immemorial rights. Yet a close examination of the legal proceedings and participants involved completely overturns this view.

> The disafforestations, rather than being arbitrary enclosures, were excellent examples of enclosure by agreement: substantial freeholders and copyholders were asked to grant their consent to the enclosure and the consequent extinction of their rights of common in return for compensating allotments of land. Contrary to accepted opinions . . . the property rights of . . . freeholders and copyholders claiming rights of common on the forest were scrupulously protected in quite elaborate legal proceedings.[7]

Protests against the enclosure came not from dispossessed copyholders and yeomen cultivators but from already-landless squatters in the forest, primarily artisans who relied on grazing, game poaching, and gathering wood for construction, woodworking, and firewood to supplement their incomes.

In addition, much enclosure in the sixteenth and seventeenth centuries was land newly reclaimed from the swampy fens or the forests. Therefore, many enclosures were made on land where common rights had never been important.

The verdict that enclosures were disruptive came from cries against enclosures that first appeared in the sixteenth century. Yet experts have since shown that this outcry was largely a case of scapegoating. In fact, "the great outbursts of public outrage against inclosure [sic] in the century before the Civil War probably do not tell us much about the progress of conversion, for most coincided with runs of bad harvests, in which unease about the food supply [created] an uproar."[8] To better understand the effects of enclosures on tenants, we must look at recent detailed studies of rural unrest throughout sixteenth and early seventeenth century England.

In the far northern counties of Cumberland and Westmoreland, Appleby's studies of enclosure show that population pressure and not the growth of capitalism created a landless and rebellious agrarian proletariat. As population grew, landlords could have profited by enclosing the common, converting it to arable lands, and renting out these new lands to a more numerous tenantry, but they did not do so. Instead, they carefully guarded the common rights of their tenants to maintain the vitality of their patronage relationships. But this protection did not free their tenants from difficulties:

> [E]ach customary tenant . . . had security of tenure on his small tenement or cottage holding. Each tenant also enjoyed the right of pasture on his manorial common. . . . In other words, the tenant retained all his old rights and privileges. But this was no longer enough. . . . The great population surge of the sixteenth century had added too many men to the rural structure, straining it to the point of collapse.[9]

Tenements were fragmented and the traditional commons overburdened as "all competed for limited land and pasture."[10] Younger sons, unable to secure new arable land on the manor lands, became landless migrants or squatters who made piecemeal enclosures in the adjacent forests.

As for the far South, Peter Clark, studying agrarian riots in Kent between 1558 and 1640, found that attacks on enclosures were usually by artisans and pastoral forest dwellers on woodlands newly enclosed for grain and not attacks by displaced cultivators on sheep-folds. Moreover, most riots were not attacks on landlords but on corn merchants in times of high prices.

> It was within the grain producing regions which in normal harvest years produced a surplus which went to feed other areas, notably the larger towns, that grain riots were most likely to occur. . . . [R]iots in Norfolk, Essex, Kent, Sussex, Hertfordshire, Hampshire, and the Thames Valley were commonly provoked by the fear of the siphoning off of local grain supplies to meet [London's] demand. . . . Elsewhere, urban demand played a similar role in provoking disorder.[11]

As for the West, Buchanan Sharp's studies of rioters in the Royal Forests of western England also stress that higher food prices generated disorders. Copyholders protesting loss of land did not cause the majority of disturbances in this region; established and skilled rural artisans, long exposed to the market, whose protests were keyed to shrinking wages, high unemployment, food scarcity, were the culprits. Food riots, far more common than enclosure riots, recurred in 1586, 1594–1597, 1622, 1629–1631, and 1641–1642.

As for the East, Walter's study of the 1629 grain riots in Essex mirrors Sharp's results. His analysis of the participants in the riots shows they were artisans, chiefly clothworkers, suffering from unemployment and high prices, who directed riots against grain merchants exporting corn form the county. Walter carefully delineates the riots' political overtones. Disorder followed a series of peaceful petitions to the King asking him to relieve the distress of the clothworkers; yet "the inability of those in authority (for all their promises) to relieve the poor threatened the implicit contract between rulers and ruled."[12] Not the failure of the Crown to protect cultivators from enclosure but its failure to provide relief to workers in times of unemployment and rising prices produced the disorders.

Even the great peasant revolts of the sixteenth century, such as Kett's rebellion in East Anglia in 1549, that experts once widely attributed to enclosures, have recently received a reinterpretation in which enclosures have played a lesser role. Cornwall's detailed study of Kett's rising concludes that "It might have been possible to assimilate the new ways in agriculture, had they been the only problem. But from the third decade of the sixteenth century at least, the situation became bedevilled by two further crises which had infinitely more immediate and universal effect: population growth and price inflation."[13]

In sum, we can no longer characterize the agrarian structure of England before the Revolution as being the result of an "enclosure crisis" due primarily to the spread of capitalist commercial farming. The sixteenth and early seventeenth centuries were a period of significant enclosure, but largely of virgin lands, largely by agreement of yeomen and tenants, and largely for the purpose of more intensive grain farming. A far greater portion of rural unrest in the sixteenth and early seventeenth centuries consisted of food riots by rural artisans concerned about unemployment, high prices, and food shortages.

Moreover, we must take a closer look at the enclosure of Crown lands. *The monarchy too* participated in the enclosure movement, particularly the enclosure of waste and fen;

in fact its efforts to turn a greater profit form the Royal Forests and fens made the Crown probably the single largest encloser of the early seventeenth century. Pressed by growing financial needs, the Crown spearheaded enclosure projects, often in conjunction with local gentry, splitting the profits from enclosure and rental of reclaimed fens and forests. For example, in Lincolnshire in the 1630s a group of gentry joined the Crown in a fen drainage project; the same gentry emerged as the core of the royalist faction in the county in the Civil War. In the north, the Crown led the way after 1600 in raising rents and entry fines, positioning itself in the forefront of the region's movement toward free market rents. If enclosure for improvement, leasing, and profit is a mark of commercial progressiveness, then in light of the Crowns's activity we cannot attribute the seventeenth century crisis to a conflict between a commercial, progressive gentry and a conservative, feudal Crown. In fact, in the relations between landlords and the Crown by the early seventeenth century enclosures were more often a source of cooperation than of conflict.

In short, the gradual increase in enclosures for commercial, capitalist farming in the sixteenth and early seventeenth centuries cannot be held accountable for most of the increase in rural disorders. Rising food prices, shortages of land due to population pressures, and a growing population of urban consumers drawing grain from rural areas seem to have been far more important factors. In addition, examining enclosure practices shows few differences between landlords and Crown. Enclosures evidently were not the source of conflicts that lay behind the revolution..

Can we say the same of the growth of trade and manufacture?

The Growth of Market Relations

Marx had argued that the growth of English trade led to new relationships and new commercial interests that joined the opposition to the King. Yet we must look closely at the growth of English trade and marketing. For the increase in marketing and trade generally did not stimulate the growth of new and distinctively capitalist relationships but did encourage the expansion of traditional markets and trades. Indeed, most of the growth in market relations was simply an increase in scale as the English economy struggled to adjust to its increased numbers.

The most important factor in the growth of market relations was the growth of towns, particularly of London. As surplus rural population streamed to the towns to seek employment, the number of people who had to buy their daily bread on the market sharply increased. The crowds who harried the bishops, signed petitions, and overthrew the Common Council were struggling guild artisans and apprentices in the traditional crafts.

Similarly, the significance of the expansion of the domestic cloth industry prior to 1640 was not the creation of a distinctive proletariat nor of a distinctive capitalist merchant interest. Mere numbers of traditional workers were the critical problem. Parish relief systems designed to cope with modest numbers of workers simply broke down in the face of ever-larger crowds of artisans dependent on trade. By the seventeenth century, in the major cloth-producing areas, "depression [in the cloth trade] spawned unemployment on a scale which the individual parish was not really designed to encounter, let alone solve."[14]

Moreover, the merchants themselves were not a united opposition; they were divided between the large merchants dealing in overseas trade and the smaller domestic traders and even within income groups between the merchants of the outer ports versus those of London. For the most part, the wealthiest merchants, who profited from monopolies on overseas trade granted by the King, supported the Crown in the Civil War. It was chiefly smaller merchants, hurt most by royal monopolies on trade and royal taxes, who supported Parliament.

The great significance of the expansion of manufacturing and markets was the simple demographic fact that as population growth outran employment opportunities in agriculture, more and more people depended on nonagricultural employment. Such people depended more on the vicissitudes of markets and the predations of rising food prices and falling wages than did agriculturalists. With their increased numbers driving up food prices and making employment harder to find, the lot of almost all workers and artisans was sharply deteriorating.

England's commercial expansion did produce pockets of more modern, larger-scale enterprises: glass-works and iron-works grew substantially before 1640, and coal production underwent spectacular growth. Yet the role played by these ventures in the economy as a whole was minor. And iron-workers or coal miners did not play any significant role in the events of 1640–1660; the prime actors among the populace were the yeomen of the countryside and the artisans, traders, shopkeepers, and apprentices of London. Indeed, a closer look at urban politics provides another curious irony. A center of truly modern capitalist enterprise in seventeenth century England fed industrial markets by production with wage labor: the enormously expanding coal trade centered in Newcastle. Yet as a recent study of its Civil War politics shows, "Newcastle . . . provides a clear case in point of a commercial and industrial center that sided with the King rather than with Parliament."[15]

An Alternative View

Why then did England have a revolution in 1640? Three questions need answering. First, why did the gentry come into conflict with the Crown? Second, why were England's elites so divided among themselves that the political conflicts of 1640 led to civil war? Third, why did so much "combustible material" which made popular disorders likely to accompany the breakdown of the central government exist among the populace?

The conflict between the Crown and the gentry was not over enclosure or commercial practices. The main problem was one found in most pre-revolutionary situations: the attempt of the central government to wrest more money from the elites by raising taxes and attacking elite privileges. The English Crown, like the French monarchy, faced a landed elite that held strategic positions in government and resisted royal attempts to reform taxation. According to England's customary constitution, the English Parliament, composed of landlord representatives, had to give its consent to all new taxes. English landlords also controlled local law enforcement as Justices of the Peace. In addition, local landlords served the Crown as tax collectors and tax assessors. However, they generally took advantage of these roles to set their own assessments unrealistically low and so avoided taxation. The Crown could overcome this resistance only by reducing landlords' role in local and national government and attempting to reform the system of taxes and elite privileges.

From 1600 to 1640, the Crown began to sell royal offices and elite titles on a large scale. It sold monopoly rights to groups of wealthy merchants to trade with certain regions and to sell certain products. The King also sought to reform and raise taxes without Parliament's consent and interfered more and more in local county government—the traditional preserve of county gentry—in order to raise more revenue. Thus in 1640, when Charles's attempts to raise money in Scotland triggered a rebellion and he asked Parliament to levy taxes for a settlement with the Scots, Charles received not money but angry complaints against his abuses of England's constitution and traditions.

Why did the English Crown need to increase its revenues? In her study of the French, Russian, and Chinese Revolutions, Skocpol suggested that traditional governments often come under economic and military pressure from more economically advanced states abroad. This cause will not explain England's problem, however, for by 1640 England was already one of the most economically advanced states in Europe. In England the need for the Crown to increase its income came partly, as elsewhere, from the expense of waging war. Yet fiscal pressures came even more strongly from rising prices, largely a consequence of England's growing population.

In the fifteenth century, England's population was making a very slow recovery from the Black Death of the 1340s. Restoring the population levels of the early 1300s probably took nearly two hundred years. During this period of population stagnation, prices were extremely stable. From the 1380s to the early 1500s prices went almost unchanged, decade after decade, differing merely 5 percent by the first decade of the 1500s from their level in the last decade of the 1300s. During this period, the Crown amassed land and established its tax base; by 1510 Henry VII was able to tell Parliament that, except in case of war, the Crown revenues were sufficient for him "to live of his own," without need for taxes.

Yet the situation soon changed. England's population, which in 1520 was probably roughly the same as it was in 1320, suddenly began to increase. From 1520 to 1640, England's inhabitants increased from just over two million to well over five million. Increased demand, pushing on a slowly improving agricultural economy, drove up prices. Prices doubled and then doubled again. By the late 1630s prices had risen to six times their level of 1500–1510.

This sustained rise in prices drained royal finances, leading the Crown first to sell its lands, then to sell monopolies, offices, and honors and later to raise taxes ruthlessly and to assault the financial privileges of the elites. The main issues in the struggle between the King and gentry were thus the scope of the Crown's authority, royal taxes, and royal interference in the counties. On these issues, the vast majority of the gentry could agree to oppose the King.

Yet one of the striking aspects of the English Revolution is the manner in which the gentry, fairly unified against the King in 1640, suddenly fractured in to a host of national and local factions in 1642. Why were various county and national conflicts so much sharper and more intense than they had been in the days of Elizabeth or than they were in the later seventeenth and early eighteenth centuries? Certainly part of the reason is the extent of the political crisis posed by the Crown's bankruptcy, the Scots invasion, and uprisings in Ireland, in London, and throughout the countryside. But at least part of the answer also lies in the extraordinarily strong personal competitiveness and insecurity that afflicted the gentry in the early seventeenth century.

The rise in prices drained some gentry fortunes and created opportunities that produced others. Prudent investments by smaller gentry and many yeoman propelled them upwards in wealth and status. On the other hand, gentry and noble families who spent freely or neglected their lands and other investments sank deeply into debt and eventually lost their lands and social position to newcomers. The sixteenth and early seventeenth centuries were thus a period of massive shifts of individual fortunes with families entering and leaving the gentry and nobility at unprecedented rates. In many counties in 1640 over half of the leading gentry families were "newcomers" who had become established after 1500.

Nor were these economic effects the only consequences of rapid demographic growth. For rapid growth meant more families and more surviving children among the gentry which increased even more rapidly than the population as a whole. From 1540 to 1640, the number of gentry families increased roughly from 5000 to 15,000. Faced with a relatively limited system of land, civil and church offices, and royal patronage to sustain them, these greater numbers brought a sharp increase in the competitiveness and insecurity of elite society. The competitiveness showed in a flood of applicants to the universities and the inns of Court who hoped to qualify for posts in the Church or State administration and in increased demands for royal patronage. Stone has gone so far as to assert that "the hostility of the majority of the Peers to Charles I in 1640 can be ascribed in large measure to the failure of the King to multiply jobs to keep pace with the increase of titles."[16] And the increased numbers of gentry and nobles intensified hostility on the part of the Royalists as well, for many of the King's supporters showed the same desperation:

> The situation [in 1642] seems to have been aggravated by the remarkable surplus of landless younger sons in the King's armies, with no estate to root them in the countryside, no career but the army open to them, and little to support their pretensions to gentility.[17]

Under conditions of increasing competitiveness and insecurity, the discipline and high deals of Puritanism increased their appeal to many of the gentry. But to others, insecurity and competition seemed to call for an increase in the order and hierarchy of the established Church of England. Thus religious conflicts further sharpened elite differences.

It appears that the recomposition of the elites, due to great rates of individual mobility occurring in the wake of massive changes in prices and the reproductive behavior of elites, had the effect on the elites *as a whole* of increasing insecurity and sharpening local rivalries and national divisions. Lacking a written constitution and an established bureaucracy, the English state depended on consensus among its elite for its stability. Yet the recomposition of the elites made such a consensus elusive in the face of the mounting political crisis of 1640–1642. Confronted with the pressing problems of royal bankruptcy, religious divisions, and popular disorders, the myriad divisions among the elite gave rise to adversary politics that paralyzed the government. Reluctantly, the English gentry found recourse to open conflict increasingly necessary to resolve both its conflict with the King and its own divisions and rivalries.

Still, we must explore the causes of popular unrest. For the popular uprisings in London and to a lesser degree in the countryside proved a catalyst in the conflicts with the King and among the gentry. In 1640 when the King called Parliament to ask for increased taxes, instead he received demands that he refrain from interfering with gentry privileges, gentry independence, and gentry local government. Yet when the lower and middle classes of England began rioting in London and the countryside, the gentry became divided. Some felt that popular uprisings, especially the urban revolt in London, offered an opportunity for people to frighten the King into concessions. Others felt that popular uprisings threatened gentry dominance so that it was now necessary to rally around the King as the symbol of traditional authority. Thus Parliament, united against the King in 1640, gradually separated into Parliamentarian and Royalist camps in 1641–1642.

The chief source of popular unrest was the vast increase in the portion of the population which depended on wages. In the countryside, rural laborers and artisans protested rising food prices and attacked grain merchants. In the capital, the flow of the landless into London depressed wages and provided recruits whose discontents with grain shortages and unemployment, the elites, in their conflict with the King, could exploit.

In examining whether population growth or the action of enclosing landlords was the main factor behind this growth in "combustible material" among the lower classes, we need to answer two questions: (1) What do studies of English villagers show regarding how they lost their lands? and (2) Could population growth alone have led to the precise changes in property-holding that occurred?

Village studies in Cambridgeshire by Spufford show unambiguously that, while middle-size property disappeared and dwarf holdings multiplied prior to 1640, actions by manor lords were *not* responsible: "Vulnerability to seigneurial action and legal factors did not underlie the change."[18] Rather, in each case, husbandmen had divided family plots among their progeny while holders of such diminished properties often sold out to other copy-holders during times of economic difficulty.

Thirsk and Everitt have shown that in Suffolk, Bedfordshire, and Lincolnshire, husbandmen commonly divided property among surviving heirs, leading to shrunken holdings: "As the number of labourers increased, . . . small holdings were either divided up amongst children, and subdivided again till they shrank to mere gardens, or else bequeathed to the elder son alone, so that the younger children were left propertyless."[19] Thirsk cites Edward Lande, an octagenarian of Dent, who in 1634 declared:

> If a customary tenant died . . . without having [a] will, then it descended to all his sons equally to be divided amongst them. . . . By reason of such division of tenements, the tenants are much increased in number more than they were, and the tenements become so small in quantity that many of them are not above three or four acres apiece.[20]

As to the likelihood that population growth alone could account for the size of the observed shift in landholding, let us look at the available data. Table 1(a) presents data compiled by Everitt on the shift in size of 447 holdings on 28 manors. Experts have sometimes cited the marked reduction in the size of holdings shown in this data as evidence that landlords were depriving tenants of their lands.

Yet simple subdivision by inheritance can account for the observed shifts as well. From 1540 to 1630, England's population increased by three-fourths. Assuming roughly thirty years per generation, finding out what effect this growth rate would have on landholdings is simple. To increase by three-fourths in three generations, the population must have a net reproduction rate of 1.2. This means that for each generation, 80 percent of the fathers have only one surviving son; 20 percent have two surviving sons. Let us make the simplest possible assumption: that for those 80 percent of fathers with one surviving son, the property is handed down intact, while for those fathers with two

TABLE 1

Patterns of landholdings of English laborers c. 1540–1640

(a) Data: 447 holdings on 28 manors (percent of holdings of each size)

PERIOD	COTTAGE W/GARDEN	UNDER 1 ACRE	1–1³/₄	2–2³/₄	3–3³/₄	4–5
Before 1560	11	31	28	7	11	11
1600–1610	35	36	13	6	5	5
After 1620	40	23	14	8	7	7

(b) Simulation: 100 families in 1535, net reproduction rate 1.2, partible inheritance (percent of holdings of each size)

PERIOD	COTTAGE W/GARDEN	UNDER 1 ACRE	1–1³/₄	2–2³/₄	3–3³/₄	4–5
c.1540	11.0	31.0	28.0	7.0	11.0	11.0
c.1600	31.6	28.5	21.9	8.1	4.9	4.9
c.1630	41.1	26.3	18.9	7.0	3.3	3.3

Source: Data in (a) from Alan Everitt, "Farm Laborers," in The Agrarian History of England and Wales, ed. H. P. R. Finberg, 8 vols. (Cambridge: Cambridge University Press, 1967–), 4 (1967): 402.

surviving sons, the property is divided equally between them. Table 1(b) presents the results of a simulation of the pattern of landholdings that would result from this growth rate and inheritance pattern.

As can be seen, this simplest possible demographic model provides a nearly exact fit. Given the result of such simple demographic simulations, and the results of local studies, it is likely that demographic changes were primarily responsible for the shifts in property seen in the century before the Revolution.

The reduction of holdings and the growth of landlessness, the marked rise in prices and unemployment, the fall of real wages, and the massive expansion of urban centers form a complex pattern we might call the "rapid population growth" syndrome. These factors sharply differentiate the period of rising conflict in the century before the Revolution from the succeeding, more stable century. In the century prior to 1640, while population almost doubled and prices rose several-fold, real wages fell by half, and London grew at an annual rate of 1.5 percent. By contrast, from 1640 to 1740, England's population grew by no more than 10 percent; grain prices leveled off and then declined; London's growth rate fell to .6 percent per annum; and real wages rose by more than a third.

Unlike the French or Russian peasants, English peasants lacked the autonomous village communities that could have sustained a successful revolt against landlords. By 1640 English peasant villages were generally loose settlements of small farmers, tenants, and laborers under the close supervision of local landlords. Local landlords' control of militias for law enforcement allowed them quickly to put down most threats to their authority, and in only a few counties did lower and middle class groups take over local government from landlords. For the most part, peasants and workers were conscripted into Royalist and Parliamentary armies, led on both sides by landlords, before they had a chance to organize for themselves. Only in London, which swelled enormously from perhaps 60,000 inhabitants in 1520 to 400,000 in 1650 with the flow of migrants from the overburdened countryside, did popular discontents give rise to a major revolt.

Still, the widely scattered riots of 1640–1641 played an important role in unsettling Parliament and splitting the gentry. And the urban revolt in London was crucial to Parliament's early assault on the King's authority. Of course, the small merchants and artisans who rebelled in London supported Parliament not through love of Parliament, but because of hatred of the King's monopolies and taxes as well as anger against rising prices and falling real wages. When Parliament itself began to levy similar taxes on the city to finance its war with the King, Londoners again rebelled, this time against Parliament, and only the action of the Parliamentary army restored order.

Conclusion

Let us review and compare the effects of emergent capitalism and population pressure on the various conflicts that contributed to the revolutionary crisis.

Figure 1 compares the Marxist view with the alternative I have sketched here. The Marxist view stresses enclosure as leading to conflict between landlords and peasants and

FIGURE 1

The origins of the English Revolution: Two views

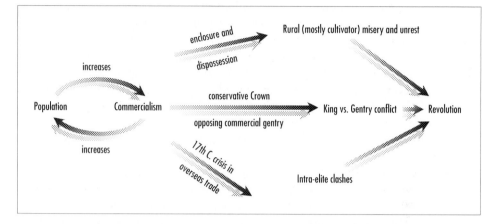

A neo-Marxist view of the origins of the English Revolution

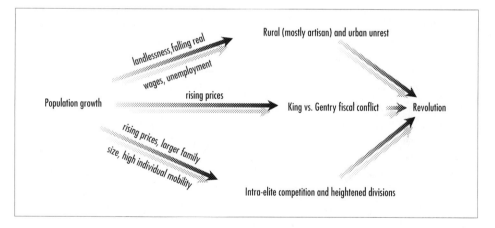

An alternative view of the origins of the English Revolution

between Crown and gentry. The Marxist view also explains conflict among the elites in terms of conflict between commercial (Parliamentarian) and noncommercial (Royalist) forces. Yet these views do not fit the details of the revolution well.

Not enclosure but population growth and rising prices led to the massive growth of London and to popular unrest. Not enclosure but conflict over taxation and Crown interference in local government led to conflict between Crown and gentry. Finally, we cannot simply identify Parliamentarians as capitalists and Royalists as feudal. Many royalist gentry had cooperated with the Crown in enclosure projects an royal monopolies of overseas trade. Many large merchants and commercial centers (such as Newcastle) supported the King. The division between Parliamentarians, and Royalists depended much more on who had benefitted from royal policies and cooperation with the Crown in the 1620s and 1630s and who had been left out as well as on attitudes of individual members of the gentry toward popular uprisings and royal authority.

Rising population and consequent rising prices and widespread fiscal distress were hardly uniquely English. These pressures were felt in many places in seventeenth century Europe and generally increased conflict over taxation and state authority. What gave the English Revolution its particular character was the structure of English society at the time of these increased pressures—a Crown that faced an entrenched gentry elite able to resist increased taxes; a greatly expanded capital city flooded with small merchants, artisans, and workers oppressed by royal monopolies and tax increases; and a peasantry that lacked strong community organization and was closely supervised by local landlords. The result was a revolution dominated by landlord opposition to the king and urban revolt in London, with only scattered and unsuccessful uprisings in the countryside.

In sum, demographic pressures and structural weaknesses help to explain the origins of the English Revolution. This structural–demographic explanation appears more accurate than the Marxist view and more satisfying than a simple emphasis on the incompetence of Charles I. Moreover, paying attention to demographic pressures and structural weaknesses may help to explain the origins of other revolutions far removed from seventeenth century England.

REFERENCES

1.   Elton (1974), p. 160.
2.   Sharpe (1978), p. 42.
3.   Hill (1980), p. 129.
4.   Moore, Jr. (1966), pp. 9, 11–12, 14, 19.
5.   Wallerstein (1974), pp. 25, 116; Wallerstein (1980), p. 142.
6.   Anderson (1974), p. 142.
7.   Sharp (1980), p. 127.
8.   Holderness (1976), p. 54.
9.   Appleby (1975), p. 580.
10. Appleby (1975), p. 580.
11. Walter and Wrightson (1976), p. 27.
12. Walter (1980), p. 74.
13. Cornwall (1977), p. 18.
14. Walter (1980), p. 73.
15. Howell (1979), p. 112.
16. Stone (1965), p. 743.
17. Everitt (1969), p. 49.
18. Spufford (1974), p. 85.
19. Everitt (1967), p. 399.
20. Thirsk (1961), p. 70.

THE MEXICAN REVOLUTION

Walter L. Goldfrank

The Mexican Revolution, begun in 1910 and culminating in the land reforms of 1934–1940, has a colorful and fascinating cast of characters: the president of Mexico from 1876 to 1911, Porfirio Díaz, who ruled Mexico with a combination of *"pan y palo"* ("bread and a club"); the peasant leader Zapata and the bandit leader Pancho Villa, both of whom led revolutionary armies; the moderate Madero, who raised the first challenge to Díaz; the counter-revolutionary general Huerta, who attempted to reestablish a conservative regime after Díaz's fall; the Constitutionalist generals Carranza and Obregón, whose victory sealed the success of the revolution; and the reforming president Cárdenas, whose land reforms helped fulfill the revolution's promise.

Yet behind the personal victories and tradegies of these great men lay complex structural relationships that shaped Mexican history, relationships between Mexico and the international states system, between the Porfirian state and Mexican elites, and between landlords and peasants. In this essay, Goldfrank analyzes these structural relationships and the ways they combined to create a revolutionary situation in early twentieth-century Mexico.

For a long time the Mexican revolution has fascinated laypersons and engaged scholars from different disciplines and many countries. Numerous confusions surround its interpretation. For the most part, attention has been focussed on several aspects: on the heros and villains of the violent struggles of 1910–1920; on the reorganization and reforms instituted by President Lázaro Cárdenas (1934–1940); on the so-called economic miracle of the decades since then (Gross Domestic Product averaged a 6.5% annual increase from 1940 to 1970); and on the victims of that miracle, the children of Sánchez in the cities and their compatriots in the countryside. Yet the great transformation of Mexico began well before 1910, in the last third of the nineteenth century. While not ignoring the dramatic years of armed struggle nor the remarkable changes that have occurred since, this essay concentrates rather on the earlier time. It attempts to account primarily for the outbreak and character of the revolution which, in the long view of the last hundred years, appears to have decisively enhanced Mexican national autonomy, economic growth, and, to a lesser extent, the well-being of the rural and urban workers. Yet these "successes" can be, and typically are, exaggerated: Mexican autonomy is gravely restricted by the country's dependent position in the world economy and by the low level of political mobilization; Mexican economic growth has greatly profited foreign corporations, left the state with a large foreign debt, and owed much to Mexico's proximity to the U.S.; and the reforms alleged to benefit the working class have neither halted the trend toward increased inequality nor substantially affected a large number of so-called "marginal" persons, serving, rather, as a means of social control.

Why, though, did the social controls of the previous years collapse, so that alone among Latin American countries Mexico experienced a revolution before World War II? After some prefatory considerations, this question leads us first to examine competing theories of revolution; second, to see how those theories help with explaining the Mexican case; and third, to sketch and apply an alternative framework which draws upon yet goes beyond existing conceptions.

Popular Views of Revolution

The popular notions of ordinary laypersons and untheoretical historians can be treated briefly. They are basically covered by two metaphors, focussing far more on rebellion than on transformation. One is the "pressure cooker" model, the other, an "outside agitator" model. In the first, too much misery and oppression lead "the people" to revolt against the unjust conditions that constrain them. Or, in the more elaborated accounts of standard historians, a cumulation of serious problems—in foreign policy, banking and finance, taxation, social conflict, government corruption, among them—so overburdens a government that it falls while at the same time popular aspirations are sufficiently frustrated to lead people to rebel. In the second model, otherwise contented people have their baser political passions inflamed by self-serving propagandists; neurotic, misguided, foreign-inspired.

These conceptions are not wholly illusory, but as theory they do not take us very far. Both widespread oppression and inflammatory agitation occur with far greater frequency than revolution, or even rebellion. Further, in the conventional historian's list of "factors" one finds little connective tissue, and typically little sense of the relative importance of the various ingredients in the pressure cooker.

Popular conceptions—too much misery and oppression, too many problems for the existing government, and the work of outside agitators—can introduce the Mexican revolution but they cannot explain it. Misery and oppression were indeed widespread. In the countryside and the cities, wages were very low, working and living conditions pitiable, governmental abuses legion. Given these conditions, revolution might well have occurred at almost any time during the rule of Porfirio Díaz (1876–1911) but it did not. Given similar conditions elsewhere in Latin America, revolutions could have been expected but did not occur. Further, many of the most miserable and oppressed Mexicans took no part in the original insurgencies or in later struggles: this holds for most victims of the tropical plantations—including the scandalously brutal Yucatan henequen fields, for the urban poor, and for the resident agricultural laborers (*acasillados*) on central Mexican haciendas.

Historians' and others' lists of "causes" of the revolution are the other variant of the "pressure cooker" metaphor. These lists can expand to include the results of long term factors such as the original Spanish conquest, the hacienda system, problems unsolved since the achievement of national independence, and the consequences of the Reform Wars of the mid-nineteenth century, middle term problems of the Porfirian era such as widespread foreign investment, increasing concentration of landed and commercial wealth, expansion of the hacienda system, labor troubles in the new industrial and mining centers, and political repression; and short term strains such as the drought and crop failures of 1909 and 1910, fiscal difficulties following conversion to the gold standard in 1905, the agitation of exiles in border communities, and Díaz's infirmities in old age (he was 80 in 1910). Such lists tend to confound the motives of the participants (their "causes" they fought for) with analytic explanations ("causes" in quite another sense). They also tend to ignore the connections between the various problems indicated, because they lack a model of society as a whole.

Toward a Structural Explanation of the Mexican Revolution

How then to account for the Mexican revolution? Logically, we need a conception that brings together elements which by themselves are insufficient conditions. That is, "x," "y," and "z" may be necessary conditions but will not be sufficient conditions unless they occur simultaneously or in a particular sequence. Substantively, we need to identify those conditions in a way that goes beyond the uniqueness of the particular Mexican case (rendering the Mexican revolution comparable with others). But we need to avoid going so far beyond it as to reduce it to an instance of "collective violence," irregular change of regime, or rebellious movement.

Four conditions appear to be necessary and sufficient, although as these conditions interact and overlap with one another, it is difficult to say exactly where one leaves off and another begins. For any particular national society, they are: (1) a tolerant or permissive world context; (2) a severe political crisis paralyzing the administrative and coercive capacities of the state; (3) widespread rural rebellion; and (4) dissident elite political movements.

WORLD CONTEXT

In her work on the major social revolutions in France, Russia, and China, Skocpol has made the case explicitly for the second and third conditions while treating the first and fourth in the course of analyzing outcomes. She has fully appreciated the role of international competition in spurring states to undertake politically difficult modernizing efforts and directly in bringing on potentially revolutionary crises. Perhaps because the cases she has treated are all states with great power ambitions if not great power results, she does not explicitly raise as a causal necessity favorable configurations of the world system as a whole and of the immediate international context. As one moves toward the present temporally and toward the periphery of the world system spatially, this condition becomes increasingly critical.

In the case of lesser and/or more peripheral states, the world system variables assume great importance. Wallerstein has shown how the Netherlands revolt against Spain in the

1570s was furthered by the international situation: England wanted the Hapsburgs weakened and so did France, while France also did not want to see the cause of Protestantism advanced and was thus paralyzed.[1] The successful independence movements in Latin America in the early nineteenth century reflected the ascent of Great Britain to world hegemony and the decline of Spain, perhaps more than any internal changes. The Cuban revolution in our own day depended at first on the division of opinion within the U.S. and later on Cold War rivalry to sustain its momentum. And the Vietnamese revolution is in part clearly a creation of determinate great power configurations: the displacement of the French by the Japanese and the former's attempt to reestablish sovereignty; the U.S. effort to stop the spread of communism; and the Soviet and Chinese capacities to thwart that effort.

In general terms it is sufficient to reduce the variety of favorable world contexts to a single formula. Provisionally, several possibilities can be suggested. First, when the cat's away, the mice will play: the preoccupation of major powers in war or serious internal difficulty increase the likelihood of revolution. This holds both in a general sense for the world system as a whole, and in it specific application to instances of revolution in societies dominated by a single power. Second, when major powers balance one another, especially if that balance is antagonistic, the likelihood of revolution is increased. Third, if rebel movements receive greater outside support than their enemies, the likelihood of revolution is increased. (At the same time, it is worth noting that "outside intervention" in support of the old order may deepen and further the revolutionary process if it comes too little or too late).

What was the favorable world situation that helped to cause the Mexican revolution? First, the changing balance of world power in the Caribbean region made it progressively less possible for Mexico to continue the diplomatic balancing act of playing off European versus U.S. interests. The U.S. had invested heavily in Mexico, where in 1911, 45.5 percent of U.S. (compared to 5.5 percent of Europe's) foreign investments were. This had two principal consequences: it meant that diplomatic pressure from the U.S. could put the Díaz government in a bind, since it owed its financial prospects to foreign investors but its political support to increasingly nationalistic Mexicans. It meant that especially given the European convulsions of World War I, little help would come to Mexican conservatives from abroad. And it also meant that internal U.S. politics would make a greater difference to Mexico than before.

Second is the shape of U.S. politics in the critical years from 1910–1913. This was a period of domestic realignments in the U.S., such that no clear policy emerged towards Mexico and the initial rebellions. U.S. opinion ranged from the plutocratic conservatism of most foreign investors to the openly anarchist and socialist sympathies of the more radical workers. At the top, the Republican president faced a Democratic congress in 1911 and 1912, as well as the division in his own party that resulted in Theodore Roosevelt's Bull Moose campaign. Both before and after 1910 domestic political considerations restrained Taft from vigorously suppressing rebels north of the border, as did hopes for pressuring Díaz into reorienting his policies in a more pro-U.S. direction. With the election of Wilson in 1912 came a period of confusion, as the new president preached popular sovereignty and free elections for Mexico while the holdover ambassador in Mexico City abetted the right-wing movement to overthrow the government of Madero.

Third, the increasing U.S. involvement in World War I left Mexico alone for a time after Perching's abortive and uninvited hunt for Villa. By then the U.S. had settled on the eventual winning side, so that when it helped Obregón mop up pockets of resistance in 1919–1920, the way was clear for renewing U.S. influence and thwarting for almost twenty years—until the Great Depression gave Cárdenas an opening—much of the nationalist impulse of the revolution.

It is not accidental that more than the Mexican revolution occurred in the period around World War I, when the great powers were fighting one another: revolution from above in Turkey, leftward movement in Argentina and Uruguay, a spurt of nationalism in India, and of course the beginnings of revolution in Russia and China. But this general world context had to be complemented by a favorable situation in the United States. Otherwise, the Díaz regime might have been more firmly supported in its last days and an orderly succession worked out. Otherwise, sanctuary and arms supplies would have been denied insurgents at several critical junctures. Otherwise, armed intervention could have thwarted the continuation of the revolutionary process (as for example in the Sandino affair in Nicaragua). And otherwise, Mexican state bureaucrats and private capitalists would not today share so strongly in the control of Mexico's political economy.

POLITICAL CRISIS

A second necessary condition of revolution is the breakdown of the administrative and coercive capacities of the state in a political crisis—a revolutionary "situation." While from the point of view of some revolutionists (especially those wedded to class conflict models), such situations may appear accidental, from an analytic stance above or outside the rush of history, they are determinate if not exactly predictable. For France in 1788–1789 the crisis came with the bankruptcy of the royal treasury and the convening of the Estates General; for Russia in 1917 it was the Tsarist government's failure at war; for China in 1911 it was the Manchu autocracy's inability to mange reforms without losing control to regional gentry cliques. Each of these crises was determined by a significant disjunction between state and the upper classes.

In Mexico, the rough picture is not dissimilar. The precipitating trigger was the failure of the government to snuff out quickly the initial Madero insurgency (itself a typical Latin American *pronunciamento*). This failure occurred in the context of a succession crisis, as Díaz himself was eighty years old in 1910, and had been unable through the recently created institution of the vice-presidency to pave the way for a successor. The crisis deepened after Madero took over the presidency in 1912, as he was unable to carry out promised reforms with an army and civil administration held over from the Porfiriato, yet from the perspective of many powerful groups was too open to such reforms and the loss of social power it would entail for them.

What brought the Mexican state to such a critical passage was a set of contradictions inherent in the political economy of the Porfiriato as it developed. The most serious was the relationship of the state to elite groups, though also grave were the political practices strengthening Díaz's personal rule and the difficulties of representing the Mexican nation while relying heavily on foreign capital.

Díaz's rise to power coincided with the great worldwide expansion of industrial capitalism in the last quarter of the nineteenth century, as the competitive search for markets, materials and investment outlets sent European and U.S. firms into new territories and invigorated their activities in old ones. Mexico in this period experienced rapid growth, in mining, commercial agriculture, and manufacturing for the national market. In this situation, three social groups shared power. There were first the older estate-owners who relied on indebted resident laborers to turn a small profit; Catholic in religion, conservative in politics, this group was conciliated by Díaz but never allowed to exercise influence at the national level. The most important group was the entrepreneurial bourgeoisie, a heterogeneous lot including promoters, import-export merchants, bankers, estate owners who modernized their operations (using more machinery and more wage-labor), and manufacturers. Varied in ethnic origins and regional loyalties, oriented to diverse markets, increasingly differentiated as the economy became more complex, and content with the state's protection of property, these "modern" bourgeois had little incentive to organize as a class, beyond distinct interest groups. The third important group was the political machine of Díaz: governors, generals, local bosses, mostly *mestizo,* socially excluded, culturally distinct.

Before the turn of the century and increasingly after that time, the second group—particularly those with extensive foreign connections—came to dominate economic policy. They also endeavored to institutionalize their future control over Mexico by insisting on a vice-presidency and by forming a political party. Their political rivals, especially in the third group, fought back, with Díaz playing the one off against the other. The ruler in fact became "indispensable," as he feared armed foreign intervention if he handed the government over to nationalistic *mestizo* politicians and even greater foreign economic dominance (and possibly open revolt) if he entrusted the future to the unpopular bourgeoisie. The disjunction between state and ruling class that was a source of leverage for the regime in its hey-day weakened it severely in the crisis.

Díaz's political methods were likewise successful in the short run but disastrous in the long run. Fearing the military, he juggled commands, reduced the budget (also helpful for impressing foreign investors), and allowed corruption to flourish; the result was a federal army unable quickly to suppress the Madero insurgency. In civil politics, he destroyed the potentially self-correcting liberal institutions (free speech and press, independent judiciary, meaningful legislative assemblies and elections) that elsewhere regulated conflict within ruling groups and helped them to absorb popular demands—in that period of Latin America typically originating among the urban middle strata. A personal political machine was enhanced at the expense of liberal institutions, while the ideology of liberalism was paid lip service. Thus it is not accidental that the Madero insurgency began as an electoral campaign for the presidency, and that demands for reinvigoration of liberal institutions were the most important points in his program. In addition to concentrating power in his own person, Díaz carried the techniques of discrediting potential rivals to such a point that no strong-man successor was available.

Finally, the Mexican state was weakened by its compromises with foreign capital and foreign governments, particularly the U.S., at a time when business rivalry, imperialist penetration, and the use of U.S. personnel in managerial and highly skilled occupations were generating increasingly potent nationalist interests and sentiments. A number of diplomatic incidents from 1907 to 1910 increased tensions, incurring Washington's displeasure with the Díaz regime without reestablishing the nationalist credentials Díaz had earned for himself in the war against the French almost fifty years before. As Díaz was also favoring a British oil firm in its competition inside Mexico with U.S. firms, the U.S. government was even less friendly to him. At the end Díaz's diplomatic balancing act—attempting to maintain diversified dependence—failed, as the British ceded primacy in Mexico to the U.S. As the Madero insurgency gathered momentum (in large part from the participation of refugees and sympathizers in Texas), the U.S. government did not move vigorously to help suppress it. Díaz then chose to resign rather than invite a protracted struggle that risked armed intervention by the U.S.

WIDESPREAD RURAL REBELLION

However, a political-administrative crisis and a favorable world context are insufficient conditions for revolution, as the cases of Meiji Japan (and perhaps present-day Portugal) remind us. Rural rebellion is a third necessary condition, interacting with the previous ones. In the French and Russian cases peasant revolts facilitated by the crumbling of royal power furthered its collapse; in the Chinese case the Communist Party was able to mobilize peasant rebellion faster than the KMT could squash it. In Mexico the rural revolt was neither so widespread as in France or Russia nor so nationally organized and ideologically sophisticated as in China. This relative weakness contributed to the fact that the Mexican revolution was relatively less successful in removing the landed upper class from power. But as in the other cases, so in Mexico it was the country people who fueled the revolutionary process, pushing would-be reformers further than they would otherwise have gone, and preventing the landed class from playing an important role in stabilizing elite coalitions at the national level.

The heterogeneity of rural Mexico increased greatly during the period preceding the revolution. Thus several distinctive rural rebellions accounted for the greater part of revolutionary participation, and the regions and groups that were relatively quiet also showed considerable differences in the nature of cultivation, the organization of labor, and the extent and kind of political organization. In general terms, it can be said that *rural rebellion was strongest where two conditions obtained simultaneously: first, where the newly dynamic capitalist (though not exclusively export) agriculture had most deeply penetrated; second, where the rural labor force enjoyed what Wolf terms "tactical mobility"—meaning village organization and/or relative autonomy from supervision and/or geographical-military advantages.*[2] [See the essay by Wolf in this volume.—Ed.]

TABLE 1

		Rural labor force: "Tactical mobility"	
		+	−
New capitalist penetration	+	Chihuahua Sonora Morelos	Yucatán
	−	Oaxaca	Central plateau haciendas

Table 1 presents both the array of centers of rural revolt and instances where only one of or neither of the necessary conditions obtained. Yet this level of analytical abstraction is insufficient for capturing important differences among the rebel groups, differences that severely limited their capacity for concerted, as opposed to parallel, political action.

In the thirty years before the revolution, capitalism spread over the Mexican countryside unevenly and in different forms. In the Yucatán, henequen plantations were established to grow the raw materials for binding wheat in the U.S. and Canada. Much of the indigenous Mayan population was pushed or fled further and further into the jungle, so that the labor force had to be partly imported from other parts of Mexico, and most notably from the northwestern state of Sonora where other indigenous groups, the Yaqui and Mayo, were defeated by the federal army as part of a land grab. The heterogeneous, brutally exploited, plantation workers took no part in the revolutionary events, while a Constitutionalist army took over the state in 1915 and used henequen revenues to help finance the struggle against the rural revolutionaries from Morelos and from the North.

In Oaxaca, the peasantry was notably quiet during the revolution. In this case, however, it was more because modern agricultural capitalism had not penetrated the state, and less due to the weakness of the cultivators' organizational and geographical potential for political action. Estate owners were less prominent in the state's political elite, and they encroached little on the lands of Mixtec and Zapotec peasants after 1880. Sugar was grown in small quantities by old methods; where coffee was introduced it was primarily grown by small scale producers. "With the salient exception of the La Cañada and Tuxtepec regions, the only parts of Oaxaca that sustained any significant peasant revolutionary action, capitalism in the form of modern agricultural enterprises did not over-run the countryside."[3]

The third non-revolutionary combination of variables includes neither significant capitalist transformation of agriculture or large degrees of peasant autonomy, organization, and military-geographic potential. This combination describes a large portion of the central Mexican plateau. In most of this region, the conventional hacienda predominated with its well known underutilization of land and technology and over exploitation of labor. While scattered estates went over to intensive cultivation of the century plant (a cactus yielding juices fermented into *pulque,* an alcoholic beverage popular with the demoralized urban poor) or to dairying, the majority took advantage of favorable land legislation to expand their holdings without measurably increasing production. One result was that the cultivation of food crops lagged behind the growth in agriculture for export and for domestic processing, not to mention a considerable growth in population. Another result was to incorporate the majority of the formerly autonomous peasant communities into the *hacienda,* and to encourage migration out of the region. Residents, perpetually indebted peons (*acasillados*), comprised the stable labor force, which was supplemented at peak seasons by day laborers and migrants. Probably because they enjoyed the advantage of job security and suffered the disadvantage of close supervision, the resident estate laborers were notably absent from revolutionary participation.

Rural rebellion then arose where both new capitalist thrusts occurred and for one or another reason large numbers of workers were tactically mobile. But the three principal loci of revolt differed greatly from one another, both in the developing patterns of capitalist agriculture and in the organizational structure and capacity of the working population. In Sonora and some others parts of Northern Mexico, small to medium scale commercial farmers rallied against discriminatory taxation, high freight rates on the foreign controlled railroads, and preferential treatment of U.S. firms and individuals in land deals. The Sonoran rebels were also able to recruit among the defeated Yaqui and Mayo Indians whose lands had been distributed to large-scale agricultural operations and whose compatriots had been deported to the *henequen* plantations. This combination, with provincial professionals as well as commercial farmers in the lead and recently subjugated peasant cultivators in the ranks, readily lent itself to the standard military organization of companies and battalions. Remote from Mexico City, separated from the Northern desert plateau by the Sierra Madre, and bordering on the U.S. so that arms could be rather easily acquired, Sonora was a stronghold of rebellion throughout the decade, once the political changes following Díaz's fall weakened the pre-existing apparatus of coercion. On the other hand, the Sonoran rebels were led by elements of the middle strata who allied themselves with the moderate Constitutionalists after 1914 to defeat the more plebeian armies of Villa and Zapata. They also parlayed their military success into control of the Mexican presidency until the nineteen-thirties.

In other parts of the Mexican North, particularly Chihuahua, capitalist agriculture expanded mainly in cattle ranching, although cotton production and the cultivation of India rubber (*guayule*) were also important. Debt peonage was on the wane in the North, with sharecropping, cash rentals and wage labor becoming common. The mining and railroad booms stimulated food production for local and export markets. The giant ranches provided spectacular examples of *latifundismo* yet were increasingly modern enterprises well suited to the terrain. Their owners controlled local and state politics, making life difficult for cultivators. They employed hundreds of cowboys—often irregularly employed—and sustained the uncertain livelihood of numerous illegal operators, involved in smuggling, banditry, and cattle rustling. When in 1909 the Northern Mexican economy was hurt as a consequence of a downturn in the U.S., workers returned from across the border only to find stagnation in mining and then drought in agriculture. They were available to join the relatively rootless proto-cavalrymen who eventually formed the core of Villa's army, after first providing the bands that enabled Madero to oust Díaz. Yet the background that made this popular cavalry strong, the development of fierce independence and equestrian skill, was also a limitation: their contempt for settled cultivators made them very parochial in their land policy and their exclusion from civic life rendered them politically inept, unable to consolidate their military gains.

The third major locus of rural rebellion was Morelos, a small state strategically located over the mountains from the capital city. There—and in adjacent portions of Guerrero, Mexico, and Puebla, as well as non-contiguous places like Huaesteca—independent villagers whose livelihoods were being squeezed by the expansion of newly capitalized haciendas spearheaded rural rebellion. In Morelos it was the capitalization of sugar cultivation after 1880 that set in motion the squeeze on the villagers. In order to pay for new milling machinery and to reach markets that the railroads put within reach, the haciendas that had formerly coexisted with peasant production came utterly to dominate it. Some villagers lost lands and water, others (15% of the state's total) disappeared completely. Villagers turned to stock raising in the mountains, to sharecropping the worst hacienda lands, to day labor in contracted gangs, even to the hated alternative of becoming resident peons. Increased competitive pressure (from beet sugar and other regions) after 1900 pushed the planters to higher investment and greater expansion at the villagers' expense,[4] but the Madero insurgency in the North furnished the occasion for a counter-attack by the villagers. Protected by the mountains they drew upon a tradition of rebellion stretching back almost a century to the independence war against Spain and organized into a classic guerrilla army defending its homeland. Their pressure on Mexico City helped Madero win in 1911, and when reforms were slow to come, they resumed armed struggle for the better part of a decade while carrying out their own agrarian reform in between extermination campaigns against them. But the village organization that gave their backward-looking egalitarian idealism its awesome tenacity also entailed a localistic orientation that gravely impaired their capacity for political action at the national level. The Zapatistas made agrarian reform a national priority but were shut out of the victorious coalition that would eventually, haltingly, carry it out.

Together these three sorts of rural rebellion made a moderate stabilization impossible, whether under the reformist liberal Madero or the more conservative but by no means reactionary Huerta. From the standpoint of comparative analysis, however, two points deserve emphasis. First, the rural rebellion in Mexico was not a nationwide conflagration, a general rising against landlords or peonage or "fuedal" forms of surplus extraction. Except for a few localities, irreversible *de facto* land reform did not occur as in revolutionary

France or Russia until the government enacted and enforced it. Second, the heterogeneity of the rural rebels, each set responding to a different form of capitalist penetration, mirrored the heterogeneity of the bourgeoisie. If the latter were unable to agree on programs and policies because of the material, cultural, and regional differences and the absence of mediating institutions at the national level, so the rural workers failed to make a coherent bid for political power. And no party, like the Communists in China, came along to do it with and for them.

DISSIDENT POLITICAL MOVEMENTS

The fourth necessary condition for revolution is the existence of dissident urban political groups capable of reshaping the state to achieve or hasten modernizing transformations and to increase its competitive standing in the world system. Dissident movements need not predate administrative breakdown and political crisis, though like the subversive moralists of pre-revolutionary France or the agitational parties of pre-revolutionary Russia they may contribute to such crisis. Nor need dissident groups link up in an organized way with peasant rebellion, as the CCP did. In varying degrees such groups arise and grow as a logical consequence of a revolutionary conjuncture, given the unusual opportunity. And since the victors typically write their own histories, we must be wary of their claims to have cleared their own paths to success.

In the Mexican case, three broad movements can be identified. First, several "precursor" movements came into existence after the turn of the century, spreading conventional liberal ideas at times tinged with anarchism and/or labor grievances. Second, Madero's presidential campaign in 1910 built on the network of liberal "clubs" that had formed in many provincial cities. Finally, the Constitutionalist movement arose to resist Huerta's government after the coup ousting Madero in 1913, then built a coalition whose armies defeated Villa and Zapata, wrote a new constitution in 1917, and became the new government. The first two movements preceded and contributed to the revolutionary conjuncture, while the third emerged from it. The first two were utterly normal political phenomena, different in local detail from protest movements and electoral campaigns elsewhere but clearly part of ordinary politics; their causal necessity can easily be overemphasized. The third was a logical outcome of governmental breakdown at the national level and of widespread rural rebellion, and it insured that neither anarchy nor a return to the *status quo ante* would result.

The "precursors" of the Mexican revolution paralleled three kinds of protest movements current in that era, in varying degrees, in the rest of the Americas, movements that either succeeded peacefully or were absorbed, deflected, and repressed elsewhere. They included civic and electoral reform spearheaded by the professional middle class, agrarian populism, and syndicalist labor agitation. Within them dissident intellectuals formulated overlapping critiques of the regime, focusing on the restoration of constitutionally guaranteed individual and community freedom, an end of favoritism to foreigners, and the elimination of labor abuses. Besides preparing the ground for Madero's electoral challenge in 1910, these movements had the important consequences of increasing the political awareness and abilities of the Mexican refugee communities in South Texas and generating support for reform in Mexico among liberals and the left in the United States generally.

Madero's presidential campaign and subsequent insurrection is conventionally regarded as the beginning of *the Revolution*. While such an understanding makes political sense for the inheritors of Madero's mantle, it misdirects analysis by uncritically taking over the Spanish "revolución" (= armed overthrow). Madero's ascent to the presidency was a temporary solution to the succession crisis of the Díaz regime, orchestrated by high officials so as to defuse incipient local rebellions by instituting an interim presidency and allowing free elections. The solution was temporary because the political freedoms of the Madero presidency facilitated the exacerbation of class conflicts and further weakened the state. Important elements of the old order were entrenched in the military and civilian bureaucracies where they first thwarted implementation of change that would satisfy popular demands. They then carried out the coup under Huerta that damaged the state beyond rescue, provoked rural rebellion and brought forth the dissident movement that would ultimately consolidate a revolutionary outcome, the Constitutionalists.

The Constitutionalists, so called because of their aim to undo the illegal coup against the duly elected Madero, began as a group of provincial landowners and professionals concentrated in the North. They formed a civilian cabinet under the leadership of their "first chief" Carranza, a minor official under Díaz and a state governor under Madero, and they gathered an army comprised of defecting federal troops and rebel groups previously loyal to Madero. They depended upon tactical alliances with the peasant and working class rural rebels until Huerta had been ousted but refused to participate in the revolutionary convention dominated by the latter in 1914. Rather, relying first on the middle class agrarians led by Obregón and then on an alliance with urban workers, they put together an army which defeated Villa and contained Zapata. But in the course of the struggle, the civilian liberals were pushed to the side, as more radical elements dominated their army, and, after elections in the provinces they controlled, dominated the 1917 constitutional convention as well. Obregón's assumption of the presidency in 1920 symbolized the shift from liberalism to populism, and the state he and his successors reconstituted fits well the model of the populist state.

Aspects of the revolutionary outcome—an end to debt peonage, the beginning of serious though insufficient land reform, the legal foundation for nationalizing foreign mineral holdings, improvement in the protection and bargaining power of labor—had been discussed before 1910 by dissidents and reformers, but no movement was able consciously to guide the revolutionary process. The "precursor" movements and Madero's electoral campaign and insurrection helped to make a revolutionary conjuncture; the Constitutionalists were finally able to reconstruct the state, though by no means with overwhelming popular support. True, their victory entailed some concessions to the radical demands represented in armed struggle by these elements of the rural poor who rebelled (and Morelos was the first state to see sizeable land reform), but that victory more importantly required the military defeat of those very forces. That the Mexican revolution did not go further to the left is in part explained by the fact that the Constitutionalists made promises to the masses but unlike the Russian or Chinese Communists did not develop or practice an ideology requiring cadre self-discipline and urging mass participation.

Analytically, we can suggest that a dissident movement capable of reorganizing the state and restoring order, which the Villistas and Zapatistas were unable to do when militarily they held the upper hand, is a necessary condition for a revolutionary outcome: otherwise, anarchy and/or reversion will occur. Yet such a movement seems in the Mexican case to follow upon the fulfillment of the other three necessary conditions and thus ought to be accorded a less independent causal status.

Conclusion

The above analysis identified four conditions as necessary and sufficient for revolution in general and the Mexican revolution in particular: a favorable world context, an administrative and coercive crisis of the state, widespread rural rebellion, and dissident elite movement(s). The first three interact to produce a revolutionary situation; the fourth, given the near-automatic existence of alternative contenders, emerges to effect political and social transformation after military superiority is proved. Other conceptions of revolution—with their foci on expectations and deprivations—were found wanting theoretically and to varying degrees unhelpful in making sense of the empirical realities of the Mexican case. The historically grounded, world-system informed structural explanation better fits the data.

The structural explanation preserves the distinction between revolution and other less far-reaching socio-political phenomena. And it suggests, sternly and surely, that in contemporary advanced societies the kind of conjuncture specified above cannot occur. The strengthening of the central state apparatus that revolutionaries typically carry out (to compete internationally, defend against counter-revolution, and enforce social reforms) makes further revolutions unlikely, perhaps impossible. If it accomplished nothing else, the Mexican revolution hastened the elimination of the reactionary elements of the landed class from national political influence, and led to the establishment of state machinery sufficiently strong both to mollify the negative effects of foreign investment and to regulate class conflict. Violent protest is far more likely than revolution in Mexico's future.

REFERENCES

1.   Wallerstein (1974).
2.   Wolf (1970).
3.   Waterbury (1975), pp. 438–439.
4.   By 1910, "the seventeen owners of the thirty-six major haciendas in the state owned over 25% of its total surface, most of its cultivable land, and almost all of its good land." Womack (1969), p. 49.

The Iranian Revolution

In this century there have been several attempts to limit the power of the Shah and give Iran a constitutional government. Most of them failed. In 1902 the Qajar Shah Muzaffar al-Din, agreeing to demands by reformers, granted Iran a constitution calling for a national assembly (the *majlis*) and a constitutional monarchy. Yet his successors often ignored the new constitution. In 1925 Reza Khan overthrew the Qajar dynasty and became the new Shah (taking the name Reza Shah Pahlavi), promising to defend the constitution. Yet Reza Shah (Shah of Iran 1925–1941) and his son Mohammed Reza Pahlavi (Shah of Iran 1941–1979) paid only limited attention to the constitution, and the power of the Shah remained virtually absolute. From 1951 to 1953 the nationalist reformer and prime minister Mohammed Mossadeq challenged the Shah, and briefly took the lead in determining government policy. But in 1953, with help from the United States, the Shah reclaimed full power through a coup d'etat against Mossadeq.

In the next twenty-five years, with oil revenues and U.S. support, the Shah built Iran's economy and army into the largest in the Middle East. Yet in 1979 the entire structure of government in Iran crumbled around the Shah in a massive revolution.

The sudden and unexpected collapse of the Shah's regime and the triumph of traditional religious leaders has been a mystery to many in the West. Abrahamian here explains the long-term background to the Iranian revolution, making clear the political and economic vulnerabilities of the Shah's regime. He argues that "tensions were aggravated not by modernization per se, but by the way modernization was implemented." The Shah's economic program benefited chiefly the rich, while the urban and rural poor were left with less land and poorer housing. At the same time, the Shah's political program rejected the claims of unions, intellectuals, merchants, religious leaders, and professionals to share in government policy-making, thus alienating virtually every major organized group in Iran.

Enmeshed in the world economy, the Shah was able to do little when in 1975–1977 rising oil and commodity prices, combined with the Shah's aggressive military and economic expansion, brought rampant inflation that undermined the incomes of most Iranians. When the economic crisis prompted strikes in 1978, leaders from every elite group sought to rally popular opposition against the Shah, and his regime collapsed amidst mass street demonstrations and national strikes. The Shah was thus brought down by a combination of factors similar to those behind the French, Russian, Chinese, and Mexican Revolutions: (1) a fiscal and political crisis (brought on by the severe inflation of 1975–1979), (2) the opposition of elite groups alienated from the regime, and (3) organized popular protests.

In the following two essays, Abrahamian first describes the background to the Revolution, analyzing the failure of the Shah's policies and the growth of a unified opposition. Green then describes the events that led to the Shah's fall.

◆

STRUCTURAL CAUSES OF THE
IRANIAN REVOLUTION

Ervand Abrahamian

The fall of the Shah will go down in history as perhaps the most dramatic revolution of modern times. In most revolutions, the collapse of the old order has paved the way for the triumph of new classes armed with modern organizations, particularly political parties, and inspired by such secular ideologies as nationalism, socialism, and communism. In the Iranian case, however, the revolution has brought to the fore the traditional clergy armed with the mosque and inspired by a seventh century political philosophy which argues that the religious leaders have the divine right to protect the community from foreigners, guide the country towards righteousness, exercise power over the elected representatives, and scrutinize the activities of all social groups.

The aim of this article is to analyze the structural causes of the revolution, focusing on the socioeconomic pressures that gradually undermined the political establishment and thereby paved the way for the crash of February 1979. The contention here is that the failure of the Pahlavi regime to make political modifications appropriate to the changes taking place in the economy and society inevitably strained the links between the social structure and the political structure, blocked the channeling of social grievances into the political system, widened the gap between new social forces and the ruling circles, and, most serious of all, cut down the few bridges that had in the past connected traditional social forces, especially the bazaars, with the political establishment.

Socioeconomic Development

In the quarter century after 1953 Iran experienced considerable socioeconomic development. The was made possible largely by increasing oil revenues. In 1953, the oil revenues totaled less than $34 million. By 1973, they reached near $5 billion. And by 1977, after the quadrupling of world oil prices, they topped $20 billion. Between 1953 and 1978, the cumulative oil income came to as much as $54 billion. Of course, some of this was wasted on princely palaces, royal grand tours, major festivals, solid gold bathtubs, nuclear projects, and ultra-sophisticated weapons too expensive even for many NATO countries. But despite the wastage, nearly $30 billion was spent on economic and social projects in the course of the Second (1955–1962), Third (1962–1968), Fourth (1968–1973), and Fifth (1973–1978) Development Plans.

As a result of these plans and the rising oil revenues, the gross national product rose at current prices from $3 billion to over $53 billion; the value of nonmilitary imports increased from $40 million to nearly $12 billion; and per capita income jumped from less than $160 to over $1600 even though the population grew from 18 million to nearly 35 million.

The socioeconomic implications of this growth can be seen best in the realms of education and industrialization. Over the quarter century from 1953 to 1977, the number of university students grew more than tenfold, from 14,500 to 154,000. Enrollment in primary and secondary schools grew from 870,000 to nearly 5,000,000. The growth of modern industry was equally impressive during these twenty-five years. The number of industrial factories grew from roughly 1,000 to more than 8,000. The output of electricity, iron, and cement increased by a factor of 100, and new industries began to produce steel and aluminum, cars, trucks, and tractors. The output of coal, sugar, and textiles also greatly increased.

This expansion in industry and education, together with growth in the state bureaucracy, increased the ranks of the two modern classes—the salaried middle class and the urban proletariat. In 1953, the modern middle class, counting all salaried employees, civil servants, professionals, engineers, managers, teachers, and other members of the intelligentsia, had numbered no more than 324,000. By 1977, however, the modern middle class totaled over 630,000, and formed as much as 6.7 percent of the labor force of 9.4 million. This total included 6726 professors, 20,300 engineers, 21,500 medical personnel, 208,241 teachers, and 304,404 civil servants. In addition, there was a large army of students who intended to join the salaried middle class: 154,315 enrolled in higher education, over 90,000 in foreign universities, and 741,000 in secondary schools.

The urban working class grew at a more rapid pace. In 1953, the wage earners employed in modern industry, oil, transport, mining, urban construction, and services located in major population centers totaled no more than 300,000—only 5 percent of the country's labor force. But by 1977, the same sectors employed over 1.7 million, 16 percent of the country's labor force. This included over 800,000 in modern factories, 30,000 in the oil industry, 50,000 in mining, 150,000, railwaymen, dockers, truck drivers and other modern transport workers, 152,000 in services, and well over 500,000 in urban construction. In addition to this modern proletariat, there were some 700,000 agricultural laborers and over 500,000 wage earners employed in rural construction, handicraft manufacturing, and small bazaar workshops. Throughout the country the wage earners totaled 2.9 million and formed more than 25 percent of the labor force.

Although the regime financed the impressive economic growth, it failed, for two major reasons, to win much support from either the salaried middle class or the urban working class. First the 1953 *coup* not only overthrew the popular leader Dr. Mossadeq, but also destroyed labor unions, professional associations, and all independent political parties, and dug a wide, even unbridgeable, gulf between the regime and the two modern classes. Second, the regime further widened this gulf by implementing policies benefiting the upper class rather than the middle and lower classes, who had no pressure groups through which they could alter or peacefully oppose government decisions.

It was true, as supporters of the regime often argued, that during the quarter century, particularly after the program of reforms known as the White Revolution of 1963, great strides were made in the areas of health, education, and public welfare: the number of doctors increased from 4500 to 13,000, the literacy rate rose from 26 percent to 42 percent, and the infant mortality rate dropped from 20 percent to less than 12 percent.

But it was equally true that after 14 years of so-called White Revolution 68 percent of adults remained illiterate, the number of illiterates actually rose from 13 million to 15 million, less than 40 percent of children completed primary school, only 60,000 university places were available for as many as 290,000 applicants, the percentage of population with higher degrees was one of the lowest in the Middle East, and the doctor-patient ratio remained one of the worst in the whole of Western Asia.

It was true that for many families the standard-of-living improved as they gained access to modern apartments and consumer goods, especially refrigerators, televisions, motorcycles, air conditioners, and private cars. But it was also true that for many urban families the quality-of-life deteriorated as the shanty towns proliferated, the air became more polluted, and the streets turned into traffic nightmares. Between 1967 and 1977, the percentage of urban families living in only one room increased from 36 to 43. On the eve of the revolution, as much as 42 percent of Tehran had inadequate housing. And, despite the vast oil revenues, Tehran, a city of over 4 million, still had no proper sewage system and no proper public transportation system. In a statement reminiscent of Marie Antoinette, the Shah's younger brother, who owned a helicopter assembly plant, asked: "If people don't like traffic jams, why don't they buy helicopters?"

It was true that the White Revolution financed the formation of farm cooperatives, drastically increased the use of tractors, harvesters and fertilizers, and, most important of all, transferred land to 1,638,00 peasant families. It was equally true, however, that 96 percent of the villagers were left without electricity, farm cooperatives were starved of credit, and agricultural production stagnated mainly because of price controls on basic commodities. For every two families that received land one received nothing, and for every one that obtained adequate land (7 hectares) three obtained less than enough to become independent commercial farmers. Thus, despite the White Revolution, land ownership remained highly unequal, as Table 1 indicates.

Income inequality in the cities was equally bad mainly because of the regime's strategy of developing the economy by helping private entrepreneurs. In the absence of statistics on income distribution, we must draw our conclusions from a number of surveys on urban

TABLE 1

Land ownership after the White Revolution

Size	Number of owners
200 plus hectares*	1,300 (including many old aristocracy)
51–200 hectares	44,000 (almost all absentee)
11–50 hectares	600,000 (many absentees)
3–10 hectares	1,200,000
less than 3 hectares	1,000,000
landless	700,000

*A hectare is equivalent to 2.471 acres.

family expenditures carried out by the Central Bank. These show that in 1959–1960 the richest 10 percent of urban households accounted for 35.5 percent of the total expenditures and the richest 20 percent for 51.7 percent. At the other end of the social pyramid, the poorest 10 percent accounted for 1.7 percent of the total expenditures and the poorest 20 percent for 4.7 percent. The middle 40 percent accounted for 27.5 percent. According to an unpublished report of the International Labor Office, this made Iran one of the most inegalitarian societies in the world. This inequality grew even worse during the 1960s. By 1973–1974, the top 20 percent of urban families accounted for as much as 55.5 percent of the total expenditures, the bottom 20 percent for as little as 3.7 percent, and the middle 40 percent for no more than 26 percent.

The public, while certainly not aware of these statistics, was constantly reminded of the gross inequalities by the rich who flaunted their wealth through conspicuous consumption and by the financial scandals which periodically shook the establishment. In 1974–1975 alone, the Commander-in-Chief of the Navy was found guilty of pocketing $3.7 million, and the Commander-in-Chief of the Air Force (the Shah's brother-in-law) was implicated in a $5 million kick-back scheme. *The Armed Forces Journal International* carried the following indictment.

> By 1977 the sheer scale of corruption had reached a boiling point. The Pahlavi Foundation had become a blatant method of grabbing wealth for the royal family. Senior officers obtained vast wealth from commissions. Senior officials who ran companies such as Iran Air and the National Oil Company hardly bothered to conceal their extortions.... Even conservative estimates indicate that such corruption involved at least a billion dollars between 1973 and 1976.[1]

Thus the structural tensions were aggravated not by modernization *per se,* but by the way the modernization was implemented.

Political Underdevelopment

While the Shah helped modernize the social structure, he did little to develop the political superstructure—to permit the formation of pressure groups, to open the political arena for social forces, to forge links between the regime and the new classes, and to broaden the base of a monarchy which, after all, had survived only because of the 1953 *coup d'etat.* On the contrary, he moved in the reverse direction, narrowed the regime's political base, and, most serious of all, broke the ties that in the past had linked, even though tenuously, the monarchy with the traditional middle class.

The traditional middle class remained important for a number of reasons. First the bazaars, the stronghold of this class, numbered as many as 250,000 shopkeepers and controlled as much as two-thirds of the country's retail trade. The Tehran bazaar alone covered some three square miles and housed over 10,000 stores and workshops. Second, the bazaars, unlike the modern classes, had been able to retain their organizations, especially their craft and trade guilds. Third, the bazaar entrepreneurs exercised considerable influence not only over their store assistants and workshop employees, but also over thousands of peddlers, small retailers, and petty brokers.

Fourth, the influence of the bazaar also reached into the countryside partly because many of the commercial farms were owned by absentee entrepreneurs, and partly because some of the 430,000 small manufacturing plants located in the villages were subsidized by urban businessmen. Employing less than 10 workers, most of whom were women, these small plants specialized in carpet weaving, shoe making, and furniture manufacturing. Finally, the bazaars had social, financial, political, ideological, and historical links with the religious establishment. This establishment retained a great deal of political influence in part because it had ideological hegemony over the shanty town poor, in part because it controlled the only nationwide organization that had remained independent of the state, and in part because it could mobilize over 90,000 clergymen—some 50 ayatollahs, 5000 hojat al-Islams, 11,000 theology students, and an unknown number of low-ranking preachers, teachers, prayer leaders, and religious procession organizers.

In the period between 1953 and 1975, the regime's policy towards the bazaars was one of "let sleeping dogs lie." It watched carefully, but took care not to arouse bazaar opposition. It spied on the trade and craft guilds, but made no attempt to destroy or replace them as it had done with the factory unions and the professional associations. It favored large entrepreneurs at the expense of small shopkeepers, but did not try to eradicate the bazaar economy. If financed clerics who supported the government, such as Ayatollah Behbehani, and exiled those who openly critized, notably Ayatollah Khomeini. But at the same time it ignored silent opposition and took precautions not to alienate the entire religious establishment.

This policy failed only twice: first, in 1954, when the bazaars organized a two-day general strike to protest the signing of a new oil agreement with the West; second, in June 1963, when Khomeini, in his first political appearance, denounced the regime for rigging parliamentary elections, allying with Israel against the Arab world, and granting "capitulations" to American military advisers. Taking up the call, thousands of shopkeepers, peddlers, and students poured into the streets to confront the army. According to conservative estimates, some 1000 demonstrators were killed. Despite the bloodshed, martial law lasted no more than a week and the bazaar soon returned to normal.

In 1975, however, the Shah abandoned the successful policy of "let sleeping dogs lie." The change was necessitated by the Shah's decision to form the Resurgence Party (*Hizb-i Rastakhiz*), and thereby transform his military monarchy into a fascist-style totalitarian regime. Citizens were given the grand choice of joining the party or "leaving the country." The aim of the party was twofold: to tighten control over the intelligentsia and the urban working class; and, for the first time in Iranian history, to extend state power into the bazaars and the religious establishment. The Resurgence Party rushed [in] where previous royalist parties had feared to tread.

Within a few months of its formation, the Resurgence Party opened branches in the bazaars, dissolved the traditional guilds, and created new ones under the direct supervision of state bureaucrats. It also set up a Chamber of Guilds in the large towns, and gave the presidency of many of these chambers to wealthy businessmen from outside the bazaar. The petty bourgeoisie considered these outsiders to be members of the "comprador oil bourgeoisie."

Moreover, the party talked of uprooting the bazaars, eradicating their "worm-ridden shops," bulldozing some of their districts to make way for major roads, and building a state-run market modeled after London's Covent Gardens. Furthermore, it spoke of the need to raise the minimum wage for bazaar workers, to force shopkeepers and workshop owners to take out medical insurance for their employees, and to extend even more credits to the prosperous entrepreneurs who had opened up large restaurants, supermarkets, and department stores. By 1976, big businessmen could go to state-subsidized banks and borrow at 6 percent interest. Small businessmen, however, had no choice but to go to private moneylenders and borrow at 20–30 percent interest. It is not surprising that during the revolution these banks became a major target for demonstrators.

The regime's attack on the bazaars further intensified during the spiraling inflation of 1975–1977. Unable to control the inflation, the regime used the small shopkeeper as the major scapegoat and declared war on the bazaars. The mass media hammered away on the theme that "bazaar profiteers" were sucking dry the blood of consumers. The Resurgence Party scrutinized store accounts with some 10,000 so-called inspectors. Meanwhile, the Guild Courts, set up to punish "profiteers," jailed some 8000 businessmen, shopkeepers and peddlers, exiled from their home towns another 23,000, and fined as many as 200,000 more.

One shopkeeper complained to the correspondent of *Le Monde* that the White Revolution had turned into a Red Revolution and that "party thugs" had official sanction to terrorize the bazaars. Similarly, another shopkeeper told the correspondent of the *New York Times*: "If we let him, the Shah will destroy us. The banks are taking over. The big stores are undermining our livelihoods. And the government will flatten our bazaars to make room for state offices."[2]

The regime waged a simultaneous war against the religious establishment. The Resurgence Party declared the Shah to be not only the "political leader" of the state but also the "spiritual guide" of the community. The Shah himself announced the coming of a "new great civilization." To hasten its arrival, he replaced the Muslim calendar with a new royalist calendar and thereby jumped overnight from the year 1355 to 2535, Parliament, disregarding the religious *shar'ia* laws, raised the age of marriage for girls from 15 to 18 and for boys from 18 to 20. The Justice Minister instructed judges to be more strict in their enforcement of the 1967 Family Protection Law, which had been designed to restrict both polygomy and men's right to obtain easy divorces. The Education Minister ordered universities not to register women who insisted on wearing the *chador* (long veil). Moreover, the newly established Religious Corps, modeled on the

Literacy Corps, intensified its activities so as to teach peasants that "true Islam" differed from that preached by "black reactionary *mullahs.*" In the words of an exiled newspaper affiliated with the clerical opposition, the aim of this corps was to "nationalize religion" and undermine the "spiritual leaders."

When the religious leaders protested these actions, the regime cracked down. Fazieh, the main seminary in Qum, was closed down. Ayatollah Shamsabadi, a prominent preacher in Isfahan, was murdered a few days after he had spoken out against the new calendar. Shaikh Hussein Ghoffari, a 60-year-old ayatollah, was detained on suspicion of aiding guerrillas and was tortured to death. Moreover, a group of prominent clerics were arrested for denouncing the Resurgence Party as "un-Islamic" and "unconstitutional." The group included not only former prison inmates, such as Ayatollahs Taleqani and Zanjani, but also many newcomers, such as Ayatollah Beheshti, Ayatollah Montazeri, Ayatollah Hassain Qumi, Hojat al-Islam Kani, and Hojat al-Islam Lahuti. Never before had so many prominent clerics found themselves in the same prison.

The clerical opposition was further reinforced by another problem—the "moral problem" created by unplanned urbanization. The dramatic influx of oil revenues led to a major construction boom. This, together with the agricultural stagnation, drew millions of unemployed villagers into the cities. The number of migrants, which had totaled 3 million between 1956 and 1971, jumped to over 380,000 annually after 1971. Since many of the migrants were young, unmarried and unskilled, and since the cities lacked housing and social services, the new shanty towns produced predictable problems: crime, alcoholism, prostitution, delinquency, and rising suicide rates. Shocked by these problems the *mullas* reacted in much the same way as many clergy would react in other parts of the world. They argued that moral laxity had endangered society and that the only remedy was to enforce traditional values and religious laws. In nineteenth century England, haphazard urbanization produced the Methodist movement. In contemporary Iran, the same problem helped to create the Khomeini phenomenon.

In a revealing speech made after the revolution, Ahmad Khomeini, the influential son of Ayatollah Khomeini, divided his fellow clergy into three groups. The first, he argued, had supported the Shah to the very end because it had received general subsidies from the state. In his estimate, this group formed only a tiny minority. The second group, by contrast, had staunchly opposed the shah because it had fundamental criticisms of his economic, social, political, and even international policies. The third group, however, which formed the vast majority, had remained silent until 1976–1977 because it had neither liked the Shah nor disliked him enough to speak out. According to Ahmad Khomeini, what had led these clerics to break their silence was not the realization that the Shah was destroying the country and selling Iran to Western imperialism, but rather the shock of seeing "moral decadence" flaunted in the streets and the double shock of finding that the authorities were unwilling, if not incapable, of cleaning up the "social filth." Having no channels through which they could communicate their grievances to the political system, they reluctantly joined the anti-regime clergy to mount the final assault on the Shah.

Conclusion

For any state to survive an economic crisis—and all states sooner or later have to confront such a crisis—it needs to have a social base and enjoy the support of a significantly large class. The Shah, despite the vast oil revenues, failed to obtain the necessary social base. He failed to win over the intelligentsia and the proletariat, and moreover, implemented socioeconomic policies that drastically expanded their ranks without altering their previous opposition. Since there were no avenues for either channeling demands into the political superstructure or reforming the social structure, more and more members of these two modern classes found themselves completely alienated from the regime. Some emigrated or joined underground parties and guerrilla groups. The vast majority, however, internalized their anger and patiently awaited the day when they could express their years of frustration.

As if the opposition of the intelligentsia and the proletariat was not enough, the Shah in 1975 embarked on a course that brought him to a head-on collision with the bazaars and the powerful religious establishment. Thus when an acute economic crisis hit the country in 1975–1977, the regime found itself first isolated, then beseiged from all sides, and eventually submerged in a flood of hatred directed not only at the monarchy and its military establishment, but also at the ruling class and their foreign patrons.

The Shah himself, in December 1978, summed up the tragicomedy of his sinking regime. When asked for a foreign correspondent where his supporters were, he shrugged his shoulders and replied, "Search me."[3]

REFERENCES

1. A. Mansur (1979), pp. 26–33.
2. J. Kendell (1979).
3. N. Gage (1978).

COUNTERMOBILIZATION IN THE IRANIAN REVOLUTION

Jerrold D. Green

Green provides a detailed account of the breakdown of the Shah's regime. He notes that the breakdown depended on the weakening of state coercion and on the mobilization of the urban poor under the direction of the religious elite. He also notes that middle class opponents of the Shah sought an alliance with religious leaders and that the latter's huge organizational network gave them a dominant role in the Revolution.

Countermobilization may be simply understood as mass mobilization against a prevailing political order under the leadership of counterelites. Due to its great magnitude, in certain cases such as process can be virtually irreversible. Reliant upon the mobilization capacity of counterelites, the anti-regime sector of a society may quickly develop the attributes of a parallel state, rendering the prevailing state structure powerless, while itself becoming impervious to attempts to undermine it. It is this process of countermobilization that is the focus of this paper. Particular attention is paid both to the conditions leading to countermobilization and to its attributes.

The Conditions Leading to Countermobilization

In order to appreciate the antecedents of countermobilization, we should enumerate and apply them to the Iranian case.

The conditions leading to countermobilization are as follows.

1. The declining coercive will or capacity of the state.
2. A simplification of politics.
3. Mass polarization.
4. The politicization of traditionally non-political social sectors.
5. Crisis-initiating event(s).
6. Exacerbating responses by the regime.

THE DECLINING COERCIVE WILL OR CAPACITY OF THE STATE

The earliest antecedents to the Iranian Revolution may be traced to a crisis of participation among Iran's most highly socially mobilized sector—the urban middle class. Prior to the 1975 elections the Shah announced his willingness to sanction electoral opposition to the government-controlled Iran-Novin Party. In part, this political liberalization was a response to sporadic terrorism as well as to the economic deterioration (for example, 40 percent inflation rate and housing shortages) resulting from the ill-conceived doubling of the expenditure level of the fifth five-year plan. Frightened by the ensuing scurry of political activity reflecting popular desires for expanded political participation, the Shah backpeddled, put an end to two-party politics, and created a single mobilization party named *Hizb-i-Rastakhiz-i-Melli* (National Resurgence Party). Yet Rastakhiz was doomed to failure from the outset. Iranians had seen parties come and go and greeted the Shah's newest attempt to generate support with ambivalence or cynicism.

By 1977 the Rastakhiz Party was but a political relic while popular dissent grew in scope. Highly socially mobilized Iranians were unable to forgive the Shah for his abolition of two-party politics. At the same time, the Shah was under pressure from President Jimmy Carter, Amnesty International, and the International Commission of Jurists, all critical of Iran's dismal human rights record. Dissident Iranian students staged well-publicized demonstrations in the United States and western Europe, while Iranians at home were losing patience as the quality of life in the country rapidly and visibly deteriorated. As Tehran was afflicted with extended electricity blackouts throughout the summer of 1977 and the police were engaged in pitched battles with indigent squatters in South Tehran, the Shah spoke loftily of his new campaign to guide Iran towards a "great civilization" and his desire to surpass Sweden by the year 2000!

Inspired by the activities of Iranian students abroad, human rights groups, and even the United States government, various middle class professional and associational groups decided to act. Frustrated by the absence of participatory mechanisms, such groups chose to go outside of the system in order to express their dissatisfaction. According to James Bill, "the middle class in Iran . . . make up over 25 percent of the population."[1] This sector, the one that felt Iran's crisis of participation most keenly, was initially reformist rather than revolutionary in character. It was only later, in coordination with the national religious sector, that opposition groups became sufficiently powerful to seek an end to the Pahlavi dynasty altogether.

Throughout this period, Iran's crisis of participation became most acute, and it is here that the first condition leading to countermobilization, the declining coercive will or capacity of the state, is most crucial. This diminished coercive capacity is reminiscent of Theda Skocpol's findings in her analysis of the French, Russian, and Chinese revolutions where, due to "the incapacitation of the central state machineries," a breakdown in the coercive ability of the state resulted.[2] Frequently induced by pressures from the international system, such breakdowns are not unlike that in Iran. Yet the rejection of the use of violence by the Shah, unlike that in the cases studied by Skocpol, was largely self-induced rather than the result of irresistible external or internal pressures. Consequently, state-sponsored coercion during the revolution was limited to particular types of situations.

In May of 1977, a group of fifty-three attorneys called for an inquiry into the lack of impartiality in the judiciary. In June, the long banned Writer's Association sent an open letter to the prime minister. Signed by forty of its members, the letter demanded greater cultural freedom and the right to reconstitute their organization. Three days later, the National Front sent a similar letter directly to the Shah in which adherence to the national constitution was demanded. The Group for Free Books and Thought was established by publishers seeking the elimination of censorship and severe government restrictions on publishing. A manifesto signed by fifty-six well-known representatives of various groups sought a return to the constitution, a cessation of human rights violations, abolition of single party rule, the release of political prisoners, and free elections. Other groups comprised of bazaaris (merchants), judges, lawyers, teachers, university professors, and students were also active in this period. Mehdi Bazargan, Khomeini's first prime minister, created the Iranian Committee for Freedom and Human Rights. Finally, on the evenings of October 10 through 19, 1977, the Writer's Association sponsored a series of poetry readings at the Goethe Institute in Tehran. The poems, in part, were extremely critical of the current order and attracted thousands of listeners—an unprecedented liberty in Pahlavi Iran.

Although unanticipated even by their most active participants, the above events heralded the earliest stages of Iran's revolution. And given the Shah's historical willingness to employ coercion, often quite brutally, we must ask why such activities were tacitly encouraged through his uncustomary tolerance. In part, the state's acquiescence may be attributed to a modest liberalization undertaken by the Shah in response to international pressure on Iran born of a heightened sensitivity in the West to human rights issues. Other more tangential explanations include the possibility of royal indecisiveness due to the Shah's early bouts with cancer and the attendant lassitude resulting from chemotherapy. Additionally, he may have been unwilling to employ coercion so as not to alienate large segments of Iranian society. Perhaps recognizing that his tenure would be prematurely curtailed, the Shah was conceivably attempting to liberalize his regime in order to facilitate the succession to the throne of his son, Crown Prince Reza. Given the Shah's accession to power at age twenty-three, he was, I suspect, keenly aware of the potential difficulties awaiting his own successor. Although none of these interpretations can be verified with any certainty, it is clear that the liberalization, what some termed the "Tehran Spring," was limited and of short duration. Yet peculiarly, it did herald a pattern of state behavior in which coercion was used in a limited and particularly inefficient manner. For the Shah resorted to coercion in a reflexive rather than preventive fashion, choosing to respond to revolutionary *symptoms* rather than *origins*. Thus, there were innumerable instances of the military repressing processions and demonstrations in which hundreds were killed (for example, at Tabriz, Qum, and Jaleh Square). Yet SAVAK was far less active in this period than usual. And the Shah, even after the imposition of total martial law, never clamped down tightly on the most vocal leaders of the revolution, many of whom, unlike Khomeini, were resident in Iran. Preference for highly public military responses alienated most Iranians while providing a series of heroes in whose martyrdom the revolution's legitimacy lay. Popular revolutionary consciousness was raised while the state never really suppressed the source of opposition to it. Had the regime put down the early middle class challenges, the revolution may have been forestalled somewhat. But it seems that from the very beginning the Shah misread the nature of opposition to him.

On January 7, 1978, the regime went on the offensive, not against its middle class opponents, but instead targeting the most troublesome segment of the religious sector. The Tehran daily newspaper *Etela'at* published a fabricated letter attacking the exiled Ayatollah Khomeini in a vicious and personal fashion. Although historically an opponent of the regime, Khomeini in this period certainly presented no greater threat to regime stability than he had in previous years. Yet ironically, the regime unwittingly designated Khomeini as the "official" head of a heretofore nonexistent national opposition. The popular response was rioting of unanticipated severity in the holy city of Qum by a citizenry outraged by the regime's attack on a respected religious leader. With these riots a cycle of violent protest began, for forty days later a commemorative gathering was held for those who died earlier. This *arba'een* led to protest, further loss of life, and another commemorative gathering forty days later. With the introduction of the religious sector into the fray and the regime's inability or unwillingness to use coercive means to halt a movement that would soon grow to uncontrollable proportions, an important watershed of the Iranian Revolution had been reached.

A SIMPLIFICATION OF POLITICS AND POLARIZATION

As an antecedent to full-scale countermobilization, a simplification of politics acted to delineate two crude groupings in Iranian society, a not insignificant development in a country of over 35 million people. The mechanics of this simplification remain as yet unclear. And to attribute it wholly to Iran's oppositional sector grants the opposition greater cohesion, power, and prescience than it deserves. Rather, the simplification of politics served as the early stage of polarization. Such polarization was begun by the Shah's introduction of the Rastakhiz Party in 1975, when he stated: "Those who [do] not subscribe to [its] principles [are] either traitors, who belong in prison, or non-Iranians who [should] be given their passports to go abroad. . . . Each Iranian must declare himself and there [is] no room for fencesitters."

Just as national leaders in such a system create an internal cold war, forbid fencesitting, and try to sanctify politics, counterelites can pursue similar goals. At first glance this may seem counterintuitive, and we must ask whether regime opponents are able even more effectively to employ the same techniques as the political order they oppose. If we remember, however, that revolutions are the products of the very forces they oppose, then such mirror image emulation, often unwitting, seems plausible. Just as elites attempt to reduce politics to their lowest common denominators, counterelites can benefit as well from such an arrangement in which potential participants are presented with two simple choices while less dramatic and/or distracting options are simply filtered out. Given a choice between what appear to be the forces of light and those of darkness, the popular choice is clear from the outset. And a contest between elite and counterelite legitimacy, charisma, and societal integration can emerge. This was the case in Iran with Ayatollah Khomeini besting the Shah on all counts. Confronted with two highly salient and conflictual poles, and little political life in between them, traditional oppositional elements in Iran flocked to the regime's critical pole.

As a society rapidly becomes polarized, in part due to a paucity of political options, its regime will soon find itself in direct competition with its critics for popular support. This competitive mobilization is in itself a de facto form of official recognition as the state chooses to vie with its competitor rather than use coercive means to eliminate it. Gradually, the oppositional pole exercises an undiscerning, almost magnetic pull, passively *attracting* supporters rather than actively recruiting them. Importantly, however, influential counterelites provide the oppositional pole with a rough shape and character while helping to focus and refine grievances against the state. In such a competitive situation, the character of counterelites is all-important. And given the infrastructural attributes and inherent legitimacy of Iran's religious sector, it found itself in an unanticipated and unique oppositional role.

Let us for a moment try to establish the basis for the religious sector's successful countermobilization. Iran contains some 80,000 mosques, 1,200 shrines, and 180,000 mullahs. Among these are roughly 100 ayatollahs, 5,000 hojats-al-Islam, and 11,000 theology students. In Tehran alone, there are more than 5,000 shrine attendants. Ironically, Iranian modernization did not weaken but rather strengthened the national religious community. For example, the number of religious pilgrims to holy places in Mashad increased tenfold, from 332,000 in 1966–1967 to 3.5 million in 1976–1977. Rises in income, improved transportation, and expansion of the roadway system, all made what was once a long journey into a relatively simple excursion, highlighting the manner in which the infrastructural attributes of Iran's religious sector were strengthened over time and benefited from national modernization.

The Qum disturbances in response to the Khomeini letter illustrated to opponents and critics of the Shah the mobilization potential of Iran's religious community. For with its introduction into oppositional political activity, the scope and magnitude of what was primarily reformist anti-Pahlavi activity grew dramatically. On January 19 and 20, 1978, the Tehran bazaar closed in response to a joint call for a general strike by Ayatollah Khomeini and Karim Sanjabi of the National Front. Recognizing its inability to generate popular support despite its petitions, letters, manifestoes, and poetry readings, Iran's secular middle class adopted a potentially more fruitful stance by throwing in its lot with the religious sector. The strike of the Tehran bazaar was the first public instance of cooperation between the two groups and illustrates the countermobilization which would provide the revolution's dynamic.

What were the mechanics of Iran's simplification of politics and polarization? Such events as the Qum disturbances and the strike of Tehran's bazaaris brought Iran's incipient revolution within reach of most Iranians, particularly those in the major urban centers. At the same time, the country was flooded with Khomeini's writings as well as taped cassettes of his *khutbehs* (sermons) delivered from his place of exile in Najaf, Iraq. The foreign press avidly followed rising dissent in Iran while the BBC ultimately became an unofficial voice of the revolution. For example, when Khomeini later moved to the outskirts of Paris, his aides would tell the BBC of a general strike called for the following day. Iranians hearing the BBC would thus learn of Khomeini's call and do as he bid. *Elamiehs* (notices) from the opposition covered the walls of Tehran and other cities giving Iranians news of the opposition while listing various demands from Khomeini and his aides. Instructions from the Ayatollah would be telephoned to Iran, while photocopying machines worked overtime reproducing revolutionary materials. For example, while in Tehran I obtained a recently received communiqué from Khomeini's supporters in Paris. I went to the clerk responsible for photocopying in the government-sponsored research institute where I was based. I quietly called him aside and asked him to make a copy of it, but he refused. After some insistence, he looked at what I had, derisively said "een copy khoob mist" (this copy's no good), and extracted a better reproduction of what I wanted from a huge pile on his machine. In and of itself this anecdote seems relatively insignificant. Yet actions such as that of a simple clerical worker, when aggregated throughout Iran, indicate a growing revolutionary force of remarkable durability and power. This man, in his own fashion, was a revolutionary. He was never recruited into a formal oppositional structure but rather responded to stimuli rampant in the Iran of 1978–1979. He had two choices open to him, support for the Shah or for Khomeini. He chose the latter, as did most Iranians, giving in to vague though irresistible instincts by supporting what most Iranians were led to believe was good over evil.

THE POLITICIZATION OF NON-POLITICAL SOCIAL SECTORS

Given the high levels of popular participation which characterize countermobilization and the different effects that political mobilization has on diverse segments of society, we must ask how popular revolutionary consciousness develops. Despite the high levels of political mobilization evident in Iran's urban centers, for example, this process was for the most part restricted to Iran's burgeoning middle class. Thus such mobilization did not reach deep enough into Iranian society to include the large numbers of peasant migrants that swelled the urban sector. Tehran's population doubled from two to four million people between 1966 and 1976. This doubling came from peasants who left the countryside to seek greater opportunity in the national capital. Though fulfilling some of the criteria for political mobilization (such as changes from traditional occupations and exposure to mass media and the products of modernity) these migrants showed little evidence of conventional politicization such as awareness of their national political leadership, membership in political parties, or voting.[3]

Yet the sudden involvement of these migrants in oppositional activities (they were the footsoldiers of the revolution) raises important questions as to their sudden politicization and commitment to oppositional values. The rapid induction of such *sans-culottes* or "shirtless ones" into revolutionary action testifies to the pervasiveness of Iran's simplification of politics and attendant polarization. Simultaneously, the persuasiveness of the national religious sector is emphasized as we begin to understand the manner in which local mullahs were able to involve their constituents in revolutionary action.

The rapid politicization of Iran's previously unpoliticized urban masses may be seen in the huge processions of *Tasuah* and *Ashura* where, in Tehran alone, over two million people took to the streets in meticulously organized, peaceful marches against the regime. The procession was led by Ayatollah Talegani and Karim Sanjabi of the National Front, the pinnacle of the coalescence of interests discussed earlier. Individual mullahs led their parishioners through the city in separate groups of men and women, leaving no doubt that even the last socially mobilized segments of Iran's urban centers were committed to the revolution. Thus, the incipient revolution itself politicized such people, albeit in a somewhat less sophisticated fashion than it politicized the middle classes, and only the stimulus of their mullahs was needed to provide a vehicle for their anti-state participation.

CRISIS-INITIATING EVENTS AND EXACERBATING REGIME RESPONSES

The final antecedent to full-scale countermobilization highlights the transition from re-formism to revolution. In Iran several events of tremendous national importance contributed to increasingly higher levels of revolutionary consciousness. For the revolution fed itself, with each triumph leading to greater heights of unity and cohesion.

The first crisis-initiating event and exacerbating regime response was the publication of the falsified Khomeini letter and the subsequent military repression of demonstrators in Qum. This led to forty-day cycles of demonstrations, military intervention, and violence in which the state provided opportunities for periodic commemorative gatherings as well as an ample supply of martyrs and heroes.

Among other particularly significant crisis-initiating events was the brief military takeover of Tabriz in February of 1978. This led to a purported shake-up of SAVAK and a censure of the military for its handling of the incident. Further contributing to the upheaval was the mysterious fire at the Cinema Rex in Abadan where 400 people perished. Widely believed to be the work of SAVAK, it was perceived as a graphic illustration of the lengths to which the Shah would go to discredit his opponents, whom he blamed for the tragedy. The religious sector, acting almost as a parallel state, imperiously opened its own investigation into the origins of the fire, helping to formalize popular views of it as a natural and legitimate competitor with and successor to the Pahlavi dynasty.

On September 8, 1978, serious rioting occurred in Tehran with hundreds being killed in Jaleh Square—a day to be known as Black Friday. Attempting to capitalize on the tragedy, Khomeini announced that Muslims could not kill other Muslims and thus the troops responsible for the massacre were Israeli. This story was given wide credence in Iran, and Black Friday was immediately enshrined in the lore of the revolution, contributing mightily to sentiment in favor of the religious sector and against the state. It also led to martial law in Tehran and in other cities.

Later in this month an earthquake struck the small city of Tabas, resulting in 15,000-20,000 deaths. It was widely believed that the religious sector sped aid to the survivors more quickly and efficiently than did the government. This further hardened opposition to the regime while strengthening the credibility of the religious sector.

On November 4, a large number of students demonstrating at Tehran University were killed by the military; this led to massive rioting. On the following day, the rioting continued, several high officials resigned, total martial law was imposed by the Shah, and General Azhari was named prime minister.

Finally, the solemn religious month of Muharram began, with the overwhelming processions of *Tasuah* and *Ashura*. The religious sector referred to the processions as a referendum against the Shah. This peaceful idiom reflected the tenor of the revolution as a whole.

Exacerbating regime responses to these crisis-initiating events took consistent forms. Demonstrations were put down with violence, except for *Tasuah* and *Ashura,* while other forms of dissent were met with offers of salary increments, lowered taxes, and other financial inducements, as well as symbolic gestures such as the closing of gambling casinos and the dismissal of the minister of women's affairs to mollify the religious community. Yet both the stick and the carrot worked to alienate most segments of Iranian society. While the former tended to emphasize the sacrifices and purity of the oppositionists, the latter served to denigrate them. That is, most regime opponents had little patience with regime attempts to "buy them off." Such cooptative techniques were a time-honored cornerstone of Pahlavi rule and represented for many Iranians what they wanted to change in their society. Additionally, these gestures served to convince the oppositional sector that it was making progress against the state, for otherwise why would the state accede to popular dissatisfaction with such uncharacteristic rapidity and concern?

Countermobilization as a Revolutionary Form

Given the high level of support for the opposition, we must investigate those factors contributing to it. Several interrelated causes can be forwarded. Of these, one of the most significant is to be found in the behavior of Khomeini and his immediate supporters in which oppositional rather than initiative issues were stressed with an emphasis on negative rather than positive goals. That is, the religious sector tended to portray itself as Iran's most legitimate and potentially effective anti-Shah force. Thus, it was viewed as an entity in opposition to something rather than one in favor of something else. By keeping its character vague and ill-defined, all anti-state elements could be drawn to it. Whether this was a conscious revolutionary technique or, as is more likely, a consequence of the opposition's inability to keep pace with rapidly changing events, is unclear. Yet the image of Khomeini contained "something for everyone" opposed to the Pahlavi political order. Thus, groups as diverse as the urban middle class and ethnic and religious minorities were able to support him due to a crucial, single-goal consensus focused on removal of the Shah. Commitment by such groups to Khomeini lay in his ability to countermobilize popular revolutionary participation rather than in this role as the architect of what at the time was vaguely defined as an Islamic Republic. For example, during a strike of the predominantly Arab oil workers in Khuzistan, Khomeini asked them to return to the fields in order to provide for domestic consumption. The workers were unimpressed by the Ayatollah's request and returned to work only after the intercession of Mehdi Bazargan, a former director of the National Iranian Oil Company under Mossadeq. Interestingly, it became clear after an interview with Bazargan in Tehran that he himself was not particularly enamored of Khomeini. Presumably, his eventual and short-lived commitment to him was pragmatic, much like that of other groups in Iranian society.

Khomeini's emphasis on his anti-Shah credentials rather than on his goal to create a theocracy in part led to a situation in which coalition-building among diverse and at times conflicting groups was simplified by a diminution in the importance of traditionally diverse ethnic, tribal, socioeconomic, generational, educational, religious, and geographic cleavages. Iran is a multiethnic society in the extreme, with Persians a minority in their own country. Yet traditional rivalries (such as those between Azarbaijanis and Kurds), which manifested themselves after the revolution, were shelved as all segments of society worked towards a common goal. This led to some surprising outcomes. For example, over several weeks Tehran was afflicted by nightly blackouts orchestrated by dissident electrical workers.

Blackouts were not engineered, however, on Christmas and New Year's eves out of solidarity with the revolution's Christian participants! Members of Tehran's large and sophisticated intelligentsia quickly supported Khomeini in his goals, their last thought being the creation of a society governed by the mullahs whom they disdained. When the newspapers went out on strike, influential mullahs paid congratulatory visits to newspaper offices while bazaaris collected money to help the striking journalists support themselves. In fact, visceral hatred of the Shah fleetingly brought Iran a degree of unanimity and national cooperation unprecedented in its history and unlikely to recur in its future.

An important aspect of Iranian countermobilization involved the gradual development of coalitions between oppositionalists and those in government. This is a common attribute of revolutions, and in Iran it assumed dramatic proportions due to already high levels of countermobilization. Although on the highest levels many such defections have yet to come to light, we can cite the case of General Hussein Fardust, former chief of the Imperial Inspectorate, which superceded SAVAK, and a close boyhood friend and classmate of the Shah from their days at a Swiss boarding school. Fardust emerged as a post-revolutionary director of SAVAMA, the Islamic Republic's version of SAVAK.

On a somewhat different level, the ouster of the Shah was strongly facilitated by the disintegration of the national bureaucracy, most of whose employees at middle and lower levels went over to the national opposition. Wildcat strikes paralyzed virtually all segments of the government. Anti-regime meetings were held in government offices, while their employees circulated petitions urging individual cabinet ministers to resign. Workers at the Central Bank of Iran provided lists of those Iranians taking large amounts of currency out of the country. Government printing presses and photocopying machines churned out anti-state materials. And, confronted with such internal and external pressures, the apparatus of state crumbled within months.

It is difficult to identify an Iranian revolutionary elite with any precision. The most viable leadership was found in Ayatollah Khomeini and his circle of advisors on the outskirts of Paris. Yet these leaders had important contacts within Iran, as the religious community closed ranks in a rare show of solidarity. Basically, the Iranian Revolution boasted a shifting, amorphous, loosely structured revolutionary leadership with no oppositional center for the regime to crush. In part, this is attributable to the distance separating Khomeini from his followers in Iran. Yet such an arrangement, which favored the Ayatollah's personal security, also entailed severe costs due to the necessity for leadership from afar and for long-range communication. Yet within Iran it would be no exaggeration to argue that countermobilization rendered virtually all of the country's 180,000 mullahs agents of revolution. At the same time, large numbers of bazaaris, professors, teachers, secondary school and university students, lawyers, doctors, and urban migrants were actively engaged in attempts to overthrow the Shah. Support for the revolution was virtually universal in Iran.

Given the extraordinary high level of revolutionary participation, Iranian countermobilization emphasized nonviolence. This is not to say that the revolution was nonviolent, but rather that the opposition eschewed its employment while the military resorted to coercive tactics in its suppression of various demonstrations, processions, and meetings.

The revolutionary sector chose to emphasize idioms of peaceful change which extended to virtually all aspects of the upheaval. The sheer size of the opposition allowed it to oust the Shah while avoiding armed conflict.

A key attribute of countermobilization is its lack of longevity, for mass revolutionary participation is time-perishable and is dependent upon quick gains, high polarity, and a truncated time-frame. Given such traits of countermobilization as a loosely structured leadership, an unwieldy and cumbersome popular following, its inherent ideological vagueness, and its oppositional, responsive character, the underlying simplification of politics which supports it cannot last indefinitely. For a society in the throes of countermobilization is like a rudderless ship. Its only link to "normalcy," the primary factor providing cohesion, is its universal opposition to the prevailing political order. People tend not to work during such an upheaval; food shortages, inflation, and other social ills are exacerbated. Yet, on the other hand, the rare society able to generate high levels of countermobilization is likely to oust a preeminent ruling elite with unanticipated rapidity.

Given these considerations, it is not surprising that, due to unnaturally high levels of unity and revolutionary participation, countermobilization is likely to culminate in rapid demobilization. Once the goal of countermobilization is achieved, disparate social groups will revert to their original niches in society. Compounding this predictable fragmentation as the bond among widely differing entities disappears, is the issue of what shape a post-revolutionary polity will take. Thus, the very factors distinguishing different groups will again become salient at a time when the polity is particularly vulnerable due to the inability of its new ruling elite(s) to consolidate its newfound power. Such demobilization was quite evident in Iran and was characterized by intense disagreements within the religious sector as to the desired character of the "new Iran." At the same time, none of Iran's not inconsiderable ethnic minorities was particularly eager to see the institution of theocracy, instead committing themselves to timeless desires for greater autonomy and cultural freedom. More liberal middle class groups were shocked by the attendant religious authoritarianism, while even the more traditional middle class, the bazaaris, felt threatened by the possible nationalization of enterprises which would adversely affect their pursuit of business. In the two years following the fall of the Shah, well-known supporters of the revolution dropped from sight (for example, Bazargan, Yazdi, Nazih, Ayatollah Shariat-Madari, Bani-Sadr, Ghotbzdeh, Matin-Daftary, Entezzam). And Iranian society was convulsed by futile attempts by the Khomeini regime to exploit unfavorable political developments in order to restore once high levels of popular mobilization (for example, the holding of American hostages, the war with Iraq, the blowing up of the headquarters of the Islamic Republican Party, and political assassinations). The very factors which contributed to the early success of the Iranian Revolution also contributed to its subsequent failures.

REFERENCES

1. Bill (1978–1979), p. 333.
2. Skocpol (1979), pp. 50–51.
3. Kazemi (1980), pp. 69–70.

THE NICARAGUAN REVOLUTION

The decade of the 1980s was not the first in which the United States fought rebellion in Central America. From 1927 to 1933, U.S. marines occupied Nicaragua to defend the government against a peasant insurrection led by Augusto Sandino. Sandino's guerrillas battled the United States to a standstill, and peace came only when the United States promised to withdraw all troops. However, before withdrawing, the United States established and trained a Nicaraguan National Guard. In 1934 the leader of the Guard, Anastasio Somoza Garcia, arranged the assassination of Sandino. In 1936, he overthrew the existing president and arranged his own election as president of Nicaragua, beginning the forty-three year rule of the Somoza family, Anastasio Somoza Garcia (in power 1936–1956), and his sons Luis Somoza Debayle (in power 1957–1967) and Anastasio Somoza Debayle (in power 1967–1979).

The Somozas' rule came to an end in 1979 as a consequence of international pressures, elite opposition, and popular revolts. International pressures came from the United States, which, under President Carter's human rights policy, forced Somoza to ease the repression aimed at his opponents, and from the International Monetary Fund, which forced Somoza to devalue Nicaragua's currency and institute economic reforms. Elite opposition grew from the Somozas' corruption and from Anastasio Somoza Debayle's exclusion of the elites from even their traditionally modest role in Nicaraguan politics. The Sandinista Front for National Liberation (known by its Spanish initials FSLN) organized neighborhood defense committees in the cities and guerrilla units in the countryside to lead the popular revolt.

In the following essays, Thomas Walker describes the economic and political background to the revolution. Ricardo E. Chavarría then describes the gradual dissolution of the Somoza regime.

◆

THE ECONOMIC AND POLITICAL BACKGROUND

Thomas W. Walker

Located at the geographic center of Central America, with Honduras to the north and Costa Rica to the south, Nicaragua is the largest country in the region. Even so, its 57,143 square miles (148,000 square kilometers) of surface make it only slightly larger than the state of Iowa. Its population of about 2.5 million is slightly smaller than Iowa's 2.8 million. Nevertheless, Nicaragua is an extremely interesting and unique country with an importance that far exceeds its size. Although there have been many revolts and coups d'etat in Latin America, Nicaragua is one of only a handful of Latin American countries to have experienced a real social revolution, by which I mean a rapid process of change in social and economic as well as political structures.

The Economic Background

There is a profound difference between what is loosely called free enterprise or capitalism in the United States and its counterpart in Latin America. Capitalism in the United States coexists with relatively high levels of social justice precisely because it is dependent on the bulk of the American people as consumers. Most of what U.S. industry produces is consumed in the United States. The economic system, therefore, would collapse if the majority of citizens were exploited to the extent that they could no longer consume at relatively high levels. Quite the opposite is true in Latin America, where the so-called "capitalist" economies are overwhelmingly externally oriented, placing great emphasis on the production of products for export. Under these dependent capitalist systems the common citizen is important as a cheap and easily exploitable source of labor rather than as a consumer. Therefore, there is little or no economic incentive for the privileged classes that dominate most Latin American governments to make the sacrifices necessary to improve the conditions of the majority of the people.

While prerevolutionary Nicaragua was not at all unusual as an example of a society distorted by dependent capitalism, it was nevertheless an exceptionally and strikingly tragic case. Unlike certain other countries—such as Bolivia, where natural resources are in relatively short supply—Nicaragua is, and always has been, a land of impressive economic potential. The population/land ratio is very favorable. Not only is Nicaragua the largest of the five Central American countries, it is the least densely populated, with fewer than 20 persons per square kilometer as opposed to 45 for the region as a whole and approximately 210 for El Salvador. The land itself is rich and varied, with different soil, climatological, and altitude characteristics suitable for the production of a wide variety of crops and livestock. The country's many rivers and volcanos offer easily exploitable sources of both hydroelectric and geothermal energy, and internal waterways facilitate inexpensive domestic transportation and present the possibility of exploitation as part of some future transoceanic waterway. Nicaragua has both Caribbean and Pacific coastlines, providing direct access not only to the food and mineral resources of the seas but also to the major markets of the world. The country has significant timber resources—from pine forests in the highlands to hardwood stands in the lowland tropics. Among the known mineral assets are silver and, particularly, gold. Finally, the Nicaraguan people, with their relatively homogeneous culture and language and their indomitable spirit and *joie de vivre,* are themselves a very important national asset.

The best way to understand the inequities of the Nicaraguan economic system is to examine its historical roots. Nicaraguan economic history prior to the Sandinist Revolution is divisible into four distinct time spans: (1) the colonial period, from the 1520s to the 1820s; (2) the first half century of independence, from the 1820s through the 1870s; (3) the period of primitive dependent capitalism, from the late 1870s through the 1940s; and (4) the rise of modern dependent capitalism, from the 1950s through the 1970s.

The Colonial Economy

When the Spaniards arrived in western Nicaragua in the early sixteenth century they found a relatively advanced agrarian society. The approximately one million native inhabitants of the region—descendants of colonizers and refugees from the Mayan and Aztec civilization to the north—lived in villages and cities ranging in population from a few hundred to tens of thousands. This was a feudal society, with chiefs, subchiefs, and commoners, in which tribute flowed from the lowly to the lofty. However, land was held collectively and each inhabitant of the villages and cities had access to a designated plot nearby. The rich soils of the region yielded agricultural products in abundance ranging from corn, cassava, and chili to beans, tobacco, and a variety of vegetables. Each population center had one or more local markets at which agricultural products were sold. Though periodic crop failure and intertribal warfare undoubtedly inflicted occasional acute hardship, the economy in general was relatively self-sufficient and self-contained. The market system, intraregional trade, and general access to rich agricultural lands provided the material wherewithal for the satisfaction of basic human needs.

The Spanish conquest had an immediate and devastating impact on this economic system. Superimposing themselves on the existing feudal structure, the *conquistadores* demanded tribute in gold and, when that was depleted, Indian slaves. Within a few decades the near total destruction of the native population through death by contact with European diseases and the export of slaves created a severe manpower shortage that all but destroyed the labor-intensive agricultural base of the region's economy. To be sure, some lands remained under intensive cultivation throughout the colonial period, providing some export products such as corn and cacao and food to meet the region's much reduced internal demand. But, for the most part, the rich lands of Nicaragua reverted to jungle or were exploited for the raising of cattle to produce hides, tallow, and salted meat for sale to other colonies.

In a few decades, therefore, the economy had become essentially externally oriented. In addition to the sale of corn, cacao, and cattle products, the tiny Spanish elite accrued wealth through the exploitation of forest products, shipbuilding, and intermittent gold mining—all to meet external rather than internal demands. The under-population of the colony and the concentration of wealth in the hands of the privileged classes made Nicaragua a prime target for attacks by pirates from England and elsewhere in Europe, further contributing to the region's status as a colonial backwater. The process of underdevelopment had begun.

The First Half Century of Independence

The partial interruption of foreign dominance resulting from the disintegration and eventual collapse of Spanish colonial rule in the early nineteenth century was reflected in important changes in the Nicaraguan economic system. It is true that British traders were quick to provide the landed elite with an outlet for their traditional export products, but the relative political anarchy and international isolation of the first half century of independence also encouraged the growth of a number of other types of economic activity. There was a rapid growth in the number of self-sufficient peasant farms or *huertas.* A fragile, indigenous marketing system was reestablished. And, in the villages and cities, various types of cottage industry began to develop.

For most of the Nicaraguan people this economic system, though certainly not highly developed, was fairly benign. Although he may have been exaggerating slightly, one observer writing in the early 1870s noted that "peonage such as is seen in Mexico and various parts of Spanish America does not exist in Nicaragua. . . . Any citizen whatever can set himself up on a piece of open land . . . to cultivate plantain and corn."

Primitive Dependent Capitalism

The relative isolation of Nicaragua and the gradual development of an internally oriented economy were abruptly interrupted by the coffee boom that hit Central America in the late 1800s. Coffee was probably introduced into the country as an exotic curiosity in the first quarter of the nineteenth century. By 1848 it was being produced commercially on a small scale. In the early 1850s it was a favorite beverage of the twenty thousand or so foreign passengers each month who utilized Cornelius Vanderbilt's Accessory Transit Company route across Nicaragua on their way to California. But it was not until the 1870s that coffee really came into its own. By then the international demand was so strong that the country's ruling elite was motivated to monopolize and redirect much of Nicaragua's productive capacity toward the cultivation of that one export product.

Two factors of crucial importance to the production of coffee are fertile land in the right climatological setting and a large, essentially unskilled work force that can be called upon to offer its services for a few months during the harvest season. In Nicaragua in the early 1870s both were in short supply. The coffee culture had already moved into most of the exploitable lands around Managua, and other promising lands in the northern highlands were occupied by independent peasants and members of Indian communes engaged in traditional subsistence farming. And as the rural masses had access to their own land, there was no pool of vulnerable and easily exploitable peons.

The traditional elite solved both of these problems with ingenuity and speed. In the late 1870s and 1880s they took the land they coveted and created the work force they needed through a combination of chicanery, violence, and self-serving legislation. Individual squatter farmers and Indians working the land through communal arrangements were extremely vulnerable to legal manipulation because, in most cases, these people held rights to the land by tradition rather than by legal title. For several decades the agrarian elite had attempted, through legislation, to abolish communal and squatter landholdings. In 1877, under the presidency of Conservative Pedro Joaquín Chamorro, an agrarian law was passed that outlawed communal holdings and gave individuals the right to buy "unoccupied" national lands. The resulting massive dislocation of Indian communal farmers and individual peasants led inevitably to the War of the Communeros in 1881 in the Pacific and north-central regions of Nicaragua. After a series of cruel battles in which as many as five thousand Indians may have been killed, the new order was imposed on the region. Coffee was free to expand into new land.

The laws that forced the small farmer off the land also helped create a vulnerable rural proletariat. To reinforce this phenomenon the elite-controlled governments also passed laws against "vagrancy" and the cultivation of plantain—the banana-like staple food of the peasants. Forced to buy staples at high prices in the plantation commissaries, many coffee workers were forced to rely on credit from these company stores. Before long they were trapped into a very effective system of debt peonage. In less than a decade, the self-sufficient peasantry of a large section of the country had been converted into a dependent and oppressed rural proletariat. Most rural Nicaraguans began to lead a life of insecurity, fluctuating between the good times of the coffee harvest, from November through February, and the hardship and unemployment of the *tiempo muerto* (dead period) between harvests.

The growth of the coffee culture also marked the birth of dependent capitalism in Nicaragua. Before this period the economy was based on traditional cattle ranching and subsistence peasant and communal farming. Neither involved a signifcant use of capital. Coffee, however, was different. First, years before the first harvest, the planter had to make a significant investment in preparing the land and planting and nurturing the seedlings. When the trees began to bear fruit, it was necessary to spend considerable sums of money on manpower and machinery. A large work force was needed for the handpicking of coffee berries, and more people and machinery were employed in weighing, pulping, drying, sorting, sacking, and transporting the product.

It is not surprising, then, that although some small farmers converted to coffee bean production, most of those who went into this new enterprise were large landholders, prosperous commercial speculators, and, in some cases, foreigners. The Conservative oli-garchy used its control of the legislative process to pass the Subsidy Laws of 1879 and 1889, which gave planters of all nationalities cultivating more than five thousand trees a subsidy of five cents per tree. Among other things, these laws encouraged foreign colonists to seek their fortunes on the fertile slopes of the central highlands. With them came an infusion of new capital.

Once established as the cornerstone of the Nicaraguan economy, coffee held that position until the 1950s. This is not to say that other forms of agriculture were completely wiped out. Some farsighted peasants chose to flee the new coffee zones entirely, moving on to subsistence farming on land in other regions that were not yet coveted by the landed elite. In addition, the traditional precapitalist cattle *hacienda* (ranch) of the lowlands, though now less important, was by no means completely eclipsed. But overall, coffee was clearly the mainstay of the country's economy.

With the growth of the coffee industry, Nicaragua developed what is often loosely referred to as a "banana republic" economy—one based heavily on a single primary export product. Typically, the benefits of the system flowed heavily to a small domestic elite and its foreign trading partners. Taxes on coffee profits, which might have helped redistribute income to the impoverished majority, were virtually nonexistent. The common citizen was an abused instrument of production rather than a benefactor of the system. The Nicaraguan economy also became subject to periodic "booms" and "busts" produced by the fluctuation of the world price of its single product. In good times the economy grew and coffee planters imported luxury goods and machinery, invested money abroad, and educated their children in the United States and Europe. The first of the Somoza dictators received his U.S. education as a result of such a boom. In bad times, such as those following the onset of the 1929 Depression, coffee prices plummeted and the economy stagnated. Planters hunkered down, lived off savings and investments, and imported fewer luxury items and less machinery.

Typical also of the banana republic syndrome was the fact that throughout most of the period little effort was made by the governments of Nicaragua to see that the economy served the purpose of genuine national development. The notable exception to this rule was the regime of Liberal strongman José Santos Zelaya from 1893 to 1909. Zelaya had no real quarrel with laissez faire economics or with coffee. Indeed, he helped the coffee industry by opening up new lands and improving Nicaragua's transportation network. Nevertheless, he also emphasized education, brought fiscal responsibility to the government, created the rudiments of a modern administrative structure, and insisted on national economic self-determination. His refusal to concede to the United States canal rights that would have diminished the economic and political sovereignty of his country and his subsequent negotiation with other powers for a more equitable canal treaty contributed to the U.S. decision to encourage, and then reinforce militarily, the Conservative rebellion of 1909. After Zelaya, the Conservatives, and later the much-chastened Liberals, provided governments whose economic policies fit the banana republic model closely. Within a few years of their ascent to power, the Conservatives gave their U.S. protectors essentially the same canal treaty Zelaya had rejected. From then until the 1950s virtually no effort was made to alter Nicaragua's established role as a provider of a single primary product.

Modern Dependent Capitalism

The quarter century preceding the Revolution was a time of economic modernization and dependent "development." New products were added to Nicaragua's portfolio of exports, technology and technocrats became faddish, the government bureaucracy grew rapidly, expanding—at least on paper—into various social service areas and the gross national product grew in respectable spurts. But the benefits of this change and growth did not "trickle down" to most Nicaraguans. Their perilous standard of living remained essentially constant as the gap between them and the tiny middle and upper classes widened relentlessly.

One of the most obvious changes to occur during this period was the diversification of Nicaragua's exports. In addition to coffee and beef products, Nicaragua now exported significant quantities of cotton, sugar, bananas, wood and seafood. The most important new product was cotton. The sharp increase in the world price of this raw material in the early 1950s, flowing out of heightened demand during the Korean War, motivated Nicaraguan planters and speculators to invest in cotton production in the Pacific lowlands. Nicaragua, which had exported only 379 metric tons of cotton in 1949, increased that figure to 43,971 metric tons in 1955. Eventually as much as 80 percent of the cultivated land on the Pacific coast was converted to cotton. Some cattle ranches became cotton plantations, but, as in the case of the coffee boom seven decades earlier, much of the land that went into the production of this new export product was appropriated in one way or another from peasant producers of grains and domestic staples. Once again independent farmers were transformed into a rootless rural proletariat in the name of "progress" and "development" for the privileged few.

Cotton, like coffee, was subject to cycles of boom and bust. The first period of bust began in 1956, three years after the end of the Korean War. Compared with coffee, cotton was a very capital-intensive activity. It required great investments of machinery, fertilizer, insecticides, and labor. In Nicaragua's case, cotton came to account for almost all of the tractors and harvesters, most of the irrigation systems, and more than three-fourths of the commercial fertilizer used in the country. Small-scale production of cotton was simply out of the question.

Another factor that affected the Nicaraguan economy in this period was the birth of the Alliance for Progress in the early 1960s. A U.S.-sponsored response to the revolutionary success of Fidel Castro in Cuba, the alliance was designed to bring about social and economic development in Latin America through politically moderate means. Enlightened reform from above would, it was hoped, defuse the "threat" of popular revolution from below. The Somozas and the traditional elite of Nicaragua found the idea of the alliance very appealing. Not that they were particularly concerned with its lofty objectives of social and economic justice. Rather, they saw it in more practical terms as a legitimizing device and a source of a variety of economic opportunities. In return for rather painless paper reforms and the creation of a modern social-service bureaucracy, they would receive increased foreign aid and technological assistance and have access to numerous new business opportunities.

Nicaragua in the 1960s was typified by a peculiar type of neopositivism reminiscent of Mexico in the days of Porfirio Díaz. Technology, foreign investment, and "development"—as defined in terms of growth in gross national product—were the new articles of faith. A group of highly trained developmentalists known as the technocrats or, less respectfully, the "miniskirts," were elevated to positions of great responsibility. The heart of their operations was the Banco Central in downtown Managua. There the dictator-president, the head of the "miniskirts" (Francisco "Ché" Láinez, the bank's director), and the cream of Nicaragua's technocratic community often met late into the night planning the country's economy as if they were the board of directors of a large corporation. Feasibility studies were ordered, foreign investment was wooed, and joint ventures were embarked upon. Once a year the Banco Central issued an annual report brimming with tables and analyses concerning the national economy. To help train even more business technocrats, Harvard University's School of Business Administration cooperated in the creation of the Central American Institute of Business Administration (INCAE), located in the outskirts of Managua.

A parallel stimulus for capitalist development in Nicaragua, which coincided with the Alliance for Progress, was the birth of the Central American Common Market in 1960. This attempt at regional economic integration provided increased incentive for both incipient industrialization and the diversification of export products. As such it was, for a while, an additional boon to the privileged domestic and international groups who controlled these activities. However, the Soccer War of 1969, between El Salvador and Honduras, brought about the demise of this integrative effort.

The developmentalist optimism of the 1960s proved to be a hollow illusion. Compared with the rest of Latin America, Nicaragua received relatively little foreign investment—perhaps because doing business in that country normally entailed paying off the Somozas in one way or another. Though economic growth did take place, its benefits were concentrated in relatively few hands. The Somozas and their allies simply used their control of the expanded governmental apparatus and the country's new technocratic expertise to increase their own fortunes. Eventually, in the late 1960s and early 1970s, the technocrats themselves were pushed aside as the corrupt and intemperate Anastasio Somoza Debayle replaced skilled administrative personnel with National Guard officers and other cronies to whom he owed rewards for personal loyalty.

Government and Politics

If one had been foolish enough to take seriously the constitutional formalities and stated objectives of the Nicaraguan government during the Somoza years, one would surely have come to the mistaken conclusion that Nicaragua was blessed with a modern democratic form of government that was pursuing praiseworthy developmental goals. According to the constitution, there were free elections, separation of powers, and a full gamut of explicitly guaranteed human rights. To insure minority participation, the largest opposition party was automatically awarded 40 percent of all seats in the legislature and minority representation on boards of government agencies, judgeships, etc. What is more, there were a variety of public agencies and institutions such as the Central Bank, the National Development Institute, the Nicaraguan Agrarian Institute, the Institute of Internal-External Commerce, and the Social Security Institute, which were ostensibly designed to cope with the problems faced by a modernizing society. The stated policies of the government were also impressive. The major expressed goal was to develop the country through the modernization and diversification of the economy. Accordingly, highly trained technocrats were given important roles in the development process and lofty five-year plans were issued and subsequently endorsed by lists of international agencies.

All of this, of course, was simply a facade. Under the Somozas, democracy was nonexistent, corruption was elaborately institutionalized, and public policy consistently ignored the well-being of the majority of the population.

Nicaragua was a democracy in name only. Although there were constitutional provisions for the separation of power—with a bicameral legislature, an executive, and a judiciary—in reality, all power was concentrated in the hands of the president. The National Guard was the president's private army. His command over the Liberal party—which in turn dominated both houses of the legislature and all government agencies—meant that the president was, in fact, the only decision maker. Mandated minority participation served only to legitimize the system and to co-opt Conservative politicians. There was never any possibility that the opposition would come to power legally since elections were thoroughly rigged. During campaign periods, there was frequent censorship of the press and intimidation of opposition candidates. On election day, there was multiple voting by the pro-Somoza faithful, tampering with the ballot boxes, and, cleverest of all, the use of a translucent secret ballot that, even when folded, could easily be scrutinized by government election officials as it was deposited in the ballot box.

Given the hopelessly undemocratic character of elections under the Somozas, party organization and activity were shallow and essentially without meaning. The two major parties, Liberal and Conservative, were crusty relics of the nineteenth century. The original ideological differences between them had long since faded into insignificance. Both represented the interests of a small privileged minority and, by the middle of the twentieth century, both had been co-opted and emasculated by the Somoza system.

Officially, the Somozas were Liberals and their governments were Liberal administrations. In fact, however, throughout most of the period, the Liberal party was simply a cosmetic appendage of a system that depended on brute military force. One apparent exception occurred in the late 1950s and early 1960s when Luis Somoza—who enjoyed the trappings of democracy and party politics—encouraged the Liberal party to have a life of its own. In that period, new Liberal leaders emerged and there was some hope that they might turn into real presidential prospects. In the late 1960s, after the "election" of the less politically minded Anastasio Somoza Debayle, these hopes were quickly dashed. Independent upstarts left or were drummed out of the party as the dictator began to maneuver to perpetuate himself in power, and the Liberal party lapsed into its more traditional cosmetic role.

The official Conservative opposition played an even less dignified role. If the Liberal party was the neglected wife of the Somoza system, the Conservative party was its kept woman. Since the facade of democracy was so important to the Somozas, it was imperative that there always be an opposition to run against during elections. Enticed by personal bribes and/or lucrative opportunities inherent in mandated minority participation in congress, the judiciary, and government agencies, the leaders of the Conservative party frequently agreed to provide a legitimizing opposition during the rigged elections. Even on those infrequent occasions when the leaders of the Conservative party mustered the dignity to refuse to participate, the dictators were usually able to convince less important Conservatives to carry that party's banner to defeat.

There were a number of microparties during the Somoza period. A few of the more notable were the Independent Liberal party (PLI), composed of Liberals who, from 1944 on, chose to dissociate themselves from the parent party over the issue of Somoza's continuing dominance; the Nicaraguan Social Christian party (PSCN), formed by young Catholic intellectuals in 1957; and the Nicaraguan Socialist party (PSN), which was founded by local Communists in 1944.

One of the more interesting of the microparties was the Social Christian party. Inspired by progressive papal encyclicals, lay Catholic humanism, and Christian Democratic ideas emanating from Europe, this party attempted to take advantage of Luis Somoza's somewhat more open attitude toward competitive political activity. Stressing the importance of platform, ideology, organization, and tactics, the Christian Democrats not only won a significant popular following, but also penetrated the labor movement and came for a while to dominate the national students' organizations. Though many young Christian Democrats freely admitted their admiration for the courage and audacity of FSLN guerrillas, they felt at that time that a peaceful, democratic solution might still be possible. When it became clear in the early 1970s that they were wrong, the more progressive members of the party split from the PSCN to form the Popular Social Christian party (PPSC), which espoused an increasingly revolutionary position.

Mass-interest articulation through legal channels was also a fairly hopeless activity under the Somozas. Peasants and urban labor, for instance, had almost no input into the political system. Ignorant, illiterate, and geographically scattered, the peasantry and rural proletariat were subject to constant abuse by landowners and the National Guard. An agrarian reform program legislated in the early days of the Alliance for Progress had virtually no impact on the misery of the rural poor. From 1964 on, a private Social Christian-oriented organization—the Institute for Human Promotion (INPRHU)—did struggle to organize and raise the consciousness of the peasants, but in the face of government roadblocks, its efforts were largely ineffectual. In the end, clandestine activity proved to be the only viable alternative. In the late 1970s, the FSLN began organizing rural workers and landless peasants in workers' committees. In 1978, these were fused into a national organization—the Rural Workers' Association (ATC). In the following year, as the Revolution neared its successful conclusion, ATC-organized peasants made their contribution by digging trenches and felling huge trees across roadways to block troop movements and by maximizing the first post-Somoza harvest through the seizure and immediate cultivation of *Somocista*-owned lands in the newly liberated areas.

The urban worker was only slightly better off than his country cousin. The organized labor movement encompassed a small minority of all workers and was badly fragmented. In 1977, the major union organizations included the Marxist Independent General Confederation of Labor, with 12,000 members; the government-patronized General Confederation of Labor, with 8,000 to 10,000 members; the AFL-CIO-oriented Confederation of Labor Unity, with 7,000 members; and the Social Christian Confederation of Workers of Nicaragua, with 3,000 members. The right to strike, while formally enshrined in law, was so severely restricted that most of the many strikes that took place in the 1960s and 1970s were declared illegal. Collective bargaining was made all but impossible by Article 17 of the *Regulations of Syndical Association,* which allowed the employer to fire, without explanation, any two leaders of the striking union. In the long run, the only viable option for urban workers, too, was to organize themselves clandestinely, again under FSLN leadership. Significantly, the urban insurrections—which took place almost exclusively in working-class neighborhoods—turned out to be one of the most important ingredients in the overthrow of the dictatorship.

Not surprisingly, given the nearly complete absence of institutionalized popular input into the political system, the Somoza government was virtually oblivious to the interests of the ordinary Nicaraguan citizen. Lofty-sounding social programs—ostensibly concerned with public health, agrarian reform, low-income housing, education, social security, and the like—served mainly as devices to legitimize the system, attract foreign aid, employ the politically faithful, and diversify opportunities for the pilfering of public revenues. Very little of what the government spent actually trickled down to the people. With members of Somoza's family at the head of most government agencies, a large chunk of each agency's assets went directly to satisfy the family's greed. For instance, in the ten years in which he headed the National Institute for Light and Energy, Anastasio Somoza Debayle's uncle, Luis Manuel Debayle, allegedly siphoned off more than $30 million (U.S.). Under the Somozas were layer upon layer of corrupt bureaucrats who were expected and, indeed, encouraged to help themselves. Honesty, a threat to the system, was discouraged.

The problem of corruption had existed throughout the Somoza period. Anastasio Somoza García had encouraged corruption in his subordinates as a way of isolating them psychologically from the people and thus making them dependent on him. In a conversation in 1977, Luis Somoza's close advisor and confidant, Francisco Láinez, the chief of the "miniskirts" during that earlier period, told me an interesting story. One day Luis Somoza, in a pensive mood, asked Láinez to tell him in all frankness what one thing he, Láinez, would do, if he were in Luis's shoes, to bring development to Nicaragua. Láinez thought for a moment and then responded that he would take each of the major categories in the national budget—health, education, etc.—and see to it that *at least half* of that money actually went for the purposes for which it was ostensibly destined. According to Láinez, Luis simply smiled sadly and responded, "You're being unrealistic." This is not to say that, at the highest levels, money was being stolen openly. That would not have been acceptable to Washington—which was footing much of the bill—nor was it necessary, since the Somoza's absolute control of the government gave them the ability to apply a legalistic patina to the flow of public funds. Even after the patent and massive misuse of international relief funds following the 1972 earthquake, the U.S. government, intent on not embarrassing a good ally, was able for several years to produce audits that appeared to refute claims that these funds had been misappropriated. But by the time the dynasty was overthrown the Somoza family had accrued a portfolio worth perhaps a billion dollars, including about one-fifth of the nation's arable land.

The events of the 1970s accentuated the abuses and defects of the Nicaraguan economic system. In the last years of the Somoza dynasty, it had reached a state that, from the point of view of most citizens, was intolerable. For over a century, the country's rich natural resources had been plundered, appropriated, and abused for the benefit of a tiny minority. Millions of Nicaraguans had become economic instruments rather than fulfilled and participating human beings. Public revenues and foreign aid officially destined "to meet basic human needs" had been routinely laundered to end up in the pockets of the ruling family and its allies. The nation's public and private banks had been used first as instruments for the concentration of wealth and finally as conduits for the export of capital as the erstwhile ruling class began to flee into exile. The Revolution of 1978–1979 was as much a product of systemic socioeconomic factors as it was an expression of intense political opposition to a particularly venal dictator.

The Beginning of the End: 1972–1977

The half-decade following 1972 was a time of mounting troubles for the Somoza regime. Most of the responsibility for the growing systemic crisis lay in the excesses and poor judgment of the dictator himself. Somoza's first major demonstration of intemperance came in the wake of the Christmas earthquake of 1972, which cost the lives of more than ten thousand people and leveled a 600-square block area in the heart of Managua. Somoza might have chosen to play the role of concerned statesman and patriotic leader by dipping into the family fortune (which, even then, probably exceeded $300 million [U.S.]) in order to help his distressed countrymen. Instead, he chose to turn the national disaster to short-term personal advantage. While allowing the National Guard to plunder and sell international relief materials and to participate in looting the devastated commercial sector, Somoza and his associates used their control of the government to channel international relief funds into their own pockets. Much of what they did was technically legal—the self-awarding of government contracts and the purchasing of land, industries, etc., that they knew would figure lucratively in the reconstruction—but little of it was ethically or morally uplifting.

It was at this point that open expressions of popular discontent with the Somoza regime began to surface. When the quake struck, Somoza lost no time using the emergency as an excuse to proclaim himself head of the National Emergency Committee. There were many high-sounding statements about the challenge and patriotic task of reconstruction, but it soon became apparent that his corrupt and incompetent government was actually a major obstacle to recovery. The promised reconstruction of the heart of the city never took place. Popular demand for the building of a new marketplace to replace the one that had been destroyed went unheeded. Emergency housing funds channeled to Nicaragua by the Agency for International Development (AID) went disproportionately into the construction of luxury housing for National Guard officers, while the homeless poor were asked to content themselves with hastily constructed wooden shacks. Reconstruction plans for the city's roads, drainage system, and public transportation were grossly mishandled. As a result, there was a series of strikes and demonstrations as the citizens became increasingly angry and politically mobilized.

It was at this point, too, that Somoza lost much of the support that he had formerly enjoyed from Nicaragua's economic elite. Many independent businessmen resented the way he had muscled his way into the construction and banking sectors. And most were angry at being asked to pay new emergency taxes at a time when Somoza—

who normally exempted himself from taxes—was using his position to engorge himself on international relief funds. As a result, from 1973 on, more and more young people with impressive backgrounds joined the ranks of the Sandinist Front of National Liberation, and some sectors of the business community began giving the FSLN their financial support.

THE REVOLUTIONARY INSURRECTION

Ricardo E. Chavarría

From 1972 to 1974, the FSLN financed its activities with kidnapping and raids. In response, Somoza declared a state of seige, in which savage repression, including torture, strict censorship, and an expanded militarization of society forced the FSLN to go underground. However, in 1977, amid mounting publicity from Amnesty International and protests from the Catholic Church, the U.S. Congress and President Carter informed Somoza that the U.S. would stop aid unless he improved his record on human rights. Somoza grudgingly lifted the state of seige. Allowed slightly more room to operate, the FSLN and elite opposition immediately stepped up their activities. Elite opposition and international pressures sufficiently weakened Somoza and encouraged popular opposition to spark armed uprisings. Eventually, popular insurrections in the cities and guerrilla attacks from the countryside divided and harassed the National Guard, pinning it down and cutting its supply lines. The Guard, divided by corruption and losing faith in Somoza, began to dissolve as Somoza prepared to flee. The revolution had won.

The FSLN reappeared in October 1977, operating with more modern weapons and carrying out hit-and-run raids throughout the country. Meanwhile, a new political organization, "The Twelve," a highly respected group of business, professional, and religious leaders, demanded substantial changes in the government. They argued that the FSLN had matured politically and should be considered a legitimate political force.

The year 1978 was filled with dramatic and spectacular events. From January to September, four major events marked the rising societal crisis: (1) the assassination of Pedro Joaquín Chamorro, (2) the Monimbó Popular Armed Rebellion, (3) the Attack on the National Palace, and (4) the September Insurrection. All of this converged into a mood of national mobilization, an increasing potential for success.

The Assassination of Pedro Joaquín Chamorro

The assassination of Pedro Joaquín Chamorro (January 10, 1978), a courageous journalist who had long opposed the Somoza dynasty, was a serious political mistake apparently committed by people high in the Somoza regime.

The reaction of the Nicaraguan people was massive and immediate. Angry crowds attacked Somoza-owned business establishments and burned several buildings in the capital city of Managua. And the business community conducted an 85 percent effective "general strike," or business work stoppage which lasted for two weeks beginning January 22. Somoza's strategy was to wait it out. At the same time, he brutalized protestors when street barricades began to appear throughout Nicaragua. The financial oligarchy did not support the stoppage, and when the business community put an end to it, the popular sector became more aggressive in acting on its own. Similarly, the FSLN assumed the initiative by attacking National Guard outposts in the cities of Rivas and Granada.

In the context of mounting repression, Archbishop Miguel Abanda y Brava began to qualify the Church's nonviolent position, stating that there were circumstances when armed resistance might be legitimate. He was paraphrasing a traditional teaching of the Church. Curiously, it was at this point that U.S. Ambassador Mauricio Solaun stated that in order to restore peace it was necessary for everyone to refrain from violence and pacifically discuss the crisis.

The Armed Rebellion at Monimbó and Its Aftermath

The name Somoza was a morbid shadow which surrounded the death of both Sandino and Chamorro. The forty-fourth anniversary of Sandino's assassination was marked by a Catholic celebration by the Indian community of Monimbó, located on the southern edge of Masaya. Upon leaving the ceremony, people found themselves surrounded by National Guard troops who opened fire and threw several tear gas bombs into the crowd. That night the residents of the neighborhood closed off the main street entrance with a large FSLN banner and the conflict escalated into an all-out rebellion. With home-made weapons, machetes, clubs, and paving block barricades, the Monimboseños forced the Guard out of their *barrio,* and from February 22 to February 27, held out against 600 soldiers with tanks, machine guns and helicopters under the command of the dictator's oldest son, Anastasio III. The losses in Monimbó amounted to at least 200 people, but Monimboseños had let the whole country know that they were more determined than ever to oust Somoza. Their rebellion had illustrated one of the secrets of the Nicaraguan popular insurrection: neighborhood organizations are the backbone of revolutionary societies.

The events of Monimbó led other groups to defy the dictatorship. On April 6, more than 60,000 students became directly involved in the most massive and prolonged student strike in the history of Nicaragua. The student leadership now became the vanguard of the urban struggle. In July, another nationwide strike of hospital workers erupted. At the same time, women's and human-rights issues were heralded by AMPRONAC (The Association of Women Confronting the National Problem). Thus the political mobilization of the popular sectors was converging into the events which would take place in August.

The Attack on the National Palace

In July, President Carter sent Somoza a personal letter congratulating him on his "concern to improve human rights in Nicaragua." The insurrectionalist group, outraged that the U.S. had apparently decided to support Somoza while the people of Nicaragua were being massacred, decided to act. The target of their next operation would be the National Palace, which housed Somoza's onerous rubber-stamp congress.

The plan which the Insurrectionalists adopted was the most audacious and spectacular in the history of the FSLN. Acting as if they were the special security guard assigned to Somoza's oldest son, they abruptly entered the Palace on August 22. With only 25 guerrillas the FSLN quickly took as hostage most of the members of the Chamber of Deputies and some 2,000 public employees. Archbishop Obando and the bishops of León and Granada acted as intermediaries. After forty-five hours of frantic negotiations, Somoza gave in to most of the Sandinista demands: the release of 59 prisoners from all three FSLN sectors (including Tomás Borge); the donation of a huge amount of cash; the airing of an FSLN pronouncement; safe passage out of Nicaragua for the liberated FSLN prisoners and the commandos; and the resolution of the hospital workers strike. Unusual publicity was given to this event in the international arena, and the FSLN captured the popular imagination. From then on, many people in Nicaragua were convinced of the real possibility that the FSLN would topple Somoza.

The September Insurrection

The success of the attack on the National Palace was crucial in the development of a *sandinista* as opposed to a mere anti-Somoza movement. Simple anti-Somoza objectives had typified the National Democratic Movement (MDN), which had emerged as an outgrowth of the business-organized work stoppage of late January. Later, a Broad Opposition Front (FAO), had been founded as an alliance between the old UDEL, the MDN, The Twelve, and several labor unions. The arrival of The Twelve in late July was a turning point in the political struggle against Somocismo. The Sandinista appeal to the masses was substantially enhanced because The Twelve were identified with the most conciliatory sector of the FSLN. On July 17, a popular alternative to FAO was formed into a single block called the United People's Movements (MPU). Initially, twenty-two organizations were integrated into the MPU coalition and three principal objectives were defined: (1) to mobilize the population for the popular overthrow of Somoza; (2) to expand the coalition and unify broad popular sectors; and (3) to contribute to the process of unification of the revolutionary forces.

On August 28, a Monimbó-style popular insurrection erupted in the city of Matagalpa. This was a spontaneous action carried out by youngsters armed only with pistols, rifles, and home-made contact bombs, their faces covered with black and red bandanas. Forcing the troops back to their barracks, *los muchachos* held out against them for two weeks. The alternatives for the FSLN were either to stop such insurrectionary tactics or to lead them. The Front decided to respond positively to the popular initiative. On September 9, integrated uprisings erupted in four other cities: León, Masaya, Chinandega, and Managua, and the following day, Estelí joined the insurrectionalist movement. These cities are located in the western half of Nicaragua, where the great majority of the population live. It was anticipated that the National Guard would attempt to retake these positions all at once, thus overextending their forces. With most of its headquarters surrounded by the civilian forces and FSLN combatants, the Guard initially adopted a defensive tactic. Later, however, Somoza's air force submitted the cities to massive bombing before ground forces retook them one at a time. The FSLN fighters then retreated into the hills accompanied by thousands of youngsters and townspeople. Finally, tanks and troops went from house to house to subject those who remained to a genocidal "Operation Cleanup."

September's death toll was calculated at 5,000; more than 10,000 were injured; 25,000 were left homeless; and more than 60,000 sought asylum in other Central American countries, particularly Costa Rica. The Human Rights Commission of the Organization of American States was sent to Nicaragua to carry out investigations *in loco,* and its conclusions clearly condemned the Somoza regime.

Many of the September casualties resulted from a lack of coordination within neighborhoods and from the fragmentation of FSLN leadership. In order to overcome these defects and to prepare civilians to resist the National Guard, the MPU subsequently set up the Civil Defense Committees. These committees were organized block by block and coordinated by neighborhood and zonal steering committees. Underground preparations were conducted and several tasks were accomplished by CDC's members: the collection of medicines and first aid supplies; training in rudimentary first aid skills; storing of basic foodstuffs; surveillance of National Guard movements and of the activities of Somoza's spies; the maintenance of constant communication with the FSLN; the storage of ammunitions and preparation of homemade weapons; the building of evacuation passageways in the form of hidden wall openings and tunnels; and so on.

Whereas Somoza's genocidal tactics had tended to deplete his resources, the people were now ready to convert their military defeat into a definite victory, both militarily and politically. Somoza and his Guard had become the principal enemies of the People of Nicaragua.

The Final Offensive

Alarmed by the strength and determination demonstrated by the popular forces during the September uprisings, the United States now attempted to mediate a nonviolent accommodation between Somoza and his traditional elite opposition. The U.S. initiative within the Organization of American States materialized into a "Trinational Commission for Friendly Cooperation" involving Guatemala, the Dominican Republic, and the United States. In Nicaragua, the FAO encouraged support for the mediation effort, but its leadership sought little more than a reform of the Somoza regime. Though the Carter strategy included the application of both pressure and incentives, Somoza's obstinacy frustrated the U.S. effort. Moreover, U.S. support of the conservative sector exacerbated the situation and more liberal factions withdrew one by one from the mediation process, charging that the Commission only wanted to establish a *Somocismo sin Somoza* (Somozaism without Somoza). At this stage, Somoza's suggestion to hold a plebiscite was immediately encouraged by the U.S. This option, however, fell through because of conflicting conditions demanded by both sides. As a result, bourgeois unity disintegrated and the proletarian forces consolidated on a strategy of "parallel power." This amounted to what Charles Tilly calls "multiple sovereignty," the identifying feature of any revolutionary situation. In his words, a revolutionary situation

> begins when a government previously under control of a single, sovereign polity becomes the object of effective, competing, mutually exclusive claims on the part of two or more distinct polities. It ends when a single sovereign polity regains control over the government.

In terms of Tilly's formulation, three proximate causes of multiple sovereignty existed: (1) the appearance of contenders advancing exclusive alternative claims to the control over the government; (2) commitment to those claims by a significant segment of the subject population; and (3) governmental insufficiency and inefficiency to suppress (1) and/or (2). This formulation is more than adequate to indicate why and how a revolution took place in Nicaragua.

The strategy of "parallel power" sprang out of the creation of the National Patriotic Front (FPN) in January 1979, which united the FSLN, the MPU and the progressive sectors of the FAO. Within the FPN, the FSLN used the MPU as its basic support structure to reorganize the masses. Meanwhile, since late in 1978 the leaders of FSLN tendencies had been involved in an effort to unify themselves. Finally, on March 8, 1979, the Joint National Leadership of the Sandinista Front for National Liberation, composed of all three factions, announced the final reunification and issued their "program of national unity."

Fortunately, as the opposition was unifying itself and preparing for the final offensive, Somoza found himself facing several crises. A military crisis had forced him to beef up his Guard from 7,500 to some 10,000 and then increasingly to militarize the state apparatus. An economic crisis took place when the International Monetary Fund forced him to devaluate the currency. The unification of the revolutionary front then, simply lent the political, military and economic crises of the Somoza regime the nature of a revolutionary crisis.

By early 1979, the FSLN had increased its forces to around 2,500 and was ready to unleash the final offensive. To win a definite victory it had to coordinate and simultaneously use three tactics: (1) a national strike, (2) popular insurrection, and (3) military attacks. The central focus of the FSLN strategy sprang from "the dynamic unity which had developed between the FSLN vanguard and the popular forces."

On June 4, the FSLN joint National Leadership called for a general strike, effective June 5, and announced the beginning of the final offensive. This paralyzed the country. The so-called "Internal Front" took on central importance in this last stage of the war because of the fact that only the popular forces could lead the urban insurrection. The Internal Front was composed of MPU-CDCs, or popular insurrection forces, in each city, particularly in Managua, in coordination with the FSLN leadership. The "Rigoberto López Pérez" Western Front entered León, Nicaragua's second largest city, on June 2, and in two days of intense fighting assumed virtual control of the city. Beginning June 6, the Northern Front aimed its main offensive at Matagalpa. In order to concentrate its columns and coordinate simultaneous operations in all Fronts, the FSLN high command needed to implement a strategy to win time. It was decided to bottle up the Guard in Managua and cut its lines of supply. At this point, on June 9, the Battle of Managua began with the original plan of holding the city for only three days. As it turned out, however, the Sandinistas held Managua for seventeen days.

By mid-June, the whole FSLN military organization had launched simultaneous operations. Whereas some units attacked the border towns of Peñas Blancas in the south and Las Manos in the north, the "Carlos Roberto Huembres" Eastern Front took Juigalpa and the "Camilo Ortega" Central Front moved on Masaya. The principal roads leading into and out of the most important cities were controlled by the insurgents and most of the Guard units were either confined to their own barracks or forced into merely defensive positions. León and Matagalpa illustrated this. By June 16, the former was under FSLN control, and in the latter only a few pockets of Guard units were still resisting. Somoza was unable to counter the extensiveness of the FSLN offensive. In spite of the fact that he did submit the principal cities of Nicaragua to intense and indiscriminate aerial bombardment, Somoza was no longer able to employ his "September strategy" of retaking towns one by one. The Guard was now largely unable to supply relief forces either inside the cities or to the field.

On June 16, the Sandinista radio station announced the creation of the Provisional Government, a move which resulted in the decision by the Andean nations to award belligerency status to the FSLN, and in the OAS's dismissal of a Somoza request aimed at investigating the Nicaraguan-Costa Rican border. Later on, Panama granted diplomatic recognition to the Provisional Government, amid the OAS deliberation regarding a U.S. proposal calling for an inter-American peace keeping force to be sent to Nicaragua. On June 23, the U.S. suffered an unprecedented defeat in the OAS when the Andean proposal was approved 17-2, demanding Somoza's unconditional resignation and upholding the principle of nonintervention.

Plans for the Managua operations were basically defensive, just to win time in order to coordinate simultaneous operations elsewhere. With only 150 combatants and a few hundred popular militiamen, taking over Managua was unthinkable. After nine days of heroic resistance, a shipment of ammunition was dropped from a Navajo plane in Bello Horizonte, a neighborhood in eastern Managua. At that point, barricades no longer appeared to be the best way to stop the Guard, and a new tactic was adopted. The Sandinistas retreated in order to produce an effect of "invisibility" and take the Guard by surprise. This worked for a while. However, the resulting house-to-house tactic also had its limitations. Meanwhile, a stalemate had developed on the Southern Front, with the National Guard elite forces holding some territory while FSLN and militia units resisted in Rivas. As the Northern and Western Front were consolidated, the only real option for the forces in Managua was to engage in a tactical retreat toward Masaya. This was successfully carried out from June 25 to June 27.

The tactical retreat toward Masaya meant a qualitative step forward because it reinforced FSLN forces in that region, giving them a total of some 6,000 people (3,000 guerrillas and militia, and 3,000 *muchachos* and civilians). This permitted the consolidation of the entire Carazo region, leaving Somoza's troops in the southern areas with little or no chance to retreat back to Managua. As a result, the rebels took Jinotepe on July 5, the first territory to be liberated in Nicaragua. Two days later, León was liberated as Fort Acosasco, six kilometers south of the city, was taken by the insurgents. In a short while, the FSLN was in control of twenty-three cities and towns throughout Nicaragua, and several popularly elected town councils came into being.

Politically, the Somoza regime was isolated, both internally and internationally. The dictator misread the situation and tried to resolve a societal crisis by adopting exclusively military means. On June 24, he called a meeting of his sixteen regional military chiefs and had them swear loyalty to him. He had also relied on Salvadorean and Honduran troops and unreported numbers of foreign mercenaries. His air force napalmed the FSLN strongholds in Managua, and then Masaya. The National Guard was an army of occupation operating in enemy territory, and in spite of the "efficiency, professionalism, and responsiveness to its chain of command" that most of its officers had learned from U.S. military training schools, their efforts were doomed.

The guard failed to penetrate Masaya and León, and no progress was reported in the Southern front. By July 10, Matagalpa was also liberated. Desperate, Somoza attempted to internationalize the conflict by having his planes strafe several towns in Costa Rican territory on July 11. On July 13, he secretly flew to Guatemala for consultation with CONDECA's high ranking officials. Promising his officers that he was not going to give up, he pointed to the acquisition of an undisclosed number of T-28 planes, which, he claimed could facilitate a vigorous counteroffensive. Actually, he and his Guard had already lost the war to the people of Nicaragua. The U.S. government, which had acted as the main impediment to a decisive Sandinista victory on the one hand, and Latin American solidarity on the other, helped determine the timing of the final departure of the "last Marine" from Nicaragua.

The Guard began to dissolve. Most of its officers fled to neighboring countries, particularly Honduras. Entire contingents of Guard units also escaped, but some 7,000 surrendered to the victorious FSLN forces. The Revolutionary Junta was proclaimed in Managua, on July 19, 1979.

THE EAST EUROPEAN REVOLUTIONS OF 1989

Daniel Chirot

The year 1989 was a momentous one in world history. The communist regimes of the Soviet Union and Eastern Europe, themselves founded in revolutions earlier in this century, were overthrown. The revolutions of 1989 were remarkable both for their unexpectedness and for their lack of violence. Regimes that once seemed frighteningly powerful quietly collapsed almost overnight. In the following essay, Chirot explains the reasons for the weaknesses of Europe's communist states, pointing to both their economic and their moral deficiencies.

For those of us interested in social change, revolutionary periods offer the most important fields of observation. We cannot, of course, conduct controlled laboratory experiments that suit the needs of our research. But, in fact, revolutions are large-scale social experiments. Although they are not tailored to scholarly ends, or by any stretch of the imagination controllable, they are the closest thing we have to those major scientific experiments that have shaped our understanding of the physical world. Great revolutions, then, are better windows into how societies operate in the long run than almost any other type of historical event. Therefore, aside from being immediately and keenly interested in the events that took place in Eastern Europe in 1989 because they are reshaping the international political order, we also have a fascinating, unexpected, revealing glimpse into how seemingly stable, enduring social systems fail and collapse.

The Underlying Causes

ECONOMIC PROBLEMS

There is no question that the most visible, though certainly not the only reason for the collapse of East European communism has been economic. It is not that these systems failed in an absolute sense. No East European country, not even Romania, was an Ethiopia or a Burma, with famine and a reversion to primitive, local subsistence economies. Perhaps several of these economies, particularly Romania's, and to a more limited extent Poland's, were headed in that direction, but they had very far to fall before reaching such low levels. Other economies—in Hungary, but even more so in Czechoslovakia and East Germany— were failures only by the standards of the most advanced capitalist economies. On a world scale these were rich, well-developed economies, not poor ones. The Soviet Union, too, was still a world economic and technological power, despite deep pockets of regional poverty and a standard of living much lower than its per capita production figures would indicate.[1]

The main problem is that investment and production decisions were based largely, though not entirely, on political will rather than domestic or international market pressures. To overcome the force of the domestic market, which ultimately meant consumer and producer wishes and decisions, the quantities and prices of goods and services were fixed by administrative order. And to exclude external market forces, which might have weakened domestic guidance of the economy, foreign trade with the advanced capitalist world was curtailed and strictly controlled, partly by fiat but also by maintaining nonconvertible currencies. The aim of curtailing the power of market forces was achieved, but an inevitable side effect was that under these conditions it became impossible to measure what firms were profitable and what production processes were more or less efficient. There were no real prices.

As the inefficiencies of socialist economies became evident, it proved impossible to reform them, largely because the managers were so closely tied to the ruling political machinery. They were able to lobby effectively to steer investments in their direction, regardless of the efficiency of their enterprises. Success as a manager was measured by the ability to produce more, maintain high employment, and attract politically directed investment, not by producing marketable goods more efficiently. Equally important, the very concept of profit as a measure of efficiency was foreign to these managers.

Such systems developed inevitable shortages of desired goods. This was partly because production was so inefficient that it kept the final output of consumer goods lower than it should have been at such high levels of industrialization. And the very crude ways of measuring success, in terms of gross output, slighted essential services and spare parts, so that the very production process was damaged by shortages of key producer goods and services.

But none of this would have made the slightest sense without the ideological base of communism. Some critics of communist economic arrangements have argued that the system was simply irrational. In strict economic terms, it may have been, but that hardly explains its long life. The key is that communist economies were based on a very coherent world view developed by Lenin, Stalin, and the other Bolshevik leaders. This view then spread to other communist leaders, and was imposed on about one-third of the world's population.

Lenin was born in 1870, and Stalin in 1878 or 1879. They matured as political beings in their teens and early twenties when the most advanced areas of the world were in the industrial heartland of Western Europe and the United States, in the Ruhr, or in the emerging miracles of modern technology being constructed in the American Middle West, from Pittsburgh and Buffalo to Chicago. It is not mere coincidence that these areas, and others like them (including the major steel and shipbuilding centers of Britain, or the coal and steel centers of northern France and Belgium), became, one hundred years later, giant rust belts with antiquated industries, overly powerful trade unions, and unimaginative, conservative, and bureaucratic managers. It has been in such areas, too, that industrial pollution has most ravaged the environment, and where political pressures resistant to free trade and the imposition of external market forces were the fiercest in the advanced countries. But in 1900 these areas were progressive, and for ambitious leaders from a relatively backward country like Russia, they were viable models.

Lenin, Stalin, and all the other Bolshevik intellectuals and leaders—Trotsky, Kamenev, Zinoviev, Bukharin, and so many others—knew that this was what they ultimately had to emulate. They felt, however, that they would make it all happen more quickly and more efficiently by socialist planning than by the random and cruel play of market forces. Despite the inherent inefficiencies of socialism, these astonishing, visionary men—particularly Stalin—actually succeeded. The tragedy of communism was not its failure, but its success. Stalin built the institutional framework that, against all logic, forced the Soviet

Union into success. By the 1970s the USSR had the world's most advanced late nineteenth-century economy, the world's biggest and best, most inflexible rust belt. It is as if Andrew Carnegie had taken over the entire United States, forced it into becoming a giant copy of U.S. Steel, and the executives of the same U.S. Steel had continued to run the country into the 1970s and 1980s!

To understand the absurdity of this situation, it is necessary to go back and take a historical look at the development of capitalism. There have been five industrial ages so far. Each was dominated by a small set of "high technology" industries located in the most advanced parts of the industrial world. Each has been characterized by rapid, extraordinary growth and innovation in the leading sectors, followed by slower growth, and finally relative stagnation, overproduction, increasing competition, declining profits, and crisis in the now aging leading sectors. It was precisely on his observations about the rise and fall of the first industrial age that Karl Marx based his conclusions about the eventual collapse of capitalism. But each age has been followed by another, as unexpected new technologies have negated all the predictions about the inevitable fall of profits and the polarization of capitalist societies into a tiny number of rich owners and masses of impoverished producers.

The ages, with their approximate dates, have been: (1) the cotton-textile age dominated by Great Britain, which lasted from about the 1780s into the 1830s; (2) the rail and iron age, also dominated by Britain, which went from the 1840s into the early 1870s; (3) the steel and organic chemistry age, one that also saw the development of new industries based on the production and utilization of electrical machinery, which ran from the 1870s to World War I, and in which the American and German economies became dominant; (4) the age of automobiles and petrochemicals, from the 1910s to the 1970s, in which the United States became the overwhelmingly hegemonic economy; and (5) the age of electronics, information, and biotechnology, which began in the 1970s and will certainly run well into the first half of the next century. In this last age, it is not yet certain which economies will dominate, though certainly the Japanese and West Europeans are well on their way to replacing the Americans.

The Soviet model—the Leninist-Stalinist model—was based on the third industrial age, the one whose gleaming promises of mighty, smoke-filled concentrations of chemical and steel mills, huge electric generating plants, and hordes of peasants migrating into new factory boomtowns mesmerized the Bolshevik leadership. The Communist Party of the Soviet Union found out that creating such a world was not easy, especially in the face of stubborn peasant and worker refusal to accept present hardships as the price for eventual industrial utopia. But Stalin persuaded the CPSU that the vision was so correct that it was worth paying a very high price to attain it. The price was paid, and the model turned into reality.

Later, the same model was imposed on Eastern Europe. Aside from the sheer force used to ensure that the East Europeans complied, it must also be said that the local communists, many of whom were only a generation younger than Stalin, accepted the model. Those who came from more backward countries particularly shared Stalin's vision. In Romania, Nicolae Ceausescu held on to it until his last day in power. It was based on his interpretation of his country's partial, uneven, and highly unsatisfactory drive for industrialization in the 1930s, when he was a young man just becoming an active communist. To a degree we usually do not realize, because China remained so heavily agricultural, this was Mao's vision too. Today its last practitioner is Ceausescu's contemporary and close ideological ally, Kim Il Sung.

In the Soviet Union, in the more backward areas of Eastern Europe, in the already partly industrial areas of China (especially on the coast and in Manchuria), and in North Korea, the model worked because there were a lot of peasants to bring into the labor force, because this type of economy required massive concentrations of investments into huge, centralized firms, and because, after all, the technology for all this was pretty well worked out. Also, producer goods were more important than consumer goods at this stage. (It is worth remembering, too, that these were all areas where industrialization had begun *before* communism, either because of local initiatives, as in Russia or most of Eastern Europe, or because of Japanese colonial investments, as in North Korea and Manchuria.)

I should note, in passing, that the model is particularly disastrous for very backward economies that have no industrial base to begin with. Thus, whatever successes it may have had in East Asia and Europe, it has produced nothing but disaster when tried in Africa or Indochina.

But if the Stalinist model may be said to have had some success in creating "third age" industrial economies, it never adapted well to the fourth age of automobiles, consumer electrical goods, and the growth of services to pamper a large proportion of the general population. This is why we were able to make fun of the Soviet model, even in the 1950s and 1960s, because it offered so few luxuries and services. But the Soviets and those who believed in the Stalinist-Leninist model could reply that yes, they did not cater to spoiled consumers, but the basic sinews of industrial and military power, the giant steel mills and power generating plants, had been built well enough to create an economy almost as powerful as that of the United States.

Alas, for the Soviet model, the fifth age turned out to be even more different. Small firms, very rapid change, extreme attention to consumer needs, reliance on innovative thinking—all were exactly what the Stalinist model lacked. Of course, so did much of America's and Western Europe's "rust belt" industry—chemicals, steel, autos. But even as they fought rearguard actions to protect themselves against growing foreign competition and technological change, these sectors had to adapt because market pressures were too intense to resist. Their political power was great, but in capitalist societies open to international trade it was not sufficient to overcome the world market. In the Soviet case, such industries, protected by the party and viewed as the very foundation of everything that communism had built, were able to resist change, at least for another twenty years. That was what the Brezhnev years were—a determined effort to hold on to the late nineteenth-century model the Bolsheviks had worked so hard to emulate. So, from being just amusing, their relative backwardness in the 1970s and 1980s became dangerous. The Soviets and East Europeans (including the Czechs and East Germans) found themselves in the 1980s with the most advanced industries of the late nineteenth and early twentieth centuries—polluting, wasteful, energy intensive, massive, inflexible—in short, with giant rust belts.

Of course, it was worse than this. The struggle to keep out the world market, to exclude knowledge about what was going on in the more successful capitalist world, became more and more difficult. It also became more dangerous because it threatened to deepen backwardness. Finally, what had been possible in the early stages of communism, when the leadership was fresh and idealistic about creating a more perfect world, no longer succeeded in the face of the growing awareness and cynicism about the model's failure.

But the Soviet and East European leaders in the Brezhnev years were very aware of their growing problems. Much of their time was spent trying to come up with solutions that would nevertheless preserve the key elements of party rule, Soviet power, and the new ruling class's power and privilege. The Soviets urged their East European dependencies to overcome their problems by plunging into Western markets. That was the aim of détente. China, of course, followed the same path after 1978. This meant borrowing to buy advanced technology, and then trying to sell to the West to repay the debts. But as we now know, the plan did not work. The Stalinist systems were too rigid. Managers resisted change. They used their political clout to force ever greater investments in obsolete firms and production processes. Also, in some cases, most notably in Poland and Hungary, foreign loans started to be used simply to purchase consumer goods to make people happier, to shore up the crumbling legitimacy of regimes that had lost what youthful vigor they had once possessed and were now viewed simply as tools of a backward occupying power. This worked until the bills came due, and prices had to be raised. Societies with little or no experience with free markets responded to price increases with political instability. This was especially true in Poland, but it became a potential problem in Hungary (and China) because it created growing and very visible social inequities between the small class of new petty entrepreneurs and the large portion of the urban population still dependent on the socialist sector.

What had seemed at first to be a series of sensible reforms proved to be the last gasp of European communism. The reforms did not eliminate the rigidities of Stalinism, but they spread further cynicism and disillusionment, exacerbated corruption, and opened the communist world to a vastly increased flow of Western capitalist ideas and standards of consumerism. They also created a major debt problem. In this situation, the only East European leader who responded with perfect consistency was Ceausescu. He reimposed strict Stalinism. But neither Romania's principled Stalinism, Hungarian semireformism, nor Polish inconsistency and hesitation worked.

POLITICAL AND MORAL CAUSES OF CHANGE

If understanding economic problems is fundamental, it is nevertheless the changing moral and political climate of Eastern Europe that really destroyed communism there. There is no better way to approach this topic than by using the old concept of legitimacy. Revolutions occur only when elites and some significant portion of the general population—particularly intellectuals, but also ordinary people—have lost confidence in the moral validity of their social and political system.

There have never been advanced industrial countries, except at the end of major, catastrophic wars, in which the basic legitimacy of the system collapsed. And if some serious questions were raised in Germany after World War I, France in 1940, or Germany and Japan in 1945, there were no successful revolutions there. It would be laughable to claim that Eastern Europe's economic problems in the 1980s approached such levels of massive crisis as those brought about by utter defeat in international war. To have had such revolutionary situations developing in times of peace and relative stability, in societies with a strong sense of their nationhood, with functioning infrastructures, police forces, armies, and governments, in the absence of foreign invaders or international crises, without precipitating civil wars, famines, or even depressions, is unprecedented. No mere recitation of economic problems can provide sufficient explanation.

To see how this loss of legitimacy occurred, it is necessary to go back to the beginning. In the mid to late 1940s, at least among cadres and a substantial number of young idealists, communism had a considerable degree of legitimacy, even where it had been imposed by force, as in all of Eastern Europe. After all, capitalism seemed to have performed poorly in the 1930s, the liberal European democracies had done little to stop Hitler until it was too late, and Stalin appeared to be a leader who had saved the Soviet Union. The claim that Marxism-Leninism was the "progressive," inevitable wave of the future was not so farfetched. In fact, many intellectuals throughout Europe, East and West, were seduced by these promises.

In the Soviet Union itself, as in China after 1949, communism benefited from the substantial nationalist accomplishments it had to its credit. Foreigners had been defeated and national greatness reasserted. For all of the problems faced by these regimes, there was clear economic growth and extraordinary progress.

The repressions, terror, and misery of life in the early 1950s soured some believers, but after Stalin's death, reform seemed possible. And after all, the claims made about rapid urbanization, industrialization, and the spread of modern health and educational benefits to the population were true. Not 1956, when the Hungarian revolution was crushed, but 1968 was the decisive turning point. That was when the implications of the Brezhnev policy became clear. Fundamental political reform was not going to be allowed. It must be said in Brezhnev's defense that what happened in 1989, in both Eastern Europe and China, has proved that in a sense his policy of freezing reform was perfectly correct. To have done otherwise would have brought about an earlier demise of communism. Economic liberalization gives new hope for political liberalization to the growing professional and bureaucratic middle classes and to the intelligentsia. It further increases the appeal of liberal economic ideas as well as of democracy. The demand for less rigid central control obviously threatens the party's monopoly of power.

Whatever potential communist liberalism may have had in the Prague Spring of 1968, the way in which it was crushed, and the subsequent gradual disillusion with strictly economic reform in Hungary and Poland in the 1970s, brought to an end the period in which intellectuals could continue to hope about the future of communism.

But this was not all. The very inflexibility of communist economies, the unending shortages, and the overwhelming bureaucratization of every aspect of life created a general malaise. The only way to survive in such systems was through corruption, the formal violation of the rules. That, in turn, left many, perhaps almost all of the managerial and professional class, open to the possibility of blackmail, and to a pervasive sense that they were living a perpetual lie.

Then, too, there was the fact that the original imposition of the Stalinist model had created tyranny, the arbitrary rule of the few. One of the characteristics of all tyranny, whether ideological and visionary, as in this case, or merely self-serving and corrupt, is that it creates the possibility for the dissemination and reproduction of petty tyranny. With tyrants at the top, entire bureaucracies become filled with tyrants at every level, behaving arbitrarily and out of narrow self-interest. The tyrants at the top cannot hope to enforce their will unless they have subservient officials, and to buy that subservience they have to allow their underlings to enjoy the fruits of arbitrary power. In any case, arbitrary, petty tyranny becomes the only model of proper, authoritative behavior.

This is one of the explanations given in recent attempts to explain the almost uncontrolled spread of purges in the USSR in the 1930s, and of course the ravages of the Chinese Cultural Revolution from 1966 to 1976. Once the model is set from the top, imitating that behavior becomes a way of ensuring survival for officials. But even beyond that, a tyrannical system gives opportunities for abuse that do not otherwise exist, and lower level officials use this to further their own narrow ends. (This is not meant to suggest that in some way the tyrants who ruled such systems, and their immediate followers, can be absolved of responsibility for the abuses; it does imply that the way tyrannies exercise power is necessarily deeply corrupt.)

Daily exposure to petty tyranny, which at the local level rarely maintains the ideological high ground that may have inspired a Lenin, Stalin, Mao, or even a Ceausescu, also breeds gradual disgust with corruption and the dishonesty of the whole system. In the past, peasants subjected to such petty tyranny may have borne it more or less stoically (unless it went too far), but educated urbanites living in a highly politicized atmosphere where there are constant pronouncements about the guiding ideological vision of fairness, equality, and progress could not help but react with growing disgust.

In that sense, the very success of communism in creating a more urban, more educated, more aware population also created the potential for disintegration. The endless corruption, the lies, the collapse of elementary social trust, the petty tyranny at every level—these were aspects of life less easily tolerated by the new working and professional classes than they might have been by peasants. (This remains, of course, the advantage of the Chinese communists; they can still rely on a vast reservoir of peasant indifference and respect for authority as long as agriculture is not resocialized.)[2]

The whole movement to create alternate social institutions, free of the corruption and dishonesty of the official structures, was the great ideological innovation that began to emerge in Poland in the 1970s and 1980s in the efforts to establish a "civil society." Traditional revolutionary resistance, taking to the streets, covert military actions, and assassinations were all generally fruitless because they provoked heavy military intervention by the Soviets. But by simply beginning to turn away from the state, by refusing to take it seriously, Polish and then other Central European intellectuals exposed the shallowness of communism's claims, and broke what little legitimacy communist regimes still had. Because of his early understanding of this fact, and his excellent descriptions of how this new ideology grew in Central Europe, Timothy Garton Ash has earned his justly deserved fame.[3]

Certainly, in the Soviet Union all these forces were at work, too, but the patriotism engendered by superpower status (though it has turned out that this was largely Russian, not "Soviet" pride and patriotism), the sheer size of the military, and the long history of successful police terror and repression kept the situation under better control than in much of Central Europe. Yet, combined with the slow erosion of legitimacy was the fundamental economic problem of failure to keep up with the rapidly emerging fifth industrial age in Western Europe, in the United States, and—most astonishingly for the Soviets—in East Asia.

There is no doubt that in the mid-1980s, after Solidarity had apparently been crushed in Poland, with the Soviets massacring Afghan resistance fighters, with Cuban troops successfully defending Angola, and with Vietnam controlling all of Indochina, it seemed to the rest of the world that Soviet military might was insurmountable in countries where the Soviet system had been imposed. But underneath, the rot was spreading. So the question is not "What was wrong with Eastern Europe" or "Why was communism so weak?" Every specialist and many casual observers knew perfectly well what was wrong. But almost none guessed that what had been a slowly developing situation for several decades might take such a sudden turn for the worse. After all, the flaws of socialist economic planning had been known for a long time. Endemic corruption, tyranny, arbitrary brutality, and the use of sheer police force to maintain communist parties in power were hardly new occurrences. None of them answer the question, "Why 1989?" Almost all analysts thought the Soviet system would remain more or less intact in the USSR and in Eastern Europe for decades.

To understand why this did not happen requires a shift in analysis from a discussion of general trends to a review of some specific events in the 1980s.

The Events of the 1980s

If there was a central, key series of developments that began to unravel the entire system, it has to be in the interaction between events in Poland in the early 1980s and a growing perception by the Soviet leadership that their own problems were becoming very serious.

As late as 1987, and throughout most of 1988, most specialists felt that the Soviet elite did not understand the severity of their economic situation. Gorbachev almost certainly did, as did many of the Moscow intellectuals. But there was some question about the lesser cadres, and even many of the top people of the government. But as Gorbachev's mild reforms failed to have a beneficial impact, as the original impact of his policy of openness, encouragement, and antialcoholism ran into sharply diminishing returns, the Soviet economy began to slip back into the stagnation of the late Brezhnev years.[4]

Serious as rising discontent in the Soviet Union might have seemed to Gorbachev, of more immediate concern was the direct military threat of the Soviet's inability to keep up with the developments of the fifth industrial age. While the Soviet nuclear deterrent was unquestionably safe and effective in preventing a frontal attack by the United States, the growing gap between Western and Soviet computer and electronic technology threatened to give NATO (and ultimately Japan) a striking advantage in conventional weapons. This is almost certainly why the Soviets were so worried about "Star Wars," not simply because the illusion of an effective antiballistic missile defense was likely to unbalance the nuclear arms race. Pouring billions into this kind of research was likely to yield important new advantages in lesser types of electronic warfare that could be applied to conventional air and tank battles. This would nullify the Soviet's numerical advantage in men and machines, and threaten Soviet military investments throughout the world.

Given the long-standing recognition by the major powers that nuclear war was out of the question, a growing advantage by the capitalist powers in electronic warfare threatened to turn any future local confrontation between Western and Soviet allies into a repetition of the Syrian-Israeli air war of 1982. From the Soviet point of view, the unbelievable totality of Israel's success was a warning of future catastrophes, even if Israel's land war in Lebanon turned out to be a major failure.

There was one other, chance event that precipitated change in the Soviet Union by revealing to the leadership the extent of the country's industrial ineptitude. This was the Chernobyl catastrophe. But unlucky as it may have been, it served more to confirm what was already suspected than to initiate any changes. The fact is that many such massive industrial and environmental accidents have happened in the Soviet Union. When they occurred in the past, they had little effect, though throughout the 1970s and 1980s there was a growing environmental movement. But on top of everything else, the 1986 nuclear plant accident seemed to galvanize Gorbachev and his advisers.

Meanwhile, in Eastern Europe, the communist orthodoxy imposed under Brezhnev was seriously threatened in Poland. Rising discontent there had made Poland ungovernable by the mid-1980s. It seemed that Hungary was going to follow soon. Economic reforms were not working, the population was increasingly alienated, and while there was no outward sign of immediate revolt, the Jaruzelski regime had no idea how to bring the situation under sufficient control to carry out any measures that might reverse the economic decline and help regain the trust (rather than the mere grudging and cynical acceptance) of the population.

In retrospect, then, the events in Poland in the late 1970s, from the election of a Polish pope, which galvanized the Poles and created the massive popular demonstrations that led to the creation of Solidarity, to the military coup that seemed to destroy Solidarity, had set the stage for what was to happen. But the slow degeneration of the situation in Poland, or in all of Eastern Europe, would not have been enough to produce the events of 1989 had it not been for the Soviet crisis. On the other hand, had there been no breakdown of authority in Poland, and a looming, frightening sense of economic crisis and popular discontent in Hungary, and probably in the other East European countries as well, the Soviets would certainly have tried to carry out some reforms without giving up their European empire. The two aspects of the crisis came together, and this is why everything unraveled so quickly in the late 1980s.

Gorbachev must have realized that it was only a matter of time until there was an explosion—a bread riot leading to a revolution in Poland, or a major strike in Hungary—which would oblige the government to call out the army. The problem was that neither the Polish nor the Hungarian army was particularly reliable. The special police could always be counted on, but if they were overwhelmed, it would be necessary to call in Soviet troops. This the Soviet economy could not bear if it was also to reform itself enough to begin to meet the challenges of the fifth industrial age, especially if this involved increased trade and other contacts with the advanced capitalist countries.

I believe that sometime in 1988 Gorbachev decided he must head off the danger before it was too late to prevent a catastrophic crisis. I cannot prove this, because the documentation is not available, but I am almost certain that because of this decision, in discussions with the Poles there emerged the plan to allow partly free elections and the reopening of talks with Solidarity. The aim would be to relegitimize the regime, and give it enough breathing room to carry out economic reforms without risking strikes and massive civil disobedience. The idea of "roundtable" talks between Solidarity and the regime was proposed in a televised debate between Lech Walesa and a regime representative on November 30, 1988. The talks themselves began February 6, 1989.

It did not work. The reason is that everyone—Gorbachev, the communist parties of Eastern Europe, foreign specialists, and intelligence services in NATO and the Warsaw Pact—vastly underestimated the degree to which the moral bankruptcy of communism had destroyed any possibility of relegitimizing it.

There was something else, too—an event whose import was not fully appreciated in the West, and which remains almost unmentioned. In January 1989, Gorbachev tried an experiment. He pulled almost all of the Soviet army out of Afghanistan. The United States and the Pakistani army expected this to result in the rapid demise of the communist regime there. To everyone's surprise, it did not. I think this might have been an important card for Gorbachev. He could point to Afghanistan when his conservative opponents, and especially his military, questioned his judgment. Afghanistan was proof that the Soviets could partly disengage without suffering catastrophe, and that in some cases it might even be better to let local communists handle their own problems. I suspect that a rapid victory by the anticommunist guerrillas in Afghanistan would have slowed progress for Eastern Europe, if not ending it entirely.

We know how rapidly event followed event. Despite the patently unfair arrangements for the Polish election designed to keep the communist party in power, the electorate refused, and party rule collapsed. Since the Soviets had agreed to the process, and wanted to avoid, at almost any cost, a war of invasion, they let Poland go. Once it became obvious that this was happening, the Hungarians set out on the same path.

Then, partly out of a well-timed sense of public relations, just before George Bush's visit, the Hungarians officially opened their border with Austria. In fact, the border had no longer been part of any "iron curtain" for a long time, but this move gave thousands of vacationing East Germans the idea that they could escape to the West. We know that this set off a mass hysteria among East Germans, who had given up hope of reform, and whose demoralization and disgust with their system led hundreds of thousands to want to flee. They rushed to West German embassies in Budapest and Prague, and began demonstrating in East Germany, particularly in Leipzig and Dresden.

The failure of communism in East Germany in many ways represents the ultimate failure. Here was a country that was not poor, where there were two hundred automobiles for every thousand inhabitants, and where for years Western, particularly West German, sympathizers had said that communism was working by producing a more communal, more kindly Germany than the harsh, market driven, materialistic West German Federal Republic. It was another misconception born of wishful thinking.

It is known that Honecker ordered repressive measures. Earlier, during the summer, Chinese officials had visited East Berlin to brief the East Germans on how to crush prodemocracy movements. But during his early October visit to East Germany, Gorbachev had publicly called for change and let it be known that the Soviets would not intervene to stop reform.

Now, in October, ambulances were readied to cart away the thousands of dead and injured bodies in Leipzig and perhaps Dresden that were sure to be produced by the crackdown. This was prevented. Most accounts credit a local initiative in Leipzig led by the conductor Kurt Mazur, although the central party machinery, taken in hand by Egon Krenz, also played a pacifying role. It is likely that an appeal was made to the Soviets, and that the local Soviet miliary commander said he would not intervene. Knowing this, the East German Communist Party simply overthrew Honecker rather than risk physical annihilation.

East Germany was no China, despite Honecker's claim that it would be. It had no reserve of ignorant, barely literate peasant boys to bring into the breach; and its economy was far too dependent on the West German connection to risk a break. So, once repression was abandoned, the system collapsed in a few weeks. With East Germany crumbling, the whole edifice of communist rule in Eastern Europe simply collapsed. On November 9 the Berlin Wall was opened. It was no longer possible to maintain it when the government of East Germany was losing control over its population, and the rate of flight was increasing at such a rapid rate.

East Germany was always the key Soviet position in Europe. It was on the internal German border that the cold war began, and it was there that the military might of the two superpowers was concentrated. When the Soviets abandoned the East German hard-liners, there was no hope anywhere else in Eastern Europe. The Bulgarians followed in order to preserve what they could of the party, and Todor Zhivkov resigned after thirty-five years in power on the day after the Berlin Wall was opened (November 10). This was surely no coincidence. A week later demonstrations began in Prague, and within ten days it was over. Only Ceausescu of Romania resisted.

Enough is now known about Ceausescu's Romania that it is unnecessary to give much background. Only three points must be made.

First, Ceausescu himself still held on to the Stalinist vision. Aside from the possible exception of Albania (which began to change in the spring of 1990), there was only one other communist country where the model was so unquestioned—North Korea. In fact, Ceausescu and Kim Il Sung long considered themselves close allies and friends, and their style of rule had many similarities. Yet in Romania, and probably in North Korea, this model turned sour about two decades ago, and pursuing it meant economic stagnation, a growing gap between reality and ideology, and the progressive alienation of even the most loyal cadres.

Second, Romania was the most independent of the Warsaw Pact European countries, and so felt itself less dependent on Soviet support. But though this brought considerable legitimacy to the Romanian regime in the 1970s, when partial independence was thought to be grounds for hope, by the late 1980s that hope had failed, and the intellectuals, as well as a growing number of ordinary urban people, had noticed that the Soviet Union had become more progressive than Romania. In southern Romania they listened to Bulgarian television and radio, and when they heard that even there (for the Romanians Bulgaria had always been a butt of jokes as a backward, thick-headed, peasant nation) there were reforms, it must have had a considerable impact. In the north and west, Romanians could pick up the Hungarian and Yugoslav media, and so be informed about what was going on elsewhere. In the east, of course, they had the example of the Soviet Union, and of Romanian-speaking Soviet Moldavia, where, for the first time since the 1940s, people were freer to demonstrate than in Romania itself. I should add that aside from broadcasts from these neighboring countries, Radio Free Europe also played a major role in educating Romanians about what was going on elsewhere in Eastern Europe. The point is that, again unlike China, it proved impossible to keep news about the world out of the reach of the interior.

Finally, and this is much less known than other aspects of Romania's recent history, even at its height the Ceausescu regime relied heavily on the fear of Soviet invasion to legitimize itself. There was always the underlying assumption that if there was too much trouble, Soviet tanks would come in. Was it not better to suffer a patriotic Romanian tyrant than another episode of Soviet occupation? Once it became clear, in 1989, that the Soviets were not going to march, the end was in sight. It was only because Ceausescu himself was so out of touch with reality, and because he had so successfully destroyed his communist party by packing it with relatives and sycophants (like Kim Il Sung), that no one told him the truth, and he was thus unable to manage the more peaceful, gradual, and dignified exit of his Bulgarian colleague Todor Zhivkov.

So, in the end, communism collapsed. The ramifications are far from clear, and there is no way of knowing how things will develop in the Soviet Union. But come what may in the USSR, it is certain that the Soviet empire in Eastern Europe is dead, and that there are almost no foreseeable circumstances that would make the Soviet army invade any of its former dependencies. We cannot be sure what directions the various revolutions of Eastern Europe will take, though it is safe to predict that there will be important differences from country to country.

What happened was that the moral base of communism had vanished. The elites had lost confidence in their legitimacy. The intellectuals, powerless as they seemed to be, disseminated this sense of moral despair and corruption to the public by their occasional protests and veiled commentaries, and the urban public was sufficiently well educated and aware to understand what was going on. The cumulative effect of such a situation, over decades, cannot be underestimated. Those who had had hope, during the 1940s and 1950s, were replaced by those who had never had hope and who had grown up knowing that everything was a lie. Educated youths, not just university students but high school students as well, knew enough about the rest of the world to realize that they had been lied to, that they had been cheated, and that their own leaders did not believe the lies.

What took everyone by surprise was the discovery that the situation was not all that different in the Soviet Union. Nor could anyone foresee the kind of panicked realism, combined with astounding flexibility and willingness to compromise, shown by Gorbachev. In the end, this was the reason revolution came in 1989 rather than in the 1990s. But sooner or later, it would have happened.

Eastern Europe and Other Modern Revolutions

This brings up a serious issue. It has long been assumed that modern methods of communication and the awesome power of tanks, artillery, and air power would prevent the kind of classical revolution that has shaken the world so many times since 1789.

Many utterly corrupt, weak African, Asian, and Latin American regimes have held on to power for a long time with little more than mercenary armies whose loyalties were purchased by allowing them to loot their own countries. This is what goes on, for example, in Burma, Guatemala, and Zaire. Cases where such regimes were overthrown show that it takes long years of guerrilla organization and warfare to carry out revolutions, and then the chances of success are slim. If revolutions occurred in Batista's Cuba and Somoza's Nicaragua, in Uganda Idi Amin held on until he foolishly provoked Tanzania into attacking him. If Baby Doc Duvalier was frightened into leaving office in Haiti, it is not clear, even today, that the Duvalier system has been removed fully.

Only internal miliary coups, as when the Ethiopian or—much earlier—the Egyptian monarchies were removed, seem to make for relatively easy revolutions.

But none of these types of revolutions fit what happened in Eastern Europe. There, even if the Romanian case is included, the total level of bloodshed was minuscule compared with other revolutions. There were no military coups. In Romania there was almost certainly cooperation between the army and the population, but no direct coup, and that was the only case where the army was involved at all. But compared with any African, Latin

American, or almost any noncommunist Asian dictatorship, the East European communist regimes were overwhelmingly strong. They had large, effective, loyal secret police forces, an abundance of tanks and soldiers led by well-trained (though not necessarily enthusiastic) officers, excellent internal communications, and no threat of external, hostile invasion. Only in Romania was the army thoroughly alienated.

Again, we are left with the same explanation: utter moral rot.

Few observers have noticed a startling parallel between events in Eastern Europe in 1989 and in Iran in 1979. There, too, the shah should have been stronger. But even though there were a lot of deaths in the final days, and months of rioting before the shah's departure in January, many were taken by surprise by the overwhelming lack of legitimacy of the regime. Even the newly prosperous middle classes and the young professionals, who had much to lose if the shah was overthrown, failed to back him.

While this is not a suitable place to discuss Iranian society and politics in the 1960s and 1970s, it is evident that the rapid modernization and urbanization of the society helped its intellectuals disseminate their feelings of disgust about the shah's regime, with its empty posturing, its lies, its torturers, its corruption, and its lack of redeeming moral values.

We can wonder, of course, to what extent the rising intellectual and professional classes in urban France in 1787 to 1789 felt the same way about the French monarchy, church, and aristocracy, and the extent to which such feelings played a decisive role in unleashing that revolution. We know that in Petrograd and Moscow from 1915 to 1917, whatever the level of popular misery, the professional and middle classes felt a good bit of disgust at the corruption and lack of morality at the imperial court.

The lesson may be that in fact we need to combine some Marxist notions of class with an understanding of John Rawls's theory of justice as fairness to understand what happened in Eastern Europe. Economic modernization did, indeed, produce a larger middle class (not in the sense of bourgeois ownership, of course, but in the cultural and educational sense, as well as in its style of life). That class was in some ways quite favored in communist regimes. But because of the flaws of the socialist system of economic management, it remained poorer than its West European counterpart, and even seemed to be falling further behind by the 1980s. That is the Marxist, or class and material, basis of what happened.

But more important, the educated middle classes in a modern society are well informed, and can base their judgments about morality on a wider set of observations than those with very limited educations. The artistic and literary intellectuals who addressed their work to these middle classes helped them understand and interpret the immorality of the system, and so played a major role. They needed receptive audiences, but it was their work that undid East European communism.

Without the social changes associated with the economic transformations that took place in Eastern Europe from 1948 to 1988, these revolutions would not have taken place. But it was not so much that new classes were striving for power as that a growing number saw through the lies on which the whole system was based. That is what utterly destroyed the will of those in power to resist.

Once these conditions were set, the massive popular discontent with material conditions, particularly on the part of the working classes in the giant but stagnating industries that dominated communist economies, could come out into the streets and push these regimes over.

REFERENCES

1. A review of the condition and prospects for the East European economies can be found in *Eastern European Politics and Societies* 2:3 (Fall 1988), "Special Issue on Economic Reform," edited by John R. Lampe.
2. Yet it is difficult to believe that China will not follow the same course as Eastern Europe in future years. The crisis of the Democracy Movement in the spring of 1989 was caused by all the same conditions that led to the collapse of communism in Eastern Europe: the contradictions of economic reform in a system still run by communist officials, growing corruption, loss of faith in the official ideology, and increasing disgust with the endless hypocrisy of those in power. The main difference, of course, was that China in 1989 was much less developed, much less urbanized than the East European countries, and also much more insulated from the effects of the economic and political crisis in the Soviet Union. For a brief review of the events in China and their causes, see Spence (1990), pp. 712–47.
3. His major essays from the late 1980s have been collected in Timothy Garton Ash, *The Uses of Adversity* (1989).
4. Each new report from the Soviet Union makes the Brezhnev years and the prognosis for the future seem bleaker. For years the CIA reports painted a more pessimistic economic picture than the official Soviet reports, but recently Soviet economists have said that even the CIA reports were too optimistic. None of this is new to the academic specialists; see, for example, Goldman (1983).

THE SOCIAL SOURCES OF THE STUDENT DEMONSTRATIONS IN CHINA, 1989

Martin King Whyte

China's politics have shown many twists and turns since the communist revolution of 1949, led by Mao Zedong. Until his death in 1976, Mao fought strenuously to overcome private property, inequality, and individualism, which he saw as elements of the capitalist economies that had, in the nineteenth century, reduced China to semicolonial dependence on Western imperial powers. Mao's efforts to create an ideal socialist society are described in the essay by Whyte in Chapter 5.

However, Mao was never fully successful in his quest. After his death, China's new leadership, dominated by Deng Xiaoping, recognized that private property, inequality, and individualism were not merely capitalist errors, but unavoidable elements of a growing economy (see the essay by Kelley and Klein in Chapter 5). Deng thus sought to permit these elements to take root in China, while preserving much of the socialist structure of heavy industry, and preserving the dominant political role of the Communist party.

Deng's reforms have not solved the problem of creating harmony among China's diverse elites and popular groups. Instead, a variety of student, worker, and bureaucratic groups have pressed for greater reforms, including free markets and democratic politics. Against these groups, military and party officials have sought to preserve the Communist party's control of government and the economy. These divisions burst forth in the spring of 1989, in student-led demonstrations in Tiananmen Square, in Beijing. In this essay, Whyte describes the social and political changes that led to the student demonstration, and the consequences of this event for China's current leadership.

As 1989 began, China could boast a population that was much better clothed, fed, and housed than it had been a decade earlier, when a program of sweeping economic and political reform was introduced. One testimonial to the magnitude of the country's transformation came from Chinese who had the opportunity to travel to the Soviet Union and Eastern Europe at the end of the 1980s. They reported back incredulously that frustrated East European consumers were trying to buy the clothing off their backs, as well as any food items and consumer durables they had happened to bring along. It was almost as if they were visitors from the rich and capitalist West. This was quite a turnabout from the 1950s, when China had taken lessons from her socialist elder brothers. Deng Xiaoping's version of "goulash communism" appeared to be outpacing the original East European version.

The reforms not only improved economic conditions; they also increased cultural diversity. The rigid political restrictions of the Mao era governing acceptable proletarian literature, art, and popular ideas were relaxed, and an increasing variety of cultural forms became available to the Chinese. The "open" policy produced a proliferation of Western cultural products, ranging from politically "rehabilitated" classics (for example, Shakespeare and Beethoven) to newly "liberated" foreign radio broadcasts and translations of the likes of Sigmund Freud, Henry Kissinger, Herman Wouk, and Sidney Sheldon. New imports even included such choice samples of Western proletarian culture as motor-cross racing, Rambo movies, and bodybuilding. With foreign tourists, teachers, and businesspeople streaming into China and with increasing numbers of Chinese going abroad, contact with Western individuals, ideas, and institutions began to reach beyond the small circle of the Chinese political elite.

The relaxation of restrictions based on ideology extended to China's own cultural heritage as well. Temples were restored and monasteries reopened, Confucius and his ideas were reexamined, and in general an effort was made to retrieve artistic, musical, and literary products of the past. This revival of tradition was not confined to high culture. The restoration of family farming helped to fuel revivals of ancestor worship, wedding feasts, elaborate funerals, geomancy, and other customs the authorities had earlier branded "feudal remnants." Peasants appreciated the new opportunities these changes offered to pursue family goals and participate in culturally meaningful rituals. The restoration of temples and sacred sites and the new tolerance for religious activity also resulted in revivals of temple worship, religious pilgrimages, and the manufacture of ritual items (for example, spirit incense, sacred charms, coffins), all of which had been banned during the Mao era.

The general relaxation of control in the political sphere, combined with growing incomes and increased leisure, led to a boom in domestic tourism. Foreign travelers accustomed to having a near monopoly on sites such as the Great Wall found themselves increasingly bumped and jostled by throngs of Chinese, who were able to enjoy the sights of their native land.

Better economic conditions and greater cultural diversity were accompanied by social healing. Large numbers of people who had been condemned to political purgatory during the many struggle campaigns of the Mao era were rehabilitated and allowed to resume normal lives. The system of class labels used to stigmatize individuals and families and to foster class struggle in the Mao era was formally dismantled. Millions of urban youths who had been sent to the countryside were allowed to return to the cities, there to resume interrupted educations, careers, and spouse searches. Many couples separated by arbitrary job assignments or by reeducation campaigns were able to arrange transfers so that they could live together for the first time in decades. Such developments made it possible for individuals to retreat from the scars and battles of public life without apology and devote more time and attention to affairs of the home and family. In general, the frazzled nerves produced by the tumult of the late Mao era began to be soothed.

Given these considerable improvements in the quality of people's lives, one would have expected the reforms, and the post-Mao leadership responsible for them, to be hugely popular. Since no popular elections or referendums on the reforms were held, and since the public opinion polls that began to be carried out during the 1980s were for the most part officially sponsored and rather unscientific, readings of popular opinion can only be impressionistic. Many observers would argue that had a referendum on the reforms been conducted in, say, 1984 or 1985, the result would have been overwhelming approval. Yet by the close of the decade the rule of Deng Xiaoping and his cronies had to be maintained by massive force of arms against widespread public disapproval. To reform-minded Chinese, at least, Eastern Europe seemed to have leapt ahead of China once again.

The Social Roots of Popular Discontent

Why was popular discontent increasing despite the apparent success of the reforms? In addressing this question I shall distinguish three separate groups within the population: those who felt the reforms had not gone far enough, those who thought that they had gone too far, and those who were generally satisfied. For the sake of simplicity, I shall call these groups the "not far enoughs," the "too fars," and the "satisfieds."

China's post-Mao reforms introduced dramatic changes in society initially; however, increasingly after the mid-1980s the reform momentum stalled, leaving a partial transformation of the system that made nobody very happy. The reasons for rising disaffection in the late 1980s, though, differed sharply between the "not far enoughs" and the "too fars." The social dynamite that exploded in the spring of 1989 was formed by a combination of circumstances that made it possible for social groups holding quite contrary views to overcome their differences and unite in their common hostility to the leadership.

TOO LITTLE REFORM

The Beijing Spring demonstrations were spearheaded by those who believed that the reforms had not gone far enough. These included not only students but also many intellectuals and a newly emerging group, urban entrepreneurs.[1] In part the "not far enough" reaction of these groups involved frustration that political reforms had been repeatedly placed on the national agenda and just as often taken off without producing any concrete results. For example, Deng Xiaoping's August 1990 speech calling for fundamental changes in China's political structure was republished on three separate occasions in the 1980s, each time stimulating discussion that led nowhere.

Students and their allies found the economic reforms insufficient as well. The slogans and goals of the reformers implied that intellectuals and experts would have a leading role in plotting China's future and that intellectual talent and expertise would play the central role in China's modernization drive. Improved treatment of intellectuals and future intellectuals (that is, students) became a standard slogan voiced by officialdom, and reforms were launched aimed at giving such individuals greater autonomy, more comfortable working conditions, greater rewards, and increased freedom to select where and on what they would work. The idea that the leadership would increasingly rely on the advice of the experts in formulating national policies held enormous appeal for most students and their allies, for whom this notion resonated with ancient ideas about the active incorporation of intellectuals into state service.

When students looked at the society around them, however, they perceived that not much had changed. State investment in education was pitifully low, even compared with many other Third World countries, and the material conditions and prospects of most students remained bleak. Most could look forward to lives earning modest and largely fixed salaries in jobs not of their choosing, under less well-educated supervisors who often did not appreciate their talents and aspirations, and with only limited chances to cash in on the new opportunities created by the reforms. Student optimism about the future was further dampened by a spate of articles published during the mid-1980s claiming that middle-aged intellectuals were not only poorly paid but also had greater health problems and shorter life spans than people in other occupations.

Intellectuals similarly saw a large gap between reform goals and present realities under reform. Instead of being able to work unobstructed and contribute to China's future, many found themselves locked into the same jobs as before. Bureaucratic overseers and constant shifts in the national political atmosphere presented repeated reminders of the Mao era, when intellectuals were presumed to be infected with bourgeois tendencies. Successful and aspiring entrepreneurs faced blatant hypocrisy as well. Instead of competing in a fully developed market, they had to make their way through a mine field of changing regulations and petty regulators. Access to the resources and opportunities they needed to run their businesses was never fully secure. As one bitter description put it, "A 'visible foot' is stepping on the 'invisible hand.' "

---

[1]This combination is symbolized by the leadership-in-exile that emerged in Paris after the June crackdown, composed of student Wuer Kaixi, intellectual/reformer Yan Jiaqi, and the founder of the Stone Computer Company, Wan Runnan.

Although the specific ways in which the "not far enough" sentiment was felt by these groups varied, they were united in their anger at the hypocrisy involved in the meritocratic vision of the reforms. Although the reforms were supposed to produce a society in which the educated, the skilled, the hardworking, and the innovative would receive the most rewards and prestige, the reality often looked quite different. A few individuals were benefiting disproportionately, even though they had done relatively little to merit such benefits. These included suburban peasants and children of high-ranking officials who happened to be situated favorably in relation to new market opportunities and who had personal access to scarce resources and foreign contacts.

Those groups angered by these inequities found they had little opportunity to vent their grievances or effect change. Their resulting frustration produced increased pressure for political reforms whose general goal would be to create a more equitable society. It is well to keep in mind the distinction between equity and equality. In political terms the "not far enough" groups wanted to reduce the power of the party/state bureaucracy, but their preferred alternative was not in most cases some sort of mass egalitarian democracy. Rather, they were concerned with gaining their own deserved places in the political sun. Many would have been horrified at the idea that an intellectual should have no more say in society than a worker or a peasant. Equity was thus seen as demanding not equality but rather a society in which the educated and technically skilled would increasingly take over from the politically loyal. This frankly elitist picture of the good society is expressed most clearly in the speeches and writings of astrophysicist Fang Lizhi, "China's Sakharov," whose views aroused such indignation within the CCP leadership that he was ousted from the party in 1987 and had to seek refuge in the American embassy during the June 1989 crackdown.

It would be a mistake, however, to see all the discontent of the Deng era in economic or political terms. Perhaps equally important in undermining support for the regime were critiques stressing the loss of cultural and moral cohesion in post-Mao China. China's leaders were seen as jettisoning the cultural and ideological orthodoxy of the Mao era without providing a coherent alternative. A long period during which individuals knew precisely what was good and bad and how they should behave gave way in the Deng era to a confusing variety of cultural practices and moral arguments. Official slogans such as "socialism with Chinese characteristics" provided only the vaguest of guidance.

In this arena of moral confusion, most of those who shared the "not far enough" view came to the conclusion that the institutional reform agenda of the May Fourth Movement (China's other great student-led, Western-oriented reform movement, launched in 1919) should be resumed. They felt that the failures of Maoist socialism represented, in large part, the continuing influence of China's long feudal legacy, and that only a thorough critique of both Marxism-Leninism and the traditional legacy, combined with institutional renewal drawing on modern Western models, could save China. Throughout the 1980s these sentiments led to increasingly sharp and systematic critiques of both China's traditional legacy and its bureaucratic socialism.

Too Much Reform

The sentiment that the reforms had not gone far enough in dismantling the bureaucratic system of state socialism was by no means the dominant view in society at large. In terms of sheer numbers, more people probably leaned toward the opposite view that the reforms had already gone too far. It is one of the persistent dilemmas of reforms in China, and elsewhere, that changes that are not sufficient to satisfy critics threaten and alienate other previously satisfied groups. This tendency makes the task of building popular support for further reform problematic. In China those who were increasingly worried that the reforms were going too far included industrial workers, low-level bureaucrats and party officials, the army, and the police. The members of these groups are much more numerous than intellectuals, students, and entrepreneurs, even if they are not as articulate.

China's workers had seen job and income security as among the greatest achievements of the revolution. Lives that before 1949 were characterized by constant fear of unemployment, inflation, and impoverishment were transformed by the socialist system. Those on the state payroll were provided with permanent employment, compensated with secure wages, and protected by a range of health care and other benefits that were unusually broad for a developing society. Even though opportunities for advancement and wage increases were limited, and were terminated almost entirely in the last decade or so of Mao's rule, the enhanced security provided by state employment made it possible for workers to plan their lives and build families in a more secure environment.[2] The efforts by the reformers to destroy the "iron rice bowl" system of job security in favor of limited-term employment contracts, the right of managers to demote and fire workers, and newly promulgated bankruptcy legislation threatened this proud victory of socialism. Even though these reforms were not fully implemented, the Chinese media came to be filled with accounts of disgruntled workers who retaliated with threats or even violence against those pushing such reforms locally.

Women workers were particularly upset that, as a consequence of the industrial reforms, many enterprises began to selectively lay off female employees or to refuse to hire any but males, using the justification that male workers were less troublesome and more productive.[3] Although advocates of these changes argued that returning women to the home would open up more employment opportunities for young males and provide more nurturance and discipline within families, women employees, accustomed to slogans of the Mao era that said that women "hold up half of heaven," were often hard to convince. The normally sluggish Women's Federation took up this issue and denounced the increasing discrimination against female workers that the reforms spawned.

---

[2] Of course, greater economic security was combined with increased political insecurity in the Mao period, and individuals who got into political trouble forfeited all claims to the security provided by Chinese socialism.

[3] In the Mao era, when enterprises had no power to retain their own profits and could request funds freely to cover any deficits, there was no incentive to economize on either labor costs or fringe benefits. Under the reforms, enterprises can retain a share of their profits for reinvestment or for spending on employees, and this change produces increased incentive to minimize labor costs and fringe-benefit expenditures. Employers claim that women are more costly due to higher absenteeism, maternity leave, and earlier retirement, and on this basis they may resist hiring and retaining female employees.

When in 1988 and 1989 the government experimented with contracting out the management rights over failing state firms to private entrepreneurs, not only many workers but also bureaucrats and even some intellectuals were outraged. Although the justification for this measure was that it would turn failing enterprises around and preserve jobs, it was widely seen by workers as representing a sellout of socialism and a return to dependence upon exploitative capitalists. (Not surprisingly, such experiments were repudiated after the crackdown, despite the claims of China's gerontocrats that the reforms would proceed.)

Workers at least could see that [despite higher risks] the reforms provided them with new opportunities to increase their salaries and bonus payments. Most other groups in the "too far" camp were not in this situation. Low-level bureaucrats, party officials, soldiers, and police shared with intellectuals the complaint that their modest and mostly fixed incomes prevented them from benefiting as much as others from the reforms. In addition, they perceived that the reforms threatened their power and prestige within their local bailiwicks as well as within society generally. Indeed, in many cases they were being blamed for the abuses and inefficiencies of the Mao era. Subordinates, colleagues, and neighbors who had formerly paid them deference now treated them with disrespect or even hostility. For individuals in these groups who felt that they had followed the call of Mao and devoted their lives to the revolution, the perception that others regarded them as political Neanderthals or worse was particularly galling. In rural areas such sentiments often led grassroots cadres to resign in order to free themselves to concentrate on getting rich, but this was not an option readily available to their urban counterparts. The changes introduced by the reforms created morale problems in organizations such as the army and the police and complicated recruitment of young people into careers in these organizations, careers that had once commanded great respect.

The "too far" groups' vision of the good society was decidedly not one in which party bureaucrats would be replaced at the top of the social pyramid by meritocratic experts. While some of the members of these groups may have yearned for a more ideal socialist society in which the actual producers would be the masters of the state, most were more realistic and assumed that Chinese society would remain sharply hierarchical. However, they were generally more comfortable with "reds" than "experts" in charge at the top. For many this preference resulted in nostalgia for the perceived benevolent concern of Mao Zedong for the problems of workers, peasants, and soldiers. They saw precious little of such benevolence in the policies and pronouncements of the reform-era leadership, and many feared the elitism and arrogance of China's intellectuals. (These groups found the slogans about favoritism toward experts convincing, even if the experts themselves did not.)

The resentments generated in such "too far" groups were aimed at a variety of targets. For some the villains to be blamed for their loss of privileges and prestige were the new entrepreneurs and the well-educated experts and managers who were taking over leadership at the grass roots. However, equally likely to receive blame were the higher-level leaders who were pushing through the changes that left grass-roots cadres and party officials feeling scapegoated and powerless. One of the weak points of a

Leninist system is that it substitutes the very visible hand of the state (or the "foot" alluded to earlier) for the invisible hand of the market. When groups feel that they are being treated unfairly, they are not likely to blame fate, their own imperfections, the market, or even rival groups. Their angry glances are quite likely to be directed upward at those who command the entire system.

The increased alienation of the "too fars," like that of the "not far enoughs," had cultural and moral dimensions beyond the economic one. The "too fars" saw the preferred remedy of the "not far enoughs" for China's cultural malaise, Westernization, as precisely the wrong solution. Indeed, when they looked around and saw such things as the revival of open prostitution, an upsurge in Christianity, and a fever among the young for foreign ideas and culture, they could agree with the claim of party conservatives that China was being "spiritually polluted" as a result of the "open" policy. For example, the 1988 documentary television series "River Elegy," with its highly unfavorable comparisons between China's bureaucratic lethargy and the dynamic West, deeply offended many "too fars" on patriotic grounds. But within this group ideas about the preferred alternative to Western culture varied. Some felt the solution to China's problems was to be found in a return to China's Confucian tradition. Such critics of complete Westernization began to produce laudatory evaluations of how Confucian values had contributed to economic development in Taiwan, South Korea, and Japan. Other opponents of the new infusions of Western culture tried to resurrect the democratic spirit of original Marxism from under the distortions introduced by Lenin, Stalin, and Mao, or even yearned for the perceived moral purity of the Mao era.

The "not far enoughs" and the "too fars" saw the world in very different terms. However, they agreed that the economic situation in the late 1980s was unacceptable and that China in the Deng era had become an unsatisfying mixture of cultural confusion and moral decay. Two factors acted together to make the economic frustrations experienced by many particularly severe. First, there were the long years of enforced spartan living of the Mao period, which left every group in society feeling that its just demands for material improvement urgently needed to be met. One effect of this backlog of unmet material aspirations was to make the early post-Mao grass-roots discussions of pay increases particularly angry and tearful. This phenomenon helps to explain why so many raises and bonus payments that were supposed to be distributed to the most worthy ended up being doled out equally to all. The second aggravating factor was inflation, which became increasingly serious after the mid-1980s. Many groups found their hard-won gains in buying power undermined and reversed; for some the fight to stay on top of the inflation treadmill brought back memories of the (much more serious) inflationary spiral of the late 1940s.

SUFFICIENT REFORM

The reader may wonder whether there were any groups at all in China who perceived that they were benefiting from the reforms. The answer is yes. Within both the "not far enough" and the "too far" groups there was, of course, diversity of views, and some students, intellectuals, workers, soldiers, and others were quite content with their lot in life. But in addition, there were two groups with particular cause for satisfaction, who felt gratitude rather than hostility toward the reformers.

One such group was the peasantry. Many if not most peasants felt that the reforms had rescued them from years of state-enforced poverty. Rural incomes initially increased more rapidly than did urban incomes and peasants created a boom in construction of new housing and competed with urbanites for the televisions, washing machines, and other new symbols of reform-era prosperity. As noted earlier, the new rural prosperity also found more traditional outlets—in elaborate weddings and funerals, in restoration of local temples and lineage halls, and in pilgrimages and tourism. No doubt the renewed ability of families to escape from the day-to-day supervision of rural cadres and plan their own lives and work activities was also a source of considerable satisfaction. However, satisfaction on this score was tempered by one increasingly severe and unpopular way in which the lives of peasant families were regulated by the state in the Deng era—the mandatory birth-control program which culminated in the one-child policy after 1979. Even among the peasants, of course, views varied widely. In many disadvantaged regions, and among disadvantaged peasant families within every region, there were strong reasons for feeling that the benefits of the reforms were not trickling down the way they were supposed to. Even peasants who prospered under the reforms often felt anger at the shifts in rules and regulations and the demands for "contributions" and bribes that kept them from enjoying their economic success. In addition, localities and families that had prospered in the Mao era often felt threatened by official demands that they disband organizational forms painfully developed over the years in order to revive competition in the marketplace. Both "not far enoughs" and "too fars" could be found in the Chinese countryside, although they were in the minority.

Because peasants make up the single largest group in Chinese society, constituting between 70 and 80 percent of the total, one might have thought that their general satisfaction with the reforms would have provided the leadership with a powerful source of support. However, those peasants who had prospered under the reforms and who felt they could now operate successfully under them did not form a well-organized group that could make its influence felt effectively in support of the leadership. The difficulty of mobilizing peasants, short of revolution, combined with their concentration on local horizons and activities, made them a negligible factor in the political battles that erupted in the late 1980s. [Moreover] trends such as stagnation in grain production after 1984, continued state niggardliness in investing in agriculture, and budget deficits that required some peasants to be paid for their grain in IOUs rather than cash had, by 1989, eroded support for Deng and his colleagues even in the countryside. Toward the end of the decade, outbursts of anger directed at the state agents became increasingly common in rural areas.

The other major group with cause to be satisfied with the reforms as they were was, of course, the high-ranking bureaucrats and their friends and families. The stalled nature of the reforms made available many opportunities for gaining new riches and prestige without providing a level playing field that would enable all groups to compete for those new opportunities. The continued substantial bureaucratic obstacles that restricted access to resources, information, and opportunities worked to the advantage of those who had the personal connections to take advantage of them, and the official slogans about the desirability of getting rich provided legitimation for their pursuit of gain. Since this small and privileged group was increasingly seen by both the "too far" and the "not far enough" groups as the cause of the problem, its satisfaction with the situation in 1989 was not an effective barrier against growing popular discontent.

From Discontent to Mass Demonstrations

The existence of widespread popular discontent in the reform era is not a sufficient explanation for either the student demonstrations or the mass response to them. Widespread popular discontent has existed in many societies, and it certainly existed during a number of periods in the Mao era, without producing anything comparable to the events of the Beijing Spring. A number of other developments were required in combination to produce those events.

One such element was the relaxation of political controls that occurred in the reform era. Political study and mutual criticism sessions in schools and work units were less intense and less frequently held than in the Mao era. As noted earlier, large numbers of individuals and groups were "rehabilitated," and although many of those who lost their negative labels concentrated on lying low and enjoying their restored lives, others began to seek out audiences for the critiques of the system that their years in political oblivion had nurtured. Similarly, former Red Guards who had survived factional battles, years in rural exile, and university entrance exams took their place as teachers of the young and found enthusiastic disciples for their unconventional analyses of the ills of Chinese society. Exposure to China's cultural legacy and to the growing flood of ideas and models from the outside world provided a new awareness of political and cultural alternatives. Images of "people power" sweeping aside Marcos in the Philippines and of the legalization of alternative parties in Taiwan also provided examples of how to organize to bring about desired changes. These concrete models were probably more influential than accounts of the separation of powers in the American political system.

Over the years, as people could see public declarations of formerly heterodox views being raised without those raising them getting into political trouble, the feeling began to grow that dissent and efforts to change the system were safe. By the mid-1980s, avowedly autonomous clubs and associations began to emerge all over China. Even though most of these were apolitical and cautious, they provided a venue within which growing numbers of individuals (mostly urbanites, and disproportionately educated ones) could acquire a sense of being able to organize activities without CCP guidance and control. Although no major changes in the structure of the political system were carried out during the 1980s, the loosening of the political atmosphere created increased opportunities for critical views to be shared beyond the boundaries of family and close friends. China did not produce a fully formed "civil society," but individual grievances found new opportunities to coalesce into group dissent.[4]

Critical voices were more widely heard in the 1980s, and groups sharing common grievances began to emerge. Still, if the political elite had remained united and consistent in opposing any mass political action, the events of the Beijing Spring would not have escalated out of control. The previous rounds of student demonstrations were successfully contained, even though they showed an ominous tendency (from the standpoint of the leaders) to revive each time in enlarged form. What made the situation different in 1989 was the crumbling of unity within the elite and the implicit and explicit encouragement that the more ardent reformers within the leadership gave to students and others to raise critical voices. That encouragement seems to have been motivated by the increasing frustration that Zhao Ziyang and his followers felt over their difficulties in reviving reform momentum. Eventually many students and intellectuals came to feel that mass pressure was not only needed to promote the reform cause within a divided leadership, but that such pressure could also be effective in turning the tide against the conservatives within that leadership. The confidence (misguided, as it turned out) that bold public voicing of discontent not only would not be penalized but might actually produce desired results helped to energize active participation among the students and their allies. To be sure, there were some students who were very pessimistic about the prospects for change and who were willing to risk martyrdom nonetheless for their cause. However, if such pessimism had been generally shared, and if discontented students had faced a united and hostile elite, no escalating mass demonstrations would have occurred.

Even in the presence of widespread popular discontent, an opportunity to share that discontent with others, divisions within the elite, and some high-level encouragement of the demonstrators, the resulting demonstrations need not have gotten out of control. Indeed, given the sharp disagreements between the "not far enough" and "too far" groups, there were considerable opportunities for the leadership to foment conflict between groups as a way of keeping the situation from getting out of hand. In the previous major wave of student demonstrations, in 1986–1987, this is precisely what happened. Leader state- ments and mass media accounts then portrayed the student demonstrators essentially as spoiled brats, concerned with improving their already privileged lives rather than with the problems of workers and peasants. The student demonstrations at that time attracted only minor public support from other groups in society and were relatively easily squelched.

By 1989 the students had learned the lessons of earlier rounds of demonstrations, although some of this learning occurred only during the course of the Beijing Spring. Initially the students tried to exclude other groups from participating in their demon- strations, and in mounting former CCP general secretary Hu Yaobang, who died on April 15, they tended to focus upon issues (political reform and intellectual freedom) that were

---

[4]Theorists of democratic transition argue that a civil society is a basic precondition for a democratic political system, and this view has been very influential among dissidents and reformers in Eastern Europe. Civil society involves the existence of a wide variety of organizations and associations that operate autonomously vis-à-vis the state. Such associations nourish a sense of citizenship that is protected from state infringement, and they provide vehicles through which group ideas and interests can be articulated and used to pressure the state. For an attempt to apply this concept to contemporary China, see Gold (1990), pp. 18–31.

mainly of concern to other "not far enough" partisans. However, eventually this exclusionary policy was dropped and replaced by active encouragement of other groups to join them. In good Chinese fashion this participation usually took organized, corporate form, with individuals taking part as members of delegations from their schools or work units, complete with banners and signs, rather than as a heterogeneous mass. The appeals and demands raised by the students increasingly focused on issues that had broad popular appeal—to the "too far" groups as well as the "not far enough" ones. Increasingly the demonstrators' anger focused on inflation and corruption within the leadership, major problems that could unite the two disparate sides in hostility against the national elite.

Still, it took a further dramatic step to overcome the political and cultural gap between the students who initiated the demonstrations and the ordinary workers, cadres, and other urbanites who later joined them. That step was provided by the hunger strike launched in mid-May. The hunger strike testified in a vivid and relatively unconventional way to the students' position that they were not simply trying to benefit themselves but were laying claim to the moral legacy of righteous intellectuals in previous dynasties who were willing to risk their lives in their quest for justice. The dramatic act galvanized popular support for the students and led to a rapid escalation in both the size of the demonstrations in Tiananmen Square and in the number of supportive acts by other groups around the city. During this crucial period, splits within the leadership as well as problems in preparing for the Gorbachev visit prevented the elite from taking timely and forceful action to prevent the alliance between the "not far enoughs" and the "too fars" from being consolidated. Once that consolidation became apparent, a bandwagon effect set in, with more and more casual onlookers and thrill-seekers augmenting the ranks of committed protesters.

The unlikely alliance that had been forged to produce this popular uprising was visible in the symbols carried in Tiananmen Square and in countless smaller squares in provincial cities and towns. It is important to remember that demonstrations were not confined to Beijing. Not only provincial cities but many county seats and even small towns witnessed student demonstrations during the period of the Beijing Spring. Prominent in such demonstrations were Western symbols that conveyed themes favored by the "not far enoughs," such as slogans about freedom of the press and the Goddess of Democracy statue. However, also visible were competing non-Western symbols that reflected the views of the "too fars"—for example, the portraits of Mao Zedong that were borne aloft by many groups of demonstrators.

Consequences of the Beijing Spring

The mass demonstrations of the Beijing Spring were thus a product not merely of popular discontent but of a whole series of forces and contingencies. Furthermore, this chain of developments undermined the ability of the regime to unite the "too fars" and the "satisfieds" to fend off the challenge of the "not far enoughs." Instead, the "not far enoughs" were able to recruit support from the "too fars" in common opposition to the bureaucratic elite despite their many differences, while most of the "satisfieds" (China's peasants, in particular) remained on the sidelines. Under these circumstances, a disaffected and highly vocal minority almost succeeded in overturning the regime.

After the crackdown, the new conservative leadership coalition took a number of steps designed to stamp out organized opposition and prevent something similar from happening again. They ousted Zhao Ziyang and some of his key followers from the leadership and promoted into their ranks new leaders not closely associated in the public mind with the crackdown (notably Jiang Zemin, the new general secretary of the CCP) in an effort to forge an appearance of unity and stability. They increased political study and indoctrination activities, tightened the limits on cultural activities, and tried to stamp out harmful ideas and influences (for example, by jamming Voice of America broadcasts). They reduced enrollments in key universities and initiated mandatory military training prior to enrollment in some institutions in an attempt to inoculate the young against "bourgeois liberal" ideas. They made it abundantly clear that voicing heterodox opinions could still get people into deep political trouble. They instituted measures designed to address the twin problems of inflation and bureaucratic corruption. And they attacked those who stimulated and participated in the demonstrations as unpatriotic, a theme designed to appeal to the nationalist sentiments of both the "too fars" and the "satisfieds."

Although such measures are designed to defuse both the sources of discontent and the precipitating conditions that led to the mass demonstrations, there are reasons to believe that the success of Deng Xiaoping's new conservative coalition in regaining control can be no more than partial and temporary. First, there are questions about how thorough and sustained these measures by the elite can be. Many provinces and localities are participating in the tightening of the political atmosphere only in a perfunctory manner, and even in Beijing many units are carrying out the new political study rituals and group criticism sessions in a formalistic and superficial way. Expressions of discontent are not being totally suppressed. Some individuals who have cooperated actively in the crackdown (for example, by turning in fugitives on the official arrest list) are now being subjected to public scorn. Furthermore, many of the familiar signs of elite disarray—conflicting messages in the mass media, unexplained disappearance and reappearances, rumors about schemes to gain more power—are apparent, making it difficult to persuade the public that the leadership will follow unified and consistent policies in the future. Even with the formal retirement of Deng Xiaoping from his last posts, it is obvious to everyone that the configuration of top leaders formed after the crackdown is of his making and is not likely to survive his death or incapacity. (The shift of mood in China is symbolized by the sad fact that many who in the early 1980s used to pray for Deng's longevity now hope for his early demise.)

All of these phenomena make it very unlikely that the genie of mass discontent can be put back in the bottle of quasi-Maoist controls. In addition to the grievances that existed prior to the Beijing Spring, there are new problems that will make the attempt by the conservatives to assert control highly problematic. There is now a powerful resentment unleashed by the crackdown itself, an outraged feeling that China's conservative leadership coalition has the blood of peaceful protesters on its hands. In addition, the economic situation has turned for the worse since the crackdown, producing new fears about stagnation and unemployment.[5] These new sources of anger are likely to make the reactions of the "too fars," who ordinarily might be expected to support the sort of curtailing of reform measures that has been launched since the crackdown, less than enthusiastic. In addition, the expressed commitment of the current leaders to continue the reforms and the "open" policy has prevented them thus far from formulating policies that would relieve the pre-1989 anxieties and hostility of the "too fars."

China's conservative leaders cannot simply turn back the clock and wipe out all consequences of the Beijing Spring, and the problems produced by the crackdown provide a strong basis for a continued union between "not far enough" and "too far" groups in the future. The Chinese political scene resembles a pressure cooker and is likely to do so for some time to come. Any crisis or rupturing of the enforced unity of the leaders is likely to unleash renewed popular anger, making the present "stability" a very precarious thing.

The paradox presented at the outset of this paper—of mounting discontent amid reform progress—is not so paradoxical after all. Dissatisfaction, pent-up consumer demands, and social tensions left over from the Mao era created extraordinary hopes and pressures that made the task of China's reformers very difficult. The initial progress of the reforms created public relief and gratitude but led to a thirst for more changes among some groups while fostering anxiety about future changes among others. Even in the wake of the June crackdown, the leadership has been unable to find a formula that will defuse popular hostilities and rebuild an effective alliance between those who think the reforms went too far and those who are relatively contented, in order to isolate the smaller but more articulate groups who do not think the reforms went far enough. Unless China's conservative leaders can find ways to defuse the situation, split the alliance of popular forces that oppose them, and rebuild popular support for their program of curtailed reforms, future explosions of mass discontent are quite likely.

---

[5]The picture on the economy is somewhat mixed. Inflation was reduced in the latter part of 1989 and a record grain harvest (in absolute, though not in relative, terms given the continued growth in population) occurred in the same year. However, one of the causes of the decline in inflation is the retrenchment of the economy, and that has led to the closing of many enterprises, reductions in employment, and new efforts to force excess urban personnel to return to the countryside. These latter trends make popular perceptions of the economic situation considerably less than bullish.

The Outcomes of Revolutions

Revolutions have numerous accomplishments to their credit. They have redistributed land, done away with tyrannical dictators and oppressive systems of land tenure, and eliminated the hereditary privileges of traditional aristocracies. They have brought increases in literacy, better education and health care, greater pride in national strength, and independence to hundreds of millions. Yet revolutions have generally failed to deliver on their chief promises: greater freedom, material well-being, and equality for all. In many countries, revolutions have led to more powerful and authoritarian regimes than the ones they replaced. And often peasants' initial gains have been weakened through policies for industrialization (in both capitalist and socialist countries) that diverted resources from the peasantry to urban centers. The implementation of these policies maintained or increased inequality while the lot of peasants stagnated or even deteriorated with population increase.

Furthermore, we must always ask: Have the accomplishments been worth the price? Civil and international wars and severe economic dislocations often accompany revolutionary transformations. Experts estimate that over 100,000 Englishmen out of a population of five million died in the Civil Wars of the English Revolution; that 1.3 million of a total population of 26 million of the French died in 1789–1815 in the civil and Napoleonic wars; that over two million of a population of 16–17 million died in the course of the Mexican Revolution; that in the Civil Wars and the initial steps to collectivize agriculture in Russia and China, war and dislocations in agriculture led to tens of millions of deaths. The recent Nicaraguan Revolution caused some 50,000 deaths in a population of 2.5 million; and the casualties of Iran's war with Iraq, which followed Iran's revolution, are still being counted.

The following essays present a variety of evidence to examine these difficult issues. Though they differ in approach, all these analyses share two conclusions. First, revolutions do not create a "clean slate." The conditions and habits of people under the old regime very much affect the outcomes of revolutions. Second, these outcomes reveal zigs and zags in state policies and their results, so that these outcomes are never quite what the revolution's leaders or supporters first expected.

INEQUALITY AND STRATIFICATION

Revolutions generally seek to bring greater justice and equality to societies. They therefore aim to change the magnitude of the differences in wealth, income, and status among individuals (inequality), and the system by which rewards and status are assigned by society (stratification). Indeed, many revolutions have aimed not merely to change the basis of inequality and stratification, but to remove them entirely, creating a society in which everyone is truly equal.

However, it appears to be impossible, given human nature, to eliminate entirely inequality and stratification. In this chapter, Jonathan Kelley and Herbert S. Klein describe why, despite the efforts of revolutionaries, inequality and stratification systems are likely to reemerge in any postrevolutionary society. Alf Edeen shows how in Russia, after the Communist Revolution of 1917, the old Tsarist stratification system based on bureaucratic ranks reappeared, even including many old Tsarist officials in important roles. Martin King Whyte demonstrates that even in communist China, where Mao Zedong made perhaps the most strenuous efforts of any revolutionary in this century to abolish inequality, inequality and stratification managed to persist.

In short, revolutions may destroy the old privileged classes and open up new opportunities; nonetheless, they have not been successful in destroying inequality and stratification itself.

◆

REVOLUTION AND THE REBIRTH OF INEQUALITY: STRATIFICATION IN POSTREVOLUTIONARY SOCIETY

Jonathan Kelley and Herbert S. Klein

Kelley and Klein note that in the short run, revolutions generally reduce inequality. But in the long run, inequality is likely to reemerge. Revolutions may destroy hereditary titles and privileges and break up large landholdings. They may even do away with private property entirely.

Yet revolutions also provide new opportunities in administration and management and, where private property is maintained, in small business and services. In these pursuits, those possessing education and skills—that is, human capital—have an advantage. That advantage generally translates into higher position and higher income. In addition, industrialization places an even greater premium on academic, technical, and managerial skills. To the extent that postrevolutionary regimes aggressively pursue industrialization, inequalities of opportunity and reward are likely to increase rapidly.

In addition, individuals with advanced education, official position, and income are often able to pass some of these advantages on to their children. Thus, a new hereditary system of inequality will tend to emerge.

Humanity left to its own does not necessarily re-establish capitalism, but it does re-establish inequality. The forces tending toward the creation of new classes are powerful.

—Mao Zedong, 1965

Probably the most shattering and dramatic transformation of human society is the violent overthrow of traditional elites by a revolution of the oppressed masses. Most such revolutions have occurred in the mainly rural, peasant-dominated societies in which the majority of mankind has lived. Local landlords have been dispossessed and chiefs deposed ever since exploitative governments arose in advanced agrarian societies. Large-scale peasant revolutions appear throughout history but particularly in the modern period (e.g., in the Peloponnese in 227 B.C., England in 1381, France in 1789, Mexico in 1910, Russia in 1917, China beginning in 1921, Bolivia in 1952, and Cuba in 1958). For the old elite, the consequences of a successful revolution are clear. But for the mass of ordinary people, they are not. Revolutions generally promise peasants justice and at least some relief from rent, taxes, usury, and traditional restrictions on their movement. They surely benefit from that relief and, at least in the short run, from the more open and equalitarian society that results. But whether some benefit more than others and why is unclear. The long-term effects are even less clear. Does equality endure, or does inequality reemerge, perhaps in new and more virulent forms? Does social mobility grow or decline? Who benefits from the forces unleashed by revolution and how? In this paper we propose a theory about the effects of revolution on inequality. We show that, in the short run, a revolution can be expected to reduce economic inequality and status inheritance, as anticipated, but also to benefit its well-to-do supporters more than its poorer ones and to make human capital more important for all. In the long run, peasants will still be better off, but stratification reemerges. Economic inequality and status inheritance grow steadily, in some circumstances eventually exceeding their prerevolutionary levels.

Scope

Our theory deals with the predominantly rural, premodern, peasant-dominated societies in which most revolutions have occurred. We claim that it applies to any revolution meeting the following conditions: (1) a politically and economically dominant traditional elite has previously been able to expropriate a large fraction of the surplus produced by peasants (e.g., by control over land, forced labor, discriminatory taxation, usury, or through monopoly privileges in agriculture, trade, or government), and (2) the revolution has liberated peasants from the traditional exploitation (e.g., by redistributing land, allowing freer access to opportunities in farming and business, expropriating or destroying accumulated capital). We call this combination of events a radical revolution, and we limit consideration of short-term effects to revolutions of this kind.

The predictions about long-term effect (Hypotheses 4 through 8 below) are more general; they apply not only to radical revolutions but also to any social changes which reduce exploitation or increase economic opportunities. Such changes include economic "revolutions" which liberate people from stifling restrictions or increase their productivity by technical means: specifically, the early phases of the Industrial Revolution, the Green

Revolution in agriculture, the introduction of cash crops or a market economy in nonmarket societies, and the like. They also include political changes which have increased opportunities for blacks and women in the United States, untouchables in India, the Ainu in Japan, and other minorities.

We deal with the apolitical mass of the rural and small-town population, deliberately excluding the revolution's political and military leaders, the revolutionary intelligentsia, and other revolutionary elites. Nonetheless, their ideology and the policies of the government they establish are extremely important. The peasants' goals will generally be what they regard as simple justice—personal (or communal) control over their land, minimal taxation, and the right to sell their produce on the open market. That leads to a predominantly market economy with peasants (or peasant communities) functioning essentially as small capitalist entrepreneurs accumulating income and property. In that case our model applies with full force. But the revolutionary elite may oppose the return to a classical peasant economy, instead pursuing more radical and collectivist goals. If successful this will mean the end of a conventional peasantry and the rise of a rural working class, usually employed in state-owned communal farms. Our model still applies in this case, but the changes will be slower and somewhat attenuated, in ways we specify.

Short-term Effects

INEQUALITY

We are dealing with radical revolutions which, by definition, at least partly free peasants from their traditional exploitation and thereby improve their economic position at the expense of the traditional elite. Transferring resources from the rich to the poor clearly reduces inequality (as we define it) in the society as a whole, which is of course typically one of the revolution's main goals. In practice, the redistribution is often extensive. Radical revolutions often redistribute land, the fundamental fixed asset in peasant societies, and hence redistribute income. They usually redistribute liquid capital as well, expropriating or destroying rents, savings, debts, pensions, and monopolies; such redistribution reduces inequality, especially in the rare cases where the expropriation is partly inadvertent. Property is abandoned during the crisis, and the collapse of the old government often leads to dramatic inflation which destroys the value of savings, salaries, and rents; these are more damaging to the old rich. Taxes and rents which fall most heavily on the poor are often reduced or eliminated. In precapitalist societies, labor taxes extracted by the state or by landlords are often the main form of exploitation, and abolishing them increases the time peasants have to work for their own benefit, leading to further equalization. In modern times, revolutionary governments usually establish new health, education, and welfare programs which result in major transfers of resources to the poor and further reduce inequality.

Human Capital In the short run, we predict that radical revolutions will make human capital more valuable. In practice the range of opportunities for utilizing education, knowledge, technical skills, and other forms of human capital increases greatly. (1) Especially in previously isolated and traditional rural areas, rapid changes in marketing and the expansion of the money economy upset traditional economic arrangements and reward the adaptability, rationality, and cosmopolitan orientations that education provides. Literacy and elementary bookkeeping skills are valuable even in very primitive economies. (2) New political and economic power creates new opportunities for cultural brokers and go-betweens (politicians, lawyers, expediters, etc.) to mediate between peasant communities and nonpeasant society. To do so requires knowledge, contacts, and linguistic and political skills. Modern revolutions generally create numerous new positions in schools, health and welfare agencies, the government bureaucracy, and nationalized industry. Economic growth, a goal of almost all modern revolutions, expands the market economy and increases employment in professional, managerial, and clerical jobs and in transportation; and success in these requires educational, technical, and linguistic skills. (3) Educational credentials may become more important quite apart from any real connection with performance, since requiring fixed levels of education is an effective and convenient way of restricting access to jobs, especially in the expanding bureaucracies. (4) In societies in which there are several languages (or the educated classes speak a different dialect), skills in the dominant language often become more valuable after the revolution. They give access to new opportunities in education and commerce and are useful in dealings with the bureaucracy. With increasing contact between urban and rural areas and the atrophy of the old landlords's role as intermediary, facility in the national language helps in dealing with the police, bureaucracy, merchants, and employers.

These new opportunities will, we predict, make education, technical and linguistic skills, and other forms of human capital more valuable, giving a larger return in occupational status and income. Some will be able to take direct advantage of their skills by self-employment, taking up more attractive and profitable opportunities than were available before the revolution. To match these new opportunities in self-employment, employers will have to offer more to attract skilled employees. Also the growth in the number of jobs requiring education and linguistic skills increases the demand for skilled personnel, and, since the supply can increase only slowly, skilled workers will use their improved bargaining position to extract better wages.

Who Benefits? Radical revolutions benefit most of their supporters, since their surplus is no longer expropriated by the old elite. But we predict that revolutions do not benefit the poorest as much as those who already possessed human or physical capital. Those with human capital, already better off before the revolution, have a great advantage in the new bureaucratic, commercial, and political jobs (e.g., in the Soviet Union), and in commercial agriculture. In addition, there are typically substantial differences in the amount and value of land peasants worked before the revolution, and they are often able to maintain or strengthen their customary rights afterward (e.g., in Bolivia); then with their surplus no longer expropriated, well-to-do peasants benefit more from their advantages.

STATUS INHERITANCE

Because a radical revolution leads to the redistribution of wealth, we predict that it leads to less inheritance of status—that is, more pure social mobility—for those who came of age just after the revolution. Since many prerevolutionary elite parents lose their wealth, they have less of an advantage to pass on to their children, whereas some poor parents gain new resources and have more to give theirs. So on the average there is less variation in the wealth that parents can pass on to their children and hence less status inheritance.

But status inheritance does not disappear. Some economic inequalities are likely to remain after even the most dedicated and efficient attempts at redistribution. Human capital remains; education, literacy, technical and linguistic skills, and the like retain or even increase their value and cannot be redistributed. The old elite and others who were better off before the revolution have more of these resources and are able to pass some of their skills on to their children. So an effective means of transmitting status from one generation to the next remains; in the short run, a revolution will reduce status inheritance but not eliminate it.

SUMMARY

Hypothesis 1 In the short run, a radical revolution produces a more equal distribution of physical capital and, for those coming of age just afterward, less status inheritance.

Hypothesis 2 In the short run, a radical revolution causes a shift in the basis of stratification, making human capital (education, knowledge, technical or linguistic skills, etc.) a more valuable source of occupational status and income.

Hypothesis 3 A revolution does not immediately benefit the poorest of its supporters as much as it benefits those who possess human capital or have been able to retain physical capital.

Long-term Effects

STRATIFICATION AMONG PEASANTS

A radical revolution allows peasants to obtain a higher return on their physical capital since, by definition, it reduces exploitation. (1) By reducing rents or taxes on land, it allows peasants to retain more of what they produce. The destruction of corvee labor obligations—the crucial tax in many agrarian societies—allows peasants more time to work their land for their own benefit (e.g., an additional one to three days per week in medieval Europe and three or more days in twentieth-century Bolivia). (2) Revolution is likely to reduce the costs peasants pay for goods and services by destroying traditional monopolies on trade, credit, and justice. Monopolies allowed traditional elites to charge exorbitant prices; even where the revolutionary government makes no deliberate attempt to reduce prices, competition is likely to drive them down. (3) Prior to the revolution, peasants' opportunities are often restricted to the least profitable sector of the rural economy. However, the destruction of serfdom, corvee labor, and other laws tying peasants to the land opens up new opportunities. They can sell their own produce and take up wage-paying jobs in addition to agriculture, which in some cases increases their income dramatically. Some become traders and merchant middlemen, replacing the old elite's commercial monopolies. (4) Economic change may have the same effects, with or without revolution. The introduction of new cash crops or new agricultural techniques, the opening of new markets, and the like all provide new and often profitable opportunities. Ending economic discrimination against blacks, untouchables, the Ainu, etc. opens up opportunities for them.

These new opportunities will, we predict, lead eventually to greater economic inequality among peasant proprietors and the mass of the previously exploited population. Even in prerevolutionary times, peasants differ in their physical capital (e.g., size and quality of usufruct landholdings), in human capital (e.g., agricultural or linguistic skills, education, experience with the outside world), and in ability, motivation, luck, and the like. By expropriating the surplus and restricting opportunities to use capital effectively, the old system prevented fortunate peasants from getting the full benefit of their advantages and so restrained the growth of inequality. Revolution removes the restraints, allowing them to take full advantage of their resources. In the long run, that creates steadily growing inequality among peasants and other previously exploited groups. This leads to what might be called the kulak stage—the rise of a newly enriched sector of the peasant population and the emergence of an essentially capitalist rural stratification system. Since fortunate peasants have increasingly large advantages to pass on to their children, we predict that revolution will in the long run lead also to steadily increasing status inheritance among them. The same reasoning applies to those economic revolutions and social changes that reduce exploitation, and in fact there is evidence that they increase both inequality (e.g., in agriculture following the Green Revolution) and status inheritance (e.g., among American blacks in the past decade).

Human Capital In the long run, a radical revolution leads to greater inequality in human capital among the peasantry and previously exploited masses. (1) Revolution provides additional reasons for acquiring human capital. Education, linguistic skills, and other forms of human capital are always valuable, and if anything, revolution makes them more so. Peasants can expect greater benefits from education after the revolution, since they have new opportunities to use it and can keep more of what they earn. Investing in education therefore becomes more attractive on straightforward economic grounds. Economic revolutions often have the same effect. (2) Modern revolutions supply the means. Whether from conviction or because of peasants' new political power, revolutionary governments generally expand the school system, making education available where it was not before. (3) Educational inequality increases because some children benefit more than others. Able and motivated children have an advantage, as do children from privileged families. Throughout the world, well-educated, high-status families are much more successful in getting their children educated (e.g., in tribal societies, in socialist societies, and in industrial societies); they provide encouragement and role models, teach linguistic and academic skills, force their children to work harder, and the like. Schooling is usually expensive, both in direct costs (fees, supplies, clothing, etc.) and indirect costs (income the student could otherwise have earned); prosperous families can better afford these costs.

This growing inequality in human capital will, we predict, in the long run lead to greater economic inequality and more status inheritance among peasants. Since education and other forms of human capital are quite valuable, greater inequality in human capital leads to greater inequality in income and wealth. That, we have argued, leads to greater status inheritance. Educational changes also increase status inheritance directly. As educational inequality grows among parents—that is, as the gap between well- and poorly-educated parents increases—it becomes more of an advantage to be born into a well-educated family.

Government Intervention A revolutionary government can try to restrain these forces by limiting the private accumulation and inheritance of capital. Populist and middle-class revolutionary parties are unlikely to have either the ideological justification or the dedicated cadre with which to do so, although many socialist and communist governments make the attempt. But it is unlikely to succeed. Expropriating large landowners, large capitalists, and foreign investments and thereby securing the "commanding heights" of the economy will not be enough, since accumulation by the mass of upper peasants and the educated middle class leads, we have argued, to inequality. To restrain these groups, private capital will have to be abolished throughout the economy. In practice this is usually accomplished by socializing the industrial economy and collectivizing the land and sometimes by the physical extinction of the kulaks. Many people have something to lose from such actions, and they are not without recourse. Small businessmen have money and can threaten to withdraw valuable services; the upper levels of the peasantry know they have much to lose; the educated middle class and party workers newly ensconced in the bureaucracy will want to secure their advantage by accumulating wealth. To fully overcome the opposition of these groups requires from the party's cadres a level of commitment, dedication, and resistance to temptation that is difficult to maintain over the years; it also requires an extensive and efficient bureaucratic apparatus which can extend its control to the very grass roots, an apparatus few societies have ever possessed. China's cultural revolution may have been in part an attempt to overcome this kind of opposition and prevent the reemergence of inequality. Even in China, however, the costs were great, opposition was strong, and success uncertain; other examples are not easy to find.

But the abolition of private capital is not in itself enough to prevent the long-term growth of inequality, since much (indeed most) inequality arises from differences in education, skills, language, and other forms of human capital which are almost immune to redistribution. Human capital is crucial; to run even a moderately complex society requires an educated elite—business, industry, and government require a variety of administrative and technical skills, and even farming and small trading are greatly facilitated by literacy, bookkeeping, and specialized technical skills. Although it is sometimes claimed that schools impart few skills of any genuine importance but merely screen or certify or are otherwise dispensable, that claim is inconsistent with detailed evidence for modern industrial societies and with the clear importance of education in societies with very different economic and institutional structures. Ignoring these skills in favor of political or equity considerations is exceedingly costly; to date only China has systematically and persistently attempted it after the revolutionary government was firmly established and the threat of counterrevolution past. Nor can governments effectively prevent human capital from being passed from one generation to the next without draconian changes in the family. The knowledge, values, culture, and language skills acquired in elite homes give children an enormous and enduring advantage in socialist as well as capitalist societies; discriminatory admissions policies for higher education and government can reduce the advantage somewhat but not eliminate it, save at enormous cost. Thus a revolution able to abolish private property will slow the long-term growth of inequality and status inheritance but will not prevent it.

STRATIFICATION IN THE SOCIETY AS A WHOLE

In the long run, a radical revolution will, we have argued, create more inequality and status inheritance among peasants and the previously exploited rural masses. But its effects on the society as a whole are less clear. We will argue that inequality and status inheritance first decrease and then remain low for a period; in most circumstances they then increase steadily and, in some circumstances, eventually exceed their prerevolutionary levels.

Economic development increases inequality. Even if everyone retains the same relative position, development increases the absolute size of the gap between rich and poor and therefore increases inequality. If, for example, the introduction of new cash crops doubles everyone's income, it also doubles the gap between poor peasants and rich merchants, so the peasant has twice the obstacle to overcome if he is to live as well as a merchant, and a peasant's son has twice the handicap to overcome if he is to catch up with a merchant's son. In addition, anyone with physical capital, human capital, or other advantages will be better able to take advantage of new opportunities opened up by economic development and that increases inequality by any definition.

The benefits that revolution provides for peasants and the exploited rural masses will at first decrease inequality in the society as a whole. Peasants' income, wealth, and human capital almost always begin well below the average for the whole society, while the commercial and administrative sectors in rural towns and most urban groups are markedly better off initially. The revolution reduces exploitation, improving the economic position of all peasants. That reduces inequality. Most peasants go no further. But those with physical or human capital or other resources will continue to improve their position, especially if the revolution is one which produces economic development. As they surpass the average income level in increasing numbers, inequality first stabilizes and then (depending on how many surpass it and by how much) may increase. So there is a standard sequence following the revolution. Inequality first declines and then stabilizes. If peasants continue to improve their economic position, the decline lasts longer, but eventually inequality begins to increase again and eventually may exceed its prerevolutionary level.

How far along this sequence a society proceeds depends not only on what happens to the peasants but also on how high the average income is to begin with and how it changes subsequently. Most prerevolutionary peasant societies are very poor, with a small surplus extracted by a tiny elite. The average is low and, other things being equal, that makes it easier to surpass, and the society will then go through the sequence quickly, often reaching the stage where inequality increases. In richer societies (e.g., Eastern Europe following the communist revolutions), peasants have further to go, and the society passes along the sequence more slowly. The average also depends on what happens to the urban population and the postrevolutionary elite, but that reflects the power and ideology of the revolutionary leadership, the society's economic and administrative capacity, international political and economic restraints, and a variety of other factors beyond the scope of our theory.

There may be further redistribution after the revolution; this too affects inequality. Particularly where there is no sustained economic growth, gains by rich peasants are someone else's losses. If they gain entirely at the expense of the elite, there will be more equality. But in practice, their gains will most probably be at the cost of poor peasants and lower and middle classes in the towns. As rich peasants take over marketing, credit, and middleman functions, they displace middle- and lower-class urbanites, and liberated peasants compete for desirable urban jobs. Successful peasants will produce cash crops more efficiently, undercutting poor peasants' market positions and driving them off the land. When rich peasants begin to pass the mean, inequality will eventually increase as long as their gains are mainly at the expense of groups below the average.

A revolution's effects on inequality in the society as a whole thus depend crucially on the speed of economic development, the economic position of urban groups and the postrevolutionary elite, and government policies toward accumulation. We predict that inequality will increase most dramatically if the revolution generates economic development (which directly increases inequality) and if the entire society was poor to begin with (since rich peasants exceed the mean sooner). Since modern revolutions in poor societies (e.g., Mexico in 1910, Bolivia in 1952) almost always promote economic development, we predict that they will eventually create more inequality than existed before the revolution unless governments make strenuous efforts to prevent it. The scattered evidence now available suggests that inequality does increase. Economic revolutions—the decay of feudalism, the early stages of industrial revolution, the introduction of cash crops and a money economy in premarket Asian and African society, the Green Revolution in agriculture, etc.—lead to economic development. We predict that therefore they will cause inequality in the long run; the evidence indicates that they do. In contrast, we predict that classical peasant revolutions in traditional societies in which urban areas remain richer than the countryside and no economic development results will reduce inequality (e.g., Punjab in the late nineteenth century). Changes in status inheritance in the society as a whole will, we predict, parallel changes in inequality for the reasons set out earlier.

SUMMARY

Hypothesis 4 In the long run, peasants are better off after a radical revolution.

Hypothesis 5 By allowing peasants to utilize their resources more fully, radical revolutions set loose forces which tend in the long run to produce steadily increasing economic inequality among them.

Hypothesis 6 In the long run, radical revolutions produce increasing educational inequality among peasants.

Hypothesis 7 Among peasants, radical revolutions create forces which tend in the long run to produce more status inheritance through both economic advantage and education.

Hypothesis 8 In the society as a whole, inequality and status inheritance following a radical revolution will first decrease, then stabilize, then (a) remain low if nonpeasants remain well off and there is no economic development in the countryside but (b) steadily increase and perhaps in time exceed prerevolutionary levels in poor societies in which there is substantial economic development.

Hypotheses 4–8 apply not only to radical revolutions but also to any social changes which reduce exploitation or increase economic opportunities, with the poor and exploited taking the role of peasants.

THE SOVIET CIVIL SERVICE:
ITS COMPOSITION AND STATUS

Alf Edeen

Edeen charts the development of the Soviet Civil Service after the Revolution of 1917. The Revolution destroyed the old privileged nobility while the industrialization of the Soviet economy, and the enormous expansion of the bureaucracy, provided vast opportunities for upward mobility. However, the bureaucracy itself became similar to the Tsarist system it replaced; moreover, as the Soviet system matured the bureaucracy grew more stable, and social mobility declined.

The Old Nobility

With the Bolshevik seizure of power in 1917 a social order with roots in a backward agrarian society was destroyed. The leading social group in this old order was the nobility. This nobility was divided into a class of hereditary landowning nobility, whose members were mostly recruited to the higher civil-service stratum, and a nonhereditary titular or civil-service nobility, the main body of which—together with untitled civil servants—appeared in the lower administration. Persons from other social levels were continually being taken into the nobility, primarily through advancement in the civil and military administrations, but also through the bestowal of orders and even through purchase of titles. Entrance into the nobility occurred automatically in virtue of the Table of Ranks which Peter the Great introduced in 1722. The purpose of this measure was to make room in the civil service for representatives of the low nobility (*dvorianstvo*), who were granted titles and prestige on the basis of the table. Thus the Table of Ranks meant that an aristocratic hierarchy, founded on birth and family trees, was replaced by a bureaucratic hierarchy, founded on merit and years of service. This reform did not have such thorough-going effects, because once the *dvorianstvo* was established in its new position, the hereditary branch in this nobility grew, in its turn, into a new high nobility, which in the following centuries saw to it that birth and family trees did not lose their significance in recruitment to the state service.

The nobility could for a long time maintain its leading position within the administration for a very simple reason: the overwhelming majority of the population was completely disqualified in this connection since they were not even literate—in 1897, for example, 80 percent of the population was illiterate. The nobility and the civil servants—along with the clergy—had by far the highest percentage of literacy; but it may be inserted parenthetically that no less than about 25 percent of the members of these culturally leading classes were illiterates. For the nobility there were also special schools and educational institutions which were closed to other social groups—for example, the lycées in Petersburg and Moscow and the page and cadet schools. Until 1880 the Alexander Lycée in Petersburg was so exclusive that only the sons of the hereditary nobility were admitted. And this lycée—like the others—was intended "for education of youth destined for important areas in the state service." On the military side, the cadet schools were mainly intended for the sons of officers. Concerning the recruitment of the officer corps—and of the clergy too, for that matter—something of a caste system had been developed, since the occupation passed from father to son and "outsiders" entered these careers only in exceptional cases.

During the latter part of the nineteenth century and up to 1914, definite progress was made, particularly in the field of public education. In leading circles, however, there was a desire to prevent this progress from encouraging an undesirable social mobility. From the notorious instruction published by the Ministry of Education in 1887, the following deserves to be quoted:

> Gymnasiums and progymnasiums are freed from receiving the children of coachmen, servants, cooks, laundresses, small tradesmen, and the like, whose children, with exceptions, perhaps of those who are gifted with extraordinary capacities, ought by no means to be transferred from the sphere to which they belong and thus brought, as many years' experience has shown, to slight their parents, to feel dissatisfied with their lot, and to conceive an aversion to the existing inequality of fortune which is in the nature of things unavoidable.

The occupations listed above show that the authors were especially concerned about the diffusion of "unnecessary" knowledge among particular sectors of the urban population. Of interest also is the open recognition of the problem of how to maintain an authoritarian and hierarchical social order in a time of industrialization and urbanization with growing demands for increased formal education—a development which might lead to the undermining of the established order.

Education and the Civil Service

The question of the increased social differentiation in the towns—connected with Russia's industrialization in the late nineteenth century—became particularly important with regard to the recruitment of the universities. The statistics concerning the social composition of the university students are incomplete, but one can discern certain rather clear trends. As a consequence of the official school policy, the social selection was, on the whole, quite naturally completed at the time of entrance into universities. The dominating group consisted of sons of the nobility and the civil servants. For 1911 there is a distribution which shows that the sons of civil servants and titular nobility represented 46 percent of the university students. A further 9 percent came from the hereditary nobility. The most striking trait, however, is the advancement of the other social groups during the latter part of the nineteenth century: the sons of peasants increased percentagewise very notably from a low initial figure, and the lower middle class in the towns appears as an important group. After having finished their studies, representatives of these groups took employment to a great extent as civil servants in local administrations in the provinces. This "rural intelligentsia" came into strong opposition to the authorities, reflecting a tendency which was also being expressed among the craftsmen and the lower level of civil servants in the towns. The authors of the instruction from the Ministry of Education that was quoted above must have thought that their worst apprehensions had come true.

Birth, personal connections, and a certain educational level opened the door to a career in the state administration. After his entry into the service, the person in question was placed according to the Table of Ranks. During the time of Peter the Great, capable men from the bottom of society could make overnight careers and consequently gain entry to the highest estate. With increasing bureaucratization, however, restrictions were gradually introduced. The order of advancement became fixed: the civil servants had in principle to pass the different ranks successively—without "skipping"—and seniority was the universally decisive factor at the advancement from one rank to another.

The marked differentiation in rank among the civil servants was combined with a similarly sharp differentiation in salary—a few top salaries for the highest civil servants and extremely modest salaries for the great mass of lower officeholders. The widespread corruption for which the Russian administration was notorious was connected with this unsatisfactory remuneration system and the almost obligatory "prestige expenses," which were pressing for precisely these last-mentioned groups. State service was nonetheless extremely sought-after, primarily because of the social prestige which the possessor of rank enjoyed. The rank table comprised the standard by which a person's social position was measured. The impressive titles and uniforms, which grew all the more dazzling and decorative with the rise in rank, invested the civil servant with dignity and authority over the general public. This title-and-rank mania, however, was not a phenomenon prevalent only in the civil service. On the whole, when a person or a group—artists, scientists, teachers, and merchants—was to be especially distinguished before the public, grants of title and rank were resorted to as a panacea. Merchants in the First Guild, for example, had been granted the right to wear special uniforms and—after twenty years' membership in the guild—to receive the title "Counselor of Commerce and Manufacturing."

The Russian Revolution

When the Bolsheviks seized power in 1917, they immediately concentrated on a consolidation of their positions and on practical administrative work. The aim was to build up a completely new social order with no roots in the past, and the heritage from the overthrown Tsarist regime was formally severed by means of a series of governmental decrees. The administrative apparatus was rebuilt from the ground up and was provided with new labels. The rank system was formally "liquidated" by means of a decree as early as November 1917, entitled "On the Abolition of the Estates and of the Civil Ranks." With the stroke of a pen, Peter's Table of Ranks, which for nearly two centuries had formed the cornerstone of the Russian administrative structure, disappeared. A revolutionary terminology was also introduced concerning the names of the civil servants' duties. "Minister" and "ambassador," for example, were replaced by "people's commissar" and "plenipotentiary representative," and in the armed forces the customary officers' ranks were replaced by the single term, *komandir* (commander). A new salary scale was put into effect in the state administration, motivated by the universal leveling spirit.

The decisive and eminently practical task with which the Bolshevik leaders were faced was to make the administrative machinery function and to man the various apparatuses. First of all, they had to organize the armed forces and next bring order into the civil administration. The dilemma was to meet, on the one hand, the political demand to recruit an administrative corps from social groups which were loyal and not infected with the old Tsarist bureaucratic spirit and, on the other hand, to meet the technical-administrative demand for competence and expert knowledge. These two interests, however, were in conflict: the sources of the new regime's personnel—the workers and peasants—were to a considerable extent illiterate; and the competent cadres—that is to say, the civil servants from the old regime—had demonstrated their attitude toward the new regime through (among other things) repeated strikes which took place in 1917 and 1918 within the state administration. The government was up against a grim fact and had no other choice but to gamble on the civil-service cadre that was at hand—despite its manifest enmity to the regime. This circumstance, which has probably been of great significance for the formation and character of the Soviet administrative corps, has to a considerable extent been lost sight of. Nor have the Soviets, for their part, mentioned this fact until very recently. In 1957 it was pointed out in an authoritative journal: "During the course of nearly *two decades'* development of the Soviet state, persons who originated in the petty-bourgeois group, formerly the exploiting classes, comprised the dominant element in the composition of the civil-service corps. A large group of these civil servants, of course, was comprised of people who, at least in earlier stages, "wintered the storm" in hopes of a change of regime.

This reliance on the "capitalist" civil servants necessitated a rigorous political control over the civilian and military functionaries. It also promoted a further acceleration of the expansion of the educational system for the purpose of producing from the worker and peasant population an administrative corps which would be more acceptable from a political point of view. During the 1920s many improvisations in the area of education were temporarily adopted—for example, facilitation of entrance into the university and different kinds of preparatory short courses. The educational level of the resulting cadres was naturally extremely low. As has been mentioned, however, the dominant group within the state administration was of civil-servant origins. Because of their suspect background, functionaries were exposed to a systematic social and, in certain respects, economic discrimination with regard to entrance into the party, admittance to educational institutions, the receiving of social benefits and rations, and the rate of taxation.

During the 1930s the internal situation radically changed. In connection with the rapid industrialization, the consequent enormous increase of administrative authorities and personnel, and the expansion of the educational system, the "radical" experimental spirit and amateurishness of the 1920s had to give way to the demand for internal unity, stability, and competence. This altered situation, partly brought about by a conscious policy on the part of the government, partly necessitated by the very pressure of events, produced particularly striking consequences in the social and economic status of the administrative civil servants.

The increase of the administrative apparatus resulted in a strong social mobility with new additions from the lower strata of society. The stream of workers' and peasants' sons into administrative work raised the question of the social status of the civil servants. Already in the beginning of the 1930s there appeared a clear tendency to do away with special rules which were directed against the civil servants; but they were still not welcomed into the party. The entrance requirements for this group were much stricter than those for workers and peasants. In view of the fact that the new additions were introduced "from below"—a process which was accelerated during the purges—the result of the differential entrance requirements was that the more a person did to make himself useful to the state, the more difficult it became for him to become a member of society's elite organization. The situation became untenable and the differential entrance requirements were abolished at the party congress in 1939. The measure was given particular emphasis through the fact that Stalin himself appeared with a speech in defense of the "new Soviet intelligentsia," which was not, however, elevated to a "class" but was characterized as a "stratum." The pragmatic attitude toward the question of the civil-servant stratum was clearly expressed in a pronouncement of Malenkov at the party conference in 1941:

Despite the party's directives, the situation within many party and administrative organs hitherto has been that on choosing functionaries one has given more attention to finding out the family tree of the person in question, to finding out who his grandparents were, than to investigating his practical and political qualifications, capacity and talent.

After the civil servants had been placed on a par with the other social groups, the doors were opened for their entrance into the party apparatus, where—particularly in the higher levels—the civil and military administrative corps is well represented.

During the 1930s many rules and stipulations were once again introduced for the purpose of gaining control over and at the same time granting authority to the powerfully expanding and differentiated administrative apparatus. The handbook issued in 1930 by the Worker and Peasant Inspection, "Nomenclature and Characterization of the Duties of the Civil Servants within the State Organs of the Soviet Union," included up to two hundred different duties and ranks for civil servants. It might be mentioned that already at that time the traditional ranks of "attaché" up to "counselor" existed within the diplomatic service. In 1935, the title, "Marshal of the Soviet Union," was reintroduced. With the Second World War a sharp differentiation, along with a clear fixing of position and authority, followed within the armed forces. The titles of general and admiral were reintroduced in 1940 and the Guards' regiments reappeared in 1942. The traditional, internal system of ranking was readopted for the rest of the corps in 1943.

At the same time, a completely new title, "chief marshal," was introduced in the air force and the artillery. The epaulettes were also restored to favor again, although according to the "short Soviet Encyclopedia" of 1931, they had been abolished after the October Revolution "as being a symbol of class oppression in the army." In 1943 and 1944, respectively, the Suvorov and Nakhimov schools were instituted after the pattern of the Tsarist cadet schools; titles and ranks in the generals and officers corps of the interior and security organs were brought into agreement with those of the regular armed forces in 1945; and in the same year Stalin allowed himself to be designated "generalissimo," the title which had crowned Peter's famous Table of Ranks.

A parallel development also took place in the civil administration beginning in 1941, when the titles "ambassador" and "minister" were reintroduced into the Soviet diplomatic service—followed in 1943 by a regular rank-and-title ordinance, including stipulations for uniforms, for the entire service. Within the governmental machinery, the designation "people's commissar" was abolished in 1946 and was replaced with the respectable title of "minister." During the period between 1943 and 1949 rules concerning order of rank were announced successively. Along with these there were titles and descriptions of uniforms for civil servants in ten to fifteen different civil (especially in the economic) administrations. The purpose for this detailed categorization and uniforming of the civil-servant corps was—as emphasized by Soviet experts in administrative law—"to strengthen the service discipline and raise the titled civil servant's authority."

These rules offer interesting insights into the functioning of the Soviet administration. Especially informative are the rules concerning the order of ranks within the prosecutor's office. The civil servants are here divided into eleven "classes" with exact stipulations for advancement from a lower to a higher rank or class. The principle of seniority is carried out up to the fourth class. The normal progression can, however, be avoided in exceptional cases by the stipulation that the supreme prosecutor himself can permit a civil servant to "skip," according to the ordinance, "not more than two ranks above the rank a civil servant holds." In the original ruling there was also a "table of comparisons" that is extremely indicative. Here it was shown how the different ranks within the prosecutor's office were to be compared with the military ranks. The cycle of the Russian development was herewith completed; Peter's rejected Table of Ranks was in fact re-established with its ostentatious titles, rank distinctions, and uniforms, displaying the social status of the civil servant before the general public. Only recently has the Soviet government attempted to eliminate the most grotesque manifestations of this mania for uniforms and ranks.

The economic status of the administrative corps during the first Soviet period has already been mentioned. The doctrine of equality, which had been cherished from the beginning, was, however, written off rather quickly. Thus, already during the Civil War outstanding scientists, for example, were allotted "academic rations" which were considerably larger than those of nonacademics. It appears that the average earnings for civil servants in industry were considerably above those of workers in 1928 and that the difference was even more marked in 1934, that is to say, after the first rush of industrialization. Thus, already by 1928 the abandonment of wage leveling had brought about a wage gap between the civil servants and the workers. At the same time, however—up to the early 1930s—the functionaries were subjected to an economic discrimination in matters concerning social privileges (for example, social benefits, social insurance, and pensions), taxes and rations. This policy was closely connected with the social discrimination against the functionaries that I mentioned earlier. After Stalin's speech before the business executives, which comprises one of the milestones in the advance of the managerial class during the Soviet era, this economic discrimination was abolished and was followed by a number of facilities and benefits—for example, special dining rooms and shops for, first of all, engineers and technical personnel. Later these privileges were gradually extended to other civil-servant groups.

Russian data published more recently show that the economic position of the functionaries has not been altered in comparison to that of the workers. It also appears that the wage scale within the civil-service corps reflects the social differentiation in title and rank. The Russian civil-service corps is already so differentiated socially and economically that what is now characterized as a stratum consists in reality of several distinguishable strata.

The higher-income level among the civil servants with "rank" involves a number of extra advantages owing to the particular structure of the Soviet economic system—for example, the absence of income-tax progression combined with heavy indirect taxation (turnover tax), social benefits and pensions (the size of which is determined by, among other things, income level), the right to extra living space, and the very favorable inheritance tax. In addition, there are "personal" salaries alongside the ordinary wage scale (these personal salaries are for specially qualified functionaries) and "personal" pensions for outstanding political, civil, and military functionaries.

The enormous disparities in income and the extreme rewarding of certain categories with bonuses has now aroused irritation in the Soviet Union. The new leaders, who have been anxious to wipe out the most extreme manifestations of the Stalinist regime, have also reacted on this point. At the Twentieth Party Congress, Mikoyan—referring to the Russian economic and social background—stated that the enormous disparity in wages was "natural" for the purpose of turning out highly qualified cadres rapidly. He added that "the differentiation must be retained, but the gap will be narrowed."

The Soviet Civil Service

The rise of a new Russian bureaucracy comprises one of the significant factors in an attempt to elucidate the question of continuity and change in Russian society after 1861. Certain main trends stand out distinctly from the material presented above. In some cases, the present state of affairs is strikingly similar to the old Tsarist order, which shows the force of tradition even in a society originating as a protest against that order. Again, in other cases, it is obvious that innovations have been introduced during the Soviet era.

The highly centralized government machinery and the state direction of the economy, which are often thought of as specific "communist" features, are completely in line with the Russian administrative tradition. The dominating position of state power in Russia is old, and the liberal Russian historian, Miliukov, has pointed out: "Since oldest times, the government has also regarded all areas suitable for industrial exploitation as its own property." The chronic pressure on the economic resources in the interest of the state— especially in order to satisfy the growing demands of an enormous war machine—pre-supposed a widely ramified administrative apparatus, the higher functionaries of which had, of old, a favored and central position in Russian society. "[Tsarist] Russia is ruled by 40,000 heads of bureaus," as Nicholas I expressed it. By that, of course, he meant the purely technical-administrative side of the question, not the political; for the bureaucrats at that time had just as little possibility of influencing great political decisions as do the present functionaries within the party and administration. The "inner circle" could in earlier times, as now, handle its cadres arbitrarily since the principle of the irremovability of the civil servant was and still is completely unknown. Even the top leadership is subject to frequent shifts, mysterious, inexplicable, and seemingly capricious, and the outsider is left to mere guesswork or to manipulating various kinds of more of less vague "theories." As under the tsars, the present-day Russian rulers rely heavily upon a strong, omnipresent, and harsh police power to enforce government policy and to control the conduct and loyalty of their subjects.

To the traditional features also belong the strong consciousness of rank and title in the administrative corps. It seems, however, as if an attempt is now being made to check this "tradition," which is particularly embarrassing against the ideological background. Yet the actual course of events has so far shown that this problem cannot be solved by decree. All of the evils and "beauty patches" inherent in the old rank system still exist, as is daily demonstrated in the Soviet press: abuse of power, bullying, red tape, paper drill, negligence, incompetence, and corruptibility. That these traditions have lived on so obstinately is not especially remarkable, considering the initial situation facing the Bolsheviks: the extremely low level of education among the population; the lack of qualified personnel; and the necessity of accepting in administrative work "alien" social groups from the old regime, who left their mark on the present Soviet civil-service group.

The decisive change introduced by the Soviet regime—the strong curtailment of the rights to private property—seems to be more relevant to questions which lie outside the subject treated here. However, the replacement of the right of private ownership of real estate and means of production with the right of use (which is usually attached to a post) has brought with it a specific disadvantage for the higher Soviet civil servant who has fallen into disfavor. He, in contrast to many of his Tsarist predecessors, does not have the possibility of quietly retiring, and enjoying the cozy daily life of the Russian provincial estate owner.

It is, further, an innovation to have a system with a party apparatus that parallels the ordinary administrative apparatus—even in the remotest local unit—and has the task of minutely supervising and controlling it. This supervision is the more remarkable today, since the party functionaries often hold purely administrative posts and the civil servants (including military officers), as a rule, are party members and often of high status. The higher up one goes in the hierarchy, the more difficult it becomes to decide whether a person shall be regarded as a party man or as a government official. This question is still more complex concerning the younger generation of party and state functionaries who have been trained at universities and other higher educational institutions. It seems as if these two administrations are on the way toward merging, and perhaps the development is moving toward some sort of gradual withering away of certain overlapping functions, even though it now appears still far off. The dualism of party and civil service control cannot, in any case, be regarded as rational or effective from a technical-administrative point of view. The present system can claim a "rationality" on political considerations alone.

The change which has had significant direct repercussions on the public administration is the improvement of the educational system and the extension of the recruitment to the state service. As has been pointed out above, the situation before the revolution was such that only a very small percentage of the population was recruited to the civil-servant corps. The social mobility and the rapid careers from the bottom of society during the Soviet regime—where the party in particular served as the basis for recruitment—have also been mentioned above. This mobility, however, is quite natural in a society subjected to rapid political, economic, and administrative change, especially in view of the institutional order of the Soviet Union. On the other hand, Russian society has now begun to settle or "ripen," and the earlier development should perhaps be regarded as a unique phenomenon, having to do with quite special conditions and causes. An interesting symptom is the fact that, already at the end of the 1930s, the functionaries and their descendants were clearly overrepresented at the universities in relation to their relative proportion of the total population. Since this time, the complete lack of information concerning the social composition of the institutions of higher education must be regarded as an indication that the present composition is "unsuitable" and would not support the official thesis of equal possibilities for all. The existing social, psychological, geographical, and—to a lesser degree, however—economic "barriers" have so far been passed over in silence. Concerning the condition within the administrative apparatus, it is obvious that advancement now proceeds more slowly than earlier—in accordance with a fixed and well-established pattern which indicates that the changes in a person's social status will probably take place over short social disturbances. There are also many facts and circumstances which imply that there has been a stabilization in the sense that the basis of recruitment to the administrative corps will be narrowed in comparison to the situation a few decades ago.

On the other hand, it must be pointed out that the government is endeavoring to prevent stagnation. It is extremely doubtful, however, whether such measures can essentially change the present state of affairs. The real problem is the actual need for administrative personnel. If this need should decrease, as a consequence of an effective rationalization within the administration, it is very likely, in view of the established social and economic order, that the descendents of the functionaries will be even more favored. Should the need increase, the probability is that the social mobility will not cease. It might not be too bold to maintain that, with regard to technical development, in the long run the need for functionaries tends to increase and thus secure the chances for social advancement— quite irrespective of the government's measures in this field. These additions "from below" will be absorbed in an administrative machinery which has increasingly acquired stability, authority, and competence over the last four decades. The social values and attitudes of this administrative corps are already fixed and have their roots in a social order which the Bolsheviks thought they had definitely destroyed in 1917.

INEQUALITY AND STRATIFICATION IN CHINA

Martin King Whyte

In this essay, published in 1975, Whyte describes the attempts made in China to reduce social and economic inequalities from the Communist victory in 1949 until just before Mao's death in 1976. Whyte notes that the Chinese Revolution removed the "privileged few" from the top of the old regime society. However, it was less successful in eliminating large "structural inequalities." Thus the inequality between urban and peasant consumption in 1956 appeared to be as great as before the Communist Revolution. In addition, substantial inequalities continued to exist among the peasantry.

Yet the Chinese did make a unique effort to limit subjective feelings of inequality by strongly discouraging conspicuous consumption and outward signs of rank. Moreover, in Mao's later years, following the Cultural Revolution of 1966–1968, the government made efforts to reward revolutionary fervor and ideological purity rather than "expertise" and rank. These efforts included attacks on cadres and party leaders and the "sending down" of numerous urban youth and intellectuals to the countryside to engage in manual labor. Finally, China made strenuous efforts to prevent a party elite from perpetuating itself and had some success, although the advantages of family wealth and education remained considerable.

However, after Mao's death many of the measures designed to reduce inequality gave way to policies designed to encourage greater individual efforts. Thus since 1976, an emphasis on educational qualifications, training and expertise—in short, on human capital—has returned, as Kelley and Klein suggested it might. Some of these recent policy shifts appear in a brief postscript to Professor Whyte's essay.

Vague and often somewhat contradictory impressions of equality and inequality in China abound. Some recent visitors to China have reported that income differentials there have been reduced to nominal levels. At the same time the recurring themes of class struggle and the dangers of revisionism alert us to the continuing conflict within China over the inequalities that still exist. In this paper I try to draw together the scattered pieces of information already available in order to examine, first, the kinds of inequalities that do continue to exist in China, and then the policies designed to affect the transmission of these inequalities over time and from generation to generation, or, in other words, stratification.[1] Although the available information is not precise enough to permit any systematic comparisons with other countries, I hope to be able to arrive at some rough impressions of the extent to which the Chinese elite has been successful in producing a society with more equality and less stratification than is generally the case elsewhere.

Income Inequalities in a Revolutionary Egalitarian Society

There is no question that the revolution did sweep away the most glaring inequalities in income of pre-1949 China, and in particular the fortunes of the privileged few. But important differentials remain, and official policy does not advocate the elimination of all of these. Although material incentives are not supposed to be used in China as a primary motivating factor in work performance and labor allocation, proper differential rewards to compensate for differing contributions to socialist construction are to be allowed. Let us examine the system of income differentials in China.

In 1956 a major reform institutionalized a system of ranks and differentiated wages for people working in state enterprises of various types: government offices, factories, transportation lines, educational institutions, and so forth. Officials and employees in the state bureaucracy were ranked from level 1 (top national leaders) to level 30 (e.g., miscellaneous service personnel), and the wage differential between the highest and lowest levels was about 28:1. In December of 1956 the wage rates for the top 10 ranks in the scale were lowered, so that the top to bottom ratio was reduced to only 25.2:1. On the assumption that comparing one's income with that of Mao Ze-dong is not the most meaningful reference, I should add that under the 1956 wage rates secretarial and other office staff earned monthly wages about twice those of menial service personnel, cadres in administrative sections earned roughly 3–4 times as much, and heads of sections and higher administrative divisions within the same unit earned anything from 4 to 10 times as much. Technical personnel (engineers and technicians, primarily) were ranked on a separate 18-grade scale, with a differential of roughly 10:1 between levels 1 and 18. Industrial workers in state enterprises were ranked in scales of 8–10 levels, with gradations of roughly 3:1. Personnel working in state enterprises, to which such scales apply, are of course only a minority of the labor force (a little over 24 million people in 1957). There are also urban personnel working in co-operative enterprises, in street factories, as temporary laborers, and so forth, and they are not covered by these rankings. Our information about their incomes is minimal, but since wages are generally dependent upon the profits of these less well-endowed enterprises, they will often be considerably lower than those in state enterprises.

This urban incomes picture is complicated by the existence of certain other policies and programs. People with low incomes do of course receive benefits from public investment in cheap housing, parks, health care systems, and so forth, which are not reflected in their wages, although even here those working in state enterprises enjoy some benefits over others (e.g., greater coverage of the medical expenses of family members). At the same time for those in official positions there is what can be considered an expense account system, under which cars, meals, travel and other expenses connected with their official duties do not come out of their own pockets.

Then there are the people who make up the bulk of the working population, the peasants. The communes and their predecessors, the agricultural producers' co-operatives, are classed as co-operative enterprises, with payments for labor again depending on the profits of the unit, or in this case on the harvests, less the various obligations placed on them (state tax, investment, the cost of seeds, the welfare fund, etc.). Within the rural basic accounting unit (generally the team, but in some places the brigade), the official policy is to reward those who work harder or better with more work points, and thus with a greater share of the consumption portion of the harvest. The rural income picture is considerably more complex than the urban one because, in addition to these payments for collective labor, peasants have other sources for income: private plots (to provide for their own consumption and for sale), household sideline activities (e.g., raising pigs and chickens, making handicrafts, cutting hillside grass for heating and cooking) and sometimes outside income (e.g., from family members with salaried jobs, overseas remittances). A number of visitors have recorded various pieces of information about rural incomes, but these are often incomplete or lack detail about what types of income are included. From what little is available, I can at least suggest the following: in spite of the official policy of reducing the urban-rural income gap, a large differential remains, and it is not clear that is has been reduced to any great extent since 1949.

An article published in China in 1957 cites unspecified data from the Economic Research Institute of the Academy of Sciences and the State Statistical Bureau to arrive at the following per capita consumption figures:

Per capita real consumption (in constant 1952 prices)

	(1) WORKERS AND EMPLOYEES	*(2)* PEASANTS	2/1(%)
1936	130 *yuan*	61 *yuan*	46.9%
1956	179.6 *yuan*	81 *yuan*	45.1%

One other 1957 article, covering selected regions, gives a picture of somewhat smaller rural-urban differentials in 1955, but Christopher Howe, in a recent study, derives his own estimate of the ratio of urban to rural incomes *per income earner* in 1957 as roughly 2:1. Howe also suggests that rural-urban income differentials widened somewhat in China in the 1950s, but may have narrowed slightly in the 1960s and 1970s.

A similar picture emerges if we look at reports of visitors to China in the mid-1960s. Barry Richman visited 38 industrial enterprises in 1966 and found that the average of the average wages earned at all these plants was 61.9 *yuan* a month. S. J. Burki was taken to 13 communes in 1964 and reported that the average monthly income received by an agricultural worker from collective labor was 30.1 *yuan*. Keith Buchanan gives a figure for the average monthly income received by an agricultural worker from collective labor in the 18 communes he visited in 1966 of 23.9 *yuan*. These figures leave out the bonuses then being paid to industrial workers (which varied from 3 percent to a maximum of 15 percent of the total wage fund in the factories Richman visited), and also the income peasants received from private plots and sideline activities (which, according to Burki, was about 20 percent of their total income in the communes he visited). Also left out, of course, are those urban people working in relatively low-paying bureaucratic agencies and universities, and also those in low-paying street industries and similar jobs. The communes visited by Burki and Buchanan are also more likely to have an atypically high compensation for labor than are the factories Richman visited. The latter are bound by state wage scales, while the communes are not, and those near cities, which are thus accessible to visitors, tend to be relatively prosperous. With all of these imponderables, no exact figures can be given, but it seems realistic to consider that the urban-rural income differential is something on the order of 2:1 (whether considered on a per capita or per laborer basis).

Within the rural areas, however, any national average has little significance, since there is a very great regional and even local variation in peasant incomes, due to factors such as soil fertility, weather conditions, population/land ratios and leadership skills. Buchanan noted that there was a ratio of roughly 4:1 between the average wages of the most and least prosperous communes he visited, and that among teams of the same commune the ratio was 2:1, and that among individuals in the same team the ratio was 3:1. Figures cited by Christopher Howe for the mid-1950s show a differential in per capita peasant incomes between provinces, with Jiangsu having a figure of 74 percent higher than that for Sichuan, and within Jiangsu a local variation with incomes of some areas 83 percent higher than those of others. Jan Myrdal gives figures for one village in Shaanxi province in 1961 in which the earnings from collective labor per household varied from a low of 49.30 *yuan* per year to a high of 1,800.30 *yuan*. Leaving out the figures for households in which the agricultural laborers were wives of industrial workers (and which depend mainly on outside income rather than income from agricultural labor), the differential is still from 126 *yuan* to 1,800 *yuan* per family (or from 63 *yuan* to 454 *yuan* per laborer).

Our own recent research on rural Guangzhou villages yields a similar picture. First rank laborers in nearby teams within a single commune may earn remunerations per day of labor varying as much as 3 or 4 to 1 (e.g., from 0.30 or 0.40 *yuan* to 1.20 *yuan*). Within any team, members do not all receive the same amount of pay each day, and the range between the lowest and highest is often in the order of 2:1 (e.g., 10 points per day versus 5 points). And of course people work different numbers of days in a year, and families have different proportions of their membership participating in labor. If we consider only the portion of income which comes from collective labor, then, within any one team there may be large differences between families. Some will receive each year not only the grain that the family consumes, but an additional cash distribution from the team of, say 100–400 *yuan*. With other sources of income added, these families may accumulate considerable savings, be able to build themselves new and better housing, and spend considerable sums on festivals, weddings, and consumer durables (bicycles, sewing machines, radios, etc.). They will also have a more than adequate diet, with white rice for all meals, and meat and other sources of protein fairly regularly. In contrast, some other families in the same team may be overconsuming households (*ch'ao-chin hu*), which means that the work points they earn during the year are not sufficient to pay for the grain rations they have consumed. They will not only fail to receive any cash from the team during its annual distributions, but will go into debt to the team. This debt may accumulate for several years into a sizeable sum (several hundred *yuan*), although nominal or no interest seems to be charged. If such families are to have any cash to spend on other necessities they will have to depend on their private plots and other sideline activities, and some of these earnings will have to be used to pay off their debt to the team. Unless such families can find profitable outside sources of income they will experience familiar problems of poverty: they will have to make do with the housing they have, they will have little to spend on festival occasions and consumer durables, and their sons will have difficulty finding brides. Also, depending on the level at which team and individual rations are set, they may have to subsist on congee rather than white rice for two of their daily meals, perhaps augmented with sweet potatoes, with meat only consumed during holiday and wedding feasts. These inequalities are moderated to some extent, it should be noted, by the fact that in some villages the poorest families may be able to apply for small amounts of relief grain or cash, and be eligible for certain other benefits (e.g., they will not have to pay for the tuition of their children at rural schools). And the grain ration-overconsumption system is in itself a sort of welfare mechanism which allows poor families to consume beyond their earnings in any particular year.* Nevertheless, it still seems reasonable to assume that for many peasants there are income inequalities more salient than the rural-urban gap.

Our information is still fragmentary, but it should at least be clear that the incomes of peasants, in addition to being on the average perhaps only half those of urban residents, are also widely spread with a range from people in wealthy communes, brigades and teams who are doing as well as, or better than, many urbanites, to people who are having difficulty feeding themselves, and going into debt doing so. In addition I should emphasize that, while individual and family diligence (and the ratio of family members in the labor force to total family size) have an important influence on peasant incomes, there are local and regional variations in rural productivity and wealth which the introduction of collective farming and communes has not erased, and which have a considerable effect on the income of a particular family. A family with a few capable laborers in a well-off region can do better than a very diligent and skilled family in a barren, unproductive, or overpopulated area. And the official policy of self-reliance, which implies in part the lack of large transfers of wealth from prosperous communes, brigades and teams to less prosperous ones, seems to point to the continued importance of such differentials in the future.

The foregoing discussion does not give us a clear idea of how rural income inequalities in China compare with either the pre-1949 situation or with other developing societies. Unfortunately, the only household income figures we have come from a single village in Shaanxi province, as reported by Jan Myrdal. A recent monograph calculates that the ratio of the incomes from collective labor of the top 20 percent of the families in this village to those of the bottom 20 percent is about 4.6:1 (omitting families with outside wage earners). This is at the lower end of the scale, but not "off the scale" when compared with the figures for other Asian developing societies, where this ratio of the upper 20 percent to lower 20 percent varies from 4–5 to 1 up to 10 or more to 1. But there is some reason to suspect that even before 1949 China may have had less rural inequality than many other developing societies. A modest level of inequality of landownership (not income) compared with other societies is reported by Russett. We also have a figure from a Chinese source in the 1950s which states that in 1936 the per capita consumption of landlords and rich peasants was more than four times that of the ordinary peasants. One

---

*Recent directives urge rural cadres to find ways to limit the proportion of households which overconsume, and this may entail limiting the size of the preliminary grain distribution.

can recompute the figures given by Myrdal for the village in Shaanxi to compare the top 10 percent of the population with the remaining 90 percent, and that ratio turns out to be about 2.5:1, i.e., substantially less than the 1936 rural elites-masses consumption figure for the entire country. But one remaining uncertainty in the puzzle is that even before 1949 villages in Shaanxi probably had less income inequality than was average for China. We also do not know how other sources of income besides collective income affect the distribution in Myrdal's village. I conclude that rural inequality in China is probably relatively modest in comparison with other Asian developing societies, although more in a quantitative than a qualitative sense, and that it is hard to be certain how much of this pattern is due to post-1949 changes as opposed to the prevailing situation before 1949.

To return to the issue of income inequalities within the urban areas, since the 1950s there have been some changes in the direction of smaller differentials, but by and large the structure of ranks and wages established during the mid-1950s has continued. Christopher Howe reports that in 1959, 1960 and 1963 there were some reductions in top bureaucratic salaries, perhaps bringing the total span to under 20-fold, but there are no detailed figures available to allow one to check the exact extent of any compression. (Because of the "expense account" phenomenon mentioned previously, any reduction confined to the highest ranks has little significance for overall inequality). With regard to income differentials among non-agricultural manual workers, Howe feels that both skill and occupational differentials increased in the 1950s, declined somewhat in the late 1950s and 1960s but, at least in the case of large-scale heavy industrial enterprises, are now approximately back to their pre-1958 levels. In sum, the industrial wage structure does not look too different now from what it was in the mid-1950s, when detailed rates were available to us. (From the scattered accounts of visitors, it would seem that not only the differentials, but even the actual wages of various ranks—as well as prices—have seen only modest changes over this period.)

The Cultural Revolution featured strong attacks on the privileges and soft life of China's elites, but for the most part these criticisms do not seem to have resulted in reductions in the incomes upon which that soft life was based. Howe concludes that in general during the Cultural Revolution the official wage structure did not collapse, and complaints against the existing differentials were for the most part deferred until after the Cultural Revolution was concluded (when, to judge from the evidence, little change took place). Academics and intellectuals were among those most strongly attacked, but post-Cultural Revolution visitors continue to report the existence of very wide differentials. Ross Terrill reports senior professors earning 348 and 360 *yuan* per month, about 6 times the salary of the lowest-paid instructors (60 *yuan*). Technical experts also came under attack, but a recent report mentions technicians' and engineers' wages ranging from 34 to 230 *yuan* a month, a spread of almost 7:1. Even those officials and intellectuals attacked personally during the Cultural Revolution and forced to "stand aside" and remould their errors often continued to receive their former salaries. There seems to have been a policy of not using financial sanctions to deal with political and ideological errors. We have an interesting account of Peking cadres who, sent to live in rural villages to overcome their errors, continued to receive their salaries as usual, but who were forbidden to tell local peasants how much they made, and were so constrained against conspicuous consumption that many of them salted away sizable nest-eggs while they were reforming themselves.

In regard to income differentials, then, one can say that the existing situation is quite different from the impression that the egalitarian rhetoric of the Cultural Revolution or the uniformity of dress of the population may convey. Certainly, the kinds of fortunes that can be made in capitalist economies are not to be made in China. And some of the "special" income situations which used to exist (royalties for writers, investment dividends for former capitalists) seem to have been restricted or eliminated in recent years, although precise information is lacking. In any case, it is my impression that even before 1966 these special incomes did not play as important a role as they do in the Soviet Union, where foreign royalties, large monetary prizes for Stakhanovites and other honored categories, suburban *dacha,* and so forth, help to differentiate elites of various types. But one may also note that familiar differentials between rural and urban residents, between the skilled and the unskilled, the experienced and the inexperienced, men and women, and the highly placed and lowly placed do exist. While some of these differentials are modest by international standards (factory managers earning only 5-7 times the salary of newly employed industrial apprentices), others (the figures for professors mentioned above, the differentials among bureaucrats) are by no means unusually "narrow."

Other Aspects of Inequality

In any society it is hard to generalize about forms of inequality besides income or wealth, and in China it is no less true. First, an obvious comment: political power is very unequally distributed. While the Chinese Communists have placed greater emphasis than their East European predecessors on encouraging opinions and initiative from subordinates, the basic Leninist Party structure and democratic centralist rules of discipline have still been preserved. The Party Committee or branch within any organization has an overwhelming dominance over the life of the organization and its members. And in spite of the care taken to preserve autonomy for local units in adapting to their immediate environment and problems, we have seen numerous instances over the years in which the dreams and goals of the leaders in Peking have led to the mobilization of much of the population for this activity or that struggle.

Educational skills and access to them have been in scarce supply, although the massive expansion of education both before and after 1949 has spread education more broadly. Here we might note two features of the educational distribution picture. Primary schooling is approaching universalization, with Chinese Communist authorities claiming that over 90 percent of the youths in "selected localities" are enrolled. The post-Cultural Revolution reforms aim to shorten the length of schooling at various levels, so that now complete secondary schooling has been reduced in many places from 12 years to only 9–10 years. In the larger cities this reduced span of secondary schooling is approaching universalization, while in the countryside lower-middle schooling (generally lasting 7 years) has been made more widely available than previously. A contrary trend occurs in university education, though. Soon after 1949 there were more than enough university places for all those wishing to go on with their education after secondary school, but since then university enrollments have not kept pace with lower level educational expansion. And in the post-Cultural Revolution period universities have experienced a sharp enrollment contraction, although part of this contraction seems to be only temporary. The figures below tell the story. This changing pattern has produced a situation in which secondary schooling is no longer the guarantee of a high status job that it once was (in fact to some extent the opposite is true today), and in which higher education and the opportunities that go with it have become relatively much more difficult to secure.

Full time enrollments (in thousands)

	Primary	General middle school	Higher education
1949–50	24,391	1,039	117
1953–54	51,664	2,933	212
1957–58	64,279	6,281	441
1958–59	86,400	8,520	660
1959–60	90,000	n.a.	810
1965–66	110,000	14,000	695
1972–73	127,000[a]	35,000[a]	200[b]

[a] I received these figures during a briefing in Peking in November 1973. They should be viewed as tentative, although other visitors have been quoted similar figures.
[b] The 1972–73 university figure refers to new university enrollments from 1970 (when China's universities began to reopen after the Cultural Revolution) through 1972. More recent university enrollments show signs of increasing the numbers quite markedly, although not to their former peak levels. In the autumn of 1973, 153,000 new students were reportedly enrolled in China's universities and, in the autumn of 1974, 167,000 new students were admitted.

So far I have not referred much to inequalities in China which are particularly distinctive when compared with other societies, or at least with other communist societies. I chose to present the materials in this manner to emphasize that the distinctiveness of Chinese egalitarianism is to be found not so much in its reduction or elimination of differences in income, power, and education, although some of this has occurred, but in its attempt to mute the consequences, in terms of matters like life styles, consumption patterns and interpersonal deference, of the inequalities that do exist. People in high positions in China are viewed as entitled to certain kinds of differential rewards and authority, but at the same time flaunting authority or engaging in conspicuous consumption is tabooed. There is thus a concerted effort to blunt the subjective impact which existing inequalities might have on the initiative and dedication of the have-nots in whose name the revolution was fought.

A number of kinds of policies relate to this effort to reduce the subjective consequences of existing inequalities. The elimination of ranks in the armed forces in 1965 is one example. This change did not produce a situation in which former privates were issuing commands to former generals, nor one in which their pay was equalized. Positions within the military hierarchy remain pretty much the same (e.g., soldier, squad commander, platoon commander, etc) but the external signs and symbols are gone. The ordinary soldier still knows who is where in his immediate hierarchy, but to the outsider more subtle cues (e.g., age, birth, bearing, the cut of the uniform) have to be used to distinguish the officers from the men.

Outside the military a variety of similar devices are used. Factory managers and engineers (as well as commune officials) are required to spend regular periods of time doing manual work alongside the workers and peasants they supervise. The ordinary workers and peasants do not correspondingly take turns serving as managers or engineers (although mobility into such positions is possible), and later on the superiors will return to their previous offices and routines. But by this practice the Chinese Communists hope to further both the knowledge the superiors have of the problems and views of their subordinates and the subordinates' feeling of involvement and participation in the goals of the organization.

Intellectuals, office workers and Party officials are expected periodically to be sent down from their posts to engage in manual labor, often in a rural commune or a May Seventh cadre school. While some of those sent may not return to their original posts, the present policy is that most shall, and that as a result of their experience they will be more appreciative of the value and problems of manual laborers in Chinese society, and less likely to be arrogant or divorced from reality. Both they and the manual laborers they come in contact with should then, in theory, be less likely to see these elites as a separate and alien class within society.

Party officials and superiors of other types are also supposed to stage regular occasions for criticism of their defects from below, in the form of recurrent campaigns involving "open-door rectification." Again the Party official does not stop being a Party official, but his acceptance of criticism symbolizes that he will not use his authority in a dictatorial manner, or arbitrarily retaliate against his critics. His close ties with subordinates are also symbolized by familiar terms of address (personal names, Old Wang, Little Ch'en, etc.) and the lack of sharply differentiated patterns of dress (which contrasts sharply with the use of graded uniforms within some parts of the civil bureaucracy in Russia during the late Stalinist years).

The homogenization of consumption patterns and life styles is one of the features of egalitarianism in China which has most often been remarked upon, and this homogenization is the result of a number of factors. One of these is the system of rationing used in the distribution of some consumption items. Since grains, oil, cotton cloth and some other consumer items (as well as, at certain times and places, items like meat and sugar) are rationed, they tend to be distributed more equitably than would be the case if rationing did not exist. The allocation of much urban housing is similarly controlled. Even consumer goods which are not rationed are produced in a limited range of types and prices, so that they cannot form the basis for widely differing consumption patterns. One might say that there is also cultural rationing, with strict official control over what is published and performed in China, so that, particularly in recent years, there is a very narrow range of cultural entertainment from which all strata of society have to pick. Finally, conspicuous consumption in any form is politically dangerous. Particularly during the Cultural Revolution, officials were attacked for eating well, having servants, collecting material possessions, and simply having a "bourgeois" life style. Other urban elements felt the force of similar attacks in 1966 when, during the "destroy the four olds" stage of the Cultural Revolution, Red Guards invaded homes and confiscated jewelry, religious objects, "decadent" books, and so forth. For all of these reasons the differences that do exist in income, power and education do not result in as wide a divergence as we might expect in the consumption patterns of the population. Differentials do exist, but they are confined within relatively narrow ranges: possession or absence of bicycles, sewing machines, radios, wristwatches, leather as opposed to cloth shoes, tailored as opposed to off-the-peg or homespun clothes, apartments with indoor private kitchens and bathroom facilities with running water as opposed to those without, and so on.

In the realm of inequalities, then, in China today there are sill marked differences in income, power, educational skills, and so forth, combined with vigorous efforts to moderate the effects of these inequalities on public consciousness.

One might in fact ask why the differentials that do continue to exist, particularly in the realm of income, are permitted in the first place. The official answer is that to do away with such differentials would constitute extreme egalitarianism, by ignoring the socialist principle of distribution according to labor. This answer cannot account for the total pattern of inequalities we have observed, which, on reflection, seems to result from many of the same factors we are familiar with in other societies—the efforts to reward seniority, skill, past services and differential profitability, and to encourage job commitment and performance, to adapt to past patterns of differential remuneration, and so forth.

We have seen that in at least some respects China is not as egalitarian a society as might appear at first glance. But what of the question of stratification? After the revolutionary upheaval in the class structure in China during 1949–1956, has the picture stabilized and an institutionalized system of social stratification emerged? Have the "old classes" (pre-1949 elites) regained positions of prominence? Has a Chinese "new class" of officials and technocrats arisen as in other communist countries, wishing and able to pass on its privileges to its offspring? Or have the Chinese Communists found some institutional mechanisms for regular "de-stratification," mechanisms which will prevent the differentiated set of ranks and statuses that exist in China from continuing over time and from generation to generation? To deal with these questions I shall first examine the situation of the "old class" elites, and then turn to "new class" phenomena.

Old Classes in the Chinese Countryside

In the rural areas not only have the "old class" elites not managed to regain their former positions, but in many ways in recent years the line against them has hardened and their lot in life has worsened. And this has occurred in spite of the fact that official policy stresses that "bad elements" can and should reform themselves and become accepted. Let us examine the rural trends.

At the time of the land reform campaign in rural China (roughly 1946–1948 in the northern "early liberated areas" and 1950–1953 in the rest of the country), detailed instructions were compiled for the grouping of families into class categories, based upon guidelines worked out by the Chinese Communist Party. The most important divisions were:

1. Landlords—those who possessed land but did little or no labor, and lived off land rents, hired labor, and engaged in usury.
2. Rich peasants—those who possessed land and engaged in some labor, but also lived by renting excess land to others.
3. Middle peasants—those with more or less enough land for their own needs, who neither rented out land to others nor had to rent land from others to any significant extent.
4. Poor peasants—those who possessed little or no land, and lived primarily on land rented from others.
5. Hired peasants and other workers—those with little or no land, who lived by hiring their labor out to others.

Some elements of the rural population were also given the labels of "counter-revolutionary" or "bad element," indicating not their former economic position, but their pasts as members of the local Kuomintang political structure, landlords' henchmen, active opponents of the Chinese Communists, or simply bullies and bandits. The landlords and these counter-revolutionaries and bad elements were the official enemies of the period, and, in addition to having any excess land and wealth taken away, they were struggled against, subjected to "mass control" or penal sentencing, and in many cases beaten or killed. The basic 1950 Government Administration Council document which governed this classification process stated that, if during the five years after land reform landlords labored well and did not engage in any bad conduct, they would then have their class labels changed to laborer or some other classification. This provision does not seem to have been generally carried out.

After collectivization had been completed in 1955–1956, these class labels ceased to have any clear connection with prosperity or occupation, and their importance might have been expected to decline in time. Indeed, speeches by prominent Party leaders in 1956 did suggest that these class labels were losing their significance. Changes in the villages reflected this trend to some extent. Class enemies who remained in the village were generally subjected to "control," which meant that they were deprived of political rights, had special restrictions placed on their movements, had to report regularly on their "reform" to the local security defense cadres, were required to perform certain types of corvee, and so forth. But over the years some of these people were "uncapped." As a result of laboring well, refraining from disruptive activities and obeying the Party, they had some or all of these controls removed. This did not mean, however, that their class labels were changed from, say, landlord to middle peasant. Rather the label was retained even after the "cap" was lost, and was in turn passed on to children and (paternal) grandchildren.

However, a number of official policies in more recent years have tended to reinforce the importance of the land reform class labels. These are symbolized by the cryptic quotation taken from a 1962 statement by Mao Zedong: "Never forget the class struggle." This quotation symbolizes the official view that post-1949 gains have come about through struggle against hostile classes, and that this struggle must continue into the indefinite future. As a result, in a number of mass political campaigns in China the division between former enemy classes and friendly classes has been re-emphasized. Former class enemies have been repeatedly drawn out as targets for mass struggle meetings, if not for current crimes then as symbols of pre-1949 sufferings. There have also been repeated calls for vigilance against former class enemies who have worked their way into positions of local leadership and Party membership, or have tried to spread discord and dissatisfaction among the population. As a result, in some cases rehabilitated class enemies have been "re-capped," i.e., put under mass control once again or given more severe penalties.

In 1964 the Party suggested that class lines had been allowed to blur in the countryside and should be made firm by organizing once again those who had suffered prior to 1949, and their descendants, in opposition to those others at whose hands they had suffered, and their descendants. Teachers coming from bad classes have in some cases been dismissed. Class status criteria have been emphasized more in selection of students for upper-middle schooling and university attendance, making it difficult in many cases for offspring from "bad class" families to compete for entrance. Co-operative medical schemes have been set up from which, in at least some villages, bad class elements (and sometimes their offspring) are excluded.

As a result of such policies the class lines laid down over 20 years ago continue to have great importance in rural China, greater importance in some ways than the current economic status of the person or family. The bad class elements themselves are in many cases still under control, and in addition are discriminated against in various ways: e.g., are ineligible for welfare assistance if they need it, ineligible for coverage by a co-operative medical plan, unable to get loans from the credit co-operative, and so forth. Whether or not they are under control, the stigma passes on to a considerable extent to their children and grandchildren. While the younger generations are not subjected to mass control, they will be unlikely to be able to join the Youth League or Party, the basic militia, or be chosen for local cadre posts; they may, as mentioned, have difficulty getting into upper-middle schools and universities, they often find it hard to get married (particularly males), they may be given lower work points, for the same kind of work, than the offspring of poor and lower-middle peasants, and they may have difficulty getting access to loans and welfare assistance. It is difficult to formulate a general rule, but it is clear that the stigma of class labels has important effects on the quality of life not only of former rural "bad classes," but also of their descendants.

All of this does not mean that the government advocates a theory of absolute class inheritance. Official policy stresses that the bad class status of people would be considered, but that they should be given opportunities to reform themselves and overcome the bad influence (the "class stamp") of their origins. In 1963 and 1964, during the Rural Socialist Education Campaign, directives were issued instructing rural officials not to treat the offspring of landlords and rich peasants just like their parents, but to remould them; and during the Cultural Revolution official documents rejected the slogans of "blood transmission of status" and "naturally red" under which some Red Guards were claiming that all offspring of good classes were revolutionary, and all offspring of bad classes were automatically bad. But in spite of such official qualifications, policies dealing with the future of the class struggle and the need to favor former workers and poor and lower-middle peasants seem to produce a situation in which the stigma of family origins is almost automatic.

Old Classes in Chinese Cities

The nature of class labels in the cities is somewhat more complex, with the following primary categories.

1. Bureaucratic bourgeoisie—capitalists and merchants whose capital was tied to Kuomintang and/or foreign interests.
2. National bourgeoisie—capitalists and merchants whose capital was not seen as so closely tied to Kuomintang and/or foreign investments.
3. Petit bourgeoisie—teachers, lawyers, doctors, low-level business and government employees, shopkeepers, etc.
4. Workers.
5. Idlers and drifters.

In the cities counter-revolutionary elements and bad elements were also designated who, along with the bureaucratic bourgeoisie, formed the major "enemies" to be singled out. (Mention should also be made of honorific labels which could be applied to certain families for service to the cause before 1949: revolutionary soldier, revolutionary cadre and revolutionary martyr. These honorific labels were not restricted to urban residents). In addition to more recent campaigns additional enemy political labels have sometimes been added. As a result of the 1957 anti-rightist campaign numerous people were given the label of "rightist," and this category was added to the list of "elements" seen as enemies.

The bureaucratic bourgeoisie in most cases had their enterprises confiscated soon after 1949, and the control of the national bourgeoisie over their enterprises was gradually reduced by a series of campaigns in the early years, culminating in the socialization of industry and commerce in 1955–1956, after which they became ordinary employees in their enterprises if they continued to work, and were eligible to draw interest on the much reduced official valuation of their previous capital investment. The urban capitalists were for the most part treated better than rural landlords, in keeping with the Marxist analysis of them as capitalist, rather than feudal, forces and with the importance of industry in the economic plans of the period. The loss of the direct relevance of the class labels of other urbanites was, of course, more gradual than in the countryside, since many people continued to work at the same job they had had at the time of the original classification. The offspring of teachers might continue to be influenced by the distinctive attitudes and concerns of their parents long after 1949 if their parents continued to work as teachers, and they could be expected to grow up differently from the children of factory workers.

The evidence is somewhat vague on this point, but in the cities the third generation seems to take on a class label based on their parents' occupations, rather than on that of their grandparents. Thus the grandson of a capitalist whose father became a factory worker should be able to claim worker class origins, while in the countryside the grandson of a landlord will generally still be stuck with the landlord label. This greater ease with which city residents may escape past labels may be offset to some extent by the fact that for many urbanites the personnel dossier (*tangan*) and deep examinations into past family history are more important in personal mobility than they seem to be for most peasants. Thus, a capitalist grandfather no longer determines one's class label, but still remains part of one's "social background," and if one gets into trouble in a political campaign, this may be traced back to the influence of the family connection. Even though such antecedents get lost in one's class label, they are not forgotten.

The influence of these class labels on what urban youths can expect of life is not easy to outline as in the countryside, and again varies from place to place. Access to things like welfare benefits and schooling has not been such a problem in the cities for those in unfavorable categories, and they can benefit as well from the greater anonymity of urban life. But at the same time access to leadership positions, Party and Youth League membership and possibly also to marriage mates has been more difficult for offspring of urban bad classes, and in recent years the ability of these children to get ahead by way of the educational ladder has been sharply limited by student enrollment reforms. The focus of "remembering the class struggle" seems to be on the rural areas, but in the process the old class elites and their offspring in China's cities seem to have suffered as well.

In sum, the policies of the government in China do not seem to have encouraged the pre-1949 elites and their offspring to blend into the rest of society. Rather by the use of dated class labels and various kinds of discrimination, both formal and informal, based upon them, the difficulties experienced by these people have in some ways increased over the years. We might compare this trend with the Stalinist policy of the "intensification of the class struggle" in the 1930s in the Soviet Union. The Stalinist theory was that, as class enemies were reduced in numbers due to social transformations, they would become more desperate and fight more viciously, so that more violent means had to be used to combat them. However, while this argument served as the justification for the massive purges of the period, Soviet policy was at the same time systematically eliminating the last barriers to higher education, Party membership, etc., for former exploiting families. Thus, while class struggle was seen to be intensifying, any connection between this struggle and the pre-1917 class structure was being de-emphasized. The class enemies turned up were in most cases labelled as such because of their personal associations, occupations or expressed opinions (when a rationale could be located), rather than because of their economic status 20 years previously. In China, in contrast, the line is that class enemies are not particularly diminishing in numbers (the figure of 5 percent has been used in campaigns for some years now), and that they will always be around and will continue to cause trouble. Thus one has to continue to be vigilant against them, but not necessarily to use more force than in the past. And 1949 class origins, or association with people of bad origins, continues to play a prominent role in the explanations of the enemies who are being continually "exposed." On this question, Maoist China, which is usually seen as adopting a more "idealist" and "voluntarist" approach than the Soviet Union, by empha-sizing individual thought and behavior, appears to be opting for a more severe approach in emphasizing the importance of class origins.

New Classes in China

The class labels used in China, by focusing to a large extent on economic circumstances more than two decades ago, tend to divert attention from "new class" phenomena: the children of a commune Party secretary who rose from poor peasant status at the time of land reform can still claim poor peasant origins. But "new class" phenomena and their dangers are not ignored. To a considerable extent, political campaigns in China, particularly the Cultural Revolution, have been aimed at these new class dangers. The Chinese Rev-olution brought to positions of power and prominence new elites of many types. Once in high positions, there is considerable evidence that some of these new elites showed traditional concerns for preserving their comforts and privileges and passing these on to their offspring, in spite of the dangers these aspirations posed for the Spartan revolutionary universalism of the new government.

Over the years the Party has adopted a number of policies designed to limit the influence of such tendencies. The anti-elitist measures I touched upon earlier are designed not only to prevent the emergence of antagonisms among the "non-enemy" social strata, but also to check the desire of those on top to maintain and pass on their privileges. Rectification campaigns, staff simplification and "sending down" movements and mass recruitment drives periodically replace a portion of the existing elite and promote new faces from below, while chastening those who are kept on. The problem, of course, is that before long the new officials may also begin to show signs of enjoying their rank, and of wanting to pass on their advantages to their children. To some extent this tendency was promoted by the existence before and after 1949 of some special schools for the children of high-ranking cadres, and the creation in the early 1960s of a broader network of key schools (denounced in the Cultural Revolution as "little treasure pagodas") which were given special attention and investment, and into which cadres of varying levels would endeavor to get their children placed, thus enhacing their chances for university selection and good jobs. In more recent years the apparent elimination of such special schools and the heightened emphasis on cadre participation in labor together with spells in May Seventh cadre schools have been supposed to provide stonger checks against the elitist sentiments that seem to be nutrued by the office and the salary.

While more vigorous efforts are being made to deal with the elitism of the new classes, the Party has adopted another set of measures for the problems of their offspring. These can be lumped together under the label of concern for training "revolutionary successors," motivated by the worry of China's aging leaders that future generations will become soft and careerist, as they feel youth in the Soviet Union have done. Promoting youth from the proper class origins is not enough, given the rejection of the "naturally red" slogan. Rather, youths have to be confronted with trials and tests of their revolutionary dedication, both to prepare them generally for the future, and to select those individuals who will occupy leading positions in society. In some ways the Red Guard movement of the Cultural Revolution was supposed to achieve this; by struggling against "capitalist roader" Party officials, youth could experience something like the pre-1949 revolutionary struggles.

Since 1968 a different kind of policy has been pursued towards the same goal. Before the Cultural Revolution, universities used standardized examinations to select most of their students from among middle-school graduates, although class background and political recommendations were taken into account. In the post-Cultural Revolution reforms of the educational system this has changed. All, or virtually all, middle-school graduates are assigned to work posts, selected for military service, or "sent down" to the countryside. As a result of this campaign, in the period since 1968 more than 10 million urban youths have "settled down" in the countryside, including about 1 million from the city of Shanghai alone. After at least 2 years at their posts, some of these youths may be selected for university attendance or urban jobs, but most are expected to remain in the villages for life. While to a certain extent this policy is aimed at coping with problems of urban over-population and unemployment, it is also seen as providing a testing of the mettle of the younger generation, with only those who pass the test being promoted (either to posts of rural leadership or to opportunities back in the cities).

The post-Cultural Revolution years have thus seen more vigorous efforts to check the growth of new class phenomena, but their impact and future remain uncertain. The Chinese press gives evidence of a number of ways in which official policies are unpopular, or attempts have been made to alter their character. This can be seen in the campaign criticizing Lin Piao and Confucius, where much of the emphasis has been against "restoration" (of pre-Cultural Revolution policies). Lin Piao is accused of attacking the May Seventh cadre schools as a form of disguised unemployment and of branding the sending down of intellectual youths to the countryside as a form of labor (i.e., penal) reform. He is accused of wanting to eliminate these programs and to return to policies fostering the promotion of concern for "talent." In the political life of China, of course, these changes indicate that such sentiments are held not simply by the now deceased Lin Piao, but by some people still in positions of influence. There is also some evidence that cadres are still not always complying faithfully with the obligations placed upon them to perform regular manual labor or to take their turns in the May Seventh cadre schools.

With regard to the system of educated youths going to the countryside, certain specific "new class" resistances can be noted. The first is that some families are upset about having to send their children off to become peasants, and try to find ways to keep them in the cities. To compensate, the press regularly carries stories urging urban residents to encourage their children to go, with leading cadres expected to set a good example by exerting pressure on their own children. Even if youths go to the countryside, other pressures are placed on them to keep them from putting down roots and deciding to stay. In one nationally publicized case, a woman university graduate who had been sent to a village in Hebei was pressured by friends and family not to marry a lowly educated peasant with whom she had fallen in love, and then subjected to scorn when she married him anyway. Her determination received official praise.

The new university enrollment system places great power in the hands of the local production or military unit, since its approval of a youth's desire to go to the university is supposed to be required in order to initiate an application. However, increasing emphasis has also been given to ensuring that university entrants have attained the academic levels of the middle-school graduate, and this has meant the reintroduction of entrance examinations as the final stage in the selection process (which involves student application, mass recommendation, leadership approval and university selection). This had led to more recent debates about the entire selection process, with some claims that entrance examinations defeat the entire purpose of the reform by allowing students with academic tendencies to escape the villages while youth with proper labor orientations get left behind. In another nationally publicized case a youth sat for the university entrance examinations and turned in a blank paper, claiming he had been too busy integrating himself with the peasants and laboring to cram for the exam. His note of protest was given widespread publicity, and was followed by his admission to a university. The appropriate mix of various parts of this selection process, and their implications for stratification in China, seem to be the focus of continuing debate.

Entrance examinations can be argued to work in favor of children of the new elites, who, as in other societies, will grow up in an environment more conducive to examination performance than will other children. But new elite parents have more direct means of trying to secure a good future for their children. By using personal connections and official influence they may be able to subvert the policies described above, a procedure referred to as "going by the back door." The most publicized case involved a second year student at Nanking University. His father, an army official and veteran of the Long March, had used his personal contacts and influence to get his son out of his rural exile, first into the army and then into the university. The son, a Party member, subsequently began to feel guilty about "going by the back door," and applied to withdraw from the university and return to his rural post. His request was accepted and given nationwide publicity, and was followed by numerous other accounts of similar "back door" cases.

These examples are only impressionistic, but they do reinforce the view that the Cultural Revolution and its subsequent reforms have not eliminated new class sentiments nor been fully successful in preventing elites from maintaining their positions and passing on their advantages. But the ways in which such status transmission works are somewhat different from before. Family status and reputation can still have some influence on the careers of youths, but that influence becomes more indirect or devious once the youths are removed from the home. More hurdles are now placed in the path of children of the new elites than was the case in the past, and it seems reasonable to suppose that the futures of these youths are no longer so secure. But it is not clear which other groups in society have benefited most as a result. For rural youths the opportunities for movement into urban jobs and higher education still remain highly restricted, and the influx of sent-down youths has added new competitors for work posts in commune factories, schools, health-care facilities, and in production leadership. One might speculate that the group that may benefit the most is the urban workers, whose children may be somewhat more likely to be picked for urban jobs after schooling or be able to withstand the rigors of a rural assignment than children of urban employees and officials. Children of workers would be freer from the ideological problems borne by some other urban elements, while at the same time having the advantages (in terms of education, culture, and so forth) of their urban origins. Whether this speculation is accurate or not, the new policies do clearly imply that China is trying to rely less exclusively on its educational system as a means of sorting and distributing talent than is the case in most modernizing and industrial societies.

Conclusions

In the first part of this article we have seen that China is a society in which some fairly marked inequalities still exist. Many of these are relatively modest compared with other societies, but at least in terms of income this is more a quantitative than a qualitative difference. If the income differentials which existed in the mid-1950s have stubbornly persisted since then, China can at least be credited with preventing the sort of sharp increases in inequality which often seem to accompany early industrialization in other societies. The most distinctive aspect of distribution in China, however, is not the degree of equality achieved, but the vigorous efforts which are taken to prevent existing inequalities from leading to differentiated life styles and social antagonisms.

In the second part we have seen that, in spite of the degree of social mobility that has occurred, both immediately after 1949 and in more recent years, China is still a society to which the adjective "stratified" can be fairly applied. Efforts are made to make access to position and privilege in China dependent upon individual dedication and political purity, but rigidities remain which give the "new classes" something of a head start in the race, and the "old classes" something of a handicap, when compared with the rest of the population. The devices used to check stratification in China are both fairly vigorous and relatively distinctive in comparison with other societies, although some are precedented by the experience of the Soviet Union (for example, in the more brutal "permanent purge" applied to cadres there and in the 1958 educational reform proposals). In terms of scale, at least, it is hard to find a precedent for the attack on family influence over careers presented by the sending down of youth campaign. And the targets of "de-stratification" efforts are not only the disadvantaged, as they tend to be in the compensatory education and affirmative action programs of the west, but also the new class elites. But without some sort of systematic data it is impossible to say how matters like career stability and inter-generational mobility in China in the post-1949 years compare with those in other societies. We can simply say that, while recent policies may have checked and limited the emergence of a rigid system of stratification, they have not been sufficient to remove the dangers the Chinese Communists feel that inequality and stratification still hold for their revolutionary vision.

POSTSCRIPT

Martin King Whyte and Jack A. Goldstone

Since Mao's death in 1976, and the fall of the "gang of four" (Mao's widow Chiang Ch'ing, and three of his other radical supporters) a month later, official policies have changed with dizzying speed. If many of the policies of Mao's later years described above can be labelled as efforts at destratification, the policies of his successors can be fairly labelled "restratification."

Examinations and academic qualifications are now stressed at all levels of the educational system, and are prerequisites for university admission. Assignments of intellectuals to labor in the countryside have been terminated, and many of the perquisites of leading cadres and specialists that were eliminated in the Cultural Revolution of 1966–1968—such as more spacious apartments and royalty payments—have been restored. In schools, factories, and research institutions, the revolutionary committee form of administration, with its representatives of the masses and outside workers and soldiers, have been junked in favor of a return to a system of individual managers supervised by party committees.

Among the populace at large, official policies to reward individual efforts seem likely to increase inequality. Factory workers are returning to pay according to their individual hours or output ("piece rates") instead of fixed monthly salaries, with bonuses and salary increases as further rewards for increased productivity. And in the countryside, peasant communes have been dismantled and replaced by a revived form of family farming. Crop specialization and incentive systems have been encouraged that disproportionately reward those peasants well endowed to grow cash crops or situated to supply urban markets.

Finally, the emphasis of the late Mao years on combatting "class enemies" has been replaced by official admiration for the contribution of "experts" to China's progress. Class labels are now being phased out, and marks of individual achievement, such as academic titles, have been restored. In 1984, restoration of ranks in the army was formally announced.

We cannot say with any assurance that the policy of restratification will be permanent and will not be succeeded by another dialectical swing toward destratification. And what role the switch toward more inegalitarian policies has played in China's improved economic performance since 1976 can also be debated. But it should be quite clear that in post-Mao China restratification is the order of the day, after a decade of experimentation with more egalitarian forms.

REFERENCE

1. This distinction between inequality and stratification is a useful and important one which is common in the sociological literature. See, for instance, the general discussion in Duncan (1968), esp. pp. 680–681.

INDUSTRIALIZATION, WAR, AND SOCIAL WELFARE

In addition to righting past injustices through attacks on inequality and stratification, revolutions generally aim to increase the nation's strength and to increase the population's welfare. Both of these goals are difficult even in normal times, and are complicated by revolution. Efforts to increase national strength generally revolve around creating industrial power and military might. Theda Skocpol, in her comparison of Russia and China, shows that efforts at industrialization in a postrevolutionary society are strongly affected by the legacy of the old regime. Where a concentrated industrial base already exists, as in Russia, state-led industrialization is easier than where no such base exists. Stephen Walt, in his examination of revolutionary states' habit of becoming engaged in international wars, shows that revolutionaries' pursuit of military might is often provocative, leading to miscalculations that increase the chances of war. Thus war, and heavy casualties, are a common result of revolutions. Finally, Susan Eckstein offers a comprehensive examination of how revolutions have affected social welfare in a number of Latin American states. She finds that some gains—in literacy and health care—can be claimed for certain revolutions. However, in general the gains in social welfare are sharply limited by the condition of the societies in which revolutions occur. That is, poor societies tend to stay poor, and have difficulty in changing their levels of welfare compared to other states, whether or not a revolution has occurred.

◆

OLD REGIME LEGACIES AND COMMUNIST REVOLUTIONS IN RUSSIA AND CHINA
Theda Skocpol

In the following essay, Skocpol uncovers the reasons for the many differences between the Russian and Chinese Revolutions, particularly China's greater "peasant" orientation. Skocpol traces these differences to the structural legacies of the old regimes, emphasizing the relationships between peasants and landlords and between landlords and the state and the nature of old regime industrial development.

Skocpol notes that in Tsarist Russia peasants lived in self-contained communities, the *obshchinas*, while noble landlords depended on state employment for their wealth and social position. When the stresses of World War I undermined the Tsarist state, the nobility that depended on that state crumbled and left an independent and fairly self-sufficient peasantry. However, the Tsarist government had also built up large military and industrial centers to help it compete with the European powers. By 1917, one Russian worker in twenty worked in mining, railroads, munitions, factories, and ironworks. The Bolshevik party was rooted in this industrial working class. After seizing power in the cities and industrial centers, the Bolsheviks faced the problem of extending their authority over a fairly independent peasantry. Using their urban base as a staging ground, the Bolsheviks emphasized urbanization and heavy industrial growth and forcibly extracted grain from the peasantry for the cities and for export to support industrialization. The peasants were thus reduced to little more than exploited producers.

In China, however, peasants lived not in self-contained peasant communities but in networks of villages anchored in market towns dominated by a local, educated landlord elite. Having a secure base in its domination of the countryside, this elite did not depend solely on the state for position and affluence. In addition, little in the way of urban industrial centers competed with the village economy; before the Revolution fewer than one Chinese in a hundred was involved in urban industrial enterprise. Therefore, the fall of the Manchu state in 1911 left the Chinese landlord elite still in control of China. In order to undertake a revolutionary transformation, the Chinese Communist party had to dislodge the local gentry. It could do this only by taking over their functions of village leadership and administration and by building a peasant army to counter the militias raised by local gentry and warlords. Based on a peasant army and closely involved with peasant village functioning, the Chinese Communist Revolution has been far more peasant-oriented—extolling peasant virtues, attacking intellectuals and sending them to the countryside to "learn from the peasantry," and promoting rural light industry.

This essay helps to account sociologically both for differences between broadly similar revolutions and for continuities, despite basic changes, between pre- and postrevolutionary regimes.

From a broad comparative and historical perspective the Russian and Chinese Revolutions—two of the most momentous happenings of the tumultuous twentieth century—seem very similar indeed. Both revolutions broke out in huge agrarian empires that had become subject to intense pressures from more industrialized nations abroad. Massive peasant

rebellions contributed indispensably to each revolutionary drama. Aristocratic, semi-bureaucratic, and autocratic old regimes gave way to centralized, bureaucratic, and mass-
mobilizing collectivist regimes. The revolutionary conflicts led to the expropriation of the
traditional state officials and landed upper classes, as well as foreign and domestic capitalists,
and brought to the fore in their stead the Bolshevik and Chinese Communist parties.
Certainly these similarities in the causes and outcomes of their revolutions are sufficient
to mark the national trajectories of "modernizing" Russia and China as examples of one
distinctive developmental pattern in contrast to the diverse alternative paths that have
been followed by other countries—routes such as liberal or authoritarian capitalist industrialization or neo-colonial dependent development. Nevertheless, as the Chinese Revolution has progressed into its third decade since the consolidation of national political
power by the Communists, important contrasts to the Soviet outcomes have become
strikingly apparent—differences both of official ideologies and policies and of actual patterns
of socioeconomic and political organization. This essay will attempt to show how differences
in the Chinese versus Soviet revolutionary outcomes can be attributed in part to effects
of differences in the prerevolutionary sociopolitical and economic structures of Romanov
Russia and late Imperial China. But before I proceed with this explanatory argument, let
me survey some of the important differences between Soviet Russia and Communist China.

Differences between Soviet and Chinese Communist Societies

Even though both the Russian and the Chinese Communists are dedicated to state-
directed economic development as a means of advancement toward the goal of socialist
society, significant differences show up in their ideologies and programs for economic
growth. In Soviet Russia, from the inception of planned economic development in the
1920s, the greatest emphasis has always been placed on the rapid expansion of heavy
industry. The tactics for accomplishing this have included the direct importation or imi-
tation of the technologies, large-scale organizational forms, and methods of labor discipline employed by the currently most advanced Western capitalist enterprises. Soviet
economic development has entailed rapid urbanization, often outrunning the provision of
consumer goods and public services, and the coercive exploitation or neglect of a stag-
nant collectivized agriculture and rural society. Industrialization, moreover, was at least
until the 1960s, accompanied by the maintenance or widening of wage and salary, rank,
and educational differentials among the strata of Soviet citizens. For in Soviet Russia,
progress toward socialism has been equated with the steady expansion of a planned urban-industrial economy with disciplined factory workers laboring under the guidance of
professional administrators and Party coordinators. The role of peasants has been merely
to provide a surplus of agricultural produce and manpower to fuel the expansion of the
progressive socialist industrial sector.

For a few years after coming to national power in 1949, the Chinese Communists un-
abashedly imitated the Soviet strategy and tactics for socialist economic development, but

between 1958 and 1970 there emerged the clear outlines of a distinctively Chinese strategy for economic development. In sharp contrast to any Soviet-style, one-sided emphasis on heavy industrial development, the Chinese are also channeling investment and leadership resources into the development of collectivized peasant farming and into the development of both agriculture- and consumer-oriented light industries. A concerted effort is being made to retard urbanization and to hold steady or reduce income, rank, and social status differentials both between urban and rural workers, and between leaders and led. There is official encouragement for the launching of small-scale industrial enterprises based on "intermediate technologies" by local and provincial authorities and collectives in areas outside the present regions of greatest industrial advancement. Peasants and the rural economy in general are not dismissed as mere passive auxiliaries in the march toward socialism. Rather the realization of that very goal is held to depend on the degree to which urban-rural differences are overridden, and the extent to which the peasants, as the majority of the people, become conscious makers of their own future.

How then may we explain the variations in the revolutionary outcomes? Naturally this question invites attention to antecedent differences in Russia and China. But which ones?

Already it is becoming quite commonplace for students of Russia and/or China to argue that the postrevolutionary divergences are rooted in the contrasting ways in which the two Communist parties came to national political power during the revolutionary struggles in 1917–1921 in Russia and before 1949 in China. This explanatory approach links the Bolsheviks' ascendancy through an urban insurrection and conventional defensive warfare to their subsequent preference for an urban-industrial strategy of socialist development, and links the Chinese Communists' ascendancy through rural guerrilla warfare to their ultimate commitment to a more peasant and rural-oriented strategy of socialist development. Such links and correspondences are of course very real and important, and constitute a valid proximate explanation of the divergent outcomes. The only difficulty is that the explanation does not go far enough. For one is left wondering *why* the Bolsheviks used one approach to gain national political power, while the Chinese Communists employed a very different one. Unless this question is answered sociologically, all that remains is the (frequently encountered) implication that the Bolsheviks were expedient people who "chose" a quick and easy path to power, while the Chinese Communists made "choices" with more democratic promise—or if one's silent preferences are different, that the Bolsheviks and later the Stalinists were hard-nosed and efficient, while the Maoists, at least since 1949, were impractical romantics!

If leadership choices are not enough to explain the divergent courses of the Russian and Chinese Revolutions, then a more basic place to look is at social structural legacies from the old regimes. Perhaps certain inheritances from the past helped to shape specific variations in the revolutionary outcomes, not simply by "surviving," of course, but rather because they set different limits for successful revolutionary strategies. Initially they set limits for gaining state power within the context of popular and elite struggles against the institutions and classes of the old regimes, and then for using that state power, once consolidated, to promote "socialist" economic development. Let me, in the remainder of this essay, develop this explanatory possibility, first by drawing some comparisons between the sociopolitical and economic structures of Late Imperial China versus pre-1917 Romanov Russia, and then by suggesting how the contrasting old-regime structural patterns directly and indirectly conditioned the possibilities for Communist political leadership to consolidate and then use revolutionary state power.

Contrast between Prerevolutionary Russia and China

SOCIOPOLITICAL STRUCTURES

Russia and China under the old regimes were both massive agrarian empires held together by partially bureaucratized administrative and military state organizations headed by hereditary autocratic monarchs. Nevertheless, the two agrarian autocracies differed significantly in the ways landlords related to the state organizations, and in the ways localized groups of peasants related to the powerful dominant elites and classes. I shall discuss each of these matters in turn, commencing with the structural position of the peasantry, which, after all, constituted the vast majority of the population and the chief source of politically exploitable economic and human resources in both Romanov Russia and Qing China.

THE POSITION OF THE PEASANTRY

In most of late traditional China, and in the most populous core agricultural regions of eighteenth- and nineteenth-century Russia, peasants lived in villages which cultivated, largely with their own labor, portions of the surrounding land. But as soon as we proceed from this common ground to ask how peasant villages fit into the broader structural designs of their respective societies, we immediately notice that while corporately organized peasant villages typically functioned as basic community units in Russia, in China the basic local units were the larger and more inclusive "standard marketing communities," in which peasants as a distinctive class or social stratum lacked any exclusive corporate existence.

In Russia, peasants were legally tied to *obshchinas*, corporate units typically corresponding to (or encompassing) villages, in which were vested the common possession of land and other economic resources, as well as collective responsibility for the enforcement of payments of rents and/or taxes by members. One of the most important and distinctive functions of the *obshchina* was the periodic repartitioning of its cultivable land, that is, its division among the taxable "souls" of the village in a manner calculated to ensure enough equality of access for all to the main resources needed to produce for external obligations and subsistence needs. Repartition was a powerful support for peasant community solidarity, and it continued to be practiced by many communities even after the state ceased to enforce or encourage it.

The immediate government of the *obshchina* rested in the hands of the assembly of the heads of the families of the village. Naturally the peasants were never free from the supervision and arbitrary interference of either the landlords or the bureaucratic agents of the state. Still, on an everyday basis, peasants were allowed to handle their own affairs as long as taxes, army recruits, and rents were forthcoming. Thus, either the entire assembly or else its elected part-time leaders took the responsibility for matters ranging from the distribution of repartitioned lands and the allocation of seigneurial and/or tax obligations and military draft calls, to the all-important planning of the many agricultural tasks that had to be coordinated by the *obshchina* members because their individual holdings were dispersed and intermixed and because they (typically) practiced the three-field system of cultivation. In sum, because the *obshchina* was a self-governing collective association that performed many functions that directly involved each family, it enforced solidarity among Russian peasants and afforded them considerable autonomy vis-à-vis landlords and the state.

The situation was quite different in China. A clear picture of the structure and functioning of local communities in late traditional China emerges from the empirical and theoretical investigations of G. William Skinner, who argues that

> the landscape of rural China was occupied by cellular systems of roughly hexagonal shape. The nucleus of each cell was one of approximately 45,000 market towns (as of the mid-nineteenth century), and its cytoplasm may be seen in the first instance as the trading area of the town's market. The body of the cell—which is to say the immediately dependent area of the town—typically included fifteen to twenty-five villages. . . .[1]

The Chinese market town was not, however, simply a bigger, more complex analogue to the Russian village peasant community. Although there were a variety of types of organizations or associations—e.g., lineages, temples, secret societies, self-defense militias, irrigation or water control projects—that brought peasants within the marketing community together for social events or common purposes, nevertheless the decisive fact about such bodies was that they were *not* strictly peasant groupings. Instead such bodies were normally promoted and led, either openly or informally, by leisured and literate members of the local gentry, a landlord class. What is more, the gentry leaders of the locally organized associations frequently had ties to analogous leaders in other standard marketing communities; consequently they were able to coordinate on a broader regional scale many activities which depended on peasant participation in the localities. For example, gentry managers might mobilize contributions and coordinate peasant labor from several communities to undertake water-control projects which could benefit agricultural productivity in many villages; similarly, in times of political instability, gentry leaders might unofficially tax "middle" and "rich" peasants in order to pay the upkeep of the local militia recruited from the ranks of impoverished local peasants (who might otherwise turn to banditry or rebellion).

With the gentry landlords so actively involved in local associations, there was little basis remaining for the peasants to organize "on their own" at the level of the marketing community. Nor did the peasant village per se possess land in common, or coordinate agricultural work as did the Russian communes, for Chinese agriculture was based on individual families owning or renting their own lands, each faring as it could amidst the vagaries of weather, politics, markets and demographic fortune.

LANDED UPPER CLASSES AND THE STATE

In addition to the situation of the peasantry, the other important sociopolitical contrast between Russia and China which we will survey is the relation of the landlords to the Imperial state organizations. It should be emphasized at the outset that in *neither* Russia nor China (until after 1900) were the landed upper classes able to exert formal, collective political leverage against the authority of the Tsar or Emperor. In contrast, for example, to European landed aristocracies such as the French, neither the Chinese gentry nor the Russian nobility possessed corporate organizations with traditionally legitimate rights to share in the governing process of the old regime. Nevertheless, the embeddedness of the Chinese gentry in the localities and its ramified functional links to the peasantry and the local economies provided it as a class with a much stronger basis to counterbalance and limit the reach of the Imperial power than did the weak local roots of the Russian landed nobility.

Why were the local roots of the Russian nobility so weak? After all, many nobles owned serfs and estates worked by serf labor, and these characteristics might appear to make them a stronger class than the Chinese gentry whose agricultural fortunes depended on rents from tenants. But the very same historical tendencies that created serf agriculture in Russia also shaped the nobility into an internally fragmented class nearly totally dependent on the state for its status and livelihood.

Serfdom in Russia was consolidated under the impetus of centralizing Tsars determined to extract from the Russian people sufficient resources to support military forces for defense and expansion in threatening geopolitical environments. Traditionally footloose Russian peasants had to be tied to the land if they were to be kept at work producing taxable surpluses. Concomitantly the Tsars needed military officers and officials to man the state organizations required for external warfare and internal social control. Over a period of centuries the lands of independent nobles and princes were expropriated and passed out as rewards for official careers to a new class of service nobles. As this happened, the Tsars took pains to ensure that no new groupings of independent landed aristocrats could arise. Service nobles were given rights to serf "souls" and to landed estates, yet typically their possessions were not concentrated in one locality or even one province, but were scattered over different regions of the empire. Moreover, until the eighteenth century, adult male nobles were forced to pursue service careers from youth until old age, with the Tsar reserving the right to shunt individuals from post to post, province to province, at will. Under these conditions, local and regional solidarity among nobles could not develop, agriculture was naturally regarded only as a source of income, not as an object of managerial concern, and "local government," such as it was, was the affair of serf communities and estate agents operating under bureaucratic scrutiny, not a sphere in which local landowners exerted important leadership.

During the eighteenth century Russian nobles were finally released from lifelong state service and their private property rights were fully officially confirmed. Moreover, the Russian economy experienced comparatively rapid commercial development. Nevertheless, the situation of the nobles did not change much. Now increasingly oriented to Western European upper-class life styles, the Russian nobles still gravitated toward state employment as the one sure site of opportunities to reside in the cities and to earn salaries to supplement the very meager incomes (if any) that most obtained from the serf-estates, the inheritance of which was subdivided in each generation. Nor did the vast majority of landlords possess either the capital or the knowledge or inclination to turn to commercial agriculture (and indeed the conditions for it were poor in most regions of Russia). By the mid-nineteenth century a large majority of Russian nobles were either impoverished or heavily indebted to the state and the minority of well-to-do were mostly prospering through official careers.

The reforms after 1860, including the Emancipation of the serfs, did not reverse the powerlessness and economic decline of the landed nobility. Most used their redemption payments (compensation for the loss of serf ownership) to pay off debts to the state or for education or consumption, not for economic investments. Even the formation of the *zemstvos*—local and provincial representative bodies to which nobles had privileged electoral access—could not alter the long-established pattern of noble "functionlessness" vis-à-vis the bureaucratic state on the one hand and the peasant communities on the other. For the Imperial authorities retained a monopoly of administration and coercion and continued to tax away most of the agricultural surplus, while the *obshchinas* continued to manage agriculture along traditional lines. At best the *zemstvos* established a foothold through the provision, on a very restricted fiscal basis, of educational, welfare and advisory-economic services in the localities, but this service sector grew up alongside, not within, the hierarchy of political power. The *zemstvos* were tolerated by the Imperial bureaucracy only to the extent that they did not challenge central controls and policy making prerogatives.

In Imperial China the gentry evolved quite differently from the Russian nobility. Chinese dynasties and their centrally deployed officialdoms traditionally coexisted politically with locally rooted landed notables. Indeed the Imperial bureaucracy never penetrated as extensively into the localities as did the Russian autocratic state, and Chinese officials (who were always outsiders to the areas they administered) had to cooperate with local landlords and literati in order to ensure smooth tax collections and the maintenance of order.

In traditional China local communities and elites could prosper without complete dependence on Imperial initiatives or employments. Especially in significantly commercialized areas of agrarian China, landlords could make profits by renting out lands and by usurious loans to peasants, and local people could afford to create associations (e.g., clans, religious sodalities, militias, and irrigation projects) and pay fees to support gentry directors to manage them. Besides, flourishing local and regional trading networks made it possible for merchants rapidly to accumulate fortunes—which they typically subsequently invested in land and in Confucian educations for their sons, thus transforming their heirs into gentry. By this process the gentry could be continually rejuvenated from outside agriculture, where only modest fortunes could accumulate given the practice of equal inheritance and the low rate of return to investments in land.

Another condition facilitating mobility into and out of the gentry lay in the fact that Imperial authorities in China never established any juridically closed hereditary nobility. This helped to prevent locally rooted upper classes from consolidating into corporate aristocracies, and the resulting mobility complemented the unique competitive process by which the Chinese state recruited its officials.

Indeed the reason why Chinese rulers were *able* to coexist with a partially autonomous landed upper class lies in the workings of the Confucian examination system for recruiting state officials, for this system, operating normally, helped to extend the Imperial reach informally into the heart of every local community. Under this system, Imperial authorities periodically convened examinations at graduated levels of difficulty to test candidates' mastery of the Confucian classics. There were strict quotas (adjustable according to Imperial needs and policies, such as the policy of maintaining regional balances) for what proportions could pass, and the Imperial authorities followed relatively consistent patterns of recruiting Imperial officials from among individuals who successfully passed the exams. In the local communities, meanwhile, wealthy families paid Confucian scholars, to educate their sons or protégés in what was essentially an entire style of life, or status manner, as well as a set of difficult skills requisite for obtaining the highly desired official posts. Invariably, there were in any locality always more Confucian-tutored aspirants to state service than ever either passed all of the requisite exams or obtained official appointments. Because such local literati shared the class interests and status-manner of the Imperial officials, they were normally inclined to cooperate with the magistrates to maintain order. And their cooperation was quite valuable because, as local leaders, they were familiar with local conditions and played strategic roles in the various types of peasant-based associations which (as we have seen) flourished in the local communities.

In sum, the systems of official recruitment and deployment in Imperial China ensured that there were always in any community Confucian gentry involved in local leadership roles and available for informal cooperation with similarly educated Imperial officials, who, in turn, needed the help of local leaders in order to govern. The Chinese gentry were, therefore, the indispensable support for Imperial rule.

Modern Industrial Development under the Old Regimes

Having surveyed the agrarian-based sociopolitical structures of the old regimes, it remains to discuss how and to what extent modern industry had developed in Russia and China prior to the outbreak of the revolutionary crises and the rise to power of the Communist revolutionaries. Neither Russia nor China commenced industrialization in the relatively autonomous and spontaneous manner of England, with indigenous agricultural commercialization and consumer demand as the predominant stimuli. Rather both responded to pressures and examples from more industrially advanced foreign military competitors. Yet both the timing and nature of the foreign pressures and the kinds and extent of the responses to foreign examples differed greatly between the two old regimes.

Long before they had to contend with military competition from mechanized European nations, Russian rulers were accustomed to borrowing techniques from the West and imposing them on Russian society. During the seventeenth century Muscovy came into sustained military conflict with European monarchial absolutisms. In adaptive response there came a remarkable effort, explosively initiated under Peter the Great (1682–1725), to rework the Russian state and economy by amalgamating the most efficient patterns of bureaucratic state service, manufacturing, and military technology and organization then existing in Western Europe with the inherited Russian forms of serfdom and patrimonal despotism. In fact, the reforms "from above" of Peter and his immediate successors succeeded in making Russia a formidable European military power, not to be eclipsed until the mid-nineteenth century, when the technologies and advances associated with industrialization again gave the Western powers a qualitative military advantage.

When the Crimean War of 1854 to 1856 revealed Russia's renewed backwardness and vulnerability within the European states system (of which Russia was now irrevocably a member), the Tsars and their officials responded in what was really a very traditional fashion. They instituted a progression of reforms from above, all designed in one way or another to help Russia to catch up militarily with her potential enemies. First serfdom was abolished and the military and judicial systems reformed; then a program of railroad construction through state and foreign investments was instituted; finally, from the late 1880s a crash program of government-subsidized heavy industrialization was launched. All such policies could be pursued even against resistance from social classes—in the face of landlord opposition to freeing the serfs; despite merchants' reluctance to compete with foreign capitalists or to modernize business practices; against peasant unrest and riots protesting crushing tax burdens—because the Russian autocratic state was, as always, the monopole of power in the society. Especially in the final decades before its collapse in war, the Tsarist state alone took the effective initiative in launching changes within Russia.

In absolute terms, moreover, the changes wrought at state initiative were very great. Of course when the grim reckoning of World War I came in 1914, Russia still had by no means caught up with the West economically. Judged in terms of their avowed purposes, therefore, the post-Crimean Tsarist reforms were failures—largely because the vast agricultural sector of the Russian economy remained for the most part untransformed in structure and technique. Yet, especially after 1890, Russia experienced remarkably rapid industrial growth. Mining, petroleum refining, metallurgical and chemical industries, and textiles all developed rapidly. Overall industrial expansion averaged about 5 percent per annum between 1888 and 1913, a rate higher on a per capita basis than industrial growth in either the United States or Germany during that period. Heavy industrial expansion in particular occurred through importation from the West of the very latest manufacturing technologies, which in turn were designed into the most large-scale and modern factory organizations. Nor was the industry concentrated in merely one region, or only on the margins of the empire; there were several important areas of industrial concentration including the regions around the capitals (St. Petersburg and Moscow), as well as the Ukraine, Polish Russia, the Donets Basin, and the Urals. Moreover, although the advent of World War I found Russia with a much less dense and redundant railroad network than her neighboring enemy, Imperial Germany, nevertheless there had been built up a primary grid of links connecting all of the administrative and industrial cities to one another, and these in turn to the ports and military frontiers of both European and Asian Russia. One student of Russian development, Alec Nove, has neatly summed up the economic situation of the Tsarist regime at the end: "Russia was the least developed European power, but a European power none the less."[2]

China, on the other hand, had not traditionally experienced compelling military pressure from pre-industrial European states. But from the Opium War of 1839–1842 through a series of imperialist incursions and military victories culminating after 1895 in the carving of China into spheres of foreign influence, Chinese authorities were increasingly compelled to respond to the evident economic and military superiority of the European nations (and ultimately Japan as well).

Nevertheless, the Chinese Imperial government's response to the Western industrial advantage could not resemble that of the Tsarist government after 1854. China lacked a history of cultural adaptation from above, but even more important, the Chinese central government could not wield significant leverage over the Chinese society and economy as a whole. This was true not only because Chinese emperors had never been as strong against the gentry as the Russian Tsars had always been over their service nobility, but also because by the mid-nineteenth century, at exactly the time when Western intrusions on Chinese sovereignty became militarily compelling, the Manchu dynasty was at the nadir of its influence and control over events within Chinese society. For during the middle decades of the century, the dynasty was saved from overthrow by massive peasant-based rebellions only through the military intervention of regional gentry-led armies and administrations—which, in the aftermath of the rebellions (from the 1860s on), retained de facto control of large sectors of the Imperial bureaucracy and of over 50 percent of the tax revenues officially collected within the empire. Unofficially, local gentry collected and controlled still more of the surpluses generated by the agrarian-commercial economy. Consequently, even as Imperial authorities came increasingly to recognize the need to promote industrial development, railroad building, and the technological modernization and professionalization of Chinese military forces, they found themselves without access to the financial revenues that might have allowed the central government to invest heavily in these things and thus to promote national development in a coordinated way calculated to reinforce Chinese political power vis-à-vis foreign enemies.

In turn, the weakness of the Chinese government encouraged foreign interests to encroach more and more on Chinese sovereignty. The obvious effect of this was to undermine the authority and power of the Manchus still further. Another consequence was that most of the little modern industrialization that did occur in China right up through 1949 happened within or near foreign-controlled Treaty Ports or spheres of influence. Industrial enterprises, established either by foreign investors or by Chinese capitalists seeking the legal advantage of operating in the foreign-administered areas or the economic advantages of trading with foreigners, grew up to process a limited range of Chinese raw materials or agricultural products for export or for sale within the treaty ports or their immediate hinterlands. These were primarily light industries and most enterprises were small or medium in scale. The total output of all modern industries never (before 1949, let alone 1911) exceeded 3.5 percent of the national income of China, and industrial workers remained substantially fewer than 1 percent of the labor force. (Roughly comparable figures for late Tsarist Russia were 16 percent and 5 percent respectively). In short, even the direct and indirect effects of capitalist imperialism did not produce any major structural change in the working of the Chinese economy before 1949.

Instead, the traditional Chinese agrarian-commercial economy continued to function, its operations modified mainly at the margins. G. William Skinner has estimated that about 90 percent of China's traditional marketing system remained intact through 1949. Most trade remained focused within the traditional regional and local periodic markets, served by traditional merchants and peddlers supplying goods still produced primarily by local peasants and artisans or nonmechanized workshops, rather than the products of modern industries.

In sum, modern industrial development in China before 1911 (or 1949) was very limited and marginal. Certainly it was much less extensive and transformative in its impact than Russian industrialization before 1917.

Influences of Old-Regime Legacies on the Revolutionary Processes and Outcomes

The preceding discussion has established some important differences between prerevolutionary China and Russia. Now it is time to assess how the differences of sociopolitical structure and modern economic development of the old regimes can help us to account for the later variations between the revolutionary regimes in Russia and China. I shall argue that the old-regime legacies helped to shape the revolutionary futures in three main ways, with the effects cumulating and thus reinforcing one another. First, differences between the sociopolitical structures of old-regime Russia and China guaranteed that revolutionary crises would develop differently, causing Communist revolutionaries in the two societies to be faced with different revolutionary tasks and different possibilities for mobilizing popular rebellious forces. Second, the contrasting levels of modern economic development within Russia versus China meant that post-autocratic state power could be consolidated with modern urban resources in post-1917 Russia but not in post-1911 China. And third, even once Communist revolutionaries in the two countries had consolidated national political power, the different economic conditions inherited from the old regimes favored different development strategies—which, moreover, matched well with the contrasting political capacities that had been acquired by the two revolutionary parties during their struggles for power. Let me elaborate on each of these assertions in turn.

PREREVOLUTIONARY SOCIOPOLITICAL STRUCTURES AND THE DEVELOPMENT OF THE REVOLUTIONARY CRISES

In neither Russia nor China did revolutionary crises emerge directly as a result of mass discontent or the activities of ideological radicals. In both cases, rather, the political, administrative, and military institutions of the autocracy were suddenly weakened and disorganized due to the direct or indirect effects of foreign pressures. In China, ineffective attempts by the Manchus to cope with imperialist pressures induced politically organized gentry groups, along with their provincial military allies, to depose the dynasty in 1911. In Russia, the autocracy was too autonomous and strong vis-à-vis class forces to be deposed by an internal force, even after suffering international humiliations as in the Crimean War of 1854–1856 and the Russo-Japanese War of 1905–1906. Instead, the Russian state finally dissolved only under the impact of defeat in prolonged, total modern warfare in World War I. Still, in both instances, China from 1911, and Russia from March 1917, the result of the sudden collapse of the autocracy was to open the way for spreading and deepening political and social conflicts. The traditional focus of order disintegrated and a revolutionary situation emerged.

Nevertheless the significance of the collapse of autocracy was quite different in Russia and China, because the old-regime structures that came apart from the top down had been put together differently in the first place.

In Russia the autocracy collapsed only when the Tsarist administration and armies were so overwhelmed by the burdens of unsuccessful total warfare as to be on the verge of complete disintegration. The "February" Revolution was itself occasioned by the war-induced insubordination of the Petrograd Garrison, traditionally a mainstay of Tsarist authority. Within days and weeks after the fall of the monarchy, the police and administrative organizations of the old regime dissolved, and by midsummer (as the war continued without success) even the front-line armies were beginning to disintegrate through desertions or rank-and-file revolts against officers.

In turn, once the Tsarist state collapsed, the single strong point of the old regime, the keystone of the entire edifice, was gone. Having been completely dependent on the autocracy, the nobility (officials and landlords) and the bourgeoisie (domestic and foreign) were suddenly left vulnerable to popular rebellions from below. The remnant landed gentry were supremely vulnerable, for they were functionally irrelevant to the processes of agricultural production and village level government, and yet still enjoyed property rights in lands coveted by the neighboring peasant communities. The mass of the peasants in turn (especially those of central Russia) possessed in the institution of the *obshchina* a collective organization through which they could spontaneously rebel against landlords on their own, without inducement or leadership from urban radical elites, given only the opportunity offered by the disintegration of Tsarist administrative and military power upon which the gentry depended for defense of their privileges. Not surprisingly, therefore, within a few months after March 1917, the Russian landed nobility as a class was swept away by snowballing peasant revolts. Meanwhile in the urban centers, administrators, army officers, professionals, and capitalists were attacked by striking industrial workers and mutinous soldiers. In short, all of the dominant classes and elites of the old regime were suddenly and thoroughly rendered quite powerless.

As a consequence, the revolutionary socialist parties, would-be consolidators of alternative regimes, were left to contend in a virtual power vacuum. Not until after one of the revolutionary parties—the Bolsheviks—had triumphed in the intrarevolutionary competition were there efforts to consolidate revolutionary state power. In this task, the Bolsheviks did not so much face the task of combating and defeating the dominant institutions of the old regime as they faced the imperatives of rebuilding political order out of virtual chaos. This was because the old regime had completely come apart. It took no less a crisis than the strains of defeat and prolonged participation in World War I to overwhelm the Tsarist army and bureaucracy, the central supports of the old regime; yet once these supports gave way, no significant remnants of the old regime remained intact for long.

But the bases on which a new national order could be built were quite limited, and this, too, was a legacy of the structure of the old regime. The very success of the revolt by the independent peasant communities ruled them out as a possible basis for national reintegration. Having seized the opportunity to attack the landlords and take their lands virtually unaided, the peasant communities wanted only to turn inward and to be left alone to carry on their self-governing and subsistence-oriented existence. Whatever progress toward political reintegration the Bolsheviks (or any other revolutionary elite) could make would thus have to be based upon the social and infrastructural resources of the urban centers.

Turning now to China, we can see that the revolutionary crisis developed after 1911 in quite a different manner from Russia after March 1917. Again, the explanation lies in the structural patterns of the old regime that was disintegrating. Whereas the revolutionary crisis in Russia was occasioned and characterized by the collapse of the entire framework of the old regime, in China in 1911 only the coordinating center was removed, while the local administrative and military power of the gentry and the warlords remained intact— indeed were initially enhanced by the removal of the meager restraints that the Manchus had been able to impose in the name of national unity. Nor were the Chinese peasants able to rebel spontaneously and autonomously, in the manner of the Russian peasants, against the landlords. For the Chinese gentry retained their local economic and political predominance, as they either directly usurped former Imperial administrative positions in the districts and provinces, or else came to terms with the regional warlord organizations that claimed administrative power.

Thus when modern-style revolutionary elites and parties emerged in the urban centers of China after 1919, they faced a very different situation from the one which suddenly confronted Russian revolutionaries in 1917. The dominant classes and elites of the old regime were still very much in place. The removal of the autocracy had not resulted directly in social revolution; instead the gentry and the warlords remained potent internal opponents of any revolutionary movement. Both the peasantry and the urban workers were potential supporters for such a revolutionary movement, for these classes had interests opposed to the gentry and bourgeoisie (both domestic and foreign). Yet given the continued administrative-military power of the gentry and the warlords, neither the peasants nor the workers were able carry out a successful revolution from below without leadership and protection by organized revolutionary forces. Thus, virtually all possibilities for popular alliances remained open, but only if revolutionaries could build administrative and military apparatuses to gain direct access to territories and populations over which warlords or gentry retained control. Only the disunity and competition of the provincially and regionally based warlord-gentry connections provided possibilities for maneuver for would-be revolutionary movements.

MODERN URBAN RESOURCES AND THE CONSOLIDATION OF REVOLUTIONARY STATE POWER

A second way in which old-regime legacies affected the course of revolutionary struggles in China and Russia had to do with whether or not the modern urban industrial sectors that had developed prior to the revolutions provided adequate resources for a revolutionary party to consolidate state power.

In Russia, the question of urban resources was quite compelling because, once the peasants had carried through their inward- and backward-looking revolts against the landlords and all other locally present remnants of the Tsarist system, only urban resources were easily available to any would-be consolidators of state power. Hence it was of great significance that European Russia possessed at its core and around its edges a series of major industrial and administrative cities, linked together by a network of railroad and telegraph lines.

Among the contending revolutionary parties, the tightly knit and internally disciplined Bolsheviks were in the best position to exploit these urban resources, since, especially after August 1917, they had the closest and most plentiful ties to the organized industrial workers and military garrisons within and near the most industrialized and administratively strategic northeastern urban centers. None of the other revolutionary parties was in a good position to outmaneuver the Bolsheviks, not only because the other parties were less unified and disciplined, but also because their strongest popular bases were not so centrally located. The Mensheviks had their greatest relative strength in the peripheral areas of the Caucasus and Georgia, while the Socialist Revolutionaries were strongest in the provincial cities and towns of the most heavily agricultural provinces and along the western and southwestern fronts.

With great tactical skill, the Bolsheviks, from the summer of 1917 through their Petrograd coup in "October" and on until the competing parties had been maneuvered out of all strategic positions, used their political links to workers and soldiers to consolidate and extend Party control of the cities, fronts, and railroad links within northeastern Russia. Then they were in a position to attempt to consolidate and extend urban-based administrative and police controls over the entire country.

That the Bolsheviks (or any party) could succeed at all in consolidating national power on this basis, no matter how clever and ruthless their tactics, certainly depended on the degree of modern industrial and transportation development that had been accomplished under the old regime. Most of the existing Russian war industries, and the stockpiles of arms and munitions produced by them during 1917, fell into the hands of the Bolsheviks. Industrial workers, many of them Party members, were available and widely distributed in sufficient numbers to staff such indispensable units as the food collection teams sent out to seize grain from the peasants and the Red Vanguard units interspersed among the peasant conscripts to give fighting spirit to the revolutionary armies. Besides, no strategy of consolidating the revolution by seizing and then defending the capitals and other important administrative centers could have won without the European Russian railroad network, which made it possible to move loyal troops and political cadres quickly from place to place. It is no accident that one of the most vivid and frequently encountered images of the Bolshevik revolutionary leadership is that of the Commander-in-Chief of the Red Army, Leon Trotsky, whisking from front line to front line in his command headquarters—a railroad car.

In China, modern urban resources played a far more complicated role in the revolutionary process. As in Russia, the leaderships of the principal revolutionary parties were recruited from an intelligentsia committed by educational experience and political principle to the furthering of "modern, urban" ways. But the Chinese Communists' feeble attempts in 1926–1927 to seize power through Bolshevik-style coups and guided mass uprisings only led to disaster. Unlike the Bolsheviks in 1917, they did not benefit from the war-induced disintegration of standing armies potentially loyal to counterrevolution. The Communists were pushed out of the cities (and most administrative towns) of China altogether, forced to pursue a do-or-die strategy of rural guerrilla warfare, while the rightist Kuomintang Party was left in control of the most modern urban centers.

During over twenty years in the countryside of China, between 1927 and 1949, the Chinese Communists gradually developed tactics to drive the warlords and gentry from regional and local political-military and economic power. They finally forged direct links to the peasants within the local communities—links which enabled them to mobilize peasant manpower and rural economic resources more directly and efficiently than any previous political movement in (at least recent) Chinese history. That the Communists were eventually able to do this depended, at least in a negative sense, on the fact that the Chinese peasants had not been able to rebel effectively against the gentry on their own. The peasantry "needed" direct protection by the Red Army and local leadership tied to the Communist party in order to gain collective organizational leverage to attack the gentry. In the very process of providing these factors, the Party and Red Army hierarchies replaced the landed and official gentry left over from the old regime.

Yet the CCP's ultimate success with its peasant-mobilization strategy depended not only on its ability to displace the gentry and directly mobilize the peasantry, but also on the *inability* of the Kuomintang Nationalists to consolidate nationwide centralized administrative and military control over China before 1937 (when the Japanese invaded China with full force). This was something that the Nationalists made every attempt to do, drawing to the fullest degree possible on the resources of the most modernized cities of coastal and central China, especially Shanghai and Nanking. The Nationalists milked the industrial wealth of the cities, taxed their national and international commercial flows, and manipulated to maximum political advantage the processes of modern finance institutionalized in the urban banks. But all of the urban-generated revenues the Nationalist government could lay its hands on were not enough to pay the costs of a truly national army that could supplant the military organizations of warlords (who remained in place as nominal allies in all but a few core provinces) or to pay for an administrative apparatus sufficiently extensive, loyal, and efficient to penetrate into the rural localities and divert agrarian revenues from the gentry. Nor did the Kuomintang leaders have access to any extensive and centralized primary railroad network which could be used, in the manner of the Bolsheviks, to deploy and redeploy small but loyal bodies of military, police, and administrative personnel. Instead, Nationalist "authority" in the interior and in the North and South of China depended on the maintenance, through periodic payoffs, of cross-cutting alliances with locally and provincially based authorities.

As a result, the Nationalists were unable to mobilize or coordinate Chinese national efforts to defend the country against Japanese invasion. Once that invasion came in earnest in 1937, the Nationalist government was driven completely out of the modernized cities of eastern China. After being feebly reestablished in the western hinterland cut off from its accustomed revenue sources, the regime was in an even less favorable position either to expel the Japanese or to counter the rising power of the Communists. Meanwhile, the wartime situation of foreign occupation and exacerbated military divisions among its enemies provided the Chinese Communists with especially favorable conditions to pursue and deepen their rural mobilization approach to generating the resources necessary to consolidate revolutionary state power in China—something they accomplished very rapidly once the United States defeated Japan in World War II.

The crucial point is that the Chinese Communists could never have survived as an organized political and rebellious military force after 1927 if the Kuomintang had been able to impose, from its modern urban base, as tight administrative-military controls on China as the Bolsheviks were able to impose on Russia from their urban base after 1918. And surely the difference between the Bolshevik's success and the Kuomintang's failure cannot be explained only by differences in party characteristics and policies—for the Kuomintang had advantages not available to the Bolsheviks after November 1917 (e.g., an intact military organization) to counterbalance the Bolshevik-style qualities that it lacked (e.g., centralized discipline and an orientation toward mass mobilization). But the Bolsheviks could operate within an urban network where modern industries and transportation facilities were thoroughly integrated with the urban-administrative hierarchy through which the autocratic regime had formerly exerted its monopolistic powers, while the Kuomintang had to contend with a tiny modern urban sector on the one hand, and a vast, traditional, agrarian-commercial sector on the other. In post-1917 Russia, nationwide state power could probably be reconsolidated *only* on the basis of modern urban resources; in post-1911 China, modern urban resources were hopelessly inadequate to this task. Instead, revolutionaries had to work around and destroy the remnants of the old regime in the hinterland and countryside. The way from Canton, the birthplace of modern Chinese nationalism, to Peking, the traditional administrative capital of China, lay not in a brief, smooth trip through the cities of Nanking and Shanghai, but in a long, arduous trek through the rural backlands.

REVOLUTIONARY OUTCOMES: BUILDING ON INHERITED ECONOMIC AND ACCUMULATED POLITICAL STRENGTHS

Once Communists consolidated revolutionary state power in Russia in the early 1920s and in China in the early 1950s, they had at their disposal new and powerful means to formulate and implement development policies for their entire societies. At that point the question arose whether future economic development should be based on absolute national political priority for investments in heavy industry. Russia under Stalinist direction answered yes, while China, especially insofar as Maoist policies have taken hold, has answered no.

Why the difference? The answer requires and allows us to tie together the separate strands of the overall argument developed in this paper. In brief, the Soviets and the Chinese Communists each found that future development for their country could best build on the inherited strengths of the existing economy. Equally important, the respective political capacities accumulated by each Party in the course of struggling to consolidate state power were well suited to the implementation of economic development strategies based on the different inherited economic strengths.

Stalin's strategy called for huge, sustained investments in heavy industries, coupled with administrative mechanisms (collectivization from above) to force the peasantry to grow crops, surrender surpluses, and release manpower for the sudden urban-industrial expansion. This approach called for a reversion to 1917–1920 style activism. The Party and state organizations, having been originally built up during the Revolution's early struggles and still being led primarily by men whose most vivid and rewarding revolutionary experiences had been during that period of intense struggle, were well suited and naturally inclined toward exactly the activist stance proposed by Stalin in 1928–1929. Mobilizing urban-based Party and worker teams to go out into the politically hostile countryside to seize grain from and reorganize the peasant communities was exactly the kind of activity that had led to victories for the same leaders and organizations in the recent heroic past. Not surprisingly, they were predisposed to turn to the old expedients in order to cope with still another crisis for the revolution.

But, of course, this time the task at hand was not winning a Civil War but propelling national industrial development. The Stalinist strategy, consonant though it was with Bolshevik revolutionary experiences and organizational capacities, could work at all only because Soviets could build upon economic conditions continuing from the prerevolutionary era. Stalin's successful program of crash heavy industrialization obviously benefitted from being able to build on the substantial existing heavy-industrial base. In addition, the Soviet agricultural sector *could* be squeezed as brutally and wastefully as Stalinist policies demanded only because that sector was (and traditionally has been) "slack" relative to its potential capacity for per capita production. Essentially, Stalin's approach called for the Communists to replace old-regime mechanisms for squeezing agriculture with more direct bureaucratic controls by the Soviet state. Once this was done, heavy industrialization could continue in Russia, even though the human cost, especially to the peasantry, was terrible.

In China, once the Communists had restored the industries of Manchuria and the coastal centers to their pre-War levels, they began to come up against the limits of an economy very different from that which the Russians had to deal with from the 1920s. For one thing, there was a well-developed heavy industrial base only in Manchuria. In other centers, overall industrial development was much less, and light industries and commercial enterprises were often more predominant. Even more decisive, the rural economy of China had problems and possibilities diametrically opposite to those of Russian agriculture. Chinese agriculture became, between 1400 and 1900, maximally productive within the limits of the traditional technology, social structure, and available land area, and the Chinese population expanded steadily from 1700, until it virtually saturated the expansive capacity of the agrarian sector (from roughly 1850 on). Moreover, much of Chinese economic life remained, right through 1949, oriented to and dependent upon well-developed intra-regional- and intra-local-marketing-area networks of trade and preindustrial commodity production. Thus the Chinese Communists faced a situation in which even the most brutal Stalin-style methods of appropriating agricultural surpluses and channelling them into heavy industry could not have worked as they did in post-1928 Russia, for the inherited industrial base on which the Chinese would have to build was far more restricted than that available to the Soviets, while the barriers to forcing sudden increases in agricultural production and marketing were much more formidable than they had been in Russia.

On the positive side, moreover, the Chinese Communists enjoyed some advantages that the Bolsheviks had lacked, for the economic and political orientations of the Chinese peasantry were far more suited to furthering peasant participation in national development efforts than had been those of the Russian peasantry after 1917. The Chinese peasantry was not strictly subsistence-oriented, nor was it unaccustomed to following extra-village leadership in projects to improve conditions for agricultural production. Even under the old regime, recall, Chinese peasants had been closely linked within market areas to gentry, merchants, and artisans. In addition, the Chinese Communists themselves had, during the Yenan period of the Chinese Civil War, acquired extensive experience and developed grassroots political organizations and techniques for directly mobilizing peasants to take part in efforts to increase agricultural and small-scale industrial production. Such efforts continued to be at the core of the Maoist developmental strategy. Nor should it seem surprising that this has happened, for the Maoist approach to Chinese development is not romantic or irrational. Just as the Stalinist strategy in Russia represented a practical way to bring to bear the political capacities of the Bolsheviks, as they had been forged in the Russian revolutionary struggles, on the economic situation inherited from the old regime and the revolution, so does the Maoist development strategy in China represent the logical way for the Chinese Communists to apply their accumulated revolutionary experiences and organizational capacities to propel the Chinese economy along a distinctive path to industrialization. This path takes into account the fact that this economy has always been strongest and most vital in its agrarian regions and localities.

Does this then suggest that revolutions change nothing? Not at all. Never have societies experienced such sudden and thoroughgoing transformations—of political institutions, socioeconomic structures, and legitimating formulas—as Russia and China through their twentieth-century social revolutions. The point is not that no fundamental changes occurred, but that those which did occur recapitulated certain structural patterns of the old regimes. Thus, just as Romanov Russia and Manchu China, despite very great overall resemblances, differed (a) in the ways that power was distributed within the dominant strata, (b) with respect to how peasant communities fit into the larger societal wholes, and (c) in the degrees and kinds of state-guided industrialization, so, too, do Soviet Russia and Communist China differ in parallel ways despite their many similarities as Communist revolutionary regimes.

Nor should this be an unwelcome truth. For, since old regimes vary in their structures, the implication is that all revolutions will not turn out the same, even if they are politically consolidated under like auspices. Quite possibly other old-regime legacies will contribute to more helpful developments in other revolutionary societies.

REFERENCES

1.   Skinner (1971), p. 272.
2.   Nove (1969).

REVOLUTION AND WAR

Stephen M. Walt

This paper examines the following questions: Why do revolutionary states fight foreign wars almost immediately after gaining power? Are revolutionary regimes inherently aggressive, or are they simply victims of other powers? Are these conflicts a direct result of the revolutionary process, or is the association between revolution and war largely spurious?

The Process of Revolution

Revolutions are deadly serious contests for extremely high stakes. The collapse of internal authority places all members of society at risk: until a new order is established, conflicts can be resolved only by tests of strength and no one's interests and safety are assured. Winners will take all and losers may lose everything; as a result, mass revolutions are almost always bloody and destructive.[1]

A revolution is more than the replacement of one set of rulers by another: "a complete revolution involves the creation of a new political order." By definition, a revolutionary state rests on new principles of legitimacy, displays new symbols of authority and identity (names, flags, anthems, etc.), adopts new rules for elite recruitment, and creates new political institutions and governmental procedures. In short, revolutions *redefine* the political community within a given territory by creating a "new state" that rests on principles and procedures that are a sharp departure from those of the old regime.

The process of revolution generates two factors that affect international relations: new ideologies and new uncertainties.

Revolutionary leaders energize their supporters through revolutionary ideologies.

To this end, revolutionary ideologies tend to emphasize three key themes.

"ENEMIES ARE EVIL AND INCAPABLE OF REFORM"

Revolutionary groups usually portray their opponents as intrinsically evil and incapable of meaningful reform: if the current system is unjust and cannot improve, then efforts at compromise are doomed, leaving revolution as the only morally possible alternative. Lenin broke with the "Economists" in Russia and with Social Democrats like Karl Kautsky over the possibility of reforming tsarism and capitalism, and Mao Zedong told his followers that " 'imperialism is ferocious.' . . . [I]ts nature will never change, the imperialists will never lay down their butcher knives, . . . they will never become Buddhas."[2] Similarly, the Ayatolloh Khomeini opposed compromise with the Shah by warning Iranians that "if you give this fellow a breathing spell, neither Islam nor your country nor your family will be left for you. Do not give him the chance; squeeze his neck until he is strangled."[3] In each case reform and compromise were rejected in favor of a radical solution.

"VICTORY IS INEVITABLE"

Unless potential supporters believe their sacrifices will eventually bear fruit, a revolutionary movement will not get very far. Revolutionary ideologies are thus inherently optimistic: they invariably portray victory as inevitable despite what may appear to be the overwhelming odds against it. Furthermore, the ideology may reinforce this belief by invoking irresistible or divine forces to justify faith in victory. Marxists, for example, saw the "laws" of capitalist development as leading inexorably toward proletarian revolution and the emergence of socialism. Khomeini and his followers rested their optimism on religious faith. Revolutionaries may also invoke the successes of earlier movements to sustain confidence in their own efforts; thus, the Sandinistas saw Castro's victory in Cuba as evidence that their own efforts in Nicaragua could succeed.

Optimism can also be encouraged by depicting one's enemy as a paper tiger. Mao Zedong argued, for example, that "reactionaries" were "paper tigers" who "in appearance . . . are terrifying but in reality . . . are not so powerful," and Marshal Lin Biao asserted that "U.S. imperialism is stronger, but also more vulnerable, than any imperialism of the past."[4] Lenin's assessment of imperialism was similar: as the "highest stage of capitalism," imperialism contained both the power to dominate the globe *and* the seeds of its inevitable destruction at the hands of the proletariat.[5] The method is an obvious way to sustain commitment: however hopeless things appear to be, success is nevertheless assured if only the revolutionary forces persevere.

"OUR REVOLUTION HAS UNIVERSAL MEANING"

Although exceptions do exist (such as Kemalist Turkey, revolutionary Mexico, or the Meiji restoration in Japan), the ideologies of most revolutionary states contain strong "universalist" themes. Specifically, the principles of the revolution are believed to apply to other societies as well. In the extreme case, the ideology may go so far as to reject the nation-state as a legitimate political unit and call for the eventual elimination of the state-system itself.

During the French Revolution, for example, the pro-war faction led by Brissot de Warville called for a "universal crusade of human liberty," arguing that the "liberty of the entire world" was worth a few thousand deaths. Orthodox Marxists saw the "inevitable" triumph of socialism as a worldwide process that would bring about a classless, stateless commonwealth of peace. Chinese officials emphasized that "world revolution relies on the thought of Mao Tse-tung. . . . [It] belongs not only to China but also has its international implications." And Khomeini's version of Shiite theology foresaw the eventual establishment of a global Muslim community (*ummah*) following the abolition of the "un-Islamic" nation-state system.

That revolutionary ideologies tend to include universalist elements should not come as a surprise. Such views promise adherents an additional reward for their sacrifices: a revolution is good not only for one's own country, but it will be beneficial for others as well. Moreover, if the failures of the old regime are the result of external forces (such as "capitalist imperialism"), then action beyond one's own borders may be necessary to eliminate these evils once and for all. Finally, in order to attract popular support, revolutionary ideologies tend to portray new political ideas as self-evident truths—which creates a bias toward universalism. How, that is, can a self-evident political principle be valid for one group but not for others? Could the Jacobins argue that the Rights of Man applied only to Frenchmen? Could Marx's disciples in the Soviet Union claim that his "laws of history" were valid in Russia alone? Could the Iranian revolutionaries argue that an Islamic republic was essential for Persians but not for other Muslims?

These ideological themes are neither necessary nor sufficient conditions for revolutionary success, and one or more of these elements may be missing in certain cases. Still, it is hard to imagine a mass revolution succeeding without an ideological program that both justified revolt and gave participants some reason to believe they would win. Indeed, it is a striking fact that the ideological programs of revolutionary movements as varied as those of the American Founding Fathers, the Russian and Chinese communists, or the Iranian fundamentalists all incorporated variations on these three principles.

Despite the certainties expressed in revolutionary ideologies, revolutions actually increase the level of uncertainty in the international system. Such uncertainty raises the likelihood of war.

WHY REVOLUTIONARY STATES TEND TO ENTER CONFLICTS WITH OTHER STATES

Revolutionary states are prone to international conflicts for several reasons. First, a revolutionary regime will be unsure about the intentions of other states simply because it has little or no direct experience in dealing with them. Lacking direct evidence, it falls back on ideology, and, as discussed above, the ideology of most revolutionary movements portrays opponents as hostile. Thus, even a mild diplomatic dispute is likely to escalate and concessions may be viewed with suspicion, because conflict is seen as inevitable and because compromise is viewed as naïve or even dangerous.

Second, a revolutionary movement may harbor suspicions based on its own experience. Eager to redress past wrongs (as is often the case), the revolutionary movement will be especially wary of any foreign powers that it sees as responsible for them. Thus, Mao Zedong's suspicions of the United States were based in part on past Western interference in China, and revolutionary forces in Mexico, Nicaragua, and Iran were preoccupied with the possibility of U.S. intervention for much the same reason.

Under such circumstances revolutionary regimes tend to assume the worst about other states and to interpret ambiguous or inconsistent policies in a negative light: threats or signs of opposition confirm the hostile image, whereas concessions or signs of approval are seen as insincere gestures masking the opponent's true (hostile) intentions. And indeed, the policies of other states are virtually certain to be ambiguous, if only because it takes time for those states to decide how to respond to the new situation. This problem is compounded by the difficulty in understanding how a new political order works, by ignorance about the beliefs and background of the new regime, and by the absence of reliable information that accompanies a revolution. Even when foreign powers are not especially hostile, therefore, some of their actions and statements will reinforce the suspicions of the revolutionary regime.

Third, conflict is more likely if the elite (or a faction within it) exaggerates a foreign threat in order to improve its internal position, that is, by rallying nationalist support for the new leaders or to justify harsh measures against internal opponents. Such efforts are especially effective when there is some truth to the accusations, for example, if foreign powers had been allied with the old regime and if they are clearly suspicious of the new government. This tactic can be dangerous if it magnifies a conflict that might otherwise have been avoided or minimized. The risk can be contained, however, if the revolutionary elite remains aware that it is engaging in a purely domestic gambit, so that its actual policy decisions are based on its true assessment of others' intentions rather than on the myth it has manufactured.

But maintaining such fine control is difficult. Although their creators may know that these are myths, the campaign may be so convincing that it becomes the basis for policy. Moreover, efforts to enhance domestic support by exaggerating external threats can be self-fulfilling: if foreign powers do not recognize the real motive behind such a campaign, they may take the revolutionary state's accusations and threats seriously. And if they then react defensively—as one would expect—it will merely confirm the bellicose image that others already hold.

WHY REVOLUTIONARY STATES ARE INSECURE BUT OVERCONFIDENT

To begin with, the inherent optimism of most revolutionary ideologies can encourage them to overstate their military capabilities. Thus, the Brissotin faction that led France to war in 1792 argued that the Revolution had created a power that would crush its enemies easily. As Brissot told the National Assembly: "Every advantage is on our side, for now every Frenchman is a willing soldier! . . . [W]here is the power on earth . . . who could hope to master six million free soldiers?" This sort of argument is difficult to challenge without appearing unpatriotic; if opponents are destined for the "ash-heap of history," expressing doubts about the certainty of victory betrays a lack of confidence in the revolution itself.

The optimism of revolutionary states also rests on the belief that citizens in other countries will rise up to support them. This hope reflects the universalism common to many revolutionary ideologies and implies that their opponents, lacking popular support, will be unable to fight effectively. The Brissotins used this argument to great effect: Brissot claimed that "each soldier will say to his enemy: Brother, I am not going to cut your throat, I am going to show you the way to happiness." And his associate Maximin Isnard predicted that "at the moment that the enemy armies begin to fight with ours, the daylight of philosophy will open their eyes and the peoples will embrace each other in the face of their dethroned tyrants and an approving heaven and earth."[6] Many Bolsheviks believed similarly that their success in Russia would spark the long-anticipated revolution in Germany and a cascade of upheavals in the rest of Europe. Even Lenin, who had rejected this view in 1917, supported the Russian invasion of Poland in 1920 because he believed it would trigger an uprising by socialist forces there. Mao's claim that "a single spark can ignite a prairie fire" conveys a similar faith in the catalytic effects of revolutionary action. Thus, the overconfidence of revolutionary states is fueled by the faith that the irresistible spread of revolutionary ideas will undermine their opponents.

Revolutionary states can be further misled if they give too much credence to the testimony of foreign sympathizers. The latter, desirous of external support, are prone to exaggerate the prospects for revolution back home. In 1792, for example, the National Assembly in Paris was bombarded with optimistic reports from foreign emissaries claiming that their countrymen cried out for liberation and that the old regime would collapse quickly if attacked.

Furthermore, successful revolutionary leaders may be convinced that they can triumph over seemingly impossible odds. The strength of this factor is likely to be affected by the ease or difficulty with which the revolutionary struggle was waged. The unexpected collapse of royal authority in France may have encouraged the Brissotins in their belief that their ideas would attract universal acceptance, just as the relative ease of Castro's final campaign against Batista convinced Che Guevara and others that revolutionary forces in Latin America could triumph even when conditions were unfavorable. By contrast, both Lenin and Mao tempered their optimistic proclamations with repeated warnings that revolutions must be conducted cautiously. Mao explicitly warned his followers to avoid both "right deviations" (passivity and fear of struggle) and "left deviations" (overconfident recklessness). Similarly, although Lenin was optimistic about the long-term prospects for world revolution, once in power he usually rejected direct efforts to promote this end. In his 1920 pamphlet " 'Left-Wing' Communism: An Infantile Disorder," he warned against ill-timed efforts to seize power, and his speech to the Second Comintern Congress in the same year emphasized long-range revolutionary prospects rather than immediate efforts to foment revolutionary upheaval in other countries. Having personally led prolonged revolutionary struggles, both Lenin and Mao had learned that success was often elusive and never easy.

This discussion suggests that revolutionary states are more likely to resist impetuous efforts to export the revolution if the leadership is experienced and unified and the movement highly disciplined. Thus, the Soviet Union and the People's Republic of China behaved prudently in most cases, despite their inherently optimistic ideologies and the fact that prominent members of both regimes favored a more assertive approach. By contrast, the factional infighting in France and Iran encouraged extremists to use foreign policy—and specifically support for the export of revolution—as a litmus test for devotion to the revolution itself. In the absence of a strong central authority, those who opposed such a policy risked appearing disloyal to the universalist ideals of the revolution and thus could not contain those who advocated a more aggressive foreign policy. The radicals in turn were overconfident regarding their ability to export the revolution and to overcome the opposition such efforts were certain to provoke.

Finally, and somewhat paradoxically, the very vulnerability of a revolutionary state may create additional incentive for aggression. Already fearful that their hold on power is fragile, revolutionary leaders view domestic opponents as a potential fifth column. (In light of foreign support for counterrevolutionary groups in France, the White armies in Russia, the Kuomintang in China, and the *contras* in Nicaragua, such worries are hardly fanciful.) Exporting the revolution by striking first may be seen as the only way to preserve power at home: unless opposing states are swiftly overthrown, the argument runs, they will eventually combine to crush the revolutionary state. Thus, the Bolsheviks who advocated greater efforts to export the revolution did so in part because they believed that capitalist states would join forces and destroy the new Soviet state unless they were swiftly overthrown by the spread of socialism. (At a minimum, the revolutionaries may hope that the mere threat of revolutionary subversion may deter attacks and force opponents to adopt more conciliatory policies.) This general argument was also a potent ingredient in the Brissotin recipe for war in 1792. After describing France as beset by a conspiracy of foreign powers and internal traitors, Brissot told the Assembly, "It is not merely necessary to think of defense, the [counterrevolutionary] attack must be anticipated; you yourselves must attack."[7]

WHY FOREIGN POWERS ARE INSECURE BUT OVERCONFIDENT

Other states will fear the spread of revolutionary ideas—especially when those ideas challenge their own form of government directly. But they also tend to view this as an easy problem to solve. To begin with, the disorder that accompanies a revolution encourages other states to view the new regime as weak and vulnerable. For example, most Europeans believed that the Revolution had reduced French power considerably, leading Edmund Burke to describe the French as "the ablest architects of ruin . . . in the world." When war broke out in 1792, both France and its opponents expected an easy campaign. Where the French deputies believed that "despotism was in its death throes and a prompt attack will precipitate its final agony," a Prussian diplomat commented that "France is without disciplined armies, without experienced generals, without money, and the highest degree of anarchy reigns in all departments." Another official predicted that "the comedy will not last long. The French army of lawyers will be annihilated in Belgium and we shall be home by the autumn." As T. C. W. Blanning remarks, "With all three combatants believing their side to be invincible and their opponent(s) to be on the verge of collapse, the scene was set for the final lurch into war."[8]

This tendency to overestimate the vulnerability of the revolutionary state is not surprising, given the inherent difficulty of calculating its ability to fight. By definition, revolutionary states rest on novel forms of social organization, and revolutionary movements succeed because they devise a formula for mobilizing previously untapped sources of social power. Unfortunately, the novelty of these institutions makes it difficult for others to assess their effect on national capabilities. As Clausewitz recognized, it was not surprising that the European states underestimated the military power of revolutionary France, because in large part it was based on ideas and institutions—best exemplified by the levée en masse—that were previously unknown. Similar problems led outsiders to expect the rapid collapse of Bolshevik power and prevented an accurate assessment of Iran's military potential after the revolution there. Ideological biases may compound this tendency because states based on different political principles may find it difficult to believe that a revolutionary government could be popular or effective. This problem seems to have affected U.S. perceptions of China, for example. Because U.S. leaders believed that communism was illegitimate and immoral, they saw Mao's government as an artificial Soviet satellite rather than as an independent regime commanding substantial popular support. Thus, Assistant Secretary of State Dean Rusk believed that China's "foreign masters" had forced it to intervene in Korea and that Mao's regime was "a colonial Russian government. . . . [I]t is not Chinese."[9] The belief that a revolutionary state is inherently unpopular inclines status quo powers to exaggerate their own ability to confront it successfully.

Foreign powers also exaggerate the threat of subversion because the appeal of revolutionary ideas is impossible to measure in advance and the extent to which they are spreading is difficult to determine. Having witnessed an unexpected revolutionary upheaval, mindful of the confident proclamations of the revolutionary forces, and aware that some members of their own society may harbor similar ideas, other states overstate the threat of contagion. Thus, Burke saw revolutionary France as a mortal danger because "it has by its essence a faction of opinion and of interest and of enthusiasm in every country. . . . Thus advantaged, if it can at all exist it must finally prevail." For Burke, the only option was to eliminate the source of infection. In a similar vein Winston Churchill justified the Anglo-French intervention after the Bolshevik Revolution by describing the new Soviet republic as "a plague-bearing Russia . . . of armed hordes not only smiting with bayonet and cannon, but accompanied and preceded by swarms of typhus-bearing vermin." The main threat was ideological subversion: "to make soldiers mutiny, . . . to raise the poor against the bourgeois, . . . the workmen against the employers, . . . the peasants against the landowners, to paralyze the country by general strikes."[10] Although Churchill's pleas for full-scale intervention were ultimately rejected, "the decisive factor in bringing about a continuation of . . . limited [Allied] intervention [after World War I] was the fear . . . that Bolshevism . . . might spread to other European countries."[11] Similar fears accompanied the Chinese, Cuban, and Iranian revolutions as well. The universalism of most revolutionary ideologies compounds these worries, because other states fear a growing alliance of revolutionary powers that would leave them increasingly isolated in a hostile ideological sea.

Even in the absence of evidence that the revolution is spreading, other states cannot be completely confident that subversive movements do not lurk beneath the surface. European fears of a Jacobin conspiracy and the U.S. Red scares of the 1920s and the 1950s illustrate the tendency for foreign powers to exaggerate the ideological appeal (and therefore the offensive power) of revolutionary states. Because the threat these states pose is not simply a function of material capabilities, revolutions often seem even more dangerous than they are. And the same logic applies in reverse to counterrevolutions. Even when there is no hard evidence, a revolutionary regime cannot be completely certain that foreign powers are not conspiring with its internal opponents.

The tendency to exaggerate the threat from a revolutionary regime and its susceptibility to pressure from outside is also exacerbated by testimony from self-interested émigrés, who, as one would expect, portray the revolutionary state as both a dangerous adversary and a disorganized, unpopular, and vulnerable target. R. R. Palmer has shown, for example, that the belief that revolutionary France headed a vast international conspiracy was a myth manufactured by counterrevolutionary ideologues, several of whom were prominent in émigré circles. According to Nita Renfrew, Iraq's invasion of Iran was encouraged by Iranian émigrés who exaggerated the unpopularity and military weakness of Khomeini's regime. Cuban and Nicaraguan émigrés fed U.S. fears of Castro and the Sandinistas, while encouraging the belief that these regimes would collapse once the United States applied pressure. The warning should be clear: reliance upon "evidence" either from counterrevolutionary émigrés or from prorevolutionary sympathizers is likely to entangle one or both of the adversaries in a destabilizing web of fear and overconfidence.

Taken together, the possibility of revolutionary expansion and the belief in revolutionary weakness create strong pressures for war. Because revolutionary states tend to grow stronger over time, their opponents have a temporary "window of opportunity." Thus, England's decision to enter the war against France in 1793 was based in part on Prime Minister Pitt's belief that war was inevitable and the sooner it was begun the better. Similarly, Iraq attacked Iran in 1979 because it feared the spread of Shiite fundamentalism and because it believed the revolution had weakened Iran's military capabilities. The Somali invasion of Ethiopia in 1977 reflected the belief that Ethiopia's revolutionary government was beset by internal divisions. And U.S. efforts to overthrow Castro in Cuba and the Sandinistas in Nicaragua were justified on the grounds that each would promote revolution elsewhere in Latin America and that it would be easiest to eliminate them before they had the opportunity to consolidate their positions. In all of these cases, the belief that delay would make the job more difficult encouraged opponents of the revolutionary state to take action.

To summarize: revolutions exert far-reaching effects on the balance of threats. Each side tends to view the other as a serious challenge, yet neither can estimate the danger accurately. Lacking reliable information about the magnitude of the threat or their ability to overcome it, both sides are therefore more susceptible to self-interested testimony from émigrés or from other revolutionaries, particularly when this advice confirms preexisting beliefs. Thus, on the one hand, each side fears the other, and on the other hand, each is also likely to believe that the threat can be eliminated at relatively low cost. In short, the belief that opponents are both hostile and vulnerable works in support of a policy of preventive and preemptive war.

WHY BOTH SIDES ARE WRONG

When a revolution topples an apparently viable regime, it is not surprising that other states fear that they might be next. Similarly, if the revolutionary state has suffered extensive damage and faces continued internal opposition, its leaders have reason to fear that their success will be short-lived. Yet revolutions are a relatively poor export commodity, and although counterrevolutionary efforts face somewhat better prospects, efforts to reverse a revolution from outside are usually more difficult than their advocates anticipate. Ironically, then, both sides' perceptions of threat are usually mistaken.

Contrary to the optimistic visions of the Brissotins, for example, the outbreak of war in 1792 did not spark sympathetic rebellions across Europe. To be sure, revolutionary France eventually established a set of "satellite republics" across Europe, and Napoleon expanded this to a sizable if short-lived empire. But these conquests were not the swift and bloodless victories that the Brissotins predicted, nor was the collapse of the monarchy the catalyst for world revolution that conservatives like Edmund Burke feared. Few people anticipated that the outbreak of war in 1792 was the beginning of a quarter century of bloody struggle; neither France nor its various opponents were as easy to defeat as both sides had assumed. Similarly, the Bolshevik Revolution failed to inspire other successes; attempts elsewhere in Europe were abortive. The spread of communism was still nearly three decades off, when the Soviet army imposed similar regimes in Eastern Europe following Germany's defeat in the Second World War. And contrary to the recurring fears that communist revolution would spread swiftly around the globe, containing the Red menace was in fact relatively easy.

Other cases teach similar lessons. The Mexican Revolution had little impact on revolutionary struggles elsewhere in Latin America; Cuba's efforts to promote revolutionary change in the region have been relatively unsuccessful. (True, Cuba was a source of inspiration, advice, and material aid for the Sandinistas in Nicaragua, and for other revolutionaries as well, but a single, short-lived success hardly constitutes a winning record after more than thirty years.) And although fundamentalist movements have become more active throughout the Muslim world, Iran's efforts to export its principles to other countries have proved equally abortive. Irrespective of its specific ideological character, in short, there seems to be little basis for the perennial hope and fear of world revolution.

At the same time, the belief that revolutionary regimes will collapse if attacked is equally dubious. In virtually every case of a major social revolution (France, Mexico, Russia,

China, Cuba, Nicaragua, Iran) opponents have argued that foreign intervention could remove the threat at relatively low cost. With the partial exception of Nicaragua, efforts to do so were uniformly unsuccessful. While counterrevolutions from abroad do on occasion succeed, on the whole, the ability of revolutionary states to resist such attempts is striking.

This argument does not mean that the fears harbored by revolutionary states and other powers are groundless. Rather, it means that the threat is usually exaggerated, as is the ease with which it can be eliminated. If the respective fears and hopes were accurate, the struggle would be a swift and decisive triumph for the stronger side. But instead of a wave of revolutionary upheavals or the swift collapse of the new regime, the typical result is either a brief and inconclusive clash (e.g., the Russo-Polish War of 1920) or a protracted and bloody struggle (e.g., the wars of the French Revolution, the Iran-Iraq War, the *contra* war in Nicaragua).

Why are revolutions hard to export and why do foreign interventions fail? First, the universalist rhetoric of revolutionary ideologies notwithstanding, a revolution is first and foremost a *national* phenomenon. A campaign to export a revolution would immediately bring the revolutionary state into conflict with the national loyalties of the intended recipients. And the principle that people who conceive of themselves as a nation are entitled to their own independent state has consistently proved to be a far more powerful social force than any notion of universal revolutionary solidarity. Foreign populations are likely to view efforts to export a revolution as acts of aggression, which makes it easier for the ruling elites to resist the revolutionary forces. Or as Robespierre warned in response to the optimistic predictions of the Brissotins: "No one likes an armed missionary, and no more extravagant idea ever sprang from the head of a politician than to suppose that one people has only to enter another's territory with arms in its hands to make the latter adopt its laws and its Constitution."[12] Moreover, even if conditions in other countries are broadly similar to the circumstances that produced one revolution (and they frequently are not), the special circumstances that enabled one revolution to succeed are unlikely to exist elsewhere. Thus, exporting the revolution is much more difficult than the revolutionaries expect.

Second, a revolution serves as a warning to other states: the more dangerous it appears, the greater the tendency for others to balance against it. Until a revolution actually occurs, other states may not take the possibility seriously. But once the danger has been demonstrated, potential victims will take steps to avoid a similar fate (e.g., through defensive alliances, internal reforms, or more extensive repression). Thus, the Cuban revolution inspired the U.S. Alliance for Progress in Latin America (intended to forestall additional "Cubas" by promoting economic and political development) and encouraged Latin American oligarchies to suppress their domestic opponents more vigorously. Similarly, the Iranian Revolution united Iraq, Saudi Arabia, and the other Gulf states against the danger of revolutionary infection, with tacit or active support from the United States and others. Again, the point is not that revolutions pose no danger; the point is, rather, that other states can and will do a variety of things to contain the threat.

Efforts to export counterrevolutions fail for somewhat different reasons. Revolutionary leaders are usually dedicated, highly motivated individuals who have been successful precisely because they are good at organizing support in the face of impressive obstacles. They are likely to be formidable adversaries, because they can direct those same skills toward mobilizing the nation for war. It is thus no accident that the French levée en masse and the Soviet Red Army were able to defeat their internal and external opponents or that revolutionary Iran managed to rebuild its military power with remarkable speed after the Iraqi invasion in 1980.

Foreign interventions also fail because they provide the domestic legitimacy that a revolutionary regime needs: the same nationalist convictions that make revolution hard to export also work against successful foreign intervention. The Russo-Polish War of 1920 illustrates both tendencies nicely: the initial Polish invasion helped mobilize public support for the Bolsheviks while the Red Army's subsequent counterattack aroused the traditional anti-Russian nationalism of the Poles rather than the proletarian uprising anticipated by Lenin.

The pressure for war produced by a revolution results from two parallel myths: the belief that the revolution will spread rapidly if it is not crushed immediately, and the belief that a reversal of the revolution will be easy to accomplish. Contrary to these expectations, however, is the more typical result: neither a tide of worldwide revolution nor the quick and easy ouster of the revolutionary regime but rather a prolonged struggle between an unexpectedly capable revolutionary regime and its surprisingly resistant adversaries.

REFERENCES

1. Note the following death tolls in modern revolutions: Russia, 500,000 dead; China, 3 million; Cuba, 5,000; Iran, 17,000; Mexico, 250,000; Nicaragua, between 30,000 and 50,000. See Small and Singer (1982).
2. Mao Zedong (1961), p. 428.
3. Quoted in Arjomand (1988), p. 102.
4. See Van Ness (1970), pp. 40–41; and Lin Biao, "Long Live Victory in the People's War," in Griffith (1966), p. 101.
5. See V. I. Lenin, *Imperialism: The Highest Stage of Capitalism,* in Lenin (1970), p. 675.
6. These quotations are from Schama (1989), p. 597; and Blanning (1986), pp. 108–110.
7. Brissot, quoted in Clapham (1969), p. 115.
8. Blanning (1986), pp. 78–80, 115–116.
9. Schaller (1979), p. 125.
10. Quoted in Fiddick (1990), pp. 4–5.
11. Chamberlin (1965), 2:152.
12. He continued: "The Declaration of Rights [of Man] is not like the sun's rays, which in one moment illumine the whole earth: it is no thunderbolt, to strike down a thousand thrones. It is easier to inscribe it on paper, or engrave it on brass, than to retrace its sacred characters in the hearts of men." Quoted in Thompson (1935), p. 207.

THE IMPACT OF REVOLUTION ON SOCIAL WELFARE IN LATIN AMERICA

Susan Eckstein

In this detailed study, Eckstein examines the progress made both in countries that did have revolutions (Mexico, Cuba, Bolivia, Peru) and in comparable countries that did not have revolutions (Brazil, the Dominican Republic, Colombia, and Ecuador) in the areas of inequality, land reform, economic growth, and social welfare.

Eckstein makes four major points. First, the outcome of a revolution may depend on what kind of revolution has occurred: from above or below, capitalist or socialist. Second, both those countries that have had revolutions and those that have not are constrained by their position in the world-economy and their own internal resources. Therefore, the economic course of events may be similar in countries with similar positions in the world economy whether or not a revolution has occurred. For example, although Mexico has made greater progress than Brazil on land reform, largely due to the Mexican Revolution, both countries, in trying to industrialize from a semi-peripheral position in the world economy, have had similar experiences in economic growth, inequality, and social welfare. Third, socialist revolutions allow certain options that may not be open in countries whose postrevolutionary regimes remain capitalist. Thus Cuba, although its performance in economic growth since the revolution has been weak, been able to provide a much higher level of routine health care than most Latin American nations. Eckstein suggests that this is possible because Cuba's health care system does not operate as a private-sector, profit-making endeavor; therefore it can place a greater emphasis on such low-profit activities as routine and preventive medical care. Fourth, in all the revolutions studied, whether capitalist or socialist, peasants benefited most in the decades immediately following the revolution, when the new government was being consolidated and needed popular support. Later, the pursuit of industrialization tended to increase inequality and to turn the government away from peasant concerns.

A variety of different factors thus influence the outcomes of revolutions, and affect how countries that have experienced revolutions differ from those that have not.

How do postrevolutionary societies differ from societies with no revolutionary history? What variations are there in the outcomes of revolutions associated with different class alliances and different modes of production, and of revolutions occurring in countries with different resource bases? This essay examines the specific effects of four revolutions on social welfare standards in Latin America: Mexico (1910), Bolivia (1952), Cuba (1959), and Peru (1968).

These countries which experienced revolutions were integrated into the world economy under the Spanish Colonial empire. The *conquistadores* reorganized the indigenous agricultural economies into *latifundios* and established mining enclaves. With imported slaves, they made Cuba a major sugar exporter. Despite a common colonial heritage, the political economies of these four countries differed in important respects at the time of their respective upheavals. In comparison to the other countries Mexico had a more diversified and developed economy. It had a network of roads and railroads, industries, an agricultural base that could support an urban population, and an educated "middle class." By contrast, Bolivia, at the time of its revolution, had one of the poorest and least developed economies on the continent. It had the second lowest GDP (Gross Domestic Product) and the third lowest GDP per capita in South America, and only one other South American country had a manufacturing sector contributing a smaller share to GDP than Bolivia's. A small tin- and land-based oligarchy ruled the country. Its mine sector, which employed about 3% of the labor force, operated as an enclave oriented toward the export market. Most Bolivians lived humbly off the land, primarily as tenant-farmers and share-croppers; in 1952 they still retained much of their pre-Columbian heritage. Peru, like Bolivia, had a large Indian population in the highlands associated with *latifundios.* But by the 1960s its coastal farms employed wage labor, and its industrial base and export sector were more developed and diversified than Bolivia's. Cuba was the only one of the four countries to have an agricultural economy that was heavily capitalized and dominated by foreign companies. By Latin American standards its industrial base was also well developed at the time Castro seized power.

All four countries experienced revolutions in the sense that political groups assumed control of the state apparatus through extralegal means, and, at least in the countryside, destroyed the economic base of the then dominant class so as to restructure class relations somewhat. Peru experienced a "revolution *from above*" in that the extralegal takeover and the initiation of the social transformation were organized and led by high-level state functionaries with negligible mass participation. Peru's revolution was initiated by General Velasco Alvarado, the army's top-ranking officer. After usurping power by a *coup d'etat,* he used the powers of the state to obliterate the rural property base of the oligarchy, to expropriate foreign-owned companies in the export sector, and to modify social relations and ownership in part of agriculture and industry.

Mexico, Bolivia, and Cuba, on the other hand, experienced "revolutions *from below.*" The three upheavals began as "middle class" reform movements for free elections and enforcement of electoral results, but the destruction of the *anciens regimes* rested on peasant and worker rebellions. In Cuba the nationalization of most of the economy eliminated the capitalist class and most of the independent petty bourgeoisie. In contrast, in Mexico and Bolivia, as well as in Peru, even though the state's role in the economy increased, opportunities also were created for nationally oriented bourgeoisie and petty bourgeoisie in private enterprise.

Thus the four cases involve: (1) revolutions from "above" and "below"; (2) revolutions instituting socialist and capitalist modes of production based, respectively, on state and private ownership of most of the economy, and (3) revolutions occurring in countries at different levels of economic development and in countries differently integrated into the world economy.

No study has systematically explored what impact these three variables have on outcomes of revolutions. Yet each is likely to be important, for different reasons. The role of the three forces can be formulated as hypotheses, and cross-national patterns that would verify each can be specified. After a formulation of the hypotheses will follow a discussion of the specific welfare measures on which I focus.

Hypothesis I: Postrevolutionary social welfare developments are shaped by the position of countries within the *world economy*.

World economy theory suggests that countries' relative position in the world economy limits their possibilities after revolution. According to Wallerstein,[1] there exists a single, capitalist world economy. Wallerstein also claims that countries' productive and political strength and their capacity to appropriate surplus vary with their core, semi-peripheral, or peripheral status within the world economy. Core countries are strongest and peripheral states weakest, but semi-peripheral countries have considerable potential, especially during periods of economic downturn (including the current one) to increase their share of the world surplus. He recognizes that revolutions may help countries modify their role in the world economy, but he views prospects for less developed countries as not very great, especially in the periphery.

If Wallerstein is correct, developments after revolution should differ in the *periphery* and *semi-periphery* because the two sets of countries assume different roles within the world economy, and accordingly have different resources available for internal use. Other analysts also distinguish between countries with different productive resources, but they view development from a national, not a global point of view. To test the world economy thesis I will trace, where possible, the relationship between internal and global processes. Wallerstein's criteria for classifying countries are not well defined, but Bolivia, with one of the poorest and least diversified economies and one of the most unstable governments in Latin America, was without question peripheral in 1952. Mexico had a growing industrial sector (largely foreign owned) and a strong, stable government at the eve of its revolution. While it was one of the economically most developed Latin American countries at the time, it probably still constituted part of the "periphery." By the time of the other revolutions, however, it had developed to the point of inclusion in the "semi-periphery." Peru and Cuba are more difficult to categorize; they had "peripheral" and "semi-peripheral" characteristics when their respective *anciens regimes* collapsed, although neither had so large an economy as Mexico. When Castro came to power Cuba's manufacturing sector accounted for as large a share of the national product as Mexico's then did. Yet its economy was exceptionally tied to the export of a single agricultural commodity, sugar, and much of its industrial production was sugar-related. Because of its extreme dependence on a single export item, and on one for which international demand varied greatly from year to year, it was limited in its capacity to influence world relations in its favor. Peru's export sector was more diversified than Cuba's and its economy was more productive and developed than Bolivia's. By the 1950's, then, we would class Mexico as semi-peripheral, Bolivia as peripheral, with Cuba and Peru in the middle, having some peripheral and some semi-peripheral characteristics. The world economy thesis thus would lead us to expect qualitatively different patterns in Mexico and Bolivia by the time of the upheaval in the latter. It would also lead us to expect postrevolutionary development possibilities in Cuba and Peru to be similar in important respects, despite their contrasting dominant modes of economic organization.

Hypothesis II: Postrevolutionary social welfare developments are shaped by the *class base* of insurrections.

Another line of argument suggests that outcomes of upheavals depend on which groups partake in the overthrow of the *anciens regimes*. Elites involved in "revolutions from above" might use state power to advance interests of classes other than their own, but if the socioeconomic base of political movements matters, peasants and workers should share more in the fruits of victory when they actively participate in insurrections; that is, peasants and workers should benefit more from "revolutions from below" than from "revolutions from above." If the class base of upheavals affects subsequent societal development, peasants and workers in the three countries experiencing "revolutions from below," Mexico, Bolivia, and Cuba, should enjoy benefits unavailable to their counterparts in Peru; Peru is the only one of the four countries to have had a "revolution from above."

Hypothesis III: Postrevolutionary social welfare developments are shaped by the *dominant mode of production* instituted, and the *form of property ownership* associated with it.

According to this third line of argument, the dominant mode of production should have a decisive effect on societal developments after revolution. Governments in societies based primarily on *capitalist* and *socialist* organizing principles, that is, on *private* and *state* ownership of the economy, may be equally committed to development and distributive goals, but the former may be constrained in ways that the latter are not. When private ownership is the rule, governments must provide sufficient incentive to induce individuals and corporations to invest locally. They therefore cannot readily implement policies favoring labor at the expense of capital. Because socialist regimes assume direct responsibility for production and accumulation, they are not faced with the same constraint. In principle, they are better able to award workers a bigger share of the product of their labor than are governments in capitalist societies. In practice, however, their allocative policies are likely to depend on trade-offs between consumption and investment. If the main form of ownership has a significant bearing on developments after revolution, then we should find major differences between Cuba on the one hand, and Mexico, Bolivia, and Peru on the other hand. Cuba, as noted above, is the only one of the four countries to have socialized ownership of most of the economy.

A problem arises in attempting to assess the relative importance of the three sets of factors in the countries under study: the upheavals occurred in different years. Consequently, differences among the countries could reflect different global conditions at the time of the outbreak of each, and the different time lapses since each transformation occurred. For this reason, a fourth hypothesis will be considered.

Hypothesis IV: The *historical epoch* in which revolutions occurred and the *time lapse* since the upheavals affect postrevolutionary social welfare options.

The timing of the revolution might be important for two reasons. First, at different historical junctures, options for revolutionary regimes might vary. The capacity and desire of powerful global and domestic forces to resist change is likely to depend on the international economic and political environment. Powerful nations would be unlikely to intervene when their economies are in recession and when they are engaged in major wars elsewhere in the world. Second, social welfare outcomes might vary over time, for the longer the time lapse since upheavals, the more opportunity revolutionary processes have had to be played out. But time also permits nonrevolutionary and counterrevolutionary forces to assert themselves and to redirect the course of revolutions. Were the longevity factor important, the impact of revolution should be most apparent in Mexico, and least apparent in Peru, as the time lapse is *longest* since the Mexican insurrection and *shortest* since the Peruvian. Because longevity might erode revolutionary accomplishments, trends in each country must be watched over time. Developments after revolution do not necessarily evolve in a linear manner.

The differences among these societies can be summarized as follows:

	Mexico	Bolivia	Cuba	Peru
Hypothesis I: Position in World Economy/Level of Development				
semi-peripheral/most developed	X			
peripheral and semi-peripheral characteristics/medium level development			X	X
peripheral/least developed		X		
Hypothesis II: Class Base of Upheavals				
revolutions from above				X
revolutions from below	X	X	X	
Hypothesis III: Dominant Ownership Pattern				
capitalist	X	X		X
socialist			X	
Hypothesis IV: Longevity				
long time lapse	X			
medium time lapse		X	X	
short time lapse				X

TABLE 1

GDP per capita, manufacturing share of GDP, and main export as % of total exports in selected years

GDP per capita (in constant dollars of 1980)

	BOLIVIA	EQUADOR	PERU	COLOMBIA	CUBA	DOMINICAN REPUBLIC	MEXICO	BRAZIL
1950	423	415	604	470	851	423	710	478
1955	406	465	731	519	876	489	810	566
1960	383	499	808	479	887	518	907	651
1965	393	549	951	577	921	524	1095	736
1970	477	597	1014	647	867	646	1306	924
1975	560	764	1141	754	1158	861	1460	1341
1980	568	1040	1101	922	1455	960	1863	1652

Manufacturing share of GDP (%)

	BOLIVIA	EQUADOR	PERU	COLOMBIA	CUBA	DOMINICAN REPUBLIC	MEXICO	BRAZIL
1950	15	16	15	16	na	17	21	20
1955	18	15	15	15	22	15	21	22
1960	14	14	18	18	45	17	19	18
1965	15	15	20	20	43	14	21	17
1970	13	18	21	18	48	17	23	25
1976	14	19	23	19	41	17	24	26

Main export as % of total exports

	BOLIVIA	EQUADOR	PERU	COLOMBIA	CUBA	DOMINICAN REPUBLIC	MEXICO	BRAZIL
1955	67	55	25	84	80	39	29	59
1960	81	62	17	72	79	49	21	56
1965	85	51	23	64	86	49	19	44
1970	57	57	28	64	77	45	9	34
1975	39	57	23	46	89	65	16	15

The longevity factor, in addition, raises a more general problem: how to assess which developments are byproducts of the class transformations, and which might have occurred in the absence of revolution. This problem is addressed by comparing developments in the four countries with developments during the same time period in societies that did not have revolutions. As shown in Table 1, each of the countries will be compared with the Latin American country it best resembled at the eve of its upheaval. Bolivia will be compared with Ecuador, Peru with Colombia, Cuba with the Dominican Republic (DR), and Mexico with Brazil. The rationale for the paired comparisons can also be formulated as an hypothesis:

Hypothesis V: As a result of changes in the class structure and class relations, *social welfare developments differ in societies that have and have not had revolutions.*

The specific aspects of social welfare on which this study focuses are land ownership, income, and health care and nutrition.*

Land Distribution

In societies where much of the population is involved in agriculture, land ownership constitutes an important component of social welfare. Consequently, land distribution patterns in the countries under study are analyzed, including how and why distribution patterns changed since the respective upheavals.

If land rights were a concern of the rural labor force, and if the class base of political transformations has a decisive bearing on revolutionary outcomes, then the Mexican, Bolivian, and Cuban "revolutions from below" should have resulted in a more widespread redistribution of land than Peru's "revolution from above." If, however, the dominant mode of production is the primary factor affecting land distribution, land redistribution should be greater in Cuba than in the other countries. Should world economic linkages further affect how production is organized and property distributed in agriculture, then land ownership patterns should change in the four postrevolutionary societies provided that profits from trade can thereby be increased.

In addition, the timing of the upheavals might affect land allocations. First, land reforms might take time to implement. If so, the most land should have been distributed in Mexico and the least in Peru. Second, land policies might be shaped by *general* global political and economic trends. There might for example be little resistance to reforms implemented when there is a world depression and when industry becomes a leading economic sector (especially if large landowners have diversified into industry). Comparisons between the matched countries will help us ascertain whether general historical trends are shaping land policies independently of forces associated with the revolutions.

As indicated in Table 2 (on page 270), land ownership was highly concentrated before the respective upheavals. Mexico had the highest GINI index† value of land concentration on the continent, even twenty years after the demise of its *ancien regime*. Bolivia had the second highest index of land concentration at the eve of its revolution, and Peru scored only slightly lower. Ownership in Cuba was least concentrated; by regional standards it was moderate. At the eve of the mexican upheaval less than 3% of Mexican landholders owned more than 90% of the productive land. The proportion held by Mexican peasants had declined in the late nineteenth century, after the Porfirio Diaz administration encouraged large surveying companies and private businessmen to purchase or appropriate land traditionally held by peasant communities. In 1950 in Bolivia, 6% of the landowners held 92% of the land, and in pre-Velasco Peru about 2% of the Peruvian farmowners monopolized 69% of the farmland. In prerevolutionary Cuba, 8% of the farm population controlled 71% of the land.

---

*Figures presented throughout this essay should be viewed as approximations. They undoubtedly contain a margin of error.
†The GINI index measures inequality on a scale from 0 to 1: 0 is complete equality; 1 is extreme inequality.

TABLE 2

GINI index values for land ownership concentration

Mexico (1930)	0.96	Peur (1950)	0.88
Brazil (1950)	0.84	Colombia (1960)	0.86
Bolivia (1950)	0.94	Cuba (1945)	0.79
Ecuador (1950)	0.86	Dominican Republic (1950)	0.79

All four countries announced land reforms shortly after their respective political upheavals. The land reforms transformed rural class relations, encouraged efficient land use, and ushered in more equitable land distributions. They reduced the number of large privately owned farm units and the portion of the land area held by private farmers. Between the latest prerevolutionary and the latest postrevolutionary year for which there are data, the private land area in large farms changed most in Cuba, least in Bolivia. In Bolivia the large farms of the landed oligarchy were broken up soon after the promulgation of the agrarian reform, but subsequently big tracts were awarded to market-oriented producers. The privately held land in independently-owned farms of 1000 or more hectares dropped from 92% to 65% in Bolivia, from 69% to 42% in Peru, and from 82% (in 1923, after the breakdown of the *ancien regime* but before widespread land distribution) to 32% in Mexico. In Cuba most holdings over 67 hectares were outlawed after 1963. Consequently, by 1967 approximately 5% of the land in private farms was in units over 67 hectares, and by 1981 only about 9% of the arable land on the island remained in private hands.

Still, the land reforms did not resolve the problem of *minifundismo*; plots of less than 5 hectares are considered "sub-family" in size. Since the respective upheavals the proportion of farm units with 5 hectares or less increased in Mexico and Cuba (though it decreased between 1950 and 1960 in Mexico); in Bolivia the proportion declined by less than 3%. No data are available on Peru. *Minifundismo* becomes especially problematic when successive generations of land reform beneficiaries subdivide already small parcels.

Yet even when the revolutions did not resolve the problem of *minifundismo,* they outlawed seignorial obligations and in so doing modified agrarian class relations. While agrarian property and class relations changed in all four countries as a result of their revolutions, in no country did all rural laborers gain access to land. The main beneficiaries of land reform have been the permanent workers on expropriated estates. The percentage of farm families without land has varied in each country over the years, depending on population growth, migration, and the extent to which the government has distributed new land. The percentage of farm families who are either *minifundistas* or landless farm laborers, according to available information, appears first to have decreased and then to have increased in both Mexico and Bolivia.

Cuba had two official agrarian reforms: in 1959 and 1963. As in Mexico and Bolivia, in Cuba the first reform addressed peasant concerns. It extended property rights to sharecroppers, tenant farmers, squatters, and some rural wage workers, although it allowed farmers to maintain up to 402 hectares. Unlike in Mexico and Bolivia, however, in Cuba the reform also transformed large capital-intensive holdings into state farms. The sugar plantations had initially been converted into cooperatives, but within a few years the government transformed them into state farms. The second reform nationalized most holdings over 67 hectares, leaving about 30% of the farm population in the private sector; many of the remaining private farmers had received their land in conjunction with the first reform law. Since the second reform the vast majority of the rural labor force has been absorbed into the state sector. Workers on the state farms enjoy job security and a guaranteed income that they did not on private farms before the revolution; and until the late 1960s they also enjoyed private plots.

The different land policies implemented in Cuba, on the one hand, and Mexico and Bolivia, on the other, reflect the different class biases of the postrevolutionary regimes and the different ways that the countries were historically integrated into the world economy. Before the respective revolutions, agriculture was more capitalized and export-oriented in Cuba than in Mexico or Bolivia. Cuba was the "sugar factory of the world," and a large portion of the sugar estates were foreign-owned. Although land ownership had been less concentrated on the island than in the two other countries, Cuban agriculture tended to be the most profit-oriented. In expropriating the big farm operations the government was able to gain control over the use of the domestically generated surplus and prevent foreign profit remittances. Yet market dynamics alone do not account for the different land distribution policies in the three countries experiencing "revolutions from below." Had the Castro government been primarily concerned with output maximization, including for trade, it would not have implemented the second reform. Productivity on the state farms proved to be lower than on private holdings. The second reform reflects the Castro regime's *anti-capitalist* bias. Only in Cuba has the postrevolutionary leadership opposed large-scale market-oriented private producers. Castro and his *guerrillero* collaborators used state power differently than their counterparts in the other two countries.

In Peru the Velasco regime transformed agrarian property relations in part of the rural economy shortly after assuming power in 1968. In 1969 it turned the largest and economically most important estates into agrarian cooperatives, and it expropriated all farms not managed directly by their owners. Estate workers were allowed to retain rights to plots they had tilled before the reform, but former landowners could not maintain any portion of their property (in Mexico former landowners were entitled to a portion of their holdings). The experience of Peru demonstrates that a land reform can, in certain respects, be more sweeping in a capitalist country with a "revolution from above" than in one with a "revolution from below." More farmland was redistributed in Peru in four years than in Mexico or Bolivia in the entire period since their respective upheavals. Moreover, Peru demonstrates that an "elite revolution" may leave fewer large private holdings intact than "revolutions from below." As of 1970–1972, the percentage of private farms in holdings over 100 hectares was more than twice as great in Mexico and Bolivia as in Peru.

The greater readiness of Peru's than Mexico's revolutionary leadership to respond to peasant and rural wage worker concerns is partly attributable to the different timing of the two upheavals. Extensive land redistribution occurred in Mexico in the 1930s not merely because of "pressure from below." The followers of Zapata and Pancho Villa had fought for land for two decades before any significant land allocations took place. It was only under specific circumstances that widespread land redistribution occurred in Mexico: when the World Depression weakened the landed elite's ability to resist expropriation. By 1968, though, the international political climate had changed, as had global and national economic dynamics. In the aftermath of the Castro revolution many Latin American countries implemented land reforms to *avert* revolution; the reforms in the countries under study which had no revolution reflect this concern. Before 1959 Latin American governments implemented land reforms only when pressured by agrarian rebellions. Also, as Latin American countries successfully promoted industrialization after World War II the power of landed oligarchies diminished. Many large landowners began to diversify their economic interests, so they had less to lose by an agrarian reform. This was true in Peru at the time of the Velasco coup.

Thus the experiences of these four countries suggest that revolutions, irrespective of their class origins or the political economy to which they give rise, are associated with land reforms. Yet the four paired countries also promulgated agrarian reforms in the 1960s. Whereas it might therefore appear that land redistribution programs do not distinguish countries which have and have not had revolutions, the different impact of the reforms in the two sets of countries is striking. According to available data, the proportion of the farm population receiving land and the proportion of the farmland redistributed as a result of the reforms has been greatest in the four countries that had revolutions (see Table 3).

Although the land reforms were implemented in Mexico, Bolivia, and Cuba before they were in their paired countries, the different time lapses do not account for the cross-national differences. The Velasco reform was the last to be implemented, yet it had had a greater impact than Colombia's, the DR's, Brazil's and Ecuador's. Nor do differentials in land concentration before the respective upheavals account for the cross-national variances. The data in Table 2 show that the GINI index of land concentration was greater in Mexico in 1930 than in Brazil in 1950, and greater in Bolivia at the time of its upheaval than in Ecuador, but Peru's GINI index was only slightly higher than Colombia's and Cuba's was identical to the DR's. Rather, in the four countries which have not had revolutions the landed oligarchies have thus far been successful in resisting pressure for land redistribution.

In sum, no single factor accounts for land distribution policies after revolution, but postrevolutionary societies contrast with societies that have not had revolutions in the extent to which they implement agrarian reforms. The cross-national comparison demonstrates that the class base of upheavals is not the only factor that shapes land allocation patterns. The political biases of the ruling elite are also important. For example, the national leadership in Colombia never redistributed land on the scale that Velasco did in Peru even though the Colombian countryside had been plagued by violence since the 1940s and the country was industrializing. The cross-national comparison also reveals that land distribution patterns after revolution depend in part on the dominant mode of production instituted.

TABLE 3

Proportion of the male farm population benefiting from agrarian reforms and the proportion of farmland distributed or confirmed by 1969

	Year reform initiated	% males benefiting	% land distributed or confirmed
Mexico	1916	46.5	35.1
Brazil	1964	0.4	0.4
Bolivia	1955	39.0	29.7
Ecuador	1964	3.7	2.5
Cuba	1959	63.7**	—
Dominican Republic	1963	2.0	2.0
Peru 1961–69	1961	2.4	4.8
Peru 1973*	1969	21.0	30.0
Colombia	1961	4.0	10.4

*For Peru 1973 data are included, showing the impact of the Velasco reform.
**Approximate percent of farm units eligible for *individual* land rights in conjunction with the 1959 Agrarian Reform.

Mexico, Bolivia, and Peru reduced the number of big farms and the proportion of land area such farms control, but not nearly so much as did socialist Cuba.

Income Distribution

As societies urbanize and agriculture is capitalized, land ownership becomes a less important determinant of overall welfare. Concomitantly, financial wealth assumes greater importance. It affects people's capacity both to invest and to consume. And the more equitable the distribution of wealth, the more an entire populace can share the benefits of a society's riches. Income is the best available measure of wealth, although it underestimates the economic worth of people with assets. Because revolutions, by definition, involve class transformations and because wealth tends to be class-determined, revolutions should alter the distribution of economic resources among socioeconomic groups. Accordingly, income distribution patterns should differ in the countries that have and have not had revolutions. But which aspects of revolutions affect income allocations? If groups benefit in income-producing ways from participation in revolutionary movements, then peasants and workers in Mexico, Bolivia, and Cuba should have improved their earning power more than their counterparts in Peru and their paired countries. But if the dominant mode of production that is instituted after revolution has a decisive bearing on people's income opportunities, then income distribution patterns should be similar in all the capitalist countries and different in Cuba. A major structural constraint of governments in capitalist societies is absent in societies where ownership of production is socialized: in capitalist societies businesses must expect sufficient profits or they will not invest. Partly to ensure investment, governments in such societies support inequitable income distributions. By contrast, in socialized economies individual investments need not be governed by profit considerations, especially by returns to owners and managers; consequently, to induce investment socialist governments need not skew income distribution. Accordingly, there is reason to expect that popular groups would be less able to increase their income share after capitalist than after socialist revolutions. Governments in capitalist societies, regardless of whether they had revolutions, would be expected to repress distributive pressures "from below" that threaten capital accumulation.

But capital accumulation exigencies could depend on the way in which economies are integrated into the world economy. This is not to say that distributive patterns are necessarily identical in semi-peripheral countries with different ownership patterns, but that the options in all semi-peripheral countries should differ qualitatively from those in peripheral countries. The success of semi-peripheral countries at industrialization, for example, rests partly on low wages allowing high returns to capital.

Finally, income distribution might depend on the time lapse since upheavals. There is no a priori basis, however, for predicting the effect of longevity. The income equalizing effects of revolutions might well vary over time with shifting political and economic priorities of regimes, somewhat independently of the class base of regimes, the dominant mode of production, or global economic dynamics.

Unfortunately, available data do not permit a systematic comparison of income distribution before the respective upheavals. It therefore is impossible to assess the full impact that each revolution has had on the apportionment of income. The data on the postrevolutionary periods, however, reveal that the dominant pattern of ownership most affects income allocations. In Table 4 we see that since the social transformation in Cuba the share of the national income of the poorest 40% increased from 6% to 20% while that of the richest 5% dropped from 28% to 9.5%. The poor have come to earn a larger share and the wealthy a smaller share in Cuba than in any of the other countries surveyed, whereas before 1959 Cuba's lowest income earners received the smallest share of the national income. Yet the data also reveal that the dominant mode of production is not the only factor shaping income allocations after revolution, for distributive patterns have changed within each country since the upheavals. They have changed as the economies have diversified and international and internal class pressures have shifted.

Mexican income estimates differ somewhat, but they concur that the share of the national wealth accruing both to the poorest 20% and to the wealthiest 5% declined between 1950 and the mid 1970s. The redistribution favored professionals, salaried employees, and organized workers, in a manner permitting an expansion of the internal market for goods and services while containing most labor demands. Mexican income allocations shifted

TABLE 4

Estimates of share of national income held by percentile groups

	Percentile groups						
	POOREST 0–20	21–40	41–60	61–80	81–100	91–100	RICHEST 96–100
Bolivia							
1968 [H]	4	13.7	8.9	14.3	59.1	—	35.7
1975 [E]		13*		26	61.0	44.5	—
1975 [H]		14**		29	58.0	41.7	—
Ecuador							
1960 [E]	4	—	—	—	—	—	42
1970 [?]	2.5	3.9	5.6	14.5	73.5	—	42
Mexico [H]							
1950	5.6	7.5	10.9	16.7	59.4	45.5	35.1
1958	5.5	9.0	13.5	19.0	52.9	35.7	25.5
1963	3.7	6.8	11.2	20.2	58.1	41.6	28.6
1968	3.4	7.3	11.5	19.7	58.1	42.0	27.1
1970	3.8	8.0	13.7	18.7	55.8	39.2	27.7
1975	1.7	6.0	11.5	20.0	60.2	43.4	—
1977	3.3	7.7	12.9	21.1	55.1	38.0	25.5
Brazil [E]							
1960	3.9	7.4	13.6	20.3	54.8	39.6	28.3
1970	3.4	6.6	10.9	17.2	61.9	46.7	34.1
1972	3.2	5.9	9.5	16.5	64.9	50.4	37.9
Cuba [E]***							
1953	2.1	4.1	11.0	22.8	60.0	38.5	28.0
1960	8.0	12.5	14.5	17.0	48.0	31.0	17.0
1962	6.2	11.0	16.3	25.1	41.4	23.0	12.7
1973	7.8	12.5	19.2	25.5	35.0	19.9	9.5
Dominican Republic							
1960 [E]	—	—	—	—	—	—	—
1970 [E]	5	—	—	—	—	—	26
Peru							
1961 [E]	2.5	5.5	10.2	17.4	64.4	49.2	39.0
	2	—	—	—	—	—	34.0
1972 [H]	1.9	5.1	11.0	21.0	61.0	42.9	—
Colombia							
1960 [E]	3	—	—	—	—	—	—
1964 [H]	2.2	4.7	9.0	16.1	68.1	—	40.4
1970 [?]	3.5	5.9	12.1	19.1	59.4	—	33
1974 [H]	3.6	7.2	11.0	18.1	60.2	45.1	32.8

*Poorest 10% received 3% of the national income.
**Poorest 10% received 3.1% of the national income.
***Since the nationalization of small business in 1968 about 7–8% of the labor force remains outside the state sector.
[E] Economically active population.
[H] Households.

after World War II because postrevolutionary governments became increasingly committed to capital-intensive industrialization.

It appears that the Mexican revolution initially redistributed wealth to low income groups. As peasants and workers organized in the 1920s, at times with arms, their socioeconomic situation improved. It improved in the 1930s as well, because the Depression weakened the then dominant economic elite's power to oppose income redistributing measures implemented by Cárdenas to ameliorate the country's political and economic crisis.

After World War II, though, the rural and urban poor began to bear the costs of the country's development. Once the Depression subsided and the war opened up new economic opportunities, Mexican governments started to intervene increasingly in the interests of upper income groups. The state began to provide business with infrastructure, capital assistance, and protection from import competition at the same time that it both cut back support to peasants and coopted and repressed labor. Consequently, as Mexico joined the economic vanguard of Latin America, its income distribution deteriorated. One study estimates that the richest 10% earned 15 times more than the poorest 10% in 1958, and 35 times more two decades later. There is also some evidence that suggests the absolute as well as relative income of the poorest fraction of the population deteriorated in the post-World War II period.

The postwar capital-intensive mode of development deprived many rural poor of their traditional means of satisfying basic needs. Because capital-intensive industries and farms displaced labor at the same time that the population growth rate continued to be unusually high (by world standards), a large portion of the labor force was excluded from modern sectors income opportunities. As a consequence, much of the farm population has had either to seek full- or part-time employment as farm laborers within Mexico or the U.S., or to move to the city and do low-paid work. By 1970 about one-third of the economically active urban and rural population was estimated to be underemployed.

As in Mexico, in Bolivia the revolution ushered in a more egalitarian society than the one it displaced, but in the absence of income data for the pre-1952 period it is impossible to document the extent to which it did. The agrarian reform that was implemented in response to pressure "from below" enabled peasants to appropriate the full product of their labor. The earnings of the newly propertied peasants who marketed their output accordingly improved, at the expense of former *latifundistas.* And in industry, and especially in the mines, labor received wage and fringe benefit increases, as a result of their militancy in the 1952 insurrection. In 1968 the poorest 40% received a larger portion of the national income in Bolivia than in the other capitalist countries here studied that experienced revolutions. The cross-national variance proves there is a range of income dispersion possible under capitalism, and it suggests the range may in part depend on the degree of industrialization. Not only in Mexico, but also in Brazil and Peru, industrialization has had an adverse effect on the share of income accruing to the lowest income groups. Were there income data by quintile for Mexico before its post-World War II industrial boom, we probably would find an income dispersion more comparable to Bolivia's than in recent decades. But the share of the national income accruing to the poorest 40% has deteriorated over the years in Bolivia, even in the absence of significant industrialization. It deteriorated because the set of classes in whose interests the state rules has shifted, and international policies toward Bolivia have changed. Nonetheless, the poorest 40% still enjoy a larger share of the national pie in Bolivia than in the more industrial capitalist countries under examination.

The biggest change in postrevolutionary Bolivian income policy occurred in 1956, when an International Monetary Fund (IMF) Stabilization program, enforced with U.S. military assistance, reduced labor's political power. The IMF and the U.S. made loans conditional on a wage freeze and a reduction of the fringe benefits that labor won in the revolution. The Stabilization program also hurt the national industrial bourgeoisie, because the IMF insisted that the Bolivian government retract industrial tariff protection and end industrial subsidies. The Stabilization program modified Bolivian class dynamics, although peasants and labor formally remained part of the ruling coalition until the 1964 *coup d'etat.* Since then Bolivia has been governed for the most part by conservative military regimes. The drop in the income share to the poorest 40% of the population during the 1968–1975 period reflects the "purification" (a term used by the leader of the 1964 coup) of Bolivia's capitalist revolution. The earning capacity of peasants deteriorated also because governments in the 1960s and 1970s continued to regulate prices of peasant-produced basic foods, while allowing most other prices to rise.

The information on Peru suggests that the 1968 "revolution from above" contributed to a "downward" redistribution of wealth, but not to the poorest 40% of the economically active population. While the data on income shares to percentile groups between 1961 and 1972 do not allow us to discern what change occurred before and after the Velasco takeover, there is evidence that income distribution deteriorated before 1968 and improved afterwards. Between 1950 and 1966 families in the top half of the income distribution, by and large, enjoyed a faster rate of income growth than the bottom half.

It might appear from the cross-national income figures that low income groups fare better when they partake in the destruction of the old order than when they do not. The lowest income earners captured a smaller share of the national income in Peru after its "elite revolution" than in Mexico, Bolivia, and Cuba after their respective social revolutions. But the changes reflect how the Velasco administration responded to the organization of the economy in the prerevolutionary epoch and to constraints imposed by national and foreign capital; the main beneficiaries of Peru's elite-led revolution were modern sector agricultural and industrial workers.

The cross-national comparison reveals, above all, that the dominant form of property ownership most affects income distribution after revolution. Income distribution has improved most in postrevolutionary Cuba. The share of national wealth captured by the poorest 40% increased and that captured by the wealthiest 20% decreased markedly during the first year of Castro's rule, for several reasons. First, the 1959 agrarian reform had a great effect on income distribution in the rural areas, both because large *latifundistas* lost land and because small farmers could acquire land cheaply. Second, a 1959 law reduced rents, thereby lowering the earnings of the rentier class. Third, Castro raised the minimum wage. The wage increases probably contributed to the socialization of the economy. Businesses cut back activities as concessions to labor reduced profits, and the new regime expropriated firms as they withdrew investments. Unable to curb the radicalization of the new revolution, businessmen and professionals emigrated; the exodus of upper income earners in turn served to equalize income among the remaining population. According to available information, income distribution has continued since 1960 to be more equitable in Cuba than in the other countries.

The pace of redistribution, however, has slowed down and the main beneficiaries of income redistribution from top income earners after 1960 have been middle income groups, including the 61–80 percentile group that was initially negatively affected by the revolution. This segment of the population may have benefited even more from policies after 1973, the last year for which we have data on income allocations. Since 1973 the government has increased material rewards for highly skilled and productive workers in its drive to improve production. In addition, because post-1962 Cuban income data excluded the private sector and because the earnings of some independent farmers are known to be high, in 1973 island income was less equitably distributed than the figures convey. In the mid-1960s it was not uncommon for independent farmers to earn 10–20,000 pesos a year; by contrast, cabinet ministers earned 8400 pesos and top technicians and specialists 10,000 pesos. Private farmers were the richest Cubans, with the exception of a few remaining physicians still in private practice. Nonetheless, income opportunities for private farmers in the 1970s remained much more circumscribed than in the capitalist countries, for only in Cuba could landowners own no more than 67 hectares (unless they were exceptionally productive, in which case the ceiling was set higher).

The significance of income statistics, as well as the data base, is distinctive in Cuba. Under Castro nonwage policies have eroded much of the historical importance of earnings, to the extent that income is a much less adequate indicator of overall material consumption on the island than in the other countries. The Castro government, for example, is the only government in this study that provides its poor with social security, free health care, and unemployment insurance. It also did not allow the price of basic goods and the cost of rent to rise for two decades.

However, while Cuba's nonwage as well as wage policies are more egalitarian than those of the other countries surveyed, island material consumption has been depressed. It was especially depressed in the late 1960s when the government emphasized moral incentives. Because the late 1960s strategy adversely affected productivity, after 1970 the government shifted both its wage and its nonwage policies in favor of skilled and productive workers. It for example deregulated the prices of certain non-essentials, granted exceptionally productive workers the prerogative to buy luxury electrical appliances, and reserved such valued items as new automobiles for persons in key economic and political posts. In Cuba material lifestyles vary with access to goods, and not merely with earnings, and by the early and mid-1970s both wage and consumer policies favored middle income groups.

The available data for the paired countries suggest not only that the dominant mode of production most affects income distribution patterns, but also that low income earners' share of the national product tends to decrease with industrialization in capitalist countries (except in Colombia). The data also suggest that income is not necessarily more equitably distributed after revolution, at least in the long run, if the dominant mode of production remains capitalist.

In support of the industrialization thesis, as Brazil rapidly industrialized in the 1960s, income distribution deteriorated: the share of the national income accruing to the poorest 40% of the economically active population decreased while the share to the wealthiest 20% increased. The industrial expansion resulted largely from an influx of foreign capital, after the military took power in 1964. Yet the Brazilian-Mexican comparison reveals that political forces may indeed modify the impact of capitalist economic dynamics. Although the share of the national income accruing to the poorest 40% deteriorated both in Mexico and Brazil in the 1960s, it deteriorated less during the decade in Mexico. Moreover, whereas the income share going to the top 5% declined during the 1960s in Mexico, it increased in Brazil. The Mexican social transformation, and the civilian regime to which it gave rise, appear to have helped the petty bourgeoisie and organized labor (who fall within the top 2–3 decile groups) appropriate a larger portion of the national income than their counterparts under Brazil's military rule. The more egalitarian trend in Mexico, compared to Brazil, suggests that internal class dynamics and not merely semi-peripheral status affect income distribution patterns.

Estimates of Brazilian, Peruvian, and Cuban real and relative per capita income of percentile groups, however, suggest not only that development may have a more egalitarian effect in a socialized economy than in predominantly privately-owned economies, but also that most income groups may benefit more from a repressive semi-peripheral regime than from a more populist but economically weaker regime. As shown in Table 5 (on page 280), before Castro assumed power the real and the relative per capita income of the poorest 3 quintiles was less, and the ratio between the earnings of the top and bottom 20% was greater in Cuba than in the other two countries; by the 1970s, however, the real and the relative per capita income of the three poorest quintiles was greater and the per capita income gap between the top and bottom 20% was much less in Cuba than in either Brazil or Peru. And the estimates also suggest that low income groups have benefited more from Brazil's repressive high growth-oriented regime than from Peru's "revolution from above." For one, between 1960–1961 and 1972–1976 the real income per capita of all income groups improved in Brazil; in Peru the real per capita income of the poorest 20% deteriorated, although that of all other income groups improved. Second, while the real per capita income of all groups was higher in Peru than in Brazil in 1960–1961, by 1972–1976 the poorest, as well as the two wealthiest quintiles, earned less in Peru than in Brazil. Third, during the 16 year period the relative income per capita of all but the richest 20% deteriorated both in Brazil and in Peru, but for the poorest 20% more in Peru than in Brazil. Fourth, during the period under consideration the gap between per capita income of the top and bottom 20% widened more in Peru than in Brazil. Thus the Brazilian so-called economic miracle (1967–1974) has had some trickle down effect on the poor, which Peru's more nationalist and less dynamic economy has not. The development strategy of neither country, however, has improved the relative per capita income standing of the very poor.

In sum, the experiences of the countries under study here suggest that revolutions in capitalist societies do not necessarily give rise to more egalitarian income distributions than societies experiencing no class transformation, that socialist revolutions improve income distribution more than capitalist revolutions and that low income groups benefit

TABLE 5

Per capita income by income strata in Brazil, Cuba, and Peru

A. *Estimates of real income per capita by income strata (1970 U.S. $)*

QUINTILES	BRAZIL		CUBA		PERU	
	1960	1976	1953	1973	1961	1972
0–20	59	95	33	236	68	40
20–40	135	183	66	374	159	189
40–60	234	309	176	574	296	344
60–80	342	607	365	763	489	548
80–100	916	2317	961	1044	1261	1746
(Top 5%)	(1869)	(5475)	(1792)	(1136)	(2365)	(3234)

B. *Relative income levels per capita by income strata (GDP/Capita = 100)*

QUINTILES	BRAZIL		CUBA		PERU	
	1960	1976	1953	1973	1961	1972
0–20	18	14	10	39	15	7
20–40	40	26	21	63	35	33
40–60	60	44	55	96	65	60
60–80	101	86	114	128	107	96
80–100	272	330	300	175	277	305
(Top 5%)	(555)	(780)	(560)	(190)	(520)	(565)
Top 20% / Bottom 20%	15.1	23.6	30.0	4.5	18.5	43.6
Top 5% / Bottom 20%	30.8	55.7	56.0	4.9	34.7	80.7

most from class upheavals, even under socialism, when the new regimes are in the process of consolidation. In all countries here surveyed, except Colombia, the share of income accruing to the poor diminished with the expansion of the economies. The Mexican-Brazilian comparison, however, shows that in the semi-periphery middle and low income groups benefit somewhat more and the elite somewhat less from industrialization when a postrevolutionary society institutionalizes a civilian regime than when a regime excludes popular groups from power.

Health Care and Nutrition

Well-being depends not only on material comforts but also on good health. Good health requires a well-balanced and adequate diet, including high levels of calorie and protein consumption. It also requires access to a medical delivery system that provides quality health care. The scope of the delivery system is reflected in the per capita supply of physicians, nurses, and hospital beds. The quality of health care, in turn is reflected in life expectancy rates, including infant mortality rates (deaths of infants less than one year old per 1000 live births.)

THE HEALTH CARE DELIVERY SYSTEM: THE SUPPLY OF DOCTORS, NURSES, HOSPITAL BEDS

According to information on the countries here surveyed, as long as the dominant mode of production remains capitalist revolutions appear not to have any predictable effect on the health care delivery system (see Table 6). Whereas per capita medical personnel and

TABLE 6

Health care

	BOLIVIA	ECUADOR	MEXICO	BRAZIL	CUBA	DOMINICAN REPUBLIC	PERU	COLOMBIA
Population per physician								
1958	—	—	—	—	2839	—	—	—
1960	3700	2800	1800	2170	—	—	2200	2400
1970	2300	2500	1440	1950	1400	2100	1920	2160
1976	2120	1570	—	1650	1100	1870	1580	1820
Population per nursing population								
1958	—	—	—	—	8262.0	—	—	—
1960	—	2280	2650	—	—	—	3640	3520
1966	—	—	—	—	786.5	—	—	—
1970	2730	8630	1570	3300	581.9	3930	3200	1040
1975	—	—	—	—	443.8	—	—	—
1976	3520	—	—	—	—	1330	—	—
Population per hospital bed								
1958	—	—	—	—	239	—	—	—
1960	580	520	590	275	—	440	490	580
1970	490	430	930	260	215	350	470	450
Infant mortality (per 1000 live births)								
1940–44	101.1	114.3	119.3	164.7	—	69.6	116.5	152.0
1945–49	123.1	101.8	104.5	117.5	38.9	87.6	108.6	141.8
1950–54	98.8	81.8	91.8	107.3	—	79.7	99.9	113.3
1955–59	81.8	80.4	77.9	107.6	32.4	83.5	98.8	100.9
1965	76.5	70.6	60.7	—	38.4	72.7	74.0	82.4
1970	—	66.6	68.5	110.0	38.4	50.1	65.1	91.3*
1973	—	59.1	52.0	—	28.9	38.6	—	—
1976–77	158.0	—	65.0	62.0	23.0	—	—	98.0

*1969

hospital facilities have tended to improve in each country that experienced a social transformation, the per capita supply of each has not come to be uniformly higher and it has not consistently improved more in the postrevolutionary societies than in the paired countries. The factor most affecting the availability of health care, and how the delivery system is organized, is the dominant mode of production. Cuba has the largest supply of doctors, nurses, and hospital beds per population. Because its supply of medical personnel is much greater than Mexico's and Brazil's, and because Mexico has the worst per capita supply of hospital beds of any of the countries under study, the level of development of societal productive resources does not account for cross-national differences in health care facilities.

Whereas the Mexican health care delivery system has expanded since the revolution, official commitment to health care has been low throughout the century, and it has been class-biased. Social welfare programs, which include medical care, have never received more than 6.5% of the national budget. Allocations to "public health, welfare, and assistance" did not consistently surpass prerevolutionary levels as a percentage of the total budget until 1926. They peaked under Cárdenas in the 1930s, and during the first two years of his successor's administration. The relatively high outlays under Cárdenas suggest that public outlays to social concerns are greatest when the national leadership is populist in orientation and minimally constrained by a powerful profit-oriented capitalist class. In weakening the power of the propertied class, the Depression made it easier for the government to implement social welfare measures. Postrevolutionary Mexican medical outlays not only are limited, but they also vary greatly by socioeconomic group. In the post-World War II period private and public medical assistance has been concentrated almost exclusively in urban areas, especially in the largest cities. In 1970, for example, 54% of all doctors—private practitioners and state employees—worked in the four largest cities, which contained only 18% of the population.

The expansion and reorganization of the health care delivery system in Castro's Cuba have been so great and so different from the other countries' as to suggest that socialization of the economy provides options private ownership of the economy does not. Given that half the country's doctors emigrated in the first five years of Castro's rule, Cuba's current supply of doctors is especially impressive. The Castro regime sponsored a massive campaign to attract students to medicine. With all graduates guaranteed jobs and with nearly all doctors government-employed, the expansion of the medical profession is a direct reflection of the state's commitment to upgrading health care. Cuba has expanded its per capita supply of doctors to the point that it can export them, with less cost to the domestic economy, than can most Latin American countries.

Just as Mexican governments modified their medical care priorities over the years, so too has the Castro regime. But the two countries have promoted increasingly different health care coverage. Whereas the Castro government initially invested in a costly and elitist doctor-based medical system, once it replenished its supply of doctors it began to invest in paramedical care. It promoted new types of personnel, such as medical and dental assistants (against some initial opposition of the medical and dental professions), and it upgraded established low prestige professions such as nursing. As a result, the population-health care personnel ratio dropped from 2838:1 in 1958 to 171:1 seventeen years later. And the nurse-population ratio, which had been between two to three times lower in Cuba around the time of the revolution than in the capitalist countries for which we have information, by 1970 was between approximately two and fifteen times higher. Moreover, nurses, nurse assistants, and auxiliary personnel seem to have more clinical responsibility in Cuba than do their counterparts in capitalist countries.

In sum, the qualitative and quantitative changes that the Castro regime alone initiated suggest that governments in socialized economies are apt to invest more in health welfare, and to allocate funds differently, than governments in capitalist societies. Whereas state ownership of the means of production in itself provides no *guarantee* that medical outlays and health standards will improve, it creates possibilities that private ownership does not. The inferior health care delivery system in postrevolutionary Bolivia is undoubtedly attributable in part to market dynamics and the limited public revenues governments there have had. But the different developments in Castro's Cuba on the one hand, and Mexico and Brazil on the other, demonstrate that capital resources are not the only issue.

INFANT MORTALITY

Infant mortality is the one aspect of social welfare that appears not to be affected by any of the revolutionary-linked variables under study (refer back to Table 6 on page 281). Because Cuba has a much lower infant mortality rate than any of the other countries, it would appear that societies with socialized economies have more effective health care systems than capitalist countries. But because island rates were significantly lower already before the 1959 upheaval and because, according to the data, the infant death rate during the first decade of Castro's rule was higher than when Batista fell, socialism alone cannot be the cause. Possibly, health care deteriorated under Castro until the new generation of doctors replaced the physicians who emigrated. The increase, however, may reflect an improvement in data collection, not a deterioration in health care: in 1969, for example, 98% of all deaths were reported, whereas in 1956 only 53% were.

The level of overall economic development and the position of countries within the world economy, in turn, show no consistent relationship with mortality rates. Through 1970, Brazil had the highest infant mortality rate of any of the countries under study, despite its large resource base.

NUTRITION

Whereas, in the countries under study, infant mortality rates appear to be unaffected by revolution or the overall wealth of societies, according to our indicators nutrition standards tend to vary with the level of development of economies (see Table 7 on page 284). Between 1960 and 1974 caloric and protein intake was generally lowest in Bolivia and Ecuador and highest in Mexico and Brazil. Peru is the only country where protein and caloric consumption, according to available information, declined after the revolution. It

TABLE 7

Nutrition

	BOLIVIA	ECUADOR	MEXICO	BRAZIL	CUBA	DOMINICAN REPUBLIC	PERU	COLOMBIA
Per capita caloric supply (percentage of requirements)								
1960	69	81	107	102	—	92	97	94
1970	77	89	110	109	—	91	98	97
1974	83	91	121	118	107	109	92	96
Per capita protein supply (total grams per day)								
1960	43	46	65	61	—	50	61	46
1970	46	49	65	64	64	51	62	50
1974	47	47	66	61	—	50	53	50

declined probably because only a limited portion of the rural population benefited from the land reform, because other agrarian policies (e.g., credit and pricing) did not favor the peasant sector, and because the earning power of the country's poor has deteriorated.

In Mexico, nutritional patterns appear to have changed over the years. Food consumption of low income groups, especially in the countryside, improved most under Cárdenas. Under Cárdenas peasant consumption depended as much on subsistence agriculture and informal exchanges among neighbors as on goods purchased in the market. But as rural communities were progressively integrated into the money economy after World War II, peasant food consumption came to depend on market purchasing power. With the impingement of market forces, informal networks for food distribution eroded and peasants became economically weaker and agrarian capital stronger. Consequently, even though farm output significantly improved after 1940, most peasants have not benefited from the gains. In the 1960s, Mexican upper and middle income group consumption of fruits, vegetables, and protein improved, while low income consumption deteriorated. The earning power of many Mexicans deteriorated to the point that by the end of the 1960s 40% of all farm families and 26% of all nonagricultural families were believed to earn below the minimum needed to assure an adequate diet. Although the government in the early 1970s implemented several programs to improve low income nutritional standards, the programs have thus far had little impact.

The other "revolution from below," in Cuba, also modified food consumption patterns. According to available data, however, the changes have not on the whole thus far been uniformly positive. Data on island consumption of 35 food items reveals that per capita acquisitions of 24 items dropped between 1966 and 1970. During the following four years consumption of approximately two-thirds of the products did improve, but consumption of only half the items was higher in 1974 than in 1966. Yet with basic goods rationed, low income groups may have improved their intake, even during the period when per capita food consumption declined. By contrast in the capitalist countries, where most food is allocated through market channels, consumption of low income groups may not have improved even when per capita consumption rose; post-World War II Mexican data confirm this hypothesis.

Thus, policies of governments after revolution *may* shape societal dietary patterns. But as new regimes become institutionalized in capitalist societies, nutritional standards tend to vary with the overall level of development of the economy and socioeconomic status. The situation in Castro's Cuba reveals that islanders, as a whole, fare no better under socialism than people in the more economically developed capitalist countries. Low income groups, however, may consume more calories and protein on the island than in the other countries, because the Castro government guarantees all Cubans a basic low-cost diet. The state in Cuba is freer than in the other countries to counter market tendencies, and it has used its power accordingly.

In conclusion, this analysis suggests that only in socialized economies is the health care system likely to change in ways that would otherwise be unlikely. Since the respective revolutions, Cuba's health care delivery system has been more extensive, it has expanded more, and it has been organized differently than have the delivery systems in the other countries. Furthermore, both the delivery system and policies affecting nutrition are least class-biased in Cuba. By the second decade of Castro's rule the changes appear also to have had a positive effect on infant mortality, but possibly not before then. Whereas health trends in other postrevolutionary societies have tended to be positive as well, the same is true in the paired countries. Thus, capitalist revolutions have no distinctive impact on the aspects of health welfare under investigation.

Conclusion

The foregoing analysis assessed ways that revolutions affected the social welfare of Latin Americans. It compared differences between societies of roughly similar levels of economic development that did and did not have revolutions, revolutions ushered in by different class alliances, revolutions instituting different modes of production, and revolutions occurring in countries differently situated within the world economy.

The class transformations in Mexico, Bolivia, Cuba, and Peru gave rise to more egalitarian societies than they displaced, but low income groups in each country gained most during the new regimes' consolidation of power. Subsequently, the interests of the popular sectors were sacrificed to those of middle and upper income groups. The rural masses benefited from revolution mainly in conjunction with agrarian reforms. Agrarian reforms have been promulgated in all the countries under study, but a much larger proportion of the agrarian population and a much larger proportion of the farmland has been redistributed in the four countries that had political upheavals than in the paired countries that did not. Whereas all the land reforms perpetuate *minifundismo*, recipients of land titles enjoy a modicum of security and the opportunity to appropriate the full product of their labor, which rural wage workers and peasants dependent on usufruct arrangements do not.

Examining the countries that *have* had revolutions shows that peasants and workers do not necessarily benefit most when they participate in the destruction of the old order. Peasants and rural farm laborers gained land where they were disruptive, but in Mexico only after a global Depression weakened the ability of large landowners to resist expropriation. The Peruvian experience demonstrates that rural laborers may benefit even if they are politically quiescent at the time of the extra-legal takeover of power, and that they may, under certain conditions, gain benefits sooner after revolutions "from above" than after revolutions "from below."

The level of development of the economy and the way the societies have been integrated into the world economy historically limit what Third World revolutions can accomplish, quite independently of how the upheavals originated. Global constraints have also been one factor restricting labor's ability to improve its earning power and influence over the organization of production. Labor did benefit from the upheavals, but as the postrevolutionary governments became concerned with attracting foreign investment and foreign financial assistance, and with improving profits from trade, labor was marginalized. The Mexican-Brazilian comparison, however, suggests that the "middle class" and the small proportion of workers employed in the modern industrial sector benefit more, and the richest 5% less, in societies where civilian groups have been incorporated into the political apparatus as a result of revolution. Thus revolutionary-linked forces may modify the income generating effect of capitalist industrial dynamics, though not to the advantage of the lowest income earners.

The dominant mode of production instituted under the new order is the aspect of revolution most affecting patterns of land and income distribution and health care. To the extent that ownership of the economy is socialized the state has direct access to the surplus generated. Although the Cuban state has not consistently allocated the resources it controls to low income groups, because the Castro regime need not provide a favorable investment climate it can more readily redistribute wealth "downward" than can the capitalist regimes. It accordingly has also been freer to redesign the health care delivery system in accordance with societal needs rather than business interests and market power. But the Cuban experience suggests that the distributive effects even of socialist revolutions can be limited. Although socialism allows certain allocative options that capitalism does not, the capacity to improve the welfare of Third World people by any revolutionary means is constricted by the weak position of less developed nations within the global economy, by investment-consumption tradeoffs, and by internal political and economic pressures.

REFERENCE

1.   Wallerstein (1980a)

Families, Women, and Minorities in Revolutions

Many classic and modern analyses of revolution treat individuals only in their political roles, as state officials, as members of the elite, or as urban or peasant groups mobilized for revolutionary action. However, individuals are also members of families and persons of gender, and often are identified with religious or ethnic minorities. These family, gender, and minority identities are of great importance in the unfolding of revolutions. Individuals' recruitment to revolutionary actions, support for specific revolutionary policies and goals, and treatment by the revolutionary authorities are all commonly affected by their family, gender, and minority status.

Revolutionary movements generally seek to improve the status of women and minorities; they often have idealistic goals about improving or perfecting the family, childhood, and interpersonal relations. As Judith Stacey shows in her essay on China, these goals are often employed quite flexibly by revolutionary leaders to recruit popular support for their cause. However, once in power, revolutionary leaders often find it more difficult than anticipated to alter long-standing traditions of family, gender, and ethnic/religious group relations. As Johnnetta Cole demonstrates in her essay on Cuba, revolutionary efforts to end inequality between the sexes, like many other revolutionary goals examined in the preceding chapter, have produced only modest and uneven results. Even more distressing, as Ted Robert Gurr relates, revolutionary leaders have often turned on ethnic minority groups, persecuting them in the name of building a new, uniform, and strictly loyal revolutionary society.

PEASANT FAMILIES AND PEOPLE'S WAR IN THE CHINESE REVOLUTION

Judith Stacey

China's communist party came to power through a long process of building support among China's peasantry. Lenin's strategy in the Russian Revolution was to build a base among the urban working classes and then use that base to conquer the countryside. In China, however, that strategy failed. After the fall of the last Manchu Emperor in 1911, it was the Chinese Nationalist Party, or Kuomintang

(KMT), and not the Communist Party that succeeded in building a base in the cities and first established a new, Nationalist, Chinese regime. In 1927, the KMT drove the Chinese Communists out of the cities in a wave of repression.

Over the next twenty years, through periods of Japanese invasion (1937–1945) and civil war with the KMT (1945–1949), the Chinese Communists under Mao developed an alternative revolutionary strategy. Reversing the Leninist strategy, Mao built a rural base and organized the peasants in the countryside to conquer the cities.

The success of Mao's strategy depended on the ability of the Chinese Communist Party to win the support of the Chinese peasantry. In the early twentieth century, the Chinese peasant family was in danger of disintegration. Warlord conflicts following the fall of the Manchus and heavy taxes levied by the Nationalist government had forced the majority of peasant families into poverty. Losing their land to large landlords, growing numbers of peasants were unable to afford to marry, while existing families could not afford proper birth and funeral ceremonies. Some families even had to sell their infant children to pay their rents and taxes. The traditional Chinese family was on the verge of collapse. A few wealthy gentry landlords, veritable "patriarchs" of their region, became the dominant figures in the countryside.

The Chinese Communists sought to reverse this process. Through a program of land reforms, they sought to restore the traditional family by allowing each male to become the patriarch of his own family household.

In this essay Stacey describes the development of this program of "new democratic patriarchy." Following the experiments of the Communist party from its expulsion from the cities in 1927, through its triumph in 1949, to the land reforms of 1949–1953, Stacey notes how the Communist party had to adopt the family morality of the peasantry in order to win support. Respect for peasant life and efforts to improve the economic well-being of the peasant family were the keys to the party's eventual victory.

Today, although collectivization of rural farms has changed the pattern of landholding, the patriarchal family remains the basic unit of the Chinese countryside. The origins of Mao's rural strategy thus continue to shape postrevolutionary China.

In 1932 the Kuomintang minister of foreign affairs, Dr. Wellington Koo, explained why communism was fated to fail in China:

> Communism considers society as being formed of individuals grouped according to their social functions, but not according to their personal sentiments or affections. This idea is alien to the Chinese, who regard family duties as being of great importance. Communism tends to destroy the family by the relaxation of the conjugal bonds, by entrusting the State with the care and education of children and by the abolition of private property. But tradition and the

respect for ancestors are important Chinese social characteristics. It is the family which for the Chinese is at the bottom of social structure.[1]

Dr. Koo was correct, of course. The Chinese endowed family duties with the highest significance and the family system formed the foundation of Chinese social structure. But history was about to provide an ironic demonstration that the Chinese Communists were better able to appreciate and benefit from this than were the members of his own party. Far from abolishing the family, the Communist revolution in China rescued peasant family life from the precipice of destruction. It resolved the crisis of the peasant family through the revolutionary policies and practices that established the material and ideological basis for a new family system. The Chinese Communist Party (CCP) named this the "new democratic family," but this essay demonstrates why a more accurate identification is the "new democratic patriarchy." The reconstruction of the peasant family system did not compete with broader Communist revolutionary goals. Nor was it an incidental by-product of the revolution. Instead, the reconstitution of the patriarchal peasant family economy was integral to the development of several of the most distinctive features and accomplishments of the successful revolutionary strategy known as People's War. In short, there was a family revolution at the center of the social revolution that brought the CCP to state power in China.

Origins of People's War

When in 1927 Mao Zedong and Zhu De led remnant bands of their defeated forces from urban uprisings to the Jinggang Mountains of rural Jiangxi, they unwittingly inaugurated a world-historic epoch of People's War. Banished from China's urban centers, the CCP spent more than two decades forging an alliance with the peasantry, which succeeded in defeating both the Japanese and the KMT. The successful process was People's War, a struggle that combined social revolution with a war for national sovereignty. Attempting to transform military weakness into strength, strategic necessity into virtue, the military objective of People's War is to conquer the cities from the countryside. Strategically this requires the establishment or rural base areas from which a protracted struggle of guerrilla warfare can be waged.

The three major forces of a People's War—peasants, party, and army—become interdependent. The party and army provide the coordinated leadership and protection the peasants require in their resistance to local and foreign enemies, while they depend upon peasant support for their very survival. Because all three share a stake in achieving economic self-sufficiency in the base areas, measures to insure the security of agricultural production, including direct participation by military and political personnel, must be at the heart of wartime economic policy. A viable program for rural development is integral to military success. In fact, a defining characteristic of People's War is the indivisibility of economic policy from military, political, and social goals. Mao Zedong articulated this during the anti-Japanese war.

War is not only a military and political contest, but also an economic contest. In order to defeat the Japanese aggressors . . . we must apply ourselves to economic work . . . we must achieve greater results than ever before.[2]

Clearly the success of such a strategy depends upon active support by the rural population and the elimination of sharp distinctions between "the people" and their political and military allies. A massive effort of political mobilization aims to create a militarized peasantry and a popular military. As Mao explained in "On Protracted War":

A national revolutionary war as great as ours cannot be won without extensive and thorough-going political mobilization. . . . The mobilization of the common people throughout the country will create a vast sea in which to drown the enemy, create the conditions that will make up for our inferiority in arms and other things, and create the prerequisites for overcoming every difficulty in the war. . . .[3]

Rebuilding the Basis for Peasant Patriarchy

The ironic rescue of peasant family life by the Communist revolution was the result of a family revolution the CCP and the peasantry conducted in the midst of People's War. Direct measures to reform family life proceeded under the aegis of the party's official ideological commitment to build the "new democratic family." The goals of this transitional family transformation were to destroy the remains of Confucian patriarchy and to establish a family system based upon free choice, monogamous, heterosexual marriage, with equal rights for the sexes. The party presumed that such marriages were universally desirable and the basis for stable, harmonious family life.

But the de facto family policy of the revolution was to create the new democratic patriarchy. I choose this term to take full advantage of its ironies. The new democratic patriarchy was a patriarchal system whose gender and generational relationships were reformed substantially at the same time that patriarchy was made more democratically available to masses of peasant men. It established a new moral economy in rural China, but one that still was family based. A radical redistribution of patriarchy was its revolutionary essence.

Far from distracting the Chinese Communists from more urgent tasks, their resolution of the peasant family crisis was the central social process of rural revolution. The crisis in the peasant family economy in the base areas provided the CCP with its most significant opportunity to mobilize masses around issues of immediate and urgent interest. The severity and nature of the crisis presented the party its greatest strategic challenge. In seizing the opportunity and addressing the challenge, the CCP forged the successful relationship with the peasantry that was a precondition to its victory.

Land Reform

Land reform was at the center of the comprehensive rural reconstruction program the CCP devised in response to the agrarian crisis. Its essence was a self-conscious attempt to rebuild the traditional peasant family economy. Measures the CCP took to solve the immediate economic needs of its Red Army and peasant supporters were measures to resolve the peasant family crisis by placing that family economy on a more secure and stable footing. The specific priorities and policies of land reform shifted as the military, political, and geographical conditions confronting the CCP changed and as the party gained experience in rural revolution. An analysis of the evolution of Communist land policy suggests a process in which the CCP learned first to accommodate to and then to exploit the family motives of its peasant collaborators.

Soon after their retreat from the cities, the Chinese Communists began to construct a land policy. In December 1928, the Hunan-Jiangxi border Soviet drafted the first land law of the Jiangxi Soviet period (1927–1934). The 1928 law required the confiscation of all land. The Soviet government was to become the sole legitimate landowner. Although the confiscated land would be redistributed among poor peasants, they would not receive private ownership rights. This was the most radical land policy ever promulgated by the CCP and is important as evidence of the sort of policy the party quickly learned to avoid.

The moderating effects of the Communists' experience with rural revolution were soon evident. The basic agrarian law of the Jiangxi Soviet period, the Land Law of the Chinese Soviet Republic of December 1931, remained radical in its promotion of class struggle. It required the confiscation of land as well as liquid and fixed assets of "feudal" landlords, warlords, temples, and other large private landowners. However, this time private ownership of land was not abolished. On the contrary, the chief objective of the redistribution process was to make private landownership more widely available to poor and middle peasants.

The peasants taught the CCP the need to avoid alienating the owner-cultivator class among them. Confiscating land from middle peasants had led to sabotage and counterrevolutionary action on their part. Experience gained in the Soviet period taught the party the need to form an alliance with the middle peasants. Their compliance, if not active support, would be crucial to a successful strategy. Moreover, peasants who received land certificates made greater efforts to increase production. As Mao soon learned, the middle peasant economy—a small family farming economy—was the most viable basis for People's War available to the party:

> The agrarian policy in the soviet area at the current stage of revolution is to continue the traditional form of the small farm unit as a consequence of the agrarian conditions found in the soviet area.[4]

Both these factors led the CCP to base its rural policy on the resurrection of the independent family farm.* The profound implications of the land law were not lost on the poor peasant masses. Victor Yakhontoff, a prophetic analyst of the Soviet period, pointed out an amusing consonance in the translation into Chinese of the word, "Soviet." The pronunciation of the Chinese idoegrams for Soviet is soo-wei-ai, which, he claims, sounds quite similar to she-wei-you, (shih wu you), which means "this is mine." It is easy to see how land revolution in the Kiangsi period would have given many poor peasants good and happy reason to confuse the terms.

The Jiangxi period of the Communist revolution came to a disastrous end in 1934 with the success of the KMT's fifth encirclement and extermination campaign. Not until the survivors of the Red Army's phenomenal Long March united with a small Communist outpost in a desolate area of Northwest China was the CCP again able to establish a base area secure enough for implementing social policies. Efforts to redistribute land were renewed immediately. However, the party soon entered the United front with the KMT against the Japanese invaders. The demands of Japanese military conflict and the terms of the alliance with the KMT caused the party to moderate its agrarian policy further still. During the war of resistance (1937–1945), the CCP abandoned land revolution, but its commitment to land reform continued and matured during these formative years of the new democratic strategy. Now the party turned to methods for the redistribution of land and wealth to the impoverished peasantry that were less direct than those inspiring peasants to forcibly confiscate landlord property. The major means employed were laws that reformed land rent, interest rates, and tax policies.

Agricultural tax policies went through a variety of adjustments during the anti-Japanese war, but the principle underlying all of them was consistent. The CCP sought to collect from rural households the amount of revenue it needed at the time according to its estimates of the people's capacity to pay. When revenues from confiscated properties and other sources were sufficient to meet administrative and military needs, no taxes were collected from the peasants. When military pressures precipitated fiscal crisis, peasants were sometimes taxes beyond their capacities. In most cases, the tax was a steeply progressive one that attempted to protect peasant subsistence requirements.

Concern for peasant interests was at the heart of the wartime economic reforms introduced by the Communists because peasants alone could provide the resources crucial to Communist victory. Mao understood land reform in precisely this manner:

---

*We lack reliable data on the number of peasants who achieved owner-cultivator status through the land revolution of the Jiangxi period. However, Mao's report on changes in class status in Xinguo County is highly suggestive. According to Mao, before the revolution in Xinguo, landlords and rich peasants constituting 6% of the population owned 70% of the land. Middle peasants, by definition the subsistence owner-cultivator class, owned somewhat less land (15%) than their proportion of the population (20%). Mao tells us that land and other goods were distributed to the poor peasants and farm laborers and that, on the whole, middle peasants also increased their landholdings. He does not say what proportion of rural families achieved the capacity for independent family farming in this manner. However, if he is correct that owner-cultivators subsisted on a smaller percentage of land than their percentage of the population, the redistribution of the 70% of the county's land should have made independent family farming feasible for the majority of poor peasants in Xinguo. Xinguo was a model county; it is likely, therefore, that less egalitarian effects were achieved in most other localities. Data from Mao's report are recorded in Chao (1967), p. 30.

Once the Agrarian system is reformed, even in such an elementary way as the reduction of rent and interest, the peasant's enthusiasm for production will grow.[5]

Although rent, interest, and tax relief was not the same thing as land revolution, it sought the same economic objective. Each of these measures attempted to support a small family farm economy to enable it, in return, to provide the productive resources needed for People's War. The Shenganning border region agricultural program was explicit on this point:

In the economy of the Border Region, a small peasant economy still occupies an important position. Hence, the development of agriculture must be regarded as a central chain in economic construction and carried out according to a definite policy.[6]

Promoting the health of the peasant family economy was one of those causes in which peasant and party fortunes were interdependent. Economic self-sufficiency of the base areas was a crucial wartime objective, and the agrarian reform measures of the period largely succeeded in achieving it. Production declined in many border localities with the onset of war, reaching a nadir during the heavy military and economic blockade years of 1940–1941. However, the Great Production Drive waged in 1944 accomplished a major upsurge in production that placed Communist forces in better circumstances to do battle with the KMT in the civil war years that lay immediately ahead.

After the defeat of the Japanese and the official demise of the united front with the KMT, the CCP had less reason to suppress the poor peasant's rising clamor for land. CCP land policy drifted gradually but irrevocably back toward land revolution. During the civil war, there was considerable vacillation in the party's policy toward rich peasants and in the extremity of class warfare it officially encouraged or condoned, but mobilizing poor peasants to forcibly confiscate and redistribute landlord holdings was once again the basic agrarian program. The land law of September-October 1947 was a key document endorsing land revolution, and its implementation was largely completed in the Old Liberated Areas and in the newly-captured Northeast by March 1949. This was the revolutionary tide that carried the party to national power. It overturned the rural order by eliminating landlords as a class, destroying the sources of power of the traditional rural elite, and radically equalizing the distribution of land and wealth. Land revolution was the key source of peasant support for the CCP, and thereby of Communist victory over the Kuomintang.

Almost immediately after its triumphant return to China's cities, the CCP set out to complete the land revolution nationwide. The party recruited and trained thousands of educated youth to serve as cadres in work teams it dispersed throughout the remaining areas of rural China. From 1950–1953, the cadres unleashed the forces that completed the new democratic stage of the Chinese revolution. The two basic documents that underwrote the national land revolution were the Common Program of September 1949 and the Agrarian Reform Law of June 1950. Both made explicit that economic development was the ultimate objective of agrarian reform. The Agrarian Reform Law reveals the self-consciousness with which the party had learned to promote private landholding among peasants to that end:

> The land ownership system of feudal exploitation by the landlord class shall be abolished and the system of peasant land ownership shall be introduced in order to set free the rural productive forces, develop agricultural production and thus pave the way for New China's industrialization.[7]

By now, the CCP had accumulated vast experience with rural revolution. It had become sophisticated organizationally and in its development of mass politics. The party exhibited this sophistication impressively in its approach to land revolution. It granted local cadres flexibility to adopt methods and timetables appropriate to local conditions, but it directed a nationwide process that followed a similar pattern everywhere.

Cadres were instructed first to recruit local activists, to organize a peasant association, to raise consciousness for land revolution, and to win peasant support. Then they were to mobilize the peasants to assign all the village families into social classes, whose membership criteria the CCP had by then defined in elaborate and painstaking detail. Next came the "speak bitterness" sessions where the peasants identified the major local agents of their misery and wrath. These became the primary "struggle targets" of the ensuing, often violent, drive to seize landlord and counterrevolutionary property and to eliminate the landlords as a class. Redistributing the "struggle fruits" was the next task of the peasant associations, which in the process established themselves as new organs of rural power. Demonstrating lessons learned in earlier periods, the Communists issued peasants title deeds to their land that guaranteed inheritance rights to legitimate heirs. Finally, the entire process of land revolution had to be evaluated by outside investigation teams, which typically discovered so many "deviations" from "correct" policy that the village was required to repeat most of the steps.

The party took care to conduct land revolution effectively because crucial economic and political objectives were riding on it. Economically, the party hoped that land reform would improve the livelihood of the peasants and provide the basis for increased agricultural productivity. Establishing a small-farm economy was the party's now time-tested means for accomplishing these goals. Thus, the immediate economic objective of land reform was to elevate the majority of poor peasants and farm laborers to the status of middle peasants. Politically, land revolution was the process whereby the party sought to consolidate its leadership of the nation by securing peasant support and eliminating competing holders and seekers of power in the countryside.

Land revolution succeeded in attaining both these objectives. One of the major structural transformations it accomplished was the elevation of most poor peasants to middle peasant status. After agrarian reform the majority of Chinese peasants belonged to the new middle peasant class.* But no agrarian reformers in China, least of all the

---

*A survey of selected areas in the "early liberated" districts conducted by the party in 1950 reported that middle peasants comprised 60 to 70% of farm households in the Northeastern provinces and between 80 and 90% of farm households in villages surveyed in Hebei, Shanxi, and Chahar. In the Central South region (a "later liberated" area), Shue estimates that 40% of the cultivated land was confiscated and redistributed to 60% of the population; in Hunan and Hebei, the consequence was, on average, the addition of between one and two acres of land to a peasant family's holdings (1975, p. 90).

Communists, ever imagined that a small private farm economy, even a nonexploitative one, could produce prosperity for the masses or an adequate surplus for industrial development. Stabilizing the small farm economy was an interim post on the trail to collectivization. Immediately the new government began to impose new taxes to appropriate resources for development purposes. In many areas of China peasants were soon finding it as difficult to accumulate grain stores as before land reform. Analysts of agricultural development in China agree that, overall, peasants did not experience a noticeable increase in real income due to land revolution. As Vivienne Shue aptly summarized, "Land reform made a relatively few people poorer, and a great many people somewhat better off. But it made no one rich."[8]

The fact that peasants realized limited income benefits due to land reform magnifies the significance of the political results the party achieved. The CCP cemented its relationship with the peasantry, because "the government was determined on a land policy which most peasants could agree was, in principle, morally right, and . . . in carrying it out the government tried, if it did not always succeed, to act with unusual scrupulousness, [and this] helped to create a reservoir of good will among villagers."[9] Land revolution was as much a political as an economic upheaval because the CCP had used it methodically "to *emasculate* the traditional village elite, the entire old rural power structure."[10] The party ensured its authority and eliminated the basis for the rise of future competitors for economic and political power by creating a vast class of small, private farming families dependent upon its structural and political support.

The Family Implications of Land Reform

Although changes in geographic, political, and military conditions led the CCP to modify its tactics—and experience to refine them—there was an underlying integrity to the implicit family policy of land reform in all its guises. True to its proclaimed new democratic spirit, the party sought to rescue peasant family life by simultaneously restoring and transforming its traditional material foundations. CCP land reform policy temporarily reestablished the viability of independent family farming while making it available to the poorest of Chinese peasants. The party's appreciation of family sentiment was evident throughout the revolutionary period. It scrupulously tried to avoid making demands that would confront peasants with direct conflicts between loyalty to the family and loyalty to the revolution. Indeed, land reform policy demonstrated the CCP's ability to turn familial sentiment and loyalties to its own advantage. Because that sentiment was so profoundly patriarchal, concessions to patriarchal morality came to facilitate and shape CCP mass-line politics.

The family restorationist aspects of land reform can be grasped most readily by viewing the way many policies and practices salvaged and buttressed the peasant family household under the authority of its patriarchal head as the basic unit of production. The family household was the effective unit for the implementation of all Communist agrarian policy.

In the few instances when official party policy dictated otherwise, the hegemony of family production and patriarchal morality asserted itself, and official policy was largely ignored.

The determination of a person's class status was the momentous occasion in land reform, because it established one's access to material rewards and political rights or vulnerability to revolutionary justice. It is of overarching significance, therefore, that class status was assigned to families rather than individuals. The party did recognize that the Chinese marriage system could create ambiguity in a woman's class position, and so it attempted to take length of marriage into account when women married into families with class status significantly different from that of their natal kin. However, the unambiguous bias of the classification guidelines was to maintain the solidarity of the family unit.

When the time came for a peasant association to redistribute its village's land, the effects of family-based class assignment were apparent immediately. The principle of "land-to-the-tiller" translated into "land-to-the-families-of-tillers." Land, houses, and wealth were confiscated from families. Peasant families sometimes played a vanguard role in the "speak bitterness" and "settle accounts" meetings. The "struggle fruits" these plaintiffs reaped were then distributed not to individuals but to family households. The economic unity of the peasant family made it irresistible to redistribute land in this way. The particulars of the party's distribution practices make its concern to resurrect the self-supporting patriarchal family unit patently clear. The basic principle was to distribute land to families according to the number of workers and dependents contained in each household. As Weng Kuantan, land commissioner for provinces in the Old Liberated Areas, explained to Edgar Snow, the primary purpose of the land laws "was to provide for every person sufficient land to guarantee him and his family a decent livelihood—which was claimed to be the most 'urgent demand' of the peasantry."[11] Thus craftsmen and peddlers were to receive land only when this was necessary to support themselves and their families adequately. Households consisting of only one or two ablebodied members received small extra allotments so that they could become self-supporting.

Redistributing land to the families of tillers also gave Communist agrarian reformers an opportunity to address the problem of excessive land fragmentation. Full resolution of the problem awaited collectivization, but in this pivotal new democratic phase, reformers often attempted to consolidate the holdings of family members so that much of their land would be in the same area. The implicit effect was to solidify the peasant family as an integrated productive unit. It seems likely this also facilitated the capacity of peasant patriarchs to coordinate and supervise the labor of their women and children.

Land reform promised women equal rights to land, but the centrality of the family economy and the dominance of patriarchal values effectively prevented most women from realizing any direct benefits of this sort. Land was instead distributed to the head-of-the-household, typically a male, and so decisions over allocating land to women became largely a matter of determining which family had rights to which women. Divorced and widowed women who headed households were almost the only women who received land. Land for wives was calculated into the portion distributed to their husband's families. It became quite a thorny matter, therefore, to allocate the shares of young, unmarried women.

Sometimes their shares went to their fathers. Frequently, when these women were betrothed and over age seventeen, their land was allotted to their future in-laws. Some villages avoided the problem altogether by refusing to allot any land for young, unmarried women. And, in some villages, unmarried men received additional land allotments in anticipation of the day that they would receive wives.

The peasants who received land were issued title deeds to underscore the legitimacy of their new ownership rights. Here once again, women's rights were circumvented. Title deeds were made out to households, and households, of course, were overwhelmingly headed by men. The party recognized the contradiction between this practice and its professed commitment to equal land rights for women. A resolution passed by the central committee in 1948 instructed land reform cadres to issue title deeds to women, even when their land was included in their families' allotments. Whenever this policy was implemented, it had profound symbolic significance. As Mariam Frenier has suggested, public acquisition of land could mean a woman assumed a name and a public identity. In 1938, Hsu Kuang, head of the propaganda department of the Hopei Women's Association for National Salvation, explained:

> To emphasize the fact that women had economic equality with the men we gave each woman a land certificate in her own name or wrote her name alongside her husband's on one certificate. Before, women had always been referred to by others as "so-and-so's wife and so-and-so's mother." Now for the first time in their lives many women heard their own names spoken in public.[12]

Unfortunately, but predictably, the resolution on title deeds was rarely implemented.

The tax policies that accompanied land reform also supported the patriarchal family-based economy. According to Vivienne Shue, the new government used its tax policy to encourage a widespread peasant vision of the future that land reform would enable them to *fa jia zhi fu* (set up a household and make one's fortune.) Thus, tax relief was granted to the families of refugees who had fled their villages due to famine and other disasters. These families were allowed several years in which to claim their missing relatives as dependents when computing the family tax. Most importantly, the government made the family household the basic taxable unit. The government never considered assessing individuals for agricultural taxes because this was a tax on production, and in the new democratic era, the basic agricultural production unit was the household.

Land reform gave the CCP ample opportunity to appreciate the depth of patriarchal family morality among the peasant villages, and the party's mass-line politics led cadres repeatedly to capitulate to its demands. One effective means of mobilizing male peasants was to appeal to their desire to marry. Thus a local peasant association badgered a reluctant man to participate in the rent reduction drive of the united front period: "If you reduce rent, I guarantee that you will have enough to have a wedding. If you still refuse, you had better forget the ceremony." This man rushed home and pressured his strong-willed father to join the rent reduction drive.[13]

Land reform provoked not a few peasant men to rather bald expression of their patriarchal yearnings. Many regarded the women of the wealthier classes as appropriate "struggle fruits." Peasant bachelors in Ten Mile Inn went so far as to urge "that the wives of their former exploiters should be divorced so that they themselves might marry them." In this case, party cadres took care to make explicit that the purpose of the "new democratic family" policy was "to consolidate family life, not to break it up."[14] However, there were instances when extremes of patriarchal "justice" were tolerated, and even encouraged by the party. For example, the pre-Communist family crisis had motivated many poor women to leave their husbands and marry other men to keep from starving. Ralph Thaxton reports that after the Eighth Route Army liberated areas in the Yellow River region, many of the former husbands appealed to the Communists to "liberate" and return their former wives to them. The CCP was extremely sympathetic to these men. It endeavored to persuade the women to return to their original husbands, arguing that families should suffer poverty together. The cadres relented in this persuasion only when a woman "steadfastly refused." And then they attempted to procure compensation from the second husbands for the deserted men: "The party requested these indemnity payments [!] partly as an expression of sympathy and partly as compensation for the harm done to the material well-being of the males who lost the services of their wives."[15]

In sum, the implicit family policy of Communist land reform was to establish the economic basis for the new democratic patriarchy. Land reform was the radical core of the new democratic stage of the Chinese revolution. It radically equalized the distribution of patriarchal authority in rural China. The traditionally dominant class of rural patriarchs was indeed "emasculated," when land, the economic base of their power, was forcibly confiscated and redistributed to the vast majority of impoverished peasant men. The latter, the major beneficiaries of land reform, found independent family farming—that most deeply desired but historically elusive goal of the peasantry—within their reach at last. Thereby, the traditional basis of peasant patriarchy and family security was restored, or first made accessible, to many of the victims of China's agrarian crisis.

But land reform did not simply restore patriarchy to the peasantry. By democratizing the distribution of its economic basis, land reform began also to transform the contents of patriarchal privilege. Instead of replacing one class of big patriarchs with another, land reform made small-scale patriarchy the new rural family order. No family retained or achieved the capacity to stage elaborate Confucian ceremonies or festivities. Nor could the new class of rural patriarchs afford its own retinue of concubines or servants. On the other hand, peasant families now had the means to avoid killing the infants, selling or betrothing the young daughters that landlessness had led them to discard.

Contrary to Wellington Koo's prediction, the Communists succeeded in China partly because they saved peasant family life. The Chinese Communists directly appealed to family sentiment to establish a new moral economy, but one still based on family, still patriarchal. Communist appeals to the material self-interest of the peasantry were thus the key to peasant cooperation.

REFERENCES

1.   Quoted in Yakhontoff (1934), p. 13.
2.   Mao Zedong (1967), p. 200.

3. Mao Zedong (1965), p. 154.
4. Quoted in Kim (1969), p. 83.
5. Mao Zedong (1960), pp. 80–81.
6. Quoted in Chao Kuo-chun (1960), p. 41.
7. *Agrarian Reform Law of the People's Republic of China and Other Relevant Documents,* article 1, p. 1.
8. Shue (1980), p. 90. Compatible evaluations appear in Yang, (1959); Paul Chao (1967).
9. Shue (1975), p. 125.
10. Shue (1980), p. 41 (my emphasis).
11. Snow (1968), p. 224.
12. Frenier (1978), p. 23.
13. Quoted in Chen (1980), pp. 277–278.
14. Crook and Crook (1959), p. 166.
15. Thaxton (1975), p. 200.

WOMEN IN CUBA: THE REVOLUTION WITHIN THE REVOLUTION

Johnnetta B. Cole

Revolutions promise to liberate peoples. Indeed, they often promise not only to liberate peoples as a whole from an oppressive government but also to liberate and give equality to especially oppressed groups within a society.

The largest oppressed group in many societies is women. Discriminated against in the workplace, in culture, in politics, in the home, women have often participated in revolutions in the hope of improving their conditions in society.

In socialist revolutions, such as Cuba's, the government has often made greater equality for women an explicit goal. Cuba has passed many progressive laws since the Revolution; however, the weakness of Cuba's economy continues to limit what the government can accomplish in the way of improved housing, services, and material benefits. As Coles notes, "the needs of the Cuban people exceed their capabilities at the present time." Moreover, despite some success in increasing women's opportunities in the labor market, overcoming old views has proven difficult, and women remain in a subordinate position in government and in the family.

In the following essay, Cole describes some of the successes and failures of Cuba's revolution. Although her account focuses on the situation of women, she presents a valuable account of many of the changes the revolution has made in Cuban society in general.

And if they were to ask what the most revolutionary aspect of this Revolution is, we'd tell them that the most revolutionary aspect is the revolution that is taking place among the women in our country.

Fidel Castro, December 10, 1966, Congress of the
Federation of Cuban Women

For those of us who live in the Americas, and perhaps on a global scale, the situation among Cuban women today presents, in sharp relief, the complexities, the problems, and the possibilities for the genuine liberation of women. The 1959 Revolution did not instantly provide the material means for full incorporation of women into the productive, political, and cultural life of the nation. And the revolution did not (and no revolution can) immediately wipe away centuries-old myths and attitudes concerning the "proper place" for men and women. But the Cuban Revolution presented, for the first time, the *possibility* for all women in Cuba to fully share the rewards and responsibilities of their society. In this brief essay, we will contrast the conditions of Cuban women in the 1950s before the revolution with the years after, indicating the accomplishments as well as the problem areas that still exist.

Before the Revolution

Before the Revolution of 1959 life for the majority of Cuba's people conformed to the patterns that are repeated in poor, underdeveloped Third World countries all over the world; chronic unemployment, meager health facilities, high rates of illiteracy, and grossly inadequate and unsanitary housing conditions. But while this was the condition for the majority of Cuba's people, the plight of women was particularly harsh.

In the years preceding the revolution, Havana may have been a playland paradise for the North American rich, but it was an inferno for the majority of Cuban women. Approximately 464,000 Cuban women knocked on doors of houses and offices looking for work—but no work existed for them. Over 70,000 eked out a living as servants in the homes of wealthy Cubans and North Americans, receiving between $8 and $25 a month. Of the thousands of beggars on the streets of Havana, at least 25,000 of them were women. In Havana alone, it is estimated that there were 11,500 prostitutes. The Havana of the 1950s had 270 brothels, 700 bars with hostesses (one step away from prostitution), and dozens of rent-by-the-hour hotels.

In the years immediately preceding the revolution, the educational level of Cuban women was dismally low. For example, in 1958 one out of every five women in urban areas could not read or write; two out of every five in rural areas. Of all women over twenty-five years of age, only one out of every 100 had any university education. This generally low educational level prepared the overwhelming majority of Cuban women for their jobs primarily as housewives or maids for rich folks; when all else failed, as prostitutes. Those few Cuban women who did manage to work outside their homes were mainly in tobacco (women formed 37 percent of the tobacco workers in 1953) or textiles (women formed 46 percent of the textile workers).

Housing was particularly poor in Cuba before the revolution. Eighty percent of Cuban people lived in huts with thatched roofs, dirt floors, and no running water or indoor plumbing. The dismal housing situation was doubly oppressive for Cuban women, since 85 percent of them spent the greatest amount of their time in and around the home, performing the drudgery of housework. In 1953 in his speech "History Will Absolve Me," Fidel Castro described the housing situation of the 5.8 million Cuban population:

> There are two hundred thousand huts and hovels in Cuba; 400,000 families in the country and in the cities live cramped into barracks and tenements without even the minimum sanitary requirements; 2,200,000 of our urban population pay rents which absorb between one-fifth and one-third of their income; and 2,800,000 of our rural and suburban population lack electricity.

The situation with respect to health was consistent with that in other areas of services. In 1959 over 60 percent of the population of Cuba (6.5 million) had virtually no access to health care. The people of rural Cuba and the majority of the urban poor lived under the constant threat of serious diseases and epidemics. Before the 1959 Revolution in Cuba, there were high rates of infant mortality, malnutrition, and infectious and contagious diseases such as polio, malaria, tuberculosis, intestinal parasitism, diphtheria, and tetanus.

Again, the nature of an exploitative society is such that women will often suffer additional jeopardies because they are women. For example, health care provided for pregnant women, women in childbirth, and newborns is critical in the prevention of chronic illnesses and death among mothers and infants. Indeed, infant mortality is a particularly good indicator of a nation's health and a very sharp indicator of the condition of women's health. In Cuba before the revolution, five out of every fifty children died before their first birthday.

Sports and culture, while not on the same level as health, education, and housing, nevertheless serve as excellent barometers of equality and inequality in a society. In terms of sports before the revolution, Jane McManus notes, "It would be hard to overestimate the importance of basic gymnasia for women in a country like Cuba. At the triumph of the Revolution in 1959, the 'ideal' Cuban woman was pampered and passive. Mild exercise, followed by massages and steam baths, were available only to the wealthy clients of the most expensive and exclusive beauty salons. The lower classes got their 'exercise' working. Organized mass physical fitness programs were unknown."[1] In the arts, while a few women managed to lead respectable lives based on their talents, too often Cuban women were associated with entertainment for wealthy Cubans and North Americans.

The conditions of Cuban women in the areas described above—work, education, health, housing, sports, and culture—were fundamentally outgrowths of the type of economic system in operation in Cuba. U.S. business interests owned Cuba; and specifically, those business interests were not concerned with the plight of Cuban women. There were enough Cuban men to work the jobs associated with U.S. business interests—indeed, more than enough since in 1958, 28 percent of the labor force was unemployed or underemployed.

But in addition to this primary cause of the oppression of women in Cuba (an inequalitarian economic system designed for the financial interests of a small national bourgeoisie and a sizeable group of foreign investors), there were certainly a number of traditions, attitudes, and values in Cuban society that buttressed the notion of women as the rightful occupiers of the bottom rung of society's ladder. In short, machismo was a bolster to class oppression. And for some Cuban women there was racism, too, as yet another instrument for securing the stratification of Cuban society.

Machismo, as it developed in Cuba, is more complex in derivation and current expression than what is implied in the everyday notion of attitudes of male supremacy among Latin American men, a legacy from Spanish culture. Cultural sources of male supremacy attitudes include Africa and the United States as well as Spain.

The Spanish base of machismo was strongly cast in a sexual division of expected and possible behavior within the typical prerevolutionary Cuban family. The husband and father worked, though poor men spent considerable amounts of time as victims of unemployment. The wife and mother seldom worked outside the home—the exceptions being the poor. For women, the control and dominance of their homes and children were often the only outlets they had to express themselves. They cooked heavy Spanish meals and kept spotless homes. Many Cuban men supported a legal family and one or more mistresses. The standard moral code was: "Anything goes for men"; the treasured signs of masculinity were demonstrated in a man's control of his wife and children and his conquering other women. As Margaret Randall notes, "Children grew up with these images of 'man' and 'woman'; proper young girls didn't wear pants and didn't go out unchaperoned."[2]

After the Revolution

The triumph of the revolution on January 1, 1959, marks the beginning of fundamental changes in the organization of Cuban society that have deeply affected the lives of the Cuban people. In the same sense that the ills of prerevolutionary Cuba disproportionately affected Cuban women, the benefits of the new political and economic order are dramatically experienced by Cuban women. Those who suffered the most before the revolution—Black people, women, and, in general, the poor—have gained the most. In the specific case of women, this is not to suggest that the total battle has been won; in fact, all evidence suggests that it is the area of Cuban society where old attitudes are particularly rigid. Cuba has managed to eliminate much institutionalized racism and substantially affect racist attitudes in only twenty years. A comparable statement cannot be made about sexism in Cuba—a reflection, no doubt, of the greater degree of sexism than racism in prerevolutionary Cuba.

Cuba has not eliminated sexist attitudes nor fully incorporated women into the work force and daily life of the revolution. But what has taken place over the past twenty years is a highly impressive series of changes—changes that can be accurately described as a revolution within a revolution. There are two sources of these changes in "women's place" in Cuban society: the revolution itself and specific laws, actions, and organizations within the revolution. We turn now to a discussion of these two sources of change.

IMPACT OF THE CUBAN REVOLUTION ON WOMEN

One of the first massive efforts following the triumph of the revolution was an extensive literacy campaign. In 1961 young boys and girls traveled throughout Cuba, teaching their elders to read and write (in one year 707,000 adults learned to read and write). Of those who learned to read and write, 56 percent were women. The formation of these brigades was a serious challenge to the old ideas of what was proper for young girls to do, and the success of the campaign is measured in the fact that Cuba has virtually eliminated illiteracy.

By 1975 one of every three Cubans was studying something in an educational system that provided free training from the elementary through the university level. In 1975, of the 80,000 university students enrolled, women accounted for 49 percent in science, 47 percent in pedagogy, and 33 percent each in the medical sciences and economics. The aim of "*every* Cuban with a sixth grade education" is now a realizable goal in a country where women were once the least educated in a sparsely educated population. Women are, of course, the recipients of tremendous improvements in a Cuba where eleven times more resources are put into education than before the revolution; 70 percent of the present school facilities have been built, adapted, or begun since 1959. Finally, with respect to education, we must note the importance in Cuba of the study-work principle. The entire educational system of Cuba has been remolded on this principle—that those who study can simultaneously contribute to the country's economic development through work in the countryside of urban areas. There are important long-range consequences for Cuba when young girls (as is the case with young boys) reach adulthood with the firmly rooted notion of their responsibility to *work*.

The transformation of health care since the revolution has earned the respect and admiration of even the most severe of Cuba's critics. The transformation is reflected in such measures as the eradication of diseases (for example, polio, diphtheria, and malaria), life expectancy (under 55 years before the revolution but has now gone up to 70 years), expenditure for public health (20 million pesos before the revolution; today over 400 million pesos—a 20-fold increase), and the widespread distribution of free clinics (for example, in 1958 there was not a single free dental clinic in Cuba; in 1976 there were 115 scattered throughout the island). Specifically related to questions of maternity, today pregnant women in Cuba receive an average of 8.5 medical visits each and 97 percent of all births now take place in a maternity hospital.

Of the three fundamental services, health, education, and housing, it is the latter that has been the most difficult challenge for Cubans to meet, a reflection, in part, of the severe labor and capital-intensive requirements to eradicate a situation where 80 percent of the Cuban people lived in huts before the revolution. In 1961 the revolution began to reverse its emphasis on home ownership and began to provide for the renting of new housing built by the state for a rent of not more than 10 percent of the family's income. This was a decisive move toward the ultimate goal of free housing for all Cubans. However, the attainment of this goal requires mass mobilization of Cuban men and women. Beginning in 1971 the Cuban people formed micro-brigades, a system whereby a percentage of the workers of a work center (factory or a port) spend one and a half to two years constructing houses, while the other workers in the center kept up production by extra effort. The homes built belong to the work collective, and it makes the decision on distribution. It is, of course, particularly striking that Cuban women have incorporated themselves into this process, for the idea of women doing such work is a sharp challenge to prerevolutionary notions of womenhood.

Because of the persistent association of women with housework, these new housing units with running water, electricity, and many modern conveniences bring the greatest relief to those who still do most of the housework.

The explosion in participation in cultural activities and sports includes monumental increases in the involvement of women. In the "amateur arts movement" of Cuba, women are actively involved in musical, community-based theater, and art groups. And on a national level, women have taken major responsibilities in ballet, theater, literature, and the graphic and plastic arts.

In the area of sports, Fidel Castro was able to report to the First Party Congress of Cuba in 1975: "People have been encouraged in every possible way to do physical exercises and to go in for sports. The diversification of sports has been promoted to include sports in which the country had no tradition or experience. Sports have been encouraged at work centers and in units of the Armed Forces and the Ministry of the Interior. Women's participation has grown considerably."[3] Sports and culture have been defined by the revolution as rights, not privileges, of every Cuban. The material means for participating in these rights have been provided. What is left is the destruction of the age-old attitudes and prejudices against women's participation.

Before the revolution in a typical year, 25 percent of the work force would have been unemployed. Today, Cuba has totally eliminated unemployment (indeed, Cuba suffers from a labor shortage). The elimination of unemployment has meant that with the intensive use of Cuban productive laws, the social services described above are available to all for free or at modest costs to individuals. The incorporation of women into the Cuban work force has steadily improved since the triumph of the revolution; however, there are still far too many Cuban women who choose not to work. In 1953 women occupied 9.8 percent of the total labor force (which included 70,000 domestics); today close to 30 percent of the work force are women.

For some percentage of Cuban women (it is difficult to be more precise), the opportunity to work was all that was needed to bring them into the work force. However, for the majority of Cuban women it has taken more than mere opportunity. First, the provision of basic social services at free-to-minimal cost has meant that many Cuban women chose not to work because they could remain in their homes and still enjoy the fruits of the revolution (for example, free health care and education). For many Cuban women who chose to work, the material conditions to support that choice did not (and still do not) exist. As Vilma Espin, president of the Federation of Cuban Women (FMC), has said, "Obtaining the participation of women in work requires overcoming numerous obstacles of a material nature such as day nurseries, workers' dining rooms, student dining rooms, semi-boarding schools, laundries, and other social services which would make it possible for the housewife to work."[4] And, finally, for many women attitudes and prejudices about women working keep them out of the work force.

THE CUBAN REVOLUTION MOVES ON THE QUESTION OF WOMEN

The incorporation of Cuban women into the work force, and indeed into the full productive life of Cuban society, has required more than the availability of jobs and statements by the leadership. We turn now to a brief review of the major steps taken by the revolution.

When the revolution triumphed in 1959, it immediately took measures to incorporate women into the work force. Approximately 20,000 women began to study in special "Schools for the Advancement of Domestic Servants." Many of these women became the staff workers of day-care centers. In those early days of the revolution, much of the door-to-door work of talking with women and urging them to join the work force was done by the FMC. In 1969/70 members of the FMC reached 400,000 women in their door-to-door conversations. That was a crucial year for Cuba with the thrust to harvest 1 million tons of surgarcane. Through the work of the FMC, as well as the work by the Committee for the Defense of the Revolution, thousands of women volunteered to cut cane. But as women moved into the work force, they also moved out again. For example, in the last three months of 1969, 107,000 women entered the labor force; but 80,000 left; so there was a net gain of only 27,000. Major reasons for this enormous turnover were, as Fidel Castro noted, "all the residual male chauvinism and supermanism and all those things that are still a part of us." Many men were encouraging their wives not to work; and many women grew tired of the double burden of working outside the home and then coming home to dishes, laundry, and cooking.

This period, 1959 to 1970, has been described as the period when the revolution moved on long-standing notions of the home (*casa*) as the place for women and the streets (*calles*) as the place for men. Carollee Bengelsdorf and Alice Hagerman characterize this period:

> Although it has now been made clear that women had the "social duty" to work, and although they were entering the labor force in increasing numbers, no nationally organized attempt was made during this period to challenge the assumption that children, laundry, and cooking were women's work. The expectation remained firm that women would be relieved of this work to the extent that the society could take on those responsibilities. In conditions of underdevelopment this has meant a *de facto* "second shift" for most women who work. For, given the scarcity of resources, the full services to relieve women of household tasks simply could not be immediately provided.[5]

In the years since 1970, the Cuban revolution has more seriously attacked the problem of "the second shift." The government of Cuba has placed a great emphasis on the construction of day-care centers, for it is clear that the absence of sound day care for their children is a major deterrent to many women working. By 1974 the revolution has constructed 610 day-care centers caring for over 50,000 children—but these still were not enough.

Since 1972 the shopping bag plan (*plan jaba*) has been in effect in order to give working women priority service at their local grocery stores. They may either drop off their lists in the morning and pick up their groceries in the evening, or they may immediately go to the front of each counter. In a country where the realities of underdevelopment and the U.S.-imposed blockade create long lines, this is a means of saving time for working women. Working women have also received preferential access to a variety of goods and services. For example, working women have preferential access to medical appointments, dry cleaners, shoe stores, hairdressers, and tailors.

The revolution has also worked to extend laundry services for workers at their workplaces and hot meals in workers' cafeterias. Although all workers benefit by these services, it is working women who benefit the most, for it means that these "household" tasks are done outside of their homes. The basic problem with all of these efforts is that the needs of the Cuban people exceed their capabilities at the present time.

The problem of the second shift has also put women at a disadvantage within their workplaces. "Women who must pick up children at day care centers and take care of their household often cannot stay at the workplace to attend assemblies or do voluntary work. Therefore, they have less chance to develop and display attitudes which might lead to their selection by workers' assemblies to leadership positions or for special material rewards."[6]

A structure was created to attempt to ease and, where possible, eliminate some of these jeopardies. In 1969 the Feminine Front was incorporated into the Cuban trade union structure—a secretariat within the Central Trade Union Federation to focus on problems of women in their work centers. The Feminine Front is now known as the Department of Feminine Concerns.

There are also problems in the area of women's participation in political leadership. Today, as throughout the history of Cuba, there are many examples of the heroism and strong leadership qualities of individual women. However, in a more general way, there is much work to be done in this area. Women comprise only 13 percent of the membership of the Communist Party of Cuba; 2.9 percent of the leadership at a base level and 0 percent at the top level of the politburo.

This problem is also expressed in the involvement of women in leadership roles in popular power—the municipal, provincial, and national assemblies in charge of all the service and production units operating at those various levels (schools, courts, hospitals, and the like). Before this new system of popular power went into effect, an experiment was carried out in the province of Matanzas. In the Matanzas experiment, women comprised only 7.6 percent of the individuals nominated as candidates and only 3 percent of those elected to municipal assemblies in the province. In a speech in which he discussed the results of the elections, Fidel Castro emphasized that these figures demonstrate how "we still have residues of cultural backwardness and how we still retain old thinking patterns in the back of our minds." And, he continued, "There are certain theories alleging that women don't like to be led by women. . . . If there is a speck of truth to it, it will serve to show that a hard struggle must be waged among women themselves." As a result of the efforts of many organizations in Cuba, but most especially the efforts of the FMC, the percentage of women candidates for municipal assemblies in1976 rose to 13.6 percent, a doubling of the Matanzas figure for 1974. This increase in female participation in the most important organs of mass political power in Cuba represents important changes in the attitudes of certain women and men who make the nominations as well as some of those women who agree to accept nomination.

In the past few years, Cuba has passed substantial legislation that deeply affects women. In 1975 the Maternity Law was passed, and in that same year the Family Code went into effect. These laws have the potential to cut away the very fiber of discrimination against women.

The Maternity Law of Cuba is based on certain assumptions: that every adult Cuban is a worker, that children will be borne by working women, and that children represent the future of the revolution. These assumptions, within the context of the Cuban revolution, have led to one of the most far-reaching maternity laws in the world:

> The Maternity Law requires that pregnant women take an eighteen week paid leave of absence—six weeks prior to the birth, and three months after. Pregnant women are granted six full days, or twelve half days, off for pre-natal care. Mothers are entitled to one day per month during the first year after the birth for the child's medical care; in practice, the father can also take responsibility for this assignment. At the end of the paid maternity leave, if the mother feels she needs or wants to continue to care for her child full time, she can take up to one year's leave without pay; at the end of the year she can return to her former position.[7]

The Family Code is a comprehensive piece of legislation that goes a long way toward bringing equality into social relationships that were hitherto considered "too private" for the law. Today, as a result of the Family Code, divorce is far easier than in the past; illegitimacy is no longer a viable concept. But certainly the most significant aspect of the law, and that which will take the longest to put into full effect, is the stipulation that men are required to shoulder 50 percent of the housework and child care when women work. The difficulty with such a law is, of course, in the necessity of women bringing legal action against their husbands. However, the immediate positive result is that the case for equal responsibilities and rights is given public sanction.

Conclusion

Without question, the Cuban revolution has brought enormous changes in the position of women, and it has been done so in the short period of twenty years. Serious problems remain, however—problems that grow out of Cuba's legacy of underdevelopment and that are the result of the tenacity of prejudices about women. As Cuba develops its economy, those problems that stem from the lack of a material base to support the integration of women into the work force and life of Cuba may diminish. However, the subjective problems—machismo and sexism—that keep women out of the workplace, leadership, and full participation in the life of their country are more difficult to root out. There is one particularly protective cushion for attitudes of male supremacy in Cuba, which appears all the more powerful when we realize that it never existed in the same way for racial prejudices. The perpetuation of sexist attitudes is aided by the fact that the setting for so many of the interpersonal relations between men and women is the home. Women may experience tremendous gains in their workplaces but return to situations within the privateness of the household that are filled with old myths and prejudices. Children are taught and practice equality of the sexes in schools but may come home in the evenings, or on weekends, to see their mothers, sisters, and other female relatives in statuses "reserved for women."

Clearly, it will not be easy to eliminate the sexist attitudes that stand as barriers to the full liberation of Cuban women. It will take time, perhaps generations. But many Cuban women and men are demonstrating a commitment to struggle against the myths and attitudes which block the full movement of Cuban women into the march of their society.

REFERENCES

1. McManus (1977), pp. 29–30.
2. Randall (1974), p. 27.
3. Castro (1976), p. 165.
4. Rowbotham (1974), p. 227.
5. Bengelsdorf and Hagerman (1974), p. 18.
6. Bengelsdorf and Hagerman (1974), p. 11.
7. Bengelsdorf and Hagerman (1974), p. 11.

MINORITIES IN REVOLUTION

Ted Robert Gurr

Revolutions seek to liberate people. Yet often they also seek to give new strength to countries through creating a unified and purified nation. When a country undergoing a revolution contains several distinct peoples, with different religious views or ethnic roots, minority groups may become victims of the revolution's search for unity. In far too many cases, struggles that begin as a revolution to liberate a country from oppressive rulers develop into struggles among ethnic or religious groups over who "belongs" in the new revolutionary nation. In this essay, Gurr discusses several recent cases of minority conflicts in revolutions, and points out that such conflicts can run the range from accommodation to controlled rebellion, civil war, or even genocide.

In February 1981, eighteen months after the Sandinista revolutionaries seized power in Nicaragua, Sandinista soldiers broke into a Moravian Church in the Atlantic Coast town of Prinzapolka to arrest a Miskito Indian leader who was accused of plotting secession. The indigenous people, armed with hunting rifles, fought back and four people on each side were killed. By the end of 1981 the 100,000 Miskitos in the region were at open war with the revolutionaries. Early in 1982, Sandinista soldiers destroyed all Miskito villages on the south bank of the Coco River and forcibly resettled their inhabitants in relocation camps far from their homeland. Many Miskitos escaped across the river to Honduras, where the CIA was quick to recruit them as allies in the U.S.-led effort to destabilize the revolutionary government. The Miskitos' war within a war did not begin to wind down until 1985, when the Sandinistas relaxed their heavy-handed revolutionary policies and agreed, after lengthy negotiations, to restore the Miskitos' historical autonomy.

Soon after Islamic revolutionaries consolidated their control of Iran in February 1979, they began a systematic campaign of persecution against Iran's largest religious minority, the 350,000 Baha'is. All Baha'i community assets and holy places were seized, Baha'is were denied access to education and employment, thousands were imprisoned, and more than 200 of their leaders were executed. The Baha'is did not resist or in any way threaten the revolutionary government: their doctrine calls on them to accept political authority. Rather, their sin was heresy against Islam, and international observers were deeply concerned that the Iranian Baha'is would again be victims of genocide, like the 20,000 Baha'is who were put to death in mid-nineteenth century Persia. A worldwide campaign of publicity and pressure, channeled through the United Nations, seemingly persuaded the Iranian government to moderate their policies from 1985 onward. But Iranian religious leaders continue to warn Baha'is that they must convert to the true faith or risk extinction.[1]

These accounts illustrate the general observation that when revolutionaries seize power, minorities are more likely to suffer than to benefit. The vast majority of the world's 180-plus independent states are not homogeneous nation-states but are composed of diverse ethnic and religious groups. These communal groups, to use a generic term for them, are especially large, numerous, and assertive in the countries of the Middle East, Africa, Asia, and East Central Europe. Many resemble the Miskitos of Nicaragua and the Croats of Yugoslavia: they resent the erosion of their historical autonomy and will press claims for greater independence whenever the political opportunity arises. Other communal minorities, like the Baha'is in Iran and Muslims in Yugoslavia, have lived for generations in close association with dominant groups who dislike and distrust them.

When revolutions occur in divided societies, subordinate nationalities almost always try to promote their own interest against a temporarily-weakened state. The absence of strong central authority also makes it possible for communal groups to settle old scores by attacking hated rivals. To secure their hold on power, revolutionary leaders have to control these kinds of conflicts. The nature of the revolutionary struggle shapes the ways in which minorities are treated. If revolutionaries seized power through protracted armed struggle, they usually have both the disposition and the means to suppress rebellions by the same kinds of tactics they used to gain power. Nationalist uprisings in postrevolutionary states thus often meet with fierce repression. Revolutionary leaders also may have historical or ideological grudges to settle. If so, they can turn the coercive powers of the state against old rivals and against people, like the Baha'is, who are defined by revolutionary ideology as unworthy or subhuman. Only if the revolutionary struggle has been relatively short and nonviolent is there a chance that resistant minorities will be incorporated peacefully in the new state.

Four patterns of conflict and repression between revolutionary states and communal groups can be discerned in the twentieth-century historical record. They are genocide, civil war, controlled rebellions, and accommodation. We will give examples of each pattern and sketch the kinds of circumstances responsible for each one.

Genocide is the promotion and execution of policies by a state or its agents that are intended to destroy, physically and culturally, a national, ethnic, racial, or religious group. At least four revolutionary governments in this century have targeted minorities for destruction. The "Young Turks" who seized control of the disintegrating Ottoman Empire in 1913 were responsible for the Armenian genocide of 1915–1917. The Nazis' policy of systematically eliminating Jews and Roma (gypsies) from Germany and all of occupied Europe gave the international crime of genocide its name. After the Khmer Rouge seized power in Cambodia in 1975, they systematically sought to destroy the Chinese and Vietnamese immigrant communities and the Muslim Chams as well as non-ethnic political and class groups that opposed the revolution. The Ayatollah Khomeini's government targeted the Baha'is in revolutionary Iran. The Armenians were the only targeted group who openly resisted the revolutionary state, thus providing a pretext for their victimization. The Baha'is were the only targets whose destruction was averted by international pressure.[2]

The common element in all these genocides was the ideological commitment of revolutionary elites to ethnic or national purification. Nazi ideology called for purging the so-called German race of alien elements. The Jews were easy targets because Nazi ideology built on traditional antisemitism and envy against the economic and intellectual success of some members of the Jewish community. The Jews also were political scapegoats for Germany's woes: Hitler reportedly said that "if the Jews had not existed, it would have been necessary to invent them." The militarist leaders of revolutionary Turkey sought to rid what remained of the disintegrating Ottoman Empire of their Christian Armenian rivals in the name of Turkish nationalism and pan-Islamic ideology. The Khmer Rouge's ideology called for the establishment of a strictly egalitarian and homogeneous Khmer society that was purged of alien exploiters (Chinese merchants), traditional enemies (Vietnamese), and people of different culture and belief (the Chams). The vocabularies of hate used to justify mass killing were generically similar: for the Nazis the Jews were "vermin," for the Khmer Rouge their targets were "dander."

One can ask whether similar revolutionary genocides might occur again. The answer is yes: the justifications and tactics used by Bosnian Serbs in their "ethnic cleansing" of Muslim-inhabited areas are genocidal in character and thus far have not been checked by international pressures on the revolutionary-nationalist government of Serbian-controlled Yugoslavia. The governments of postrevolutionary Armenia and Azerbaijan have thus far stopped short of genocide against their respective Azeri and Armenian minorities, but the situation could easily degenerate into deliberate mass killings.

Civil war is the second pattern that is evident in some revolutionary situations. Civil war is used here in its narrow meaning, referring to conflicts in which a national people tries to gain independence from an existing state. Attempts at secession are a virtually inevitable result of revolutions in multinational states and empires, for two reasons. The revolutionaries usually come disproportionately from the dominant nationality in the old state, which increases the fears of other nationalities that they will be unfairly treated by the new regime. Ant the new revolutionary state often is too weak at the outset either to deter attempts at secession or to bargain with national minorities from a position of strength.

Twice in this century a Russian-dominated state has come apart at its national seams. After the 1917 revolution Georgia, Armenia, the Baltic peoples and the Finns declared their independence from Imperial Russia and only the first two were promptly reincorporated in the new Soviet state. The democratic revolution of 1990 was accompanied by the complete fragmentation of the Soviet state, leaving all its fifteen successor republics with their own problems of minority and nationality conflicts. There are striking contrasts between the two situations: the 1917 revolution was a violent one, and secessionist regions were reincorporated by force. The 1990 revolution was almost entirely nonviolent and the Russian state has not tried to reestablish control over the breakaway republics by force. There are militant secessionists *within* some of the new republics, including Russia, Moldova, Azerbaijan, and Georgia. Only the last two governments have responded with military force. There is, however, a threatening possibility that economic crisis in Russia will lead to a counterrevolutionary takeover by nationalists who then will try to establish a Greater Russia by military means. Belarus, the Baltic states, and the Russian-inhabited parts of Kazahkstan are the most likely targets of such action.

Eastern Europe offers other examples of the secessionist consequences of revolution. All the Yugoslav republics held democratic elections in 1990. The elections brought non-Communist nationalists to power in four republics—Slovenia, Croatia, Bosnia, and Macedonia—which eventually declared their independence from the federation. The Communist-nationalist leadership of Serbia chose to fight rather than to let the first three republics escape but failed militarily to hold either Slovenia or western Croatia. The most likely outcome of the Yugoslav revolution will be the de facto creation of a stridently nationalistic Greater Serbia that forcibly controls or expels large Albanian, Hungarian, and Macedonian minorities. The contrast with political changes in Czechoslovakia could not be greater. Czechoslovakia's "velvet revolution" was accomplished in ten November days in 1989 without any loss of life. When elections in 1992 brought nationalists to power in both the Czech and Slovak republics, they quickly agreed to the peaceful dissolution of the federation.[3]

Ethiopia is the third multinational state that has come apart under the impact of revolution and civil war. Ethiopia had its first revolution when military leaders seized power from the Emperor Haile Selassie in 1974 and introduced radical Marxist politics. When factions among the revolutionaries fought for power in Addis Ababa in 1977, an existing civil war escalated in Eritrea, in the North, and new rebellions broke out among the Tigreans in the North Central part of the country and among the Somali in the East. Warfare continued until 1991 when a coalition of rebels seized the capital and established an interim government. This new revolutionary government is based mainly on the Tigreans, however, and the Eritrean nationalists have made it clear that they will go to war again if the interim government stands in the way of their complete independence. The Ethiopian case shows that "revolution" and "civil war" are names for transient phases of protracted communal conflict in a place where for thirty years no central government has been able to exercise effective authority over all its nominal subjects.[4]

Controlled rebellions are just as likely to occur in the aftermath of revolutionary seizures of power as are full-blown nationalist wars of independence. The case of the Miskitos, sketched earlier, illustrates the essential differences between secessionist civil wars and rebellions. The Miskitos never sought to establish their own sovereign state and could not have mustered enough force to do so even had they sought such an ambitious objective. They sought to stop the Sandinistas from expropriating their lands and managing their schools and local agencies; and, above all after 1982, they wanted to return to their home villages in peace. From the Sandinista viewpoint the Miskitos may have been troublesome and misguided, but since they lived in an isolated part of the country they were no serious threat to the revolution *except* through their support for the Contras. When it became apparent to the revolutionary leadership that the policy of relying on force was too costly, they shifted toward accommodation.

In other words, the stakes and risks in ethnic rebellions are not so high as they are in all-or-nothing civil wars for independence, and they are more susceptible to compromise solutions that stop short of massacres and genocide. An earlier example of this kind of rebellion occurred among the Kabyle Berbers in the aftermath of the Algerians' successful war of independence from France. The Berbers of the Kabyle mountains played a major part in the war but found themselves losing out in the postrevolutionary coalition government. Their dissatisfaction prompted a regional rebellion in the early 1960s, but a combination of limited force and political compromise ended the open conflict. Tensions between the Arab majority and the Berber minority have surfaced several times since then over a variety of economic, political, and cultural issues, but there is little prospect of serious interethnic violence.

Iran is another multiethnic state, one in which the Farsi-speaking Persians dominate a half-dozen tribal peoples around the country's periphery. About 40 percent of the population consists of minorities such as the Azerbaijanis in the Northeast, the Baluchi in the Southeast, the Arabs and Bahktiaris in the Southwest, and the Kurds in the Northwest. The Iranian revolution of 1979 prompted regional rebellions among all of them except the Azeris. The most serious such rebellion occurred in Iranian Kurdistan. The Kurdish rebels joined in the revolution against the Shah but soon split from the revolutionary coalition. During the revolution they had taken control of a number of towns, including Mahabad. Autonomy plans were offered to the Kurds by the revolutionary government but were not accepted or implemented because of mutual distrust. It was ultimately left to the Revolutionary Guards to recapture Kurdish-held areas in intermittent fighting that continued until autumn 1980. Serious fighting erupted again in 1985 but the outcome was no different. Over 25,000 Iranian Kurds were claimed to have died in these years of sporadic rebellion, 90 percent of them civilians. Although the Kurds gained little from their rebellions, their losses could have been worse. The Iranian government refrained from using the tactics of mass relocation and massacre that were employed by the Iraqui government against its rebellious Kurds, and sought—sometimes successfully—to enlist the Kurds' cooperation during the Iran-Iraq war.[5]

Accommodation of differences between communal groups and new revolutionary regimes sometimes occurs, as is exemplified by the peaceful dissolution of Czechoslovakia. Some minorities remain inactive throughout a revolutionary conflict: examples are the Cambodian Chams, Iranian Azeris and Baha'is, and the Hungarian minority in northern Serbia's autonomous Vojvodina province. But this does not necessarily insulate them from being targeted later by a revolutionary government on ideological or nationalist grounds, as happened to the Chams and the Baha'is. Serbian nationalists have reportedly begun to harass Hungarians in Vojvodina. If so, it is another illustration of what typically happens in multiethnic states during and after revolutions: all communal groups are at risk of being drawn into the vortex of conflict. By the time of Ethiopia's second revolution in 1991, every communal group in the country seems to have been organized and armed. The same probably will be true of what is left of Yugoslavia.

Yet accommodations are sometimes reached by revolutionary states with resistant minorities. The case of the Miskitos in Nicaragua has already been reviewed: strategic calculations and external pressures on both sides contributed to settlement after four years of violent conflict. The Philippines provides a different kind of example. The rebellion of the Moros (Muslims) in the southwestern Philippines began in the early 1970s and had largely run its course by the mid-1980s. An autonomy agreement had been worked out while President Marcos was in power but had not been acted on at the time of Corazon Aquino's people power revolution of 1986. Her new government quickly resumed negotiations with Moro leaders and pushed ahead to implement a modified agreement, one that contributed to the ending of the rebellion.

The democratic commitments of the Aquino government were a major factor in this outcome. The fact that rebellion had ebbed by the time the revolution occurred was another. One last recent example of accommodation shows the importance of democratic norms for shaping revolutionary outcomes. The one million members of the Turkish minority in Bulgaria were the targets of forcible "bulgarianization" programs in the mid-1980s and were being expelled to Turkey as late as 1989. The postrevolutionary government completely reversed the old policies from 1990 onward. Turks were guaranteed full political, economic, and cultural rights and allowed to organize their own party, which in 1992 had enough seats in the Bulgarian parliament to determine whether a socialist or anticommunist government would stay in power. Nationalist Bulgarians still resent the Turks' new status and role and may in the future reimpose restraints on them. But for the time being the Bulgarian Turks, along with the Slovaks and the peoples of the ex-Soviet republics, are testimony to the fact that democratic revolutions can have positive outcomes for communal minorities.[6] When nationalist and authoritarian leaders seize power, however, disadvantaged minorities' chances of improving their situation are slim to none. The only exceptions are those instances in which national peoples, like those of Slovenia and Croatia, can take advantage of temporary weakness at the center to establish their complete independence. The births of both these new countries were midwifed by international supporters and Croatia is being safeguarded by United Nations peace-keeping forces. In the case of Bosnian independence, however, international support has been too little and too late to make any difference, and the Bosnian Muslims are suffering a near-genocidal fate.

REFERENCES

1. A good narrative account of the Miskito conflict is Kinzer (1991). The persecution of the Baha'is is summarized by Bigelow (1992).
2. For a definition of genocide and a list of contemporary cases see Harff (1992). On the Cambodian genocide see Harff (1991). For a comparative study of genocides in Turkey, Germany, and Cambodia, see Melson (1992).
3. Ethnonational conflicts in the U.S.S.R. and Eastern Europe are analyzed by Marshall (1993).
4. Ethiopia and other African cases are examined by Scarritt (1993).
5. The later development of the Iranian Revolution is described by Moshiri (1991).
6. Democratic values also played a role in the case of the Miskitos. The Sandinista government was a quasidemocratic government and was susceptible to arguments made on behalf of the Miskitos by representatives of the global indigenous rights movement and by social democratic governments in Western Europe. Moreover Tomás Borge, the senior Sandinista official who was given the task of settling the conflict with the Miskitos in 1985, followed "democratic" practices of consultation and conciliation with local leaders.

Revolutions in World History

As we look back over world history, what can we say about when and where revolutions have occurred? Where are they likely to occur in the future? And what have revolutions accomplished or what are they likely to accomplish?

First of all, revolutions did not occur randomly throughout history. In ancient times revolutions were most common in times of rapid geographic and population expansion. Violent changes in the structure of government occurred in many Greek city-states during the phase of colonial and trading expansion (the sixth and seventh centuries B.C.) and in Rome during the period of rapid expansion of the Republic following the Punic Wars (first century B.C.). Similarly, in the Islamic world, the Abbasid Revolution occurred at the end of the great expansion of Islam under the early Caliphs. In each case, these revolutions were followed by the emergence of more powerful and more centralized governments that consolidated empires.[1]

Looking to the modern world, the same relationship recurs: In Europe, revolts and revolutions crowded the years from 1500–1650 and from 1750–1850, periods of rapid population expansion, whereas the century from 1650 to 1750, a period of little or no population growth, was one of political stability throughout Europe.[2]

How can we account for this relationship? Revolutions occur only where there is a combination of state weakness, elite conflicts, and popular uprisings. As Wolf and I have noted in this volume, rapid population growth in the context of traditional societies can simultaneously give rise to all three factors. Population growth can lead to inflation, which undermines the finances of traditional states. Inflation and the increase of elite families can heighten conflicts among elites as they compete for a limited number of positions in the Church and State bureaucracies. And finally, population growth can lead to a fall in real wages, land shortages, and unemployment among the population.

Therefore, revolts and revolutions have been particularly frequent during those eras in which population growth outran economic growth and have been relatively rare during eras of population stability. Predictably, the twentieth century has been a period of frequent revolutions, especially in the Third World where population increases have pressured the ability of states to maintain their finances, of the elites to maintain their position, and of the populace to maintain its standard of living.

While revolutions have been more frequent in eras of rapid population growth, this is not the only factor that may increase the likelihood of revolutions. Other forces—particularly in the complex world-economy and superpower politics of today—may also undermine state finances, spur elite conflict with states, and increase popular grievances. In the years since World War II, financial weakness has often arisen through a state's dependence on the international commodity and money markets. This dependence has left states vulnerable to wide swings between inflation and depression due to the fluctuation of world prices. In addition, elites have often clashed with state leaders over colonial or foreign superpower domination of the government, or military failures. And the realignment of the economy to produce goods for export has often led to the loss of land and employment and falling incomes for a significant portion of the population.

Population growth and international economic and political pressures can greatly strain the fabric of a society; yet whether such pressures lead to revolution depends on the vulnerability of a society's government and social structure. Where governments can avoid fiscal strains, where elite positions and rewards are sufficiently stable and attractive so that elites remain united in their support of the government, or where the populace is scattered and hard to organize for revolt, revolution is unlikely. In short, it is never enough to identify pressures that may lead to revolution; we must also examine carefully the condition of state finances and state relationships with elites and the capacity of popular groups to organize under elite or local leadership to assess the likelihood of revolution in future years.

In these areas, we can identify several factors that may intensify conflicts and provoke revolutionary crises: superpower policies (or especially sudden changes in policy) that antagonize elites or weaken the state's finances and repressive capabilities; shifts in the world-economy or specific commodity markets that lead to severe inflation, indebtedness, or unemployment; rapid expansion of elites that leads to increased conflicts and competition for resources among elites; and the monopolization of political authority or corruption by the state in a manner that excludes many elites from their traditional share of political and economic spoils. Readers of the selections on Iran and Nicaragua in this volume will find that all of these exacerbating factors emerged in the 1970s in those states. In the 1980s, difficulties in state finances and elite divisions also prompted revolutions in Eastern Europe and the Soviet Union. Some or all of the above problems are present or seem likely to arise in parts of the Middle East, Latin America, and Africa.

Revolutions are therefore liable to continue in the near future. What can we expect revolutions to accomplish, and what have they accomplished to date?

The most compelling accomplishment of revolutions has been to increase the centralization and power of the state. In most cases, especially in Russia, China, Mexico, and Cuba, the postrevolutionary regime has extended the power of the government deeply into the countryside, and has monopolized both elite and popular mobilization and political activity to an unprecedented degree. These regimes have been among the world's most stable in terms of the tenure of office of state leaders and the continuity of authority by a single party in the years after their revolution. A second major accomplishment, although not as widespread as the first, is providing elementary education, employment, and basic services to a vast majority of the population. Although revolutions generally have not eliminated poverty and suffering, to their credit they have sometimes greatly reduced ignorance—the Cuban and Nicaraguan Revolutions have done a remarkable job of bringing basic literacy to most of the population. A third accomplishment is that many revolutions have ended the domination of politics and the economy by a narrow and closed traditional elite.

Still, revolutions are essentially human creations, and as such they share the flaws of their creators. Revolutions have in no case provided equality, liberty, and political freedoms to all of their populace (even the American Revolution, though more successful than most in these respects, continued to maintain slavery in the United States long after it was abolished in England). In many cases, revolutions have reduced liberty and political freedoms as the more powerful postrevolutionary state has enforced the dominance of a new bureaucratic party elite to an even greater degree than the old traditional elite. And often, postrevolutionary regimes have not been able to improve their economies enough to avoid widespread shortages of essential goods. We may hope for the best, but we shall have to wait and see whether the recent revolutions in Eastern Europe and the Soviet Union prove more successful than past revolutions in overcoming these challenges.

In sum, revolutions have often resulted in the exchange of one set of problems—elite corruption and dominance of traditional elites, the financial or military failure of weak regimes, subordination of the domestic economy to foreign capital—for another set of problems. These postrevolutionary problems include domination by bureaucratic elites and lack of political liberties, the extended and often oppressive power of more powerful and more centralized states, bureaucratic inefficiency and dislocations of the economy, and subordination of the domestic economy to the military defense of the revolution and to drastic realignments of foreign trade and aid. Silvia Pedraza-Bailey, a native of Cuba who is now a professor of sociology at the University of Michigan, has compared the situation in her country to a change in marriage partners, both with flaws:

> It is better [now] than the years of Batista? Batista was horrible: corruption and repression marked his regime. . . . There wasn't a Cuban left in Cuba at the beginning of the revolution who was not against all that and for the revolution. . . . The eradication of prostitution and vice, the spread of the educational and health services all over the country: those are very good. In a society, however, where people's lives are completely controlled, [and essential goods are unavailable or in short supply], people feel that is good, but it is not enough. To my mind, the best analogy is a woman whose first husband was a wife-beater. The second husband is sweet, treats her well, brings her flowers. It just so happens that he is an alcoholic and cannot hold a job.[3]

What then are the revolutions of the recent past and the near future, of the 1970s, 1980s, and 1990s, likely to accomplish? One may always hope that a path exists, whether through revolution or reform, that will grant greater prosperity, equality, and liberty to individuals. Clearly, on the basis of past history, we cannot exalt revolution as a certain path to that end. Yet no one can doubt the impact of revolutions in strengthening states, bringing new elites to power, and changing global political alignments. We can be fairly certain that in these three aspects, the revolutions of the near future will continue to have a major impact.

Whether or not we consider the shortcomings of revolutions greater than their accomplishments, we cannot overstate their importance in framing the political and eco-nomic organization of the majority of humankind. Revolutions have created the current governments of the world's most powerful states, and changed the destiny of many smaller nations. The belief in revolution as a symbol of rebirth and liberation remains a powerful political force. In understanding world history, understanding the origins and outcomes of revolutions remains essential.

REFERENCES

1.   Forrest (1966); Syme (1939); Shaban (1970).
2.   Aston (1965); Rabb (1975); Hobsbawm (1962).
3.   From an interview with Silvia Pedraza-Bailey in Hamada (1982).

The following books further pursue the theory of revolutions and give more details on the particular revolutions discussed in this volume.

The Theory of Revolutions

The most influential recent book on the theory of revolutions is Skocpol (1979), who examined the classic revolutions in France, Russia, and China. Skocpol's work was extended and modified by Goldstone (1991), who dealt with revolutions and rebellions from 1600 to 1850 in Europe and Asia. Moore, Jr., (1966) provides a still provocative analysis of how revolutions contributed to the political development of the United States, Europe, and Asia. For a theoretical analysis aimed more at contemporary revolutions, Goldstone, Gurr, and Moshiri (1991) focus on revolutions of the late twentieth century.

On such specific topics as the character of revolutionary leaders, the causes of human aggression, the relation of war to revolution, and the like, Gurr (1980) provides a valuable survey of recent research. On the role of peasants in revolution, the major views are those of Wolf (1969), Migdal (1974), Paige (1975), Scott (1976), and Popkin (1979). The role of cultural factors in the origins of revolution, a much neglected topic, receives special attention in Eisenstadt (1978) and Sewell, Jr. (1980).

Other comparative surveys of revolutions, focusing chiefly on the modern Third World and offering valuable insights, include Dunn (1972), Chaliand (1977), Trimberger (1978), and Walton (1984).

Specific Revolutions

Stone (1972) offers a brief but excellent survey of the causes of the English Revolution; Ashton (1978) provides a more elaborate study with more detailed treatment of the Revolution's main events.

The best short account of the coming of the French Revolution is still Lefebvre (1947). Doyle (1980) offers an excellent, up-to-date account of the Revolution's origins that incorporates recent research and controversies, and Schama (1989) provides a lively and detailed chronicle of events.

For Russia, Trotsky's (1959) account is a literacy masterpiece and a joy to read; Chamberlin (1965) offers a more objective, but still accessible, history.

China's long history and recent revolution are both covered in lively fashion by Fairbank (1983). Heng and Shapiro (1983) is a gripping firsthand account of life in revolutionary

China. The most accessible and thorough account of China's current struggle with modernization is Spence (1990).

Regarding Latin America, Womack, Jr., (1969) has written a moving narrative of the Mexican Revolution; Cumberland (1968) provides a more analytical survey. Kelly and Klein (1980) discuss the Bolivian Revolution, and Dominguez (1978) surveys the Cuban Revolution well. Walker (1985) provides a fine introduction to the Nicaraguan Revolution, and Diskin (1984) offers an overview of Central America in general.

Among the many fine books on Iran's Revolution, Abrahamian (1982) stands out. Keddie (1981) is also excellent and somewhat easier reading.

Eastern Europe's recent changes are superbly surveyed by Goldfarb (1992). Ash (1989) is highly readable on the events of the late 1980s, and Chirot's (1991) edited volume offers a variety of useful perspectives.

Abrahamian, Ervand. 1982. *Iran between Two Revolutions*. Princeton, NJ: Princeton University Press.

Adams, Richard N. 1966. "Power and Power Domains." *America Latina* 9:3–21.

Agrarian Reform Law of the People's Republic of China and Other Relevant Documents. 1952. 4th ed. Peking: Foreign Languages Press.

Anderson, Perry. 1974. *Lineages of the Absolutist State*. London: NLB.

Appleby, Andrew B. 1975. "Agrarian Capitalism or Seigneurial Reaction? The Northwest of England 1500–1700." *American Historical Review* 80:574–94.

Arendt, Hannah. 1963. *On Revolution*. New York: Viking Press.

Arjomand, Said Amir. 1988. *The Turban for the Crown: The Islamic Revolution in Iran*. London: Oxford University Press.

Ash, Timothy Garton. 1989. *The Uses of Adversity*. New York: Random House.

Ashton, Robert. 1978. *The English Civil War: Conservatism and Revolution 1603–1649*. London: Weidenfeld and Nicolson.

Aston, T., ed. 1965. *Crisis in Europe 1560–1660*. New York: Basic Books.

Bengelsdorf, Carollee, and Alice Hagerman. 1974. "Emerging from Underdevelopment: Women and Work." *Cuba Review* 4:3–18.

Bigelow, Katharine R. 1992. "A Campaign to Deter Genocide: The Baha'i Experience." Pp. 189–196 in *Genocide Watch*, edited by Helen Fine. New Haven, CT: Yale University Press.

Bill, James. 1978–1979. "Iran and the Crisis of 1978." *Foreign Affairs* 57:323–42.

Blanning, T. W. 1986. *The Origins of the French Revolution Wars*. London: Longmans.

Brinton C. 1938. *The Anatomy of Revolution*. New York: Vintage Books.

Calhoun, Craig. 1983. "The Radicalism of Tradition" *American Journal of Sociology* 88:886–914.

Castro, Fidel, 1976. *First Congress of the Communist Party of Cuba*. Moscow: Progress.

Chaliand, G. 1977. *Revolution in the Third World: Myths and Prospects*. New York: Viking Press.

Chamberlin, William Henry. 1965. *The Russian Revolution 1917–1921*, 2 vols. New York: Grosset and Dunlap.

Chang, P'eng-yuan. 1968. "The Constitutionalists." Pp. 143–83 in *China in Revolution: The First Phase, 1900–1913*, edited by Mary C. Wright. New Haven, CT: Yale University Press.

Chao Kuo-chun. 1960. *Agrarian Policy of the Chinese Communist Party, 1921–1959*. Bombay: Asia Publishing House.

Chao, Paul. 1967. "The Marxist Doctrine and the Recent Development of the Chinese Family in Communist China." *Journal of Asian and African Studies* 2:161–73.

Chen, Yung-fa. 1980. "The Making of a Revolution: The Communist Movement in Eastern and Central China, 1937–1945." Ph.D. dissertation, Stanford University.

Chirot, Daniel, ed. 1991. *The Crisis of Leninism and the Decline of the Left*. Seattle, WA: University of Washington Press.

Chorley, Katharine. 1943. *Armies and the Art of Revolution*. London: Faber and Faber.

Clapham, J. H. 1969. *The Causes of the War of 1792*. London: Octagon Books.

Cobban, Alfred. 1957. *A History of Modern France, Volume I: 1715–1799*. Baltimore, MD: Penguin Books.

Cornwall, Julian. 1977. *Revolt of the Peasantry 1549*. London: Routledge and Kegan Paul.

Crook, Isabel, and David Crook. 1959. *Revolution in a Chinese Village: Ten Mile Inn*. London: Routledge and Kegan Paul.

Cumberland, Charles C. 1968. *Mexico: The Struggle for Modernity*. New York: Oxford University Press.

Davies, J. C. 1962. "Toward a Theory of Revolution." *American Sociological Review* 27:5–19.

Diskin, Martin, ed. 1984. *Trouble in Our Backyard: Central America and the United States in the Eighties.* New York: Pantheon.

Dix, Robert. 1983. "The Varieties of Revolution." *Comparative Politics* 15:281–93.

Dominguez, Jorge. 1978. *Cuba: Order and Revolution.* Cambridge, MA: Harvard University Press.

Dorn, Walter L. 1963. *Competition for Empire, 1740–1763.* New York: Harper and Row.

Doyle, W. 1980. *Origins of the French Revolution.* Oxford: Oxford University Press.

Duncan, O. D. 1968. "Social Stratification and Mobility: Problems in the Measurement of Trend." Pp. 675–719 in *Indicators of Social Change,* edited by E. Sheldon and W. Moore. New York: Russell Sage Foundation.

Dunn, John. 1972. *Modern Revolutions: An Introduction to the Analysis of a Political Phenomenon.* Cambridge: Cambridge University Press.

Eckstein, S. 1982. "The Impact of Revolution on Social Welfare in Latin America." *Theory and Society* 11:43–94.

Edwards, L. P. 1927. *The Natural History of Revolution.* Chicago: University of Chicago Press.

Eisenstadt, S. N. 1978. *Revolution and the Transformation of Societies: A Comparative Study of Civilizations.* New York: Free Press.

Elton, G. R. 1974. *Studies in Tudor and Stuart Politics and Government: Papers and Reviews 1946–1972,* 2 vols. Cambridge: Cambridge University Press.

Everitt, Alan. 1967. "Farm Laborers." Pp. 396–465 in *The Agricultural History of England and Wales, Vol. IV: 1500–1640,* edited by H. P. R. Finberg. Cambridge: Cambridge University Press.

———. 1969. *Change in the Provinces: The Seventeenth Century.* Leicester: Leicester University Press.

Fainsod, Merle. 1953. *How Russia Is Ruled.* Cambridge, MA: Harvard University Press.

Fairbank, John King. 1983. *The United States and China,* 5th ed. Cambridge, MA: Harvard University Press.

Farhi, Farideh. 1990. *States and Urban-based Revolutions: Iran and Nicaragua.* Urbana and Chicago: University of Illinois Press.

Feuerwerker, Albert. 1970. *China's Early Industrialization.* New York: Atheneum.

Fiddick, Thomas C. 1990. *Russia's Retreat from Poland, 1920.* New York: St. Martin's Press.

Fincher, John. 1968. "Political Provincialism and the National Revolution." Pp. 185–226 in *China in Revolution: The First Phase, 1900–1913,* edited by Mary C. Wright. New Haven, CT: Yale University Press.

Ford, Franklin L. 1965. *Robe and Sword.* New York: Harper and Row.

Forrest, W. G. 1966. *The Emergence of Greek Democracy, 800–400 B.C.* Oxford: Oxford University Press.

Fox, Edward Whiting. 1971. *History in Geographic Perspective: The Other France.* New York: W. W. Norton.

Frenier, Mariam Darce. 1978. "Women and the Chinese Communist Land Reform, 1946–1952." Mimeographed. Morris, MN: University of Minnesota.

Gage, N. 1978. "Iran: Making of a Revolution." *New York Times,* December 17.

Gillis, John R. 1970. "Political Decay and the European Revolutions, 1789–1848." *World Politics* 22:344–70.

Gold, Thomas. 1990. "The Resurgence of Civil Society in China." *Journal of Democracy* 1:18–31.

Goldfarb, Jeffrey. 1992. *After the Fall: The Pursuit of Democracy in Central Europe.* New York: Basic Books.

Goldman, Marshall. 1983. *USSR in Crisis: Failure of an Economic System.* New York: Norton.

Goldstone, Jack A. 1983. "Capitalist Origins of the English Revolution: Chasing a Chimera." *Theory and Society* 12:143–80.

———. 1991. *Revolution and Rebellion in the Early Modern World.* Berkeley and Los Angeles: University of California Press.

Goldstone, Jack A., Ted Robert Gurr, and Farrokh Moshiri, eds. 1991. *Revolutions of the Late Twentieth Century*. Boulder, CO: Westview.

Griffith, Samuel B., ed. 1966. *Peking and People's War*. New York: Praeger.

Gugler, Josef. 1982. "The Urban Character of Contemporary Revolutions." *Studies in Comparative International Development* 17:60–73.

Gurr, T. R. 1970. *Why Men Rebel*. Princeton, NJ: Princeton University Press.

Gurr, T. R., ed. 1980. *Handbook of Political Conflict: Theory and Research*. New York: Free Press.

Hagopian, Mark. 1974. *The Phenomenon of Revolution*. New York: Dodd, Mead & Co.

Hamada, Tarek. 1982. "Reflections on a Revolution." *Washington University Magazine* 52:12–16.

Hampson, Norman. 1963. *A Social History of the French Revolution*. Toronto: University of Toronto Press.

Harff, Barbara. 1991. "Cambodia: Revolution, Genocide, Intervention." Pp. 218–34 in *Revolutions of the Late Twentieth Century*, edited by J. A. Goldstone, T. R. Gurr, and F. Moshiri. Boulder, CO: Westview.

———. 1992. "Recognizing Genocides and Politicides." Chapter 3 in *Genocide Watch*, edited by Helen Fine. New Haven: Yale University Press.

Heng, Liang, and Judith Shapiro. 1983. *Son of the Revolution*. New York: Vintage Books.

Hill, Christopher. 1980. "A Bourgeois Revolution?" Pp. 109–39 in *Three British Revolutions: 1641, 1688, 1776*, edited by J. G. A. Pocock. Princeton, NJ: Princeton University Press.

Hobsbawm, Eric. 1962. *The Age of Revolution, 1789–1848*. New York: New American Library.

Holderness, B. A. 1976. *Pre-Industrial England: Economy and Society 1500–1750*. London: J. M. Dent.

Hopkins, Terence K., and Immanuel Wallerstein. 1967. "The Comparative Study of National Societies." *Social Science Information* 6:25–58.

Howell, Roger. 1979. "The Structure of Urban Politics in the English Civil War." *Albion* 11:111–27.

Huntington, Samuel P. 1968. *Political Order in Changing Societies*. New Haven, CT: Yale University Press.

Johnson, C. 1966. *Revolutionary Change*. Boston: Little, Brown.

Joint Economic Committee, U.S. Congress. 1977. *East European Economies Post-Helsinki*. Washington, DC: U.S. Government Printing Office.

Kazemi, Farhad. 1980. *Poverty and Revolution in Iran: The Migrant Poor, Urban Marginality and Politics*. New York: New York University Press.

Keddie, Nikki. 1981. *Roots of Revolution: An Interpretive History of Modern Iran*. New Haven, CT: Yale University Press.

Kelley, J., and H. S. Klein. 1977. "Revolution and the Rebirth of Inequality: A Theory of Stratification in Post-revolutionary Society." *American Journal of Sociology* 83:78–99.

———. 1980. *Revolution and the Rebirth of Inequality: Stratification in Post-Revolutionary Bolivia*. Berkeley, CA: University of California Press.

Kendell, J. 1979. "Iran's Students and Merchants Form an Unlikely Alliance." *New York Times*, November 7.

Kim, Ilpyong J. 1969. "Mass Mobilization Policies and Techniques Developed in the Period of the Chinese Soviet Republic." Pp. 78–98 in *Chinese Communist Politics in Action*, edited by A. Doak Barnett. Seattle, WA: University of Washington Press.

Kinzer, Stephen. 1991. *Blood of Brothers: Life and War in Nicaragua*. New York: Putnam.

Lasch, Christopher. 1967. *The New Radicalism in America*. New York: Vintage Books.

Lefebvre, Georges. 1947. *The Coming of the French Revolution*. Translated by R. R. Palmer. Princeton, NJ: Princeton University Press.

———. 1963. *Etudes sur la Revolution Francaise*. Paris: Presses Universitaires de France.

Lenin, V. I. 1970. *Selected Works*. Vol. 1. Moscow: Progress Publishers.

Liu, Michael Tien-Lung. 1988. "States and Urban Revolutions: Explaining Revolutionary Outcomes in Iran and Poland." *Theory and Society* 17:179–210.

Mansur, A., (pseud.). 1979. "The Crisis in Iran," *Armed Forces Journal International* (January):26–33.

Mao Zedung (Mao Tse-tung). 1960. *On Coalition Government.* Peking: Foreign Languages Press.

————. 1961. "Cast Away Illusions, Prepare for Struggle." *Selected Works of Mao Tse-tung.* Vol. 4. Peking: Foreign Languages Press.

————. 1965. "On Protracted War." *Selected Works of Mao Tse-tung.* Vol. 2. Peking: Foreign Languages Press.

————. 1967. "Production Is Also Possible in the Guerrilla Zones." *Selected Works of Mao Tse-tung.* Vol. 3. Peking: Foreign Languages Press.

Marshall, Monty G. 1993. "States at Risk: Ethnopolitics in the Multinational States of Eastern Europe." Chapter 7 in *Minorities at Risk,* edited by T. R. Gurr. Washington, DC: United States Institute of Peace.

McManus, Jane. 1977. "Stretching Out." *Cuba Review* 7:29–30.

Melson, Robert F. 1992. *Revolution and Genocide: On the Origins of the Armenian Genocide and the Holocaust.* Chicago: University of Chicago Press.

Migdal, J. S. 1974. *Peasants, Politics, and Revolution: Pressures toward Political and Social Change in the Third World.* Princeton, NJ: Princeton University Press.

Moore, Jr., Barrington. 1966. *Social Origins of Dictatorship and Democracy.* Boston: Beacon Press.

Moshiri, Farrokh. 1991. "Iran: Islamic Revolution against Modernization." Pp. 116–35 in *Revolutions of the Late Twentieth Century,* edited by J. A. Goldstone, T. R. Gurr, and F. Moshiri. Boulder, CO: Westview.

Nove, Alec. 1969. *An Economic History of the U.S.S.R.* Baltimore: Penguin.

Paige, J. M. 1975. *Agrarian Revolution: Social Movements and Export Agriculture in the Underdeveloped World.* New York: Free Press.

Palmer, R. R. 1959–1964. *The Age of the Democratic Revolution, I.* Princeton, NJ: Princeton University Press.

Pettee, George S. 1938. *The Process of Revolution.* New York: Harper and Row.

Popkin, Samuel. 1979. *The Rational Peasant: The Political Economy of Rural Society in Vietnam.* Berkeley, CA: University of California Press.

Rabb, Theodore. 1975. *The Struggle for Stability in Early Modern Europe.* New York: Oxford University Press.

Randall, Margaret. 1974. *Cuban Women Now.* Toronto: Canadian Women's Educational Press.

Robinson, Geroid Tanquary. 1969. *Rural Russia under the Old Regime.* Berkeley: University of California Press.

Rowbotham, Sheila. 1974. "Colony within a Colony." Pp. 200–49 in *Women, Resistance and Revolution: A History of Women and Revolution in the Modern World.* New York: Vintage.

Rudé, G. 1964. *The Crowd in History: A Study of Popular Disturbances in France and England 1730–1848.* New York: Wiley.

Russell, D. E. H. 1974. *Rebellion, Revolution, and Armed Force: A Comparative Study of Fifteen Countries with Special Emphasis on Cuba and South Africa.* New York: Academic Press.

Scarritt, James R. 1993. "Communal Contention for Power in South Africa South of the Sahara." Chapter 9 in *Minorities at Risk,* edited by T. R. Gurr. Washington, DC: United States Institute of Peace.

Schaller, Michael, 1979. *The United States and China in the Twentieth Century.* New York: Oxford University Press.

Schama, Simon. 1989. *Citizens: A Chronicle of the French Revolution.* New York: Knopf.

Scott, James C. 1976. *The Moral Economy of the Peasant: Rebellion and Subsistence in South East Asia.* New Haven, CT: Yale University Press.

———. 1977. "Peasant Revolution: A Dismal Science." *Comparative Politics* 9:231–48.

Sewell, Jr., W. H. 1980. *Work and Revolution in France: The Language of Labor from the Old Regime to 1848.* Cambridge: Cambridge University Press.

Shaban, M. A. 1970. *The Abbasid Revolution.* Cambridge: Cambridge University Press.

Sharp, Buchanan. 1980. *In Contempt of All Authority: Rural Artisans and Riot in the West of England, 1586–1660.* Berkeley, CA: University of California Press.

Sharpe, Kevin. 1978. "Parliamentary History 1603–1629: In or Out of Perspective?" Pp. 1–42 in *Faction and Parliament: Essays on Early Stuart History,* edited by Kevin Sharpe. Oxford: Clarendon Press.

Shue, Vivienne Bland. 1975. "Transforming China's Peasant Villages: Rural Political and Economic Organization, 1949–1956." Ph.D. dissertation, Harvard University.

———. 1980. *Peasant China in Transition: The Dynamics of Development toward Socialism.* Berkeley and Los Angeles: University of California Press.

Shugart, Matthew Sobart. 1989. "Patterns of Revolution." *Theory and Society* 18:249–71.

Skinner, G. William. 1971. "Chinese Peasants and the Closed Community: An Open and Shut Case." *Comparative Studies in Society and History* 13:270–81.

Skocpol, Theda. 1979. *States and Social Revolutions.* Cambridge: Cambridge University Press.

Small, Melvin, and J. David Singer. 1982. *Resort to Arms: International and Civil Wars, 1816–1980.* Beverly Hills, CA: Sage.

Smelser, N. J. 1963. *Theory of Collective Behavior.* New York: Free Press.

Snow, Edgar. 1968. *Red Star over China.* Reprint. New York: Grove Press.

Spence, Jonathan D. 1990. *The Search for Modern China.* New York: Norton.

Spufford, Margaret. 1974. *Contrasting Communities: English Villages in the Sixteenth and Seventeenth Centuries.* Cambridge: Cambridge University Press.

Stone, Lawrence. 1965. *The Crisis of Aristocracy 1558–1641.* Oxford: Oxford University Press.

Stone, Lawrence. 1972. *The Causes of the English Revolution 1529–1642.* New York: Harper and Row.

Syme, Ronald. 1939. *The Roman Revolution.* New York: Oxford University Press.

Thaxton, Ralph. 1975. "When Peasants Took Power: Toward a Theory of Peasant Revolution in China." Ph.D. dissertation, University of Wisconsin, Madison.

Thirsk, Joan. 1961. "Industries in the Countryside." Pp. 70–88 in *Essays in the Economic and Social History of Tudor and Stuart England,* edited by F. J. Fisher. Cambridge: Cambridge University Press.

Thompson, J. M. 1935. *Robespierre.* Oxford: Basil Blackwell.

Tilly, C. 1978. *From Mobilization to Revolution.* Reading, MA: Addison-Wesley.

Trimberger, Ellen Kay. 1972. "A Theory of Elite Revolutions." *Studies in Comparative International Development* 7:191–207.

———. 1978. *Revolution from Above: Military Bureaucrats and Development in Japan, Turkey, Egypt, and Peru.* New Brunswick, NJ: Transaction Books.

Trotsky, Leon. 1930. *My Life.* New York: Scribner's.

———. 1959. *The Russian Revolution.* Selected and edited by F. W. Dupee. Translated by Max Eastman. New York: Doubleday (Anchor Books).

Van Ness, Peter. 1970. *Revolution and Chinese Foreign Policy.* Berkeley: University of California Press.

Walker, Thomas. 1985. *Nicaragua: Land of Sandino,* 2d ed. Boulder CO: Westview Press.

Wallerstein, Immanuel. 1971. "The State and Social Transformation: Will and Possibility." *Politics and Society* 1:25–58.

———. 1974. *The Modern World System I: Capitalist Agriculture and the Origins of the European World Economy in the Sixteenth Century.* New York: Academic Press.

———. 1980a. *The Modern World System II.* New York: Academic Press.

———. 1980b. *The Capitalist World Economy.* Cambridge: Cambridge University Press.

Walter, John. 1980. "Grain Riots and Popular Attitudes to the Law: Maldon and the Crisis of 1629." Pp. 47–84 in *An Ungovernable People? The English and Their Law in the Seventeenth and Eighteenth Centuries,* edited by John Brewer. New Brunswick, NJ: Rutgers University Press.

Walter, John, and Keith Wrightson. 1976. "Dearth and the Social Order in Early Modern England." *Past and Present* 71:22–42.

Walton, J. 1984. *Reluctant Rebels: Comparative Studies of Revolution and Underdevelopment.* New York: Columbia University Press.

Waterbury, Ronald. 1975. "Non-revolutionary Peasants: Oaxaca Compared to Morelos in the Mexican Revolution." *Comparative Studies in Society and History* 17:410–42.

Wolf, Eric. 1969. *Peasant Wars of the Twentieth Century.* New York: Harper and Row.

Womack, Jr., John. 1969. *Zapata and the Mexican Revolution.* New York: Knopf.

Yakhontoff, Victor A. 1934. *The Chinese Soviets.* New York: Coward-McCann.

Yang, C. K. 1959. *Chinese Communist Society: The Family and the Village.* Cambridge: Massachusetts Institute of Technology Press.

COPYRIGHTS AND ACKNOWLEDGMENTS

The essays in this book have been edited and adapted from the following works. The editor is grateful to the publishers and copyright holders for permission to use the selections reprinted here.

ANNUAL REVIEWS INC. For "The Comparative and Historical Study of Revolutions" by Jack A. Goldstone. Reproduced with permission from the *Annual Review of Sociology*, vol. 8, pp. 187–207. Copyright © 1982 by Annual Reviews Inc.

BERKELEY JOURNAL OF SOCIOLOGY For "Revolutions and the World-Historical Development of Capitalism" by Theda Skocpol and Ellen Kay Trimberger. Reproduced with permission of the authors from the *Berkeley Journal of Sociology*, vol. 22, pp. 101–13. Copyright © 1978 by *Berkeley Journal of Sociology*.

CAMBRIDGE UNIVERSITY PRESS For "France, Russia, China: A Structural Analysis of Social Revolutions" by Theda Skocpol. Excerpts from *Comparative Studies in Society and History*, vol. 18, pp. 175–209. Copyright © 1976 by Cambridge University Press.

THE CITY UNIVERSITY OF NEW YORK For "Countermobilization as a Revolutionary Form" by Jerrold D. Green, from *Comparative Politics*, vol. 16, pp. 153–69 (1984). For "Does Modernization Breed Revolution?" by Charles Tilly, from *Comparative Politics*, vol. 5, pp. 425–47 (1973). All copyrights © by The City University of New York.

CONTEMPORARY CHINA INSTITUTE For "Inequality and Stratification in China" by Martin King Whyte, from *The China Quarterly*, no. 64, pp. 684–711. Copyright © 1975 by the China Quarterly, Contemporary China Institute, SOAS, London.

DOUBLEDAY & COMPANY, INC. For excerpts from *The Old Regime and The French Revolution* by Alexis de Tocqueville, translated by Stuart Gilbert; reprinted with permission of the publisher. Copyright © 1955 by Doubleday, a division of Bantam Doubleday Dell Publishing Group, Inc.

ELSEVIER SCIENCE PUBLISHERS For "The Impact of Revolution on Social Welfare in Latin America" by Susan Eckstein, abridged from an article with the same title originally published in *Theory and Society*, vol. 11, pp. 43–94 (1982). For "The Mexican Revolution" abridged from "Theories of Revolution and Revolution without Theory: The Case of Mexico" by Walter Goldfrank, originally published in *Theory and Society*, vol. 7, pp. 135–65 (1979). Both reprinted with permission of Elsevier Science Publishers, B.V., Amsterdam.

THE FREE PRESS For "Peasant Rebellion and Revolution" by Eric Wolf, from *National Liberation: Revolution in the Third World*, edited by Norman R. Miller and Roderick R. Aya. Reprinted with permission of The Free Press, a Division of Macmillan, Inc. Copyright © 1971 by The Free Press.

JACK A. GOLDSTONE For "The English Revolution: A Structural-Demographic Approach" by Jack A. Goldstone. Adapted from "Capitalist Origins of the English Revolution: Chasing a Chimera," *Theory and Society*, vol. 12, pp. 143–80 (March 1983). Copyright © by Jack A. Goldstone.

HARVARD UNIVERSITY PRESS For "The Soviet Civil Service: Its Composition and Status" by Alf Edeen, from *The Transformation of Russian Society: Aspects of Social Change Since 1861*, edited by Cyril E. Black. Cambridge, MA: Harvard University Press. Copyright © 1960 by the President and Fellows of Harvard College.

INDEX

Agrarian bureaucracy
characteristics of, 82–87
foreign pressures on, 85–87
modernization in, 84, 97–98
peasant revolts in, 83, 90–96
Aristocracy
vs. bourgeoisie, 28
overthrow of, 21

Bolivia
economy, prerevolutionary, 263–264
income distribution in, 276–277
land distribution in, 269
land reforms in, 269–272
postrevolutionary developments, 265
revolution from below, 264
Bourgeoisie
vs. aristocracy, 28
in China, 236
as destructive force, 25–27
expansion of, 23–25
Mexican Revolution and, 120
vs. proletariat, 22–30
Bourgeois revolutions, 65, 69
in England, 100
Brazil, outcomes of reform, 263, 268, 270, 272, 273, 275, 276, 279–280, 281, 282–283, 284, 286
Bureaucracy, 31–36
and democracy, 32–35
in neopatrimonial state, 72
permanence of, 35–36
and Russian Revolution, 207
Soviet civil service, 205–210
change in, 211–213
after revolution, 205–208

Capitalism
dependent, in Nicaragua, 151–154

development of, 168
emergence of, in England, 100
in Latin America, 148
Mexican Revolution and, 120
in Mexico, 122, 123
in United States, 148
as world system, 68–70
Challenger, 50
defined, 49
and revolution, 53
China
as agrarian bureaucracy, 85–86
Beijing Spring, 189–191
consequences of, 191–193
Tiananmen Square, 191
Boxer Rebellion, 89
communism, and family, 288
Communist party
and peasants, 289–290
urban resources of, 248–249
economic development of, 235–236, 250–251
egalitarianism in, 221–223
elites
rural, 223–225
and state, 240–241
urban, 226–228
industrialization in, 241–244
inequality
of education, 220–221
of income, 214–220
postrevolution, 213–214
Kuomintang party, 95
urban resources of, 248–249
land reforms in, 291–295
and family, 291, 295–298
modernization and, 88–90
peasant revolts in, 91, 93–96
peasants
mobilization of, 248–249